WORLD WATCHING

This book reflects on the author's distinguished scholarly career over half a century, linking personal biography to changes in the discipline of anthropology. Ulf Hannerz presents a number of important essays and a brand new chapter that allows readers to track developments in his own thinking and interests as well as broader changes in the field. In doing so he provides students with valuable insight into the research process and the building of an anthropological career. Featuring work conducted in the United States, Africa, Sweden, Hong Kong, and the Cayman Islands, the book spans a period in which anthropology adapted to new global circumstances and challenges. Hannerz covers the emergence of the fields of urban anthropology, transnational anthropology, and media anthropology in which he has played a significant role. The chapters demonstrate interdisciplinary openings toward other fields and bear witness to anthropology's connections to world history and to public debates.

Ulf Hannerz is Emeritus Professor of Social Anthropology at Stockholm University, Sweden.

"Ulf Hannerz has long been one of anthropology's most subtle, prescient thinkers. A scholar unusually at home in the world, his work is testimony to the creative interplay of different cultures, methods, theoretical traditions. These essays, spanning almost fifty years, offer us a brilliant mini-history of the unfolding of the late modern anthropological imagination."

Jean Comaroff, Harvard University, USA

"This is a superb introduction to the oeuvre of one of the world's leading anthropologists. In more than fifty years of fieldwork in a host of locations all over the world, Hannerz has tackled complex social problems with sly humor and an inimitably wry voice. In these pages, anthropology emerges as a cosmopolitan discipline studying other cosmopolitans."

Akhil Gupta, University of California, Los Angeles, USA

"For over fifty years Ulf Hannerz has been pioneering anthropological research and challenging disciplinary boundaries. Part-autobiographical, part-critical commentary, these writings chart his personal journey through a changing world, from postcolonial Nigeria, the Caribbean and ghetto culture in Washington to the lifeworlds of foreign correspondents and Swedish detective writers. Readers will relish the wit, insight and originality of these essays."

Cris Shore, The University of Auckland, New Zealand

WORLD WATCHING

Streetcorners and Newsbeats on a Journey through Anthropology

Ulf Hannerz

LONDON AND NEW YORK

First published 2019
by Routledge
2 Park Square, Milton Park, Abingdon, Oxon OX14 4RN

and by Routledge
52 Vanderbilt Avenue, New York, NY 10017

Routledge is an imprint of the Taylor & Francis Group, an informa business

© 2019 Ulf Hannerz

The right of Ulf Hannerz to be identified as author of this work has been asserted by him in accordance with sections 77 and 78 of the Copyright, Designs and Patents Act 1988.

All rights reserved. No part of this book may be reprinted or reproduced or utilised in any form or by any electronic, mechanical, or other means, now known or hereafter invented, including photocopying and recording, or in any information storage or retrieval system, without permission in writing from the publishers.

Trademark notice: Product or corporate names may be trademarks or registered trademarks, and are used only for identification and explanation without intent to infringe.

British Library Cataloguing-in-Publication Data
A catalogue record for this book is available from the British Library

Library of Congress Cataloging-in-Publication Data
A catalog record has been requested for this book

ISBN: 978-1-138-31512-9 (hbk)
ISBN: 978-1-138-31513-6 (pbk)
ISBN: 978-0-429-45653-4 (ebk)

Typeset in Bembo
by Swales & Willis, Exeter, Devon, UK

CONTENTS

List of figures	*vii*
Acknowledgments	*viii*

	Prospectus: stops along the way	1
1	The notion of ghetto culture	52
2	Washington and Kafanchan: a view of urban anthropology	60
3	The management of danger	71
4	Marginal entrepreneurship and economic change in the Cayman Islands	96
5	Tools of identity and imagination	105
6	The world in creolization	120
7	Flows, boundaries and hybrids: keywords in transnational anthropology	135
8	Other transnationals: perspectives gained from studying sideways	159

vi Contents

9 Being there … and there … and there! Reflections on
   multi-site ethnography   176

10 Foreign correspondents and the varieties of cosmopolitanism   189

11 Touring Soweto: culture and memory in urban South Africa   203

12 Reflections on varieties of culturespeak   214

13 A detective story writer: exploring Stockholm as it once was   227

14 Neighbors in a south Swedish village: globalization – small-scale
   and unexpected   238

Index   *252*

FIGURES

0.1 Protest march in George Town, Cayman Islands, 1970   20
1.1 James Brown, "Soul Brother Number One" appeared frequently at Howard Theatre, Washington, DC, in the 1960s   56
2.1 Conversation in a Kafanchan bar – Ben, research assistant, second from the left   65
5.1 The *sharo* duel   106
7.1 Jorge Amado, Salvador writer   136
10.1 Foreign Correspondents Club, Lower Albert Road, Hong Kong   190
13.1 Stieg Trenter, on the right, with the photographer K.W. Gullers, model for his amateur detective hero Harry Friberg   230

ACKNOWLEDGMENTS

Chapter 1, "The Notion of Ghetto Culture," first appeared in *Black America*, edited by John F. Szwed, copyright 1970. Reprinted by permission of Basic Books, an imprint of Hachette Book Group, Inc.

Chapter 2, "Washington and Kafanchan: A View of Urban Anthropology," first appeared in *L'Homme*, 22(4): 25–36, 1982. Reprinted by permission of *L'Homme*, Ecole des Hautes Etudes en Sciences Sociales (EHESS), Paris.

Chapter 3, "The Management of Danger," first appeared in *Ethnos* 46: 19–46, 1981. Reprinted by permission of Taylor & Francis.

Chapter 4, "Marginal Entrepreneurship and Economic Change in the Cayman Islands," first appeared in *Ethnos*, 38: 101–112. Reprinted by permission of Taylor & Francis.

Chapter 5, "Tools of Identity and Imagination," first appeared in *Identity: Personal and Socio-Cultural*, edited by Anita Jacobson-Widding. Acta Universitatis Upsaliensis, Uppsala Studies in Cultural Anthropology, 5, 1983. Reprinted by permission of University of Uppsala.

Chapter 6, "The World in Creolization," first appeared in *Africa*, 57: 546–559. Reprinted by permission of Cambridge University Press.

Chapter 7, "Flows, Boundaries and Hybrids: Keywords in Transnational Anthropology," first appeared (in Portuguese) as "Fluxos, fronteiras, híbridos: palavras-chave da antropologia transnacional," in *Mana* (Rio de Janeiro), 3(1): 7–39. Reprinted by permission of *Mana*.

Chapter 8, "Other Transnationals: Perspectives Gained from Studying Sideways," first appeared in *Paideuma*, 44: 109–123. Reprinted by permission of Frobenius-Institut, Goethe-Universität Frankfurt am Main.

Chapter 9, "Being There … and There … and There! Reflections on Multi-site Ethnography," first appeared in *Ethnography*, 4: 229–244. Reprinted by permission of Sage Publishing.

Chapter 10, "Foreign Correspondents and the Varieties of Cosmopolitanism," first appeared in *Journal of Ethnic and Migration Studies*, 33: 299–311. Reprinted by permission of Taylor & Francis.

Chapter 11, "Touring Soweto: Culture and Memory in Urban South Africa," first appeared in *City and Culture: Cultural Processes and Urban Sustainability*, edited by Louise Nyström, 1999. Reprinted by permission of Boverket, Karlskrona.

Chapter 12, "Reflections on Varieties of Culturespeak," first appeared in *European Journal of Cultural Studies*, 2: 393–407, 1999. Reprinted by permission of Sage Publishing.

Chapter 13, "A Detective Story Writer: Exploring Stockholm as It Once Was," first appeared in *City & Society* 25: 260–270, 2013. Reprinted by permission of John Wiley & Sons.

PROSPECTUS

Stops along the way

The title of this book, *World Watching*, deserves some comment. For one thing, ever since in my childhood I acquired the habit of reading newspapers. I have always been inclined to do that – somehow taking a special interest in foreign news. Probably it appealed to my imagination. At the time the Korean War was going on, so I also looked at the map to find those remote places: Seoul, Pyongyang, Pusan … Later I tried to use whatever opportunities came my way to catch at least glimpses of as many parts of the world as possible. But apart from that, "world watching" is one way of describing the anthropological vocation, in its shifts between close-ups and globalizing overviews.

More specifically, however, I have in mind "world watching" as a particular kind of challenge to anthropology. Now and then, I return to the writings of Alfred Kroeber, one of the discipline's ancestral figures (sometimes for inspiration, at other times for irritation or distraction). In early 1946, Kroeber traveled to Britain on board the *Queen Mary*, back in service as a passenger ship, recently released from World War II duty. In London, renewing the transatlantic dialogue with his colleagues in a Huxley Lecture, he would offer his vision of anthropology as a discipline for which the ultimate natural unit was "the culture of all humanity at all periods and in all places."[1]

Kroeber could concern himself with both very large and very small matters, but he had his own kind of preoccupation with the Big Picture, and I have continued to be intrigued by that concern with humanity in all periods and all places. Almost three-quarters of a century after he suggested that program for anthropology, the discipline has come closer to realizing it, but the facts on the ground have also continued to change. The ancient world Kroeber dwelt on in his lecture was very different from the one we live in now, and his 1940s world was not like the present either. Over the time that I have been in anthropology,

2 Prospectus: stops along the way

the quite expansive understanding of its task is one that has been inspiring. Especially when, at times, I have found myself in situations where I have sensed a need to explore how an anthropological point of view could be updated to engage with human life and its organization, in areas where the discipline had not been so active before. (And it matters here that anthropological field methods have a special potential for serendipity.) This may be "world watching" in a particular sense, turning attention outward from more established intellectual habitats.

It follows that "streetcorners" and "newsbeats" are in the subtitle to suggest an emphasis in the book on field sites, field experiences, and the further thinking they set in motion. This is not so much a book about "seminar rooms" or "academic corridors of power" – which do tend to also be necessary parts of contemporary scholarly life – although there are also some passing glimpses of such matters. That is to say, I have not included so much commentary on recent or current internal debates in the anthropological discipline. There is some, for example in Chapters 7 and 12, but anyone interested in my opinions on such matters should be able to find them elsewhere.[2] "Streetcorners" and "newsbeats" are keywords suggesting a certain variety of sites for listening, looking and learning, on my journey through anthropology. Most specifically and concretely, they relate to two of my research endeavors: the first in Black Washington, DC; the last among newsmedia foreign correspondents. Yet they connect in certain ways to other fields as well. I certainly spent time at streetcorners in a Nigerian town. Suddenly and briefly, newsbeats could also include those Washington streetcorners, that Nigerian town, and (possibly) a somewhat obscure Caribbean island, as these happened to become the sites of dramatic happenings.

One difference between streetcorners and newsbeats is that streetcorner fieldwork has resulted in some classic ethnographies that usually reach mostly an academic, perhaps intradisciplinary audience; whereas newsbeat reporting is intended for a wider public. But there may be a continuum here, rather than a sharp divide.

There is, too, a difference of scale: streetcorners are very local, newsbeats are likely to cover more territory, perhaps even stretching to a global side. The contrast between streetcorners and newsbeats, however, is also a matter of time. They tend to involve different tempos in social life. The streetcorner may in large part be a site of everyday life: repetitive; a kind of slow life even as it may be busy in its own way. The newsbeat is a matter of moving between events, from one to the next. So what becomes a stop on one person's newsbeat may long have been another person's streetcorner – however briefly, different kinds of sites may come to overlap.

The theme of time shows up in different ways at different places in this book. Again, it may be a matter of shifts in speed, between events and routines, but it can also be a matter of long-term change, in ideas and in those facts on the ground. The following chapters, actually writings from a period of almost a half-

"Being there" and "the first draft of history"

There are different ways of looking back at a working life, and constructing an account of it. Most lives probably involve a number of routines and a fair amount of relative boredom, and one may not want to dwell so much on that. In one period – more about that later – I read numerous memoirs of newsmedia foreign correspondents, and while I know that their work can also have its rather unexciting stretches, it was clear that what they chose to foreground in their life stories were more likely their engagements with colorful places and striking events. There were key phrases that they tended to be fond of: "being there" was one of these.

Anthropologists share with the foreign correspondents this preoccupation with "being there."[3] But for the newspeople, it may be a matter of parachuting in (metaphorically, not literally), and leaving again very soon. Unlike them, the anthropologists tend to identify more enduringly with particular field sites. They spend more time there, try to grasp "the native's point of view" (a notion that in itself has generated some controversy), and then struggle with the challenge of trying to make at least academic colleagues – and sometimes other audiences as well – understand what that is all about. Some return to the same place again and again. Field experiences, however, tend to become more than strictly research experiences. As phases of your life, they can become deeply-personal facets of your cumulative identity. After you have finished your research in a place, and perhaps even begin to realize that you will never come back to it, you will still be concerned with what happens to it; still imagining "being there." Particularly if you have several such experiences, your nostalgia will be distributed over the map.

Another key idea of the foreign correspondents has been to be present to "write the first draft of history" – to be a witness to critical events. Other versions, other interpretations may follow, but they still depend on the original. This is part of the reasoning behind my leaving the chapters that follow in their original state. There was a time when anthropologists entertained a somewhat practical fiction of "the ethnographic present," of fields remaining frozen in a vaguely timeless state, but we have now basically discarded that device. Fields are there in a history of the past, present and future. My personal journey through anthropology has been through a half-century (and a little more) of a changing world, and through a discipline that in some ways adapted to that, and in other ways evolved on its own. Keeping chapters in their original state allows them to bear witness to their times in various corners of the world, and to some extent in Academia (which is of course another corner). If occasionally they seem remote in time, that may be precisely the point. Alternatively, I could have chosen to put together one overall retrospective narrative, where

4 Prospectus: stops along the way

the perspective toward what happened early is to a degree shaped by the accumulated understandings and priorities of a late, even final stage. There is more room for wisdom when rewriting history perhaps, but less sense of how things looked in those earlier phases.

This introduction is therefore a kind of running commentary on the later chapters; pointing to how things looked then, and how they look in retrospect. If one were to read it all on a computer screen, I could imagine having this Prospectus in a column to the left, moving slowly – and occasionally perhaps back and forth – and the later chapters in the column to the right, moving more quickly. (But then I may confess that I still prefer reading books on paper.)

A newcomer on campus

The following chapters will relate mostly to ethnographic field experiences and preoccupations. Let me start, however, at a point a little before those.[4] I was a beginning student at Stockholm University, and I had started taking a serious interest in Africa – exciting times there, as much of the continent was moving quickly out of colonialism and into independence. But what could I do at the university to satisfy my curiosity? Not much, it seemed. In the early 1960s, the human sciences at Swedish universities were mostly complacently inward turning, occasionally concerning themselves with European themes, casting a glance toward North America mostly as it related to Swedish emigration as a topic in history, but certainly not paying much attention to the rest of the world.

The one discipline, it seemed, that might legitimate my preoccupation with Africa was something called "general and comparative ethnography" – which, reinvented, would be relabeled "social anthropology" about a decade later. Beyond a sort of academic legitimation, however, it did not at the time offer much of a response to my kind of African interests either. The minimal department was really an appendix to the rather sleepy state ethnographic museum, where elderly curators gave lectures on their specialties and showed the collections.

Yet on our first official reading lists were items like Ruth Benedict's *Patterns of Culture* (1934) and Robert Lowie's *The History of Ethnological Theory* (1937). Hardly the latest in the field even then, but as I was finishing my undergraduate work, it was thus clear to me that there was more anthropology to be had in the United States. I found my way to a one-year exchange scholarship at Indiana University, where I would be hosted by the rather new African Studies program. Numerous such programs were being set up at the time, in the period of Afro-optimism, after the almost continent-wide achievement of independence, and before the times of military coups.

So I came to Bloomington, Indiana, and a major Midwestern university campus with all its facilities. I was on my way to a Friday afternoon lecture when I heard that President Kennedy had just been shot in Dallas. Later in that academic year, Governor George Wallace of Alabama came to speak as part of his presidential primary campaign, and a small group of Southern students whistled "Dixie" from the auditorium balcony. Indiana had a big-tent anthropology department, offering me a chance to sample most of the specialties in U.S. anthropology as it was at the time: a course on "culture and personality," one on kinship, even one on British social anthropology, taught by a junior professor who had just returned from a year in Manchester. I also learned that some of my teachers were, academically, Franz Boas' "grandchildren" – they had been the students of Boas' students. Then, too, there was the African Studies program, offering great openings of interdisciplinarity. And a library with generous opening hours, which for one thing allowed me to explore anthropology's past. (It was in the university bookshop I picked up my copy of Alfred Kroeber's *Anthropology* [1948], intended as a textbook for a course I ended up not taking.)

I spent only one academic year at Indiana University, but occasionally, when I learn that a colleague from somewhere else in the world, be it someone from Cyprus or from Ghana, has also spent time in Bloomington, I greet him or her with "So you are a Hoosier, too!" This tends to lead to a puzzled look, and then a smile. For those who might not know, *Hoosier* is a native term for someone from Indiana. The Indiana University football team is "The Hoosiers," but I cannot actually remember whether there was anybody born and reared in the state among the faculty and students I got to know on campus. The recruitment to larger American graduate schools is clearly national, and increasingly transnational, even as they may belong to state institutions. In the cafeteria of the Graduate Residence Center where I stayed, foreign students would sometimes seek out the tables where they could – often rather humorously, among themselves – exchange experiences and interpretations of the natives surrounding them.

My identifying, playfully, as a Hoosier points toward to my continuous involvement with the United States and with American anthropology. From Bloomington I returned to Stockholm, and found myself in charge of teaching the introductory course in what was officially yet to become "anthropology" – to about a dozen students, mostly young, although there also happened to be one retired Air Force general. (He questioned the suggestion that I cited, from some study out of Andean anthropology, about the effect of thin air on human aggression.) Yet during my year in Bloomington I had fulfilled the course requirements for a master's degree, so back in Stockholm, I also went to work on a thesis. In the next year again, I had a chance to revisit Indiana briefly to talk to my advisor about how I was doing. After that, I continued to Denver, Colorado, for my first encounter with an American Anthropological Association annual meeting. (I had acquired a habit of doing a lot of traveling by Greyhound bus by then.) So here, in 1965, was my first full experience of the diversity of U.S. anthropology – in scholarly topics as well as personal styles. The ill-fated Project Camelot (involving undercover intelligence work by American academics abroad) was in the news, and the youngish Marshall Sahlins gave a widely noted

6 Prospectus: stops along the way

speech on the topic: "The Established Order: Do Not Fold, Spindle, or Mutilate."[5]

Meanwhile, I was considering my next step. Again, it was an interest in Africa that had taken me to anthropology (and in a way to Bloomington), and in the early 1960s I had traveled a couple of times, fairly briefly but widely, in Nigeria and along a stretch of the West African coast, trying to get to know the region in a preliminary way. I intended my first serious field study to take place somewhere there.

But then too quickly the political situation deteriorated, not least in Nigeria. After a military coup and a countercoup there was a civil war, as the part of the country identifying itself as "Biafra" attempted to secede. Obviously my research plans were becoming unwise. But it turned out I would be lucky. At that meeting in Denver, as I ran into one of my Indiana University professors, I told him that I would have to rethink my field work plans. He had himself moved on from the Midwestern campus to Washington, DC, joining the national research policy establishment. A couple of months later, when he had a conversation with someone engaged in putting together a new project, he remembered me.

Hanging out on Winston Street

All of a sudden, in my Stockholm mailbox, I had a letter inviting me to become the "staff anthropologist" for a sizeable sociolinguistic-cum-educational research effort. I did not really hesitate, and thus I came to spend two years in Washington, DC. The project office was next-door to the large edifice of Brookings Institution, the think tank, so I got an early sense of the Washington power/ knowledge landscape. Decades later, when I would come through again, some of the elegant brownstones on the side streets had become the embassies of countries that did not yet exist when I first arrived.

But more of my time was actually spent in a short street in an all-Black neighborhood, which in my writings I renamed "Winston Street." Come with me, then, in Chapter 1, to my first serious field engagement in the second-half of the volatile American 1960s. The chapter, "The notion of ghetto culture," is not so concretely ethnographic, but rather more concerned with an overall understanding of what was urban Black culture at the time. It draws on my extensive participant observation in that neighborhood, although it also responds to some of the scholarly and political arguments about the nature of Black American culture, as they were at the time.

Clifford Geertz (1998) once described the characteristic anthropological field method as "deep hanging out." That was indeed what I tried to do on Winston Street. However, in my Winston Street field work, in a fairly sensitive setting and period, I avoided marking myself as an inquisitive outsider. True, I was White, blond, and blue-eyed; but an innocent newcomer, "just off the boat" as it were, and to some extent I could play on that. I have no photographs from this field, as a camera would have been unusual and conspicuous, and did not use a tape recorder for interviews – which, at that time in history, with such bulky equipment, would have been even more awkward. In the resulting book, *Soulside* (1969), which had also been my Stockholm doctoral dissertation, an extensive appendix described the nature of my field study.[6] In the present book, the study is also discussed at some length in Chapter 2.

There was one particular time, however, when I sensed a threat to my rather unobtrusive, undramatic presence. The U.S. correspondent of a major Swedish chain of popular magazines who had caught wind of my study contacted me to ask if he could come, with a photographer, to do a reportage. I was horrified. So over a lunch downtown, we worked out an arrangement where I would write a story myself, accessible in style but choosing my words carefully in describing the ways of life I was engaging with; and I would take the photographer to a similar row-house neighborhood, far away from mine. There I was, then, a few weeks later, with a full-page picture in a mass-market weekly, describing a facet of American life to a quite sizeable foreign audience. (Some decades later, that Swedish journalist would become the editor-in-chief of one of his country's main newspapers, and after forty-some years we would have lunch again, in my Stockholm neighborhood.)

Writing – for whom?

"The notion of ghetto culture" appeared in a volume that originated as a series of broadcasts on Voice of America; so while the book, *Black America*, had a well-known U.S. publisher, the contributions may have been intended, to begin with, for an audience elsewhere. In this case, I was the only non-U.S. contributor; among the others were a number of American scholars who were prominent in African-American studies at the time. As I look over a shelf of my rather scattered writings, I note that several years later, I was again in a Voice of America project, this time in a series of interviews with scholars from elsewhere who offered their views on the United States.[7] In various ways then, these two engagements involved different positions on the interface between the United States and the outside world: in one case as an outsider among insiders, seemingly reporting to a combination of inside and outside audiences; in another as a voice within a choir of outsiders, offering their interpretations of American matters to yet other outsiders.

One may be a different writer for different readers, and this is something I have often had to think of. When I endeavor to address an international community of anthropological colleagues, I bear in mind that a great many of them are based in North America, although this need not mean that I pretend to be one of them. At times, I may make a bit more of being generally non-American, or (more rarely) specifically Swedish. Then there are also those occasions when I aim my reports or reflections about American matters more precisely at non-American audiences; but there is little of that in what follows here. In any case, my anthropology includes several varieties of cultural brokerage.[8]

8 Prospectus: stops along the way

Again, a couple of my field studies have engaged with Americans, at home or abroad: those in Washington, and those that in considerable part involved the American journalist diaspora, reporting to compatriots on foreign news. Moreover, beyond my year as a sojourner in Hoosierland, I have spent various periods at American universities and other research institutions (in Manhattan, in the Rustbelt and the Midwest, and in California); so the American connection is continuously present. In a later piece, I suggested that this has been "the theme park of my life": "a place one visits in large part for sheer enjoyment, a bit separated from the grind of everyday life."[9]

Myrdal and me: perspectives on Black America, over time

In relation to my engagement with Black America, I should point to one Swedish connection. The name of Gunnar Myrdal is by now hardly as widely recognized as it once was. A youngish economist with some breadth of interdisciplinary interests and a growing reputation, he had arrived in the United States in 1938, with an invitation to undertake a major study of what was known then as "the Negro question." The resulting work, the historically important *An American Dilemma* (1944), of some 1,400 pages, was surely an impressive collaborative effort, drawing on the knowledge and analysis not only of the invited outsider but also of a great many expert American insiders on his team. A quarter-century or so later, the project I came to work for in Washington, DC was in fact supported by the same major foundation which had funded Myrdal's study. That one-time professor of mine who had argued that I would be a good hire for a project anthropologist position may even have made the point that I was Gunnar Myrdal's compatriot – I could be marketed as part of a Swedish brand in Black American studies.

Once I got out in the Winston Street neighborhood this hardly mattered. The more interesting Swedish connection on the streetcorner was that heavyweight boxer who had fairly recently held the world championship. Most of his adversaries in the ring, of course, had been Black Americans. As it turned out, moreover, I was not really attracted by Myrdal's point of view. There was his italicized opinion that "In practically all its divergences, American Negro culture is not something independent of general American culture. It is a distorted development, or a pathological condition, of the general American culture" (Myrdal 1944: 928).

So rather I became the un-Myrdal. For one thing, my starting point was different. As my attraction to anthropology had been by way of African studies, I had early been intrigued by the work of one scholar who had been on Myrdal's team of specialists, Melville Herskovits. Here was someone whose life's work had been devoted to research on Africa and Afro-America – the two continuously intertwined, with shifting emphases. Herskovits had not come to his interest in what was African about Black America easily. Early in his academic life (he was one of Franz Boas' students at Columbia University), at a time

Prospectus: stops along the way **9**

when racist-tinged theories of eugenics had a considerable influence on public opinion, he aligned himself with the opposite anti-racist side, which asserted that White Anglo-Saxon Protestants, immigrant minorities, and Blacks were really all much the same.

He then seems to have undergone a conversion, as he became involved with the 1920s Harlem Renaissance, and its vivid intellectual and artistic expressions of Black culture. In the years that followed, Herskovits undertook a series of field studies in the Caribbean, Latin America, and West Africa – a groundbreaking contribution to a mapping of cultural connections between Africa and the Americas.[10] To begin with, his continued scholarly engagement with Africa and Afro-America was evidently a lonely enterprise. Even into the 1940s, it was mischievously suggested that an interdisciplinary conference of Africanists in the United States might meet in a telephone booth. His anthropologist colleagues were more interested in Native Americans. But then after World War II the United States was a world power, and a Cold War was building. Africa could be one of its possible battlegrounds. So as African Studies turned into a growth field among the varieties of "area studies," Herskovits became one of its founding fathers, as mentor/entrepreneur/lobbyist/public intellectual. Two of my Indiana University professors had been his students.[11]

In *An American Dilemma*, actually only one chapter (out of forty-five) was devoted to the contemporary, internal community life in Black America, and Myrdal had outsourced the writing of that chapter to one of his American sociologist collaborators.[12] The "dilemma" in question was fundamentally one for White Americans: the clash between racism and an egalitarian creed.

Melville Herskovits, however, was a recognized authority on Black American life and heritage. To a degree, moreover, Myrdal might actually have had Herskovits to thank for his American job; when that major foundation announced that it wanted a foreign, impartial scholar to lead its new project, Herskovits had evidently pushed the foundation to avoid recruiting someone from an imperial power who might merely bring another set of the established prejudices of a ruling race.[13] And then Herskovits had a certain part in the project itself. What became his classic book *The Myth of the Negro Past* ([1941] 1958) indeed began as a memorandum for it – the "myth" he questioned was that Black Americans had no past – that African cultural heritage was basically negligible. Drawing on his own field studies as well as other sources, he offered evidence of "Africanisms" traveling across the Atlantic, surviving the slave trade and plantation slavery, continuing visibly and audibly into the present.[14]

This, however, was a minority voice which Myrdal chose not to listen to very much. There may have been a personality clash as well. But during the long period when, according to American progressive opinion, the interests of racial equality would be best served by viewing Black people and White people as basically alike, Herskovits' interest in "Africanisms" could seem a bit risky.

On the other hand, even as Myrdal's work was published, there were some critical responses. In an unpublished comment in 1944, Ralph Ellison, yet to

10 Prospectus: stops along the way

become the famous novelist with his *Invisible Man*, pointed to some less impressive aspects of American mainstream culture, and asked, "Why, if my culture is pathological, must I exchange it for these?" (Later published in his *Shadow and Act*, 1964: 316.)

By the 1960s when I was in Washington, DC, I did not have to draw only on my old interest in Herskovits' writings for alternative views. In wide circles at least, the characteristics and the past and present circumstances of Black American culture were increasingly matters of argument. It is true that there were still those in public debate who were more or less solely preoccupied with the link between economic and political equality and the characteristics of Black life in American society. A "war on poverty" was on, as declared by President Lyndon Johnson, not exclusively involving the situation of Black Americans, but certainly in large part waged on their behalf.[15] In that connection, a new notion appeared that was perhaps akin to Gunnar Myrdal's notion of Black culture as fundamentally pathology. While Oscar Lewis, the anthropologist originator of the term may not have intended it that way, the "culture of poverty" was understood to link certain recurrent modes of behavior to deprived economic circumstances – but with cause-and-effect relationships variously and uncertainly interpreted.

One statement drawing much attention was the so-called "Moynihan Report," *The Negro Family: The Case for National Action* (1965) by Daniel Patrick Moynihan, then Assistant Secretary of Labor, later U.S. Senator for New York, who identified dysfunctional aspects of often female-headed Black households as an important reason behind social and economic deprivation. The commentary on such lines of argument tended to identify them as recurrent modes of "blaming the victim."[16]

In these debates, there might again be less room for any curiosity about what might be a cultural heritage of African-Americans. Yet once more, other voices could also be heard. Coming through New York on my way to these two years in Washington, I stopped by Strand Book Store at 12th Street and Broadway (I have rarely missed that whenever I have been in New York) and found a review copy of the brand-new book *Urban Blues* by Charles Keil (1966) – an impassioned ethnography of Black music, and a good read which came just at the right time as I was about to get into my own field.

It was one sign of many that America was moving beyond the largely assimilationist notion of "the melting pot." Black American nationalists elaborated on ways of identifying with Africa, in thought and style. No doubt it had something to do with the new part of the old continent in global geopolitics. In scholarship, there was a growing sophistication about how to deal with the connections between Africa and Afro-America, and between Afro-America and America as a whole as well. In that stark formulation about Black American culture as pathology, Gunnar Myrdal had made a basic analytical mistake: this culture does not have to be "independent" of the general American culture to exist and to have its own strengths.

The characteristics of Black American culture have been continuously and intricately interwoven with general American culture. In *Soulside*, I used as an opening epigraph a couple of lines from *The Souls of Black Folk* (1903), by the pioneering scholar of Black America, W.E.B. DuBois – make a quick visit to Chapter 7, and you will find those lines in full there: "It is a peculiar sensation, this double-consciousness ...."[17] This complex culture has had its own forever developing history, from African villages through the slave trade to plantations, from southern rural to urban northern life. And later students could engage in documenting and understanding its language, lore, and literature, its crafts and its cuisine, its music and religion, and the changing forms of its social and inter-personal life.[18] The enduring emphasis here was – with a book title by one of their prominent representatives, Roger Abrahams – on what was *Positively Black* (1970).

An American Dilemma, meanwhile, had turned out to be an important work. Ten years after its publication, it was cited as evidence in the Supreme Court case, *Brown v. Board of Education*, which banned segregation in American public schools. By then, Myrdal had moved on in life. In much the same period as he was putting together *An American Dilemma*, he wrote two books on America in Swedish – partly employing what has become a familiar anthropological device of using a report on a foreign land to frame a cultural critique of one's own society. But he was certainly not an anthropologist – to some degree perhaps a sociologist (Americans are somewhat inclined to describe him as such), but primarily an economist, hardly much interested in heritage and history, more inclined toward social engineering.[19] He and his wife Alva Myrdal, a pioneering power couple in Sweden, were both government ministers in their home country at different times, and both were also awarded Nobel Prizes.[20] In a period when Alva was the Swedish ambassador in New Delhi, Gunnar also stationed himself there, writing another massive book on development economics, *Asian Drama*.[21] I never met him personally. But toward the end of his life, we were near neighbors in the Old Town in Stockholm. I remember seeing him in the town square, wandering slowly, seemingly deep in his own thoughts, not to be disturbed.

The travels of the ghetto concept

The very title of "The notion of ghetto culture" raises another kind of question, about the shifting meanings of words in time and space. A "notion," I believe, is something not quite a concept, but a little looser, more tentative; and that seems an appropriate stance here. This again relates to leaving chapters as they were, on first publication.

I believe in confronting the past without trigger warnings, without deleting words and concepts and thereafter pretending that they never existed – but with a preparedness for critical scrutiny, and a sensitivity to historical and situational contexts. Words can move also in the sense of provoking emotional reactions.

12 Prospectus: stops along the way

In this chapter, for one thing, what we have since identified as "the n-word" appears; but so as to point out that while White people should avoid it, Black Americans may occasionally use it among themselves, in friendly banter.[22] (In a way, it may at such times perhaps be seen as an ironic, sideways reference to White prejudice.)

Words can make curious journeys, worth tracing in their own right. Gunnar Myrdal, again, offers one instance. At a later point, while still transatlantically influential, and perhaps with greater aplomb than real linguistic fluency, he brought from his home country the term "underclass" to insert it into the American vocabulary (Myrdal 1963). Coming from him, it was no doubt understood as a concept with somewhat radical connotations; although as time passed, it may just have taken on some of the same ambiguity as preceding concepts, like "culture of poverty." So we could again see how a debate sometimes goes on, or is reawakened, mostly by finding new terms for old facts, or claims – terms which may become just a problematic as their forerunners. With "underclass," however, there is the added twist that in a younger Myrdal's time at home, the Swedish term, *underklass*, was mostly a derogatory bourgeois epithet for lower-class behavior showing a lack of cultural skills.

Or take, from more recent history, the expression "politically correct" – first set in circulation, in an ironic mood, by Stanley Fish, literary and legal theorist, more or less from the left. He has tried to explain what he wanted it to mean (Fish 1994) but that hardly mattered on its rightward journey into general political discourse, including American presidential election campaigning, but globally as well.

But here I am primarily concerned with "ghetto." The first *gueto*, according to one view, was in medieval Venice, where it was seen as convenient to gather the community of successful Jewish international traders in one quarter. That genealogy does not seem altogether certain. In any case, Jewish ghettos then developed elsewhere in Europe, north, east, and west, often doing less well economically. Louis Wirth ([1928] 1956), one of the pioneers of urban sociology, took the concept across the Atlantic, from Frankfurt am Main to Chicago, with a classic monograph. However, Wirth also expanded its use by arguing that not only Jews had ghettos. "There are Little Sicilies, Little Polands, Chinatowns, and Black belts in our large cities ..." ([1928] 1956: 6). (In fact, Chicago had its "Swede Town" too – I suspect some of my relatives a couple of generations ago were there for a while.)

By the time I came to Washington, DC, a ghetto, in widespread American linguistic usage, was typically Black, and it was quite clear that it was also mostly low-income and inner-city.[23] The move of the term from European Jewish to Black American had certainly been expedited by the Black psychologist Kenneth B. Clark's famous book *Dark Ghetto* (1965) – with a foreword by Gunnar Myrdal. More metaphorical extensions such as "gilded ghettos" were not yet much in circulation.

So Chapter 2 uses the term "ghetto dwellers" extensively, and my book *Soulside* had the subtitle "Inquiries into Ghetto Culture and Community." It was evidently a term that I felt had a clear reference, and not particularly controversial. But it was also in a way conveniently specific. It referred not to all African-Americans, but to northern urban Blacks, mostly of low income – although with ethnicity as overriding criterion for recruitment, there could in fact be considerable diversity in other respects, including some variation in household incomes.

By 1969, there was the Elvis Presley hit *In the Ghetto*: "As the snow flies, on a cold and gray Chicago mornin', a poor little baby child is born, in the ghetto ..." The reference to Black urban poverty was clear enough. But have the connotations of "ghetto" again shifted somewhat since then? By now, in the early 2000s, it may be that the countercultural facet of at least some Black American cultural expression has become stronger. That, too, has a past.

On a visit to the City Lights Bookstore in San Francisco (another of my favorites for browsing – and the poet/proprietor Lawrence Ferlinghetti himself used to be often at the front desk), I picked up an old pamphlet by Norman Mailer, on *The White Negro* (1957). In his "superficial reflections on the hipster," Mailer argued that in a

> wedding of the white and the black it was the Negro who brought the cultural dowry ... he kept for his survival the art of the primitive, he lived in the enormous present, he subsisted for his Saturday night kicks, relinquishing the pleasures of the mind for the more obligatory pleasures of the body, and in his music gave voice to the character and quality of his existence, to his rage and the infinite variations of joy, lust, languor, growl, pinch, scream and despair of his orgasm.

Perhaps Mailer's 1950s vision of the cultural model for the existentialist White Negro hipster had a fair amount in common with Myrdal's 1940s "pathological condition," and Moynihan's 1960s "tangle of pathology". Did Mailer actually stand Myrdal and Moynihan on their heads? In present-day vocabulary, in any case, the word "ghetto", in at least some varieties of speech, may carry a little less of the sense of a syndrome tied to economic disadvantage, and more of adversary cultural expression, confrontational to whatever is White mainstream, yet as such mostly not White hipster but one particular variety of Blackness.[24]

A field remembered and revisited

Another American Anthropological Association meeting, probably in the late 1980s, in Chicago: a colleague and I were standing at the entrance of the Michigan Avenue hotel where the meeting was going on, when a rather ill-clad Black street person approached us for a donation. The two of us exchanged glances – we had both written ghetto ethnographies, in early important steps in

14 Prospectus: stops along the way

our careers. So the innocent panhandler was unaware that he faced two academics whose previous work had told them a great deal about his circumstances … he may have found these two White, middle-aged out-of-towners somewhat unexpectedly generous, and all three of us smiled for our own reasons as he continued on his way.

Move forward to January 20, 2009: I was in Stockholm and turned on my television set to watch the CNN International coverage of the American presidential inauguration. It was 11 a.m. in Stockholm, only 5 a.m. in Washington, DC – but I could see that in the darkness before daybreak, the open space in front of the Capitol was already getting crowded. In large part with Black people: this was the inauguration of the first African-American president. In the ceremony, Aretha Franklin, whom I had seen on stage and heard in "R-E-S-P-E-C-T" and other hits, sang "My Country 'Tis of Thee" in an interesting gray hat.

I had already learned that a few days before his inauguration, in the company of Washington, DC's mayor, the President-elect had been for lunch at Ben's Chili Bowl on U Street, where long before its recent fame I used to go for a "Chili Dog" (with grated cheese), in winter evenings. In a way, after some forty years, it seemed my field had arrived at the White House.

Some years later yet, as I was in Washington, DC for another meeting of the American Anthropological Association, I was browsing at the local history shelf at Kramerbooks, just off Dupont Circle, yet another of my favorite bookstores. I found that *Soulside* was turning into a source for those writing about a turbulent period in Washington, DC politics and urban life.[25] As politics as well as demographic patterns changed, the capital was described at one point as "Chocolate City", and then soon as "Cappuccino City." These shifts were by this time reflected in my Winston Street neighborhood as well. I had passed through once earlier in the new century, and described it afterwards as "lumpengentrified" – young, mostly White people of modestly comfortable means had been moving in, leaving their mark on what was acquiring a reputation as a hipster area (with hipsters not quite of Norman Mailer's type). Making my way there once more, I found that gentrification had proceeded further yet. New trees and bushes had been planted along the sidewalks, and there were more elaborate locks on front doors. Certainly of the people I had known there, and their descendants, none would be left. I checked the website of a local real-estate agent, and found that one of the street's modest two-story row houses, a house I knew from the inside fifty years earlier, was now on the market for a million dollars.

Yet some ten blocks away, I could have another nostalgic moment. In my field work, of course, I had not just hung out on Winston Street, but roamed around more freely in "the ghetto." One of my favorite locales had been the Howard Theatre, one of the prime stages of what was known as "the chitlin' circuit" (along with the Apollo in New York and the Regal in Chicago), where musical artists like Aretha Franklin and James Brown, as well as comedians like Moms Mabley and Pigmeat Markham would appear.[26]

The old Howard Theatre closed down in the 1970s, and for some time it seems to have been little more than a ruin. But then some time into the next century it reopened, extensively renovated, with a new business concept. During rather hurried Washington, DC visits, I had never had time to make it back to the neighborhood around 7th and T Streets, but when we had a little more time for a week in 2014, my wife Helena and I got ourselves tickets for a Gospel Brunch at the theater. The buffet was extensive, with a mixture of southern-style and other offerings, and there was an hour with the Harlem Gospel Choir.

The brunch guests were mostly Black, in large part middle-aged and upwards, well dressed, and perhaps reasonably prosperous if they were willing to pay the price for a not-so-modest buffet (although they would probably not come every week – perhaps more likely for birthdays, anniversaries, and the like). Then toward the end of the gospel hour, as we might all have made return visits to the buffet table, the choir inspired the guests to rise to their feet, and take such dance steps as they enjoyed in front of the stage. I could only wonder, as I watched some of the elderly ladies gyrating to the music, hands in the air: had they been at the Howard as teenagers, too, back in the 1960s when I was there?

The urban turn in anthropology

There had been anthropologists studying urban communities before, but it was really the late 1960s and early 1970s that saw the take-off of a subdiscipline of urban anthropology. There were anthropologists coming out of field studies not only in urban neighborhoods in the United States but in Latin American squatter settlements, African small towns, Asian temple cities … certainly it reflected an accelerating urbanization in the world. But it was clear that anthropologists were no longer necessarily professional villagers either. Urban anthropologists came together at conferences, started journals, wrote text books.

Chapters 2 and 3 show how my Winston Street experience had turned me into one such urban anthropologist (although it is also true that in life generally, I have always been more drawn to city streets than to mountain tops, forests, or beaches). As I began to reflect in a more organized way on what it might mean to be an urbanist in anthropology, I had to confront first the contrast that was emerging between anthropology "*in* the city" and "*of* the city." Or with more word play, the city as locus or focus.

In much of what at that point had become urban anthropology, the primary concern had not been with the nature of urbanism, but on race or ethnicity, poverty, gang delinquency, or a group or subculture of some other sort, and on neighborhoods. One pioneering contribution to this wave of urban ethnography was not by an anthropologist, but by the sociologist Herbert Gans, whose *Urban Villagers* (1962) portrayed an established Italian-American neighborhood in

16 Prospectus: stops along the way

Boston.[27] And describing it as a "village" was in his case a critical reaction to a pronounced generalizing tendency in the dominant Chicago School of urban sociology, of some decades earlier. "The contacts of the city may indeed be face to face," Louis Wirth (1938: 12) had written in his classic article on urbanism as a way of life, "but they are nevertheless impersonal, superficial, transitory, and segmental."

Much of the 1960s–1970s anthropological studies tended to be *in* the city rather than *of* the city, finding there some unit that rather readily allowed the importation into an urban site of an ethnographic method that centered on sets of rather stable and close social relationships. So if you took the anthropologists out of villages, could you take the villages out of the anthropologists? Again, the city surely also had other kinds of social life. If Louis Wirth had generalized too much, he was hardly entirely wrong either.[28]

As I tried to think about what urban studies might contribute to anthropology as a general discipline of human diversity, I sensed that it was necessary to move beyond the urban villages. It was not necessary, on the other hand, to reinvent the wheel. So one line of activity was to find what there was of a usable past: in classic, often rather ethnographic, Chicago sociology and elsewhere. I assembled that in the book *Exploring the City* (1980), which seems to have met a widely felt need – over time it was translated into French, Spanish (in Mexico), Portuguese (in Brazil), Italian, and Polish.

With a social anthropological bent, I also tried to think in an orderly way about what kinds of relationships between people there actually were in urban life – and relationships between relationships, which is to say: networks.

Now, in the twenty-first century, network concepts seem to be all over the place, in academic disciplines like history, political science, and sociology, in commentary about how to understand the future, and in everyday usage in both noun and verb forms.[29] Even economists, mostly not particularly hospitable to influences from other disciplines, are catching on to it. But we may remember that it made its debut in the conceptual toolkit in anthropology, in the mid-1950s, in a paper by a British social anthropologist on rural life in Norway. Then in what was thus its home discipline, it drew much more interest in the late 1960s and early 1970s, in large part in the context of urban studies. As I pointed out in *Exploring the City*, the research of the "Manchester School" in the mining communities of the Central African Copperbelt had a key role here. An inclination toward thinking with networks would remain with me, when I engaged with other kinds of units as well.[30] I will come back to this later.

With the urban turn, Chapter 2 takes me to Washington, DC again, but concentrates more on field methods than Chapter 1. It also introduces Kafanchan, my Nigerian field site, about which more will follow.[31] Clearly I worked in very different ways in these places. In all its internal diversity, Kafanchan became a challenge to experiment with new approaches to data gathering. Concluding that chapter, I also emphasize that all urban anthropology should not be "anthropology at home" – the latter notion was also spreading, in Europe and

Prospectus: stops along the way **17**

in North America, at much the same time as the urban subdiscipline expanded. All anthropology did not have to be "exotic," reporting on "non-western" lands, it was argued. I could sympathize with that, but I thought the discipline should stick to the ambition to deal with human diversity everywhere. (As for "anthropology at home," I get to that particularly in Chapter 14, but then it is in a village setting.)

Danger in the streets

Chapter 3 dwells on one kind of urban social relationships, and a kind of concern that readily grows in these relationships.[32] It opens with a dramatic scene, as I was mugged on a street in Kingston, Jamaica. I did not lose my life and was not seriously injured, but got a good introductory paragraph.

Cities are places where you meet with strangers – this is one way in which they are not like typical villages. Often these are quite minimal encounters to which one does not give much thought. There is this possibility though that they turn into something quite different – become dangerous. While this is a recurrent preoccupation in urban life (more so in some communities and neighborhoods than others), the conceptual tools of social anthropology, as brought into urban studies, did not really seem to foster attention for these encounters.

Focusing on them in "The management of danger" was thus a matter of adding another building block to a comparative urban anthropology. The chapter involves a special writing style: I return once more to Black Washington, DC to dwell on what counted as street wisdom, but also shift between such concrete ethnographic moments and diverse readings in anthropology, history, and other disciplines. (I recognize the style again particularly in Chapter 5, entailing rather loose comparison, perhaps an ingredient in what I have seen as "the anthropological imagination.")

Looking back at this chapter decades later, the kinds of questions raised, and ingredients of danger identified, still seem relevant, even as references to hippies, skinheads, and mods and rockers place it in time. The South African tsotsis of the apartheid era come back in in Chapter 11. Yet ideas from the sociology of deviance of the period, such as "labeling" and "moral panics," may well be retrieved and reused as we try to grasp current cultural processes. But the global map of urban danger and danger management has changed in some ways.[33] Worries have grown about terrorist attacks and suicide bombings, and such danger is in large part unmanageable. Apart from regular policing, there are now security guards in more settings, and stationary cameras are watching some public places. Motorcycle gangs with scary outfits may parade through the streets, some of them linked to organized crime. Particularly in the United States, access to guns has become a central political issue. Police and vigilante shootings of young Black men, mostly unarmed, have also been a controversial feature of danger in American cities. Back in the mid-twentieth century at least,

18 Prospectus: stops along the way

Europe mostly had less of such concerns; with greater transnational migrant streams, and greater ethnic diversity, the typing of some more or less identifiable social categories as dangerous grew, and so did vigilante groupings. "Gated communities" became increasingly common as upscale turfs, in cities in much of the world.

Again, too, there is a question of terminology. "The management of danger" is among those of my urban anthropological writings where I use the term "traffic relationships." The common term "fleeting relationships" is too vague, covers too many quite different things; so I coined the new term for that minimal "taking each other into account" in physical co-presence which is centrally a matter of not bumping into each other. "Traffic" seemed an appropriate term for the way cars or bicycles on streets, and pedestrians on sidewalks, manage what are almost non-relationships, sometimes by explicit rules (such as not moving against a red streetlight), sometimes by personal skills of navigation.

But then this, too, became a word that to a degree changed meaning with time and lost innocence. Later in the twentieth century, "trafficking" entered the vocabulary more noticeably, as in "human trafficking" involving illegal transportation of people across borders — with linkages to bondage, prostitution, and slavery. In my earlier sense, traffic relationships involve the body as a vehicle; in trafficking, the body may become a commodity.

Defending Sweden, briefly

Back in Stockholm (in the 1960s, again) after two years in Washington, DC, I had a hectic year. I hurried to finish my PhD dissertation — not least because I already had a commitment from a major university press to take it on. But that became in large part night work. In daytime, I found that student numbers were growing in the anthropology department. Moreover, here, there, and almost everywhere that universities existed, there were student upheavals, with early models in New York (Columbia University) and Paris (Nanterre), and quaint size S versions in Sweden. This all generated quite intensive activity in those academic corridors of power. From the top of the Swedish national university system there was a rather ill-informed attempt to rethink what this discipline, now officially changing its name (after some wrangling) from "general and comparative ethnography" to "social anthropology," should be about; but what happened was rather more a revolution from below, led by junior faculty and graduate students. My sense is that there were parallel changes in the discipline more or less in this period in a number of European countries, in particular those who had not had overseas empires, and no conspicuous indigenous ethnic minorities.[34] As far as I was concerned, after two years of listening to the repartee of soul-radio disc jockeys and comedians like Moms Mabley, I was possibly somewhat maladapted to the format of Swedish Academia.

Then, more in slow-motion, I did my military service, at the time still mandatory for all Swedish males, although I had managed to postpone it considerably. Perhaps

Prospectus: stops along the way **19**

this could be seen as another variant of "the management of danger," but even in the midst of the Cold War, staff service as a cryptologist at the Stockholm Coastal Defense headquarters was idyllic. Once I had to decode a message about a Soviet submarine penetrating the Swedish archipelago. As this happened during the weekend, I reached the officer on duty by telephone at his golf course. But he had already heard of it. Very occasionally I helped another older officer with his crossword puzzle. Otherwise I had plenty of time to read. In a way I might consider those ten months as another kind of field work (participant observation for a period of more or less standard length, in a setting familiar in some ways and unfamiliar in others), although I never published about it.

Just after the end of that period, however, I left for the Caribbean. Well in advance, I had an invitation to a conference on things African-American, to be held at the University of the West Indies in Jamaica, and since I was not due back at the university in Stockholm until five months later, when the fall term would start, I had recognized another field opportunity. Staying on in the Caribbean, where should I go? After an earlier brief visit to Jamaica (out of Washington, DC), I had been ticketed on a return flight with a one-hour stopover at George Town, Cayman Islands, before continuing to Miami. So I knew the Cayman Islands were there. Moreover, I found out that there was not much recent scholarly writing about them. Consequently, that is where I went, a few months into 1970 – perhaps somewhat parenthetically on my overall research path.

Cayman Islands: crisis in the Crown Colony

My Caymanian field experience is represented in this book by Chapter 4, a brief portrayal of small business enterprises. It gives a sense of what island society was like at the time, in particular with the beginnings of a tourist industry. Melville Bodden, Evelyn Watler and Bertram Wood (pseudonyms, although very typical Caymanian names) were people of a certain small-town visibility; Evelyn was actually my landlady.

As it turned out, however, I came to devote most of my work on the islands to another topic, a study of local politics (resulting in a small monograph [Hannerz 1974]). Very soon after my arrival, the local weekly *The Caymanian* – at the time, all there was of "news media" in what was still a small Crown Colony within the shrinking British empire – had carried a brief item about new planning and building regulations just issued by the administration, and the following week the same paper could say that according to reliable sources, there would be a protest march through George Town against these regulations.

Then things happened very quickly. While the new rules would hardly affect more traditional styles of land ownership and use very much, they were primarily intended to constrain the real estate and construction enterprises that had been growing quickly and a bit wildly in response to the tourist industry, and a new North American interest in "second homes" in a pleasant winter climate. So these businesses had a major part in organizing the protest campaign.

20 Prospectus: stops along the way

FIGURE 0.1 Protest march in George Town, Cayman Islands, 1970. *Drawing by Björn Ranung after a photograph by Ulf Hannerz, reprinted with kind permission of Marja Seilola.*

The march, on a late Monday morning, drew a larger crowd than anything in the previous history of the islands. In front of it, the leading real estate agent drove a cabriolet, accompanied by a star female politician in a wide-brimmed hat, with a legal consultancy as her main business. (When visiting her in her office for an interview, I could see a pile of such hats in different colors on a shelf – clearly part of her personal brand.) Behind them walked a couple of other members of the islands' legislative assembly, and then a sizeable group of young Black men, with a black letter "P" attached to their shirts. Then followed diverse members of the Caymanian public, carrying signs: against the regulations, for unity, and signaling some other current concerns as well. The Administrator, highest representative of the colonial power, came out to meet the marchers outside Government House; addressing them through a loudspeaker, in a not very conciliatory manner. The protesters, in turn, demanded that the Administrator should be recalled to London. It was announced that the legislative assembly would hold a special meeting.

That took place eleven days later – but between the march and the meeting, the political temperature rose quickly. Apparently the Administrator, and the handful of local politicians who remained closer to him, had been exposed to threats, and one morning a small British gunboat could be seen anchored outside George Town harbor. There were rumors about soldiers hiding in the bushlands outside the town. When the meeting of the legislative assembly finally took place, its oppositional members protested against the security arrangements: the windows boarded up, the policemen guarding the hall, the members of the audience being searched for arms. Yet eventually a sort of compromise was reached, the problematic regulations would be further scrutinized … and soon enough, in the following days and weeks, things returned to their normal calm.

The weeks of crisis provided me with leads for further inquiry. I went on to interview all major participants, and a variety of observers. I looked more deeply into the recent political history of the territory, seeking out such public and private documents as there were. But not least did I reflect over what I had witnessed during those weeks. Business people had enacted a populist drama, perhaps with elements of farce: in a small-scale structure the same individuals appeared in different roles.[35] There had also been rumors and conspiracy theories. Some commentators would speculate about those young men with the black "P" – could this be the beginning of a Black Power movement, like that which islanders had heard of from the United States, as well as from other Caribbean islands? (They were also known as "the Mathilda Corner Boys," after their local meeting place.) Could this be a reason why the oppositional business interests had at some point turned more conciliatory?

In some ways, too, the speculations could affect my own role. One or two of the people I interviewed found it odd that purely my own scholarly interest, and a small research grant, had taken me to the Cayman Islands precisely at this time. Was I actually a government collaborator? Through a shared acquaintance I heard that one of my interviewees had pieced together the evidence in his own way. I seemed too well-informed, I lived close to the bar where the "Mathilda Corner Boys" hung out in order to spy on them, and I was Swedish – as was that tough-minded Administrator's wife! In fact, the latter might have wanted to see a little more of me, since she seldom found a compatriot visiting the islands, but I had limited my contacts with Government House in order not to be compromised. In any case, it seemed to me appropriate that there, in my field again, was Elvis Presley – on Caymanian jukeboxes – I could again and again hear his *Suspicious Minds*.

From Mathilda Corner to Magajiya Street

I have not been back to the Cayman Islands, although I could hardly avoid learning of its continued history as a tourist spot where cruise ships would anchor, and

22 Prospectus: stops along the way

as a financial center/tax haven of global magnitude. If there had been some 10,000 inhabitants at the time when I was there, the current population is some 75,000 – hardly a natural growth. Obviously there are now not so many natives, relatively speaking, but lots of business-related expatriates.[36] By 2017, it turned out that whether she knew it or not, Queen Elizabeth II also had money in the Cayman Islands. So although the old designation is no longer officially in use, you might perhaps say that this is now literally a "crown colony".

With the "Mathilda Corner Boys" nearby, my time in George Town could have been streetcorner anthropology, but as it turned out, I found myself more "nearly" on a newsbeat. Strikingly enough, however, the crisis I happened to witness seems not to have drawn any public attention outside the islands. No foreign correspondent was stationed there: most of the time, what occurred on those tiny specks of land in a remote part of the Caribbean Sea was hardly of much continuous outside interest. And nobody who was present, and even involved, during those dramatic weeks may have wanted to spread the word. Both the government and the protesters could feel that the less the outside world learned of any unrest in the Cayman Islands, the better.

On toward Chapter 5. The chance to come back to my West African commitment came in the 1970s, as I organized a project designed to take several of my graduate students to their respective field studies, but also to allow me to spend more time in Nigeria. The project's umbrella problematic was the variable relationship between cultural diversity and social integration.[37] This was a main theme in my study in Kafanchan, with several, mostly fairly brief, off-and-on field stays over a ten-year period.

While ethnography is a form of non-fiction, it seems to me a good idea to search out whatever may be existing fiction relating to one's field: it can offer an eloquent instance of that "native's point of view." In Black America, apart from the writings of Ralph Ellison, there had been Richard Wright, James Baldwin, and others. In Nigeria, this was hardly less important. No doubt a great many anthropologists have used Chinua Achebe's *Things Fall Apart* (1958) in a class, to allow undergraduate students a view of what the coming of colonialism had meant to one African society.

Now another Nigerian novel had a direct influence on my Nigerian work. I had discovered Kafanchan, after a fashion, when I traveled in Nigeria in the 1960s. One afternoon the train I was on had stood around for an hour or so, in the habit of Nigerian Railways those days, at a station complex with lots of people milling about, in the middle of a savanna landscape. The name on the station sign had a sort of mystical appeal, different from the names of other stops. So "Kafanchan" stuck in my mind. Then later, back in Stockholm but keeping up with the beginnings of Nigerian fiction writing, I came across Onuora Nzekwu's *Blade Among the Boys* (1962). Evidently Nzekwu had grown up in Kafanchan, the child of a railway worker, and in its beginning pages this novel offered what amounted to an ethnographic snapshot of the town in its early years. On a reconnaissance trip to find a suitable field site, I decided to have a look at Kafanchan first. Being there, I concluded that I needed to look no further.

Chapter 2 has already summarized what kind of town it was: developing around that colonial-era railway junction, it had people from all over Nigeria, north and south, as well as from the nearby areas. I came to know it well, and returning to Kafanchan for more stays over a decade increasingly felt like coming home.

So at the beginning of Chapter 5, "Tools of identity and imagination," I am back on the street. There is an opening scene of street violence again, like in "The management of danger." But this time the violence is voluntary, highly organized, a ritual event intended as a public spectacle.

Magajiya Street is the home of the butchers in Kafanchan, of the Hausa ethnic group, and that also makes it a special place for the Fulani herdsmen who come into town to deliver cattle to the butchers. It is a part of their special way of celebrating a major Muslim holiday (*Id el-fitr*), at the end of Ramadan, to stage the *sharo* there: a series of duels in which their young men can show strength and bravery among themselves, and also to the young women watching. But in the version I saw, a combatant would hold up a small mirror to himself, to see that he could take the heavy blows without changing his face.

In this chapter the *sharo*, with its mirrors, becomes the point of departure for a rather wide-ranging essay on materiality in the human handling of identities (perhaps one could say the "infrastructure" of identities); again an exercise in the anthropological imagination shifting between past and present, and between settings far apart. Moving between the Renaissance invention of autobiography and our everyday uses of bathroom scales and measuring tapes, I try to show how the preoccupation with personal identity can be intricate as well as mundane. Kafanchan, however, remains there as a source of ethnography – especially by way of my encounters with urban Nigerian youth culture. By now, certainly, digital media offer a wealth of new possibilities for identity work.

A football hero gets into trouble

Apart from the *sharo*, Kafanchan had other sports events as well. At the small football (soccer) stadium, games would always draw an enthusiastic audience, but often enough one of my friends and best informants was on the field itself. He was a young Tiv – thus member of an ethnic group well-known from classic anthropological studies – although of a later generation than the Tiv who had hosted other anthropologists in their traditional home region.[38] A migrant to Kafanchan, he was again an employee of the national railway corporation, and really more or less a professional football player on the local railway team. And this accounts for the nickname by which he was well-known in Kafanchan: "Limited." For the uninitiated, this may seem like a rather undesirable identification. But in this railway community, it was a familiar fact that "Limited" trains were those that made few stops along the line – they were the fastest trains. So my friend "Limited" was recognized to move wonderfully quickly across the football playing field.

24 Prospectus: stops along the way

Since his railway job did not take up very much of his time, Limited had rich opportunities to pursue other interests apart from football. He could walk about in town, meet friends, play cards, watch television (electricity had just arrived in Kafanchan), and sing in a church choir. One of his friends was a tailor, so for fun he picked up some sewing skills from him, but mostly he would go to a larger city to check out fashions. In his living-room there was a couch, a couple of comfortable chairs, a refrigerator and a TV set. The walls were covered with pictures of pop artists and British football teams.

There was a time when Limited's popularity, in combination with his Tiv ethnic identity, briefly got him into trouble. A young Fulani girl had apparently become bored with nomadic camp life and gone into Kafanchan, where she seemed to have moved in with two young men living in the same house where Limited had his rooms. When her herdsman father came to look for her, he encountered Limited at the front door, and asked him if he knew the where-abouts of the daughter. Limited, however, had already defined the situation in a way the father had not caught onto. Between the Tiv and the Fulani there is what anthropologists know as a joking relationship: if you meet someone of the opposite group, you make fun of him, perhaps in a somewhat rough way. So in this case Limited gave the older man a slight push, and ridiculed him a little. The Fulani man walked angrily away, not quite understanding what had hap-pened, and reported Limited to the police. When a constable appeared at his door, Limited was still in a good mood, and not so respectful. Limited's father had been one of Queen Elizabeth II's soldiers – the British colonial government had indeed been somewhat inclined to recruit Tiv men for its forces – and thus he had had his shirt chest full of military decorations, going back even to World War II.[39] So now Limited pointed contemptuously to the policeman's chest, devoid of signs of merit.

The policeman got angry, and took Limited along to the Kafanchan jail. Apart from having been insulted himself, he thought Limited was exactly the kind of popular, outgoing, style-conscious young man who would have attracted the Fulani girl. Actually, anyone could easily have escaped this prison, as the old mud walls were crumbling. But Limited was treated well during the two days he spent there, as his guards were football fans and admired his talents on the field. When I came to visit him, I found that his acquaintance with me seemed to have given him certain ideas. His stay in the prison yard had taken the form of a small ethnographic field study, as he walked about taking notes about his observations, and interviewing the other prisoners.

Cultural growth in an interconnected world

The 1970s, when I got going on my work in Kafanchan, were in large part fairly good times in Nigeria. The civil war was over, and the income from the oil wells in the southeast of the country made the country reasonably prosper-ous. The national currency, the naira, was referred to in some circles as the "petronaira." Nigeria was probably never a country free of corruption, but in this period it had not reached the levels that it later would, and more of the national wealth stayed in the country. Government employees got pay raises, roads were improved, and indeed, as Kafanchan got electricity, someone like Limited could have both a fridge and television at home.

I made another of my most important contacts in Kafanchan by way of the coming of electrification. One young electrician who showed up to connect the house where I was staying to the net became curious about what I was doing in town. Ben told me about his own life, and by the time his installation contracts were largely done, he joined me as a research assistant. He was of a local ethnic group, the Kaje – among those designated "the people of the land" – but as he had had his vocational training in a town further north, and had spent some time doing a little bit of everything in what was at the time still the Nigerian capital, Lagos, on the southern coast, he was about as much of a cosmopolitan as one could be without ever leaving Nigeria. For one thing, usefully for me, he knew enough of a number of Nigerian languages to get by.

So Ben helped in translating interviews. But he was also a local guide, informant, and always good company, with intellectual curiosity and broad local knowledge. Having grown up in Kafanchan, and also by way of his electric installation work in various parts of the town, he knew a great many people. In interviews he sometimes asked sharper questions than I might have dared do myself. He could complain gently after a visit to a service in one of the mushrooming Christian revivalist churches, where he had had to fall on his bare knees in prayer on a rough concrete floor too many times – he usually wore shorts. Ben more enjoyed doing the kung fu, a China-inspired dance fashion, some evenings at one of the beer bars in town. When somehow our work day had ended late, we would stand there in the darkness at the corner of Warri Street and Emir Road, talking about what we had done that day, and what we would try to do the next day, and about life in general.

The electricity supply was really not too reliable – NEPA, which stood for the Nigerian Electric Power Authority, was also interpreted as "never expect power always." Yet more people in Kafanchan could have television sets and record players, and the few hole-in-the-wall record stores had loudspeakers in the town streets. There were good times to be had in the present, and there could be ideas of an even better future. Often, I realized, such visions involved extended horizons – in a fashion, Kafanchan was turning into a world city: an observation post for growing global interconnections. Friends like Limited and Ben helped make me aware of the creativity of new Nigerian popular culture, not least in music. From those loudspeakers I could hear some of the same Black American soul music I had heard at Howard Theatre, and some reggae from the Caribbean, but there were also genres like highlife, juju, and Afrobeat. The conventional wisdom of modernization theory, as well as of European and North American critiques of "cultural imperialism," that a more interconnected world would primarily lead to uniformity and cultural loss, seemed to

26   Prospectus: stops along the way

ignore such growth of new culture through blending and innovative combination.

While I pursued my urban anthropological agenda, then, to a degree the urban place was again becoming more of a locus, a little less of a focus in its own right. Chapter 6 is evidence of this shift. As I sought for terms to fit my street-level observations into a Big Picture, I came across several recent anthropological writings that borrowed concepts of creolization from linguistics to a wider view of large-scale cultural process – and this appealed to me not least because a couple of my linguist colleagues in the project in Washington had been Creolists, exploring traces of African heritage in Black American dialects, so I was already familiar with the general idea. "The world in creolization" shows how I felt that it could serve as a root metaphor bringing together understandings of global center-periphery structures, open cultural continua, and creativity in thought and expression.[40]

Between Chapter 6 and Chapter 7, from 1987 to 1997, there is a decade of mostly desk work – scholarly as well as administrative. As far as reading, thinking, and writing were concerned, my most general preoccupation was what to do with understandings of "culture." That this was a concept of varied uses as well as misuses was clear to me from my Winston Street phase. But then even before that, during my Hoosier year, I had come across a small book, *Culture and Personality* (1961), by the psychological anthropologist Anthony Wallace, who contrasted two understandings of culture: the more widely taken for granted "replication of uniformity" versus "the organization of diversity." Both have their uses, but the idea has remained with me ever since that if the major concern of anthropology is human diversity, then the organization of diversity must be an important aspect of that. Wallace's point of departure was very microsociological – the distribution of understandings among two parents and their baby – but the line of argument could be extended more or less infinitely in scale.

What I went on to do was in large part a matter of bringing together anthropological understandings of culture with symbolic interactionism and the sociology of knowledge, in the book *Cultural Complexity: Studies in the Social Organization of Meaning* (1992c). Anthropology and sociology, it seems to me, are inclined to handle the borderlands between them in large part by mutual avoidance; but these were territories I tried to explore.

I remember with pleasure that I had a year of concentrated engagement with such challenges in Palo Alto, California, at the Center for Advanced Study of the Behavioral Sciences – in front of a wonderful view of the San Francisco Bay, and the hills beyond it. (The study where I sat had in an earlier year been used by the economist George Shultz – by the time I was in it, he was Ronald Reagan's Secretary of State.)

One way of looking at the organization of diversity was to see culture as a network of perspectives, and of perspectives toward other people's perspectives – and with perspectives would also go variations in horizons. How much of the world would individual or collective points of view take in? Just a little more specifically than reaching for a general understanding of cultural complexity, this was also a time of working out the implications of anthropology going global – again a matter of serious world watching. One might observe here that the 1990s were the time when "globalization" really made its entrance as a new keyword in the public vocabulary. In some contexts, however, it seemed preferable to use the term "transnational" rather than "global"; partly because some of the relevant phenomena significantly crossed borders without really becoming worldwide, and partly because the term "globalization" tended to become too associated primarily with the expansive power of markets, at the expense of the variety of other linkages that also reached out widely. ("Transnational," meanwhile, was also something other than "international," which strictly speaking should refer to relations between states, as political entities.)

Increasing global interconnectedness, and awareness of it, also brought other changes in the vocabulary of anthropology and adjoining disciplines, pointing to central emergent concerns. "Borders" became more prominent – although not as absolute outer limits, but as entities to be managed, as relative obstacles for many, as resources for some. "Creolization" was joined by "hybridity" and others, to refer to the creative power of cultural mingling and mixing. "Flow," mostly understood as a term of cultural process in space, tended to involve crossing borders.[41]

In Chapter 7, which originated as a lecture to a conference of the Brazilian Anthropological Association in Salvador, Bahia, I took my point of departure in a novel by the intriguing local novelist Jorge Amado to examine this set of keywords – pointing out that while they had gained a new prominence, they also had histories in anthropology and neighboring disciplines. (Even as I moved on to the debates of the day, I could recognize here some of the references that had been with me since Winston Street: Herskovits, the Chicago sociologists, DuBois on "double consciousness.") Moreover, they belonged in clusters with related notions. As some of the central ideas and arguments were by this time not only the intellectual property of Academia, I suggested a need to relate scholarly efforts to public discourse.

Since then, these terms have continued their passages through history: entering into new combinations, confronting new realities. "Flows" are perhaps now less visible in the vocabulary; the power of cultural mixing may have become more taken for granted, and that coming of global uniformity less so. In "The world in creolization," I referred to the "been-to" as a social type portrayed for one thing in early postcolonial Nigerian fiction. A generation or two later, West African writers with one part of their life in the United States or Europe, and another wherever they have their African roots, have occasionally taken to referring to themselves as "Afropolitans," thus appearing to commute along an updated creole continuum. In anthropology itself, moreover, a growing number of colleagues acknowledge that they are themselves "halfies": "people whose national or cultural identity is mixed by virtue of migration, overseas education, or parentage" (Abu-Lughod 1991: 137).[42] As a quasi-Hoosier,

28 Prospectus: stops along the way

I feel a certain personal affinity with them. Indeed, a number of my best anthropologist friends are halfies.

Here and there, on the other hand, borders may again be more like real barriers, rather than mere metaphors.[43] In some circles, a few decades after the one in Berlin crumbled, "walls" are seen with sympathy.

Knowledge across borders: missionaries, spies, newspeople

Lingering in Salvador after the conference, I stood on a beach one morning, looking out over the south Atlantic. There, somewhere across the ocean, was West Africa. But I would not be returning to Nigeria and Kafanchan. I had thought of that, initially, as an open-ended engagement, with one field stay after another as opportunities arose. But by the mid-1980s or so, things in Nigeria again took a turn for the worse, and I sensed I might feel ill at ease in a fieldwork situation. One military dictator followed another, stashing fortunes away in foreign banks. Particularly under General Sani Abacha, it appeared, all one could expect from the state apparatus was venality and corruption: all the way down, all the way up.[44] There seemed to be no public order worthy of trust, offering some safety net for a foreign field worker's everyday activity.

Moreover, as that novelist Onuora Nzekwu had noted in his *Blade Among the Boys*, "It was the Railway that had created Kafanchan." But I learned that the trains were not running anymore. Nigerian Railways had largely closed down its operations, nation-wide.

Meanwhile, my interests had again, to a degree, also been turning in other directions. Chapter 8, "Other transnationals," was first presented in the spring of 1995 at a conference on "The question of the Other in anthropology" in Germany, on a site with a beautiful view of the Rhine River. I saw this as an occasion to engage in some anthropology of knowledge. There had been a time when there were fewer academics, fewer social scientists in other disciplines, studying in what were the exotic fields of anthropologists. On the other hand, there were also other kinds of transnational knowledge workers, engaged in production and distribution, sometimes with blurred and conflictual borderlands between them. So giving some attention to them was a matter of "studying sideways."

For one thing, there had been that old ambiguous relationship between anthropologists and missionaries: where anthropologists had come to study the thought worlds of the natives, missionaries were perhaps already there, trying to convert these natives away from such ideas. Yet there were also missionaries turning into anthropologists.

More controversially yet, there was the question of the relationship between anthropology and espionage, and other varieties of covert intelligence activity. Franz Boas had taken on the part of a pioneer whistleblower at the time of World War I. At that mid-1960s meeting of the American Anthropological Association which I referred to before, there had been the controversy over Project Camelot, primarily targeting Latin America. Soon enough there were heated arguments over what anthropologists were doing in war-time Southeast Asia. Later yet, after 9/11, the Pentagon launched a program of "Human Terrain Systems" in the Middle East and Central Asia. Indeed, I had myself been suspected of being an informer to the colonial administration during that Caymanian mini-crisis. Yet mostly, this has been a recurrent concern in American anthropology, reflecting its relationship to a world power; not so much elsewhere.[45]

My developing in-depth interest, however, was in the work of newsmedia foreign correspondents.[46] Again, they shared that preoccupation of anthropologists with "being there," but their presence in more or less remote places was of a rather different kind, and their conditions of reporting were likewise different. I end Chapter 8 with a case study of *New York Times* reporting on an earthquake disaster in Kobe, Japan, as material for some comparisons with anthropological writing.[47]

Streets and screens in the global village

I need to take several steps back here. Very quickly, as I began walking around in the Winston Street neighborhood, I noticed the mobile transistor radios, usually carried by young men, turned on to one of the soul music stations – these still rather clumsy devices became known as "ghetto blasters." Then as I was sitting in some living room in the neighborhood, even for hours, watching black-and-white television with friends from the streetcorner, I worried to begin with about what I was doing there: nothing had been said about watching television in the classic ethnographies I had been reading. They focused on face-to-face relationships only. Was I wasting my time? Gradually, however, I realized that this was part of my active field work. The audience response to programs, whether they were mainstream soap operas or boxing games, was culturally revealing.

Moreover, the disc jockeys at these Black radio stations were Very Important Persons in the ghetto. I went to a public birthday party for one of them, with the artist name "Nighthawk," and shared a table with the Black Power leader Stokely Carmichael (who most likely wondered what I was doing there). I joined in, too, as Stokely, somewhat sheepishly, led the assembled fans in singing "Happy Birthday to Nighthawk." (Carmichael was himself ironically referred to, among some of his political associates, as "Teevee Starmichael.")

Then these were also the years, in the mid-1960s, when you could hardly fail to notice that Marshall McLuhan's *Understanding Media* (1964) had introduced the phrase "the global village." It was a striking notion, although I have always felt it was rather misleading. As it was mostly about the power of television, the flow of messages was one-way in a manner hardly similar to that in ordinary villages. (Only the arrival of "social media" some decades later would come closer to that kind of back-and-forth exchange – but they would also have other implications.) Nonetheless, there was a rapidly growing public awareness of the social and cultural implications of electronic media.

30 Prospectus: stops along the way

In Kafanchan, the coming of electricity had meant the coming of television. It was also my daily habit to read the *New Nigerian*, the paper published in the nearest larger city, to get a sense of what was happening nationally. But I discovered that the coverage could be quite uneven. When soldiers (stationed in Kafanchan ever since Nigeria's late 1960s civil war) rioted in the market place, protesting a lag in the payment of their monthly wages, military police were sent in to restore order – but in the following days, the *New Nigerian* contained not a word about it.

In other words, the varied presences of media had been a recurrent ingredient in my ethnographic experiences. Here was again that challenge of stretching anthropology to take in all of current human experience. This was reflected, too, in the book *Cultural Complexity*. But in the field situations, these experiences had been mostly at the consumption end. From my own news consumer habits, however, it was a rather short step to a more active curiosity about the production of news.

Two, three, many fields – in one

In the late 1990s, I became engaged in a field study of foreign correspondents – resulting finally in my book, *Foreign News* (2004b). For one thing, this involved a new methodological trend. In Washington, much of my work had been on that block-long Winston Street. In Kafanchan, I would walk around the town in a couple of hours – pedestrian field work. (At the same time, I knew that there were in a way several co-existing sites in the single community, with people whom it might be wise to keep apart.) Now, surely linked to the concern with transnational interconnections, the insight was spreading in anthropology that the customary concentration on a single field site was not always optimal. Consequently, in my foreign correspondent study, most of my field work was in three widely dispersed cities: Jerusalem (which had Middle East correspondents), Johannesburg (Africa correspondents), and Tokyo (where most foreign newspeople focused on Japan). There was some additional work in other cities, where I found myself briefly and where correspondents were also based. Moreover, I met with some foreign news editors at headquarters: at the *New York Times*, the *Daily Telegraph* in London, the *Frankfurter Allgemeine Zeitung*, and *Dagens Nyheter* in Stockholm.

Chapters 9, 10, and 11 all relate to my foreign-correspondent study, in different ways. Chapter 9, "Being there … and there … and there!" focuses on issues of multi-site research. If Chapter 2 was mostly streetcorner methodology, this is newsbeat methodology. Not least old-timers in the discipline, aware of the challenges involved in getting to know the complexities of a single field site, could sometimes have their doubts about the quality of those new multilocal efforts. So I saw it as one task to try and make clear that these, usually, were not attempts to deal with several sites as local wholes, but rather concentrated on the particular groups and networks that tied them together. On this I could draw not only on my own experience, but also that of several colleagues in Stockholm who had taken on other multi-site projects.

On to Chapter 10. In early 2017 it was announced that Clare Hollingworth, legendary journalist, had died. At the beginning of her career, based momentarily in Poland, Hollingworth had been the very first to report that World War II had broken out: German troops were moving in across the border. In the early 1980s, she had established herself in Hong Kong. And there, a few months before her death, she had celebrated her 105th birthday, with a party at the Foreign Correspondents Club.

At that vibrant place, Chapter 10 also begins, and it focuses in large part on newspeople based in Hong Kong. This had been one of my supplementary field sites, a brief stay brought into the study because I could combine it with a conference there.[48] I focused on it in this chapter because it originated as a conference paper in Perth, Australia – and in Hong Kong I had found the only correspondent for an Australian newspaper who had become one of my important informants. His experiences, and his own analysis of the varieties of foreign correspondents, were interesting enough, but then I found others among his local colleagues very valuable informants as well.

In this chapter, however, occupational ethnography is intertwined with the theme of cosmopolitanism, a concern that has come to be with me for a long time, although not so fully grounded in specific field work. It had begun in the mid-1980s, when I gave a talk about globalization at the University of California, Berkeley, and a question came up whether I had thought about cosmopolitanism.[49] I confessed that I had not, really – it was not a concept often referred to in the human sciences at the time. But it stuck in my mind as something I ought to attend to. And then a year or so later, as I was invited to "The First International Conference on the Olympics and East/West and South/North Cultural Exchanges in the World System," in Seoul, I saw an opportunity to collect my thoughts. (This was at a time when South Korea was about to stage the 1988 Olympic Games – hence the title of this gathering.)

Inevitably, I was reminded that I had reached the country that had long ago been central to my acquisition of newspaper reading habits; not least when I crossed the 38th parallel which had been central to the Korean War. In my conference contribution in Seoul, relating to the conference topic, I dwelt on cosmopolitanism in the sense of searching for new experience, appreciating cultural diversity more or less for its own sake. Yet while increasing global interconnections offers more opportunities for this, not least through travel, not all geographical mobility in the world is intended to seek new windows of cultural experience. Migrant laborers are looking for a livelihood, refugees and exiles fleeing from oppression mostly want to survive. If they value the encounter with a new cultural habitat, fine – but it could not be taken for granted.

Active, experiential, intellectual, and aesthetic outreach would be one kind of cosmopolitanism. But there are others. Not so long after that Seoul conference, the Cold War came to an end. The world, for some time at least, particularly in the 1990s, seemed more like "a single place," and cosmopolitans could be world citizens, concerned with the needs and desires of humanity as a whole, on the

32 Prospectus: stops along the way

basis of moral and political principles. For some time at least, in Academia, this became the more conspicuous notion of cosmopolitanism in a number of disciplines, such as in political philosophy and sociology.

Yet then there is also a third, everyday sense of cosmopolitanism: a matter of simply managing cultural diversity as a fact of life, coping with it without seeking it out, mostly without attaching particular value to it. It comes to us not least in our work places and neighborhoods as they draw people of many different backgrounds, from many places, especially in big cities.

So this is the way I worked myself, gradually, through the varieties of cosmopolitanism; again one of those words that keeps moving in time and space.[50] In Chapter 10, the topic is discussed at two levels. On the one hand, foreign correspondents, based away from home, may or may not become cosmopolitans themselves. On the other hand, by way of their work, they may have an important role in turning their readers and viewers into cosmopolitans. Much of our awareness of other parts of the world, its riches and its troubles (involving especially those first two kinds of cosmopolitanism), comes by way of media reporting – so how do we respond to it?

Soweto and Sophiatown

Chapter 11, "Touring Soweto," is a by-product of the foreign correspondent project. I found a great many of the "Africa correspondents" of American and European media organizations based, remarkably, in two buildings in a Johannesburg suburb. That had its own implications. Their newsbeats could in principle cover some forty-five countries south of the Sahara, but they might get to travel to the more remote parts only when there was major bad news (coups, civil wars, major natural disasters) – not to do more ethnography-like feature stories on everyday life. Decisions on such costly travel tended to be taken at headquarters in Europe or North America, rather than by the correspondents themselves. Not that the continent was lacking in unfortunate events in the 1990s, but it seemed to me that as a notion of "Afro-pessimism" spread in the commentary of the Global North, the organization of the international news business had its part in amplifying such understandings.[51]

In this chapter, however, I visit, in a fashion, two other suburban areas of Johannesburg. Soweto is very much of the present, and at the same time a symbol of the apartheid era, a monument of both segregation and resistance. Nelson Mandela had lived there once, before he was incarcerated for a great many years. Only his release set in motion that transition of South Africa out of apartheid that became part of the world history of the late twentieth century, and made him a global hero. I could get a view of a great deal of this on a guided bus tour. (That tour could also bring to mind the ethnography of apartheid-era tsotsis in Chapter 3, on the management of danger.)

The other area is really not there anymore. Its time of efflorescence was in the mid-twentieth century, and when I came to look for any signs of what had been Sophiatown, it was basically long gone, torn down by the apartheid regime. But I had already written about Sophiatown "from afar" in an article drawing on many kinds of sources.[52] In that article (originally a conference paper from the year before apartheid finally came to an end), I had viewed it as an instance of cultural creativity through creolization. Now I could also link it to what had been one of my other interests, pursued mostly by way of historical materials: the remarkable outcome of a combination of diversity and openness, in particular cities at particular times – Calcutta, Vienna, and San Francisco had been my main cases, but historical Sophiatown could fit into the same picture.[53]

A postscript to my earlier article on Sophiatown; it seems that it came just in time as local scholarly interest in the history of the area began to develop. At an American Anthropological Association meeting some number of years later, a whole group of young researchers from one of the Johannesburg universities held a session focusing on Sophiatown – and finding me in the audience, they insisted on taking group photographs with me, to show their students at home the author of the article that had for some time been assigned course reading!

Kafanchan again: "being there," and "having been there"

While I was engaged in my foreign correspondent study, I also had periods in Stockholm. And so, even if I have always tended to be a news junkie, now I was attending more closely than usual to television news programs. There I was, then, in front of the TV set in my Stockholm living room, watching CNN International – and that evening it took me by surprise. One of the CNN Africa correspondents, otherwise based in Nairobi, was on the screen, reporting from Kafanchan. Soon after, the *New York Times*, too, had a news article datelined Kafanchan.

The story that both the *New York Times* and CNN told was that the old Emir of Jemaa, with his palace in Kafanchan, had died, at age 95. (I suspect that figure was uncertain and approximate.) The government had announced that he would be succeeded by his son. A great many in the local population had disapproved, so they had stormed the palace, burned down parts of it, and chased the new emir away on his coronation day. The uproar had also caused some deaths.

That may well have been the first and last time that Kafanchan made it into world news, and evidently it was a matter of serendipity – the newspeople had found one thing when they were looking for another. After many years of military dictatorship Nigeria was on its way to democratic politics. General Sani Abacha, that rather unsavory head of state, had died under somewhat mysterious circumstances. (As one rumor had it, people in his nearest circle had flown in some particularly pretty Asian prostitutes to entertain him, and then poisoned his Viagra pills.) The military junta that succeeded him had decided to return the country to civilian rule, and now the world's newsmedia were gathered in

34 Prospectus: stops along the way

the capital Abuja to witness the inauguration of the newly elected president –
actually another former military ruler, more recently a chicken farmer – when
they heard of some dramatic violence in another town not so far away. So at
least some of the reporters hurried over there.

Obviously these people from the global newsbeat had very soon left Kafanchan, but I could easily fill in the background of the story. It really began
almost two hundred years earlier, when an Islamic *jihad* expanded from the
emirates of what would become the far north of Nigeria. It established an
uncertain foothold in the area where Kafanchan would later come into existence, and that emirate of Jemaa had been founded then. About a hundred years
later, when the British colonialists arrived, they followed their standard practice
of establishing a low-cost "indirect rule" by way of what was taken to be
"native authorities." Which in this case had the consequence of giving that
Jemaa emirate a strength it had never had before.[54]

Time passed again; by the mid-twentieth century the local populations in the
area had been pleased to find that the newly arrived Christian missions provided
them with both ideological and organizational tools for their opposition to Islam
and that rather unimpressive emirate. Moreover, by now Kafanchan was there.
The emirate had at one point had to move its headquarters to the town, but
migrant newcomer populations were also present. Neither they nor the "people
of the land" had ever really acquiesced in emirate domination – but they had
expected that when old Emir Isa Muhammadu (whom I had met a couple of
times) died, the entire antiquated structure would be abolished. So when the
outgoing military regime in Abuja did not do so, they rebelled.

For me, back in Stockholm, this brief newsmedia experience provided some
food for thought. Again, there was that idea of "being there." A lot earlier, but
still in my mind, there was that Cayman Islands crisis, where by accident
I found myself doing a sort of parachutist anthropology. In the case of the Jemaa
emirate crisis, the correspondents of CNN and the *New York Times* had been
there, and I had not.

My general sense, however, was that there could often be a role for anthropologists here, in a division of labor and division of knowledge between newsmedia reporters and academia. What we can contribute is often a matter of
"having been there." When the parachutist correspondents submit their "first
drafts of history," or when their home-based editors try to make sense of what
is going on, anthropologists may already know a fair amount of what went
before, stored but still useful knowledge – perhaps some basis, too, for informed
speculation about what may happen next. Here may be a shift again, between
"fast" and "slow," as contrasted early in this prospectus. I think of this now and
then, when momentarily some place or area shows up on the global newsbeat
that I know something about, or that I know somebody else in anthropology
who knows something about. In fact, I had been through something like this
before. Toward the end of my time on Winston Street, in early April, 1968,
when Martin Luther King had been assassinated, there were upheavals in

Washington, DC, as in many other American cities; a headline in the *New York Times* on April 6, 1968, read "Army Troops in Capital as Negroes Riot; Guards Sent into Chicago, Detroit, Boston; Johnson Asks a Joint Session of Congress."

So the National Guard was in my neighborhood. On the sidewalk, neighborhood children playfully imitated troops marching. As my *Soulside* appeared the following year, the title of the concluding, slow-motion chapter was "Waiting for the Burning to Begin." That is, the streetcorner waiting for the newsbeat.

Newspeople, such as editors on the foreign desk, may not be able to identify possible resource persons, or may feel that they do not have time to look for them. The anthropologists, busy with campus work and with such writing as fits into contemporary academic bibliometrics, may not find the time to make themselves available, may have their doubts about journalism and media, or may be reticent for other reasons. Yet for the edification of those informed, cosmopolitan world citizens, and for public understandings of what anthropologists do, more such interactions might be a good thing. In a changing news landscape, with blogs and the like, there should be a wider range of possibilities.[55] Public anthropology can be protean – shapeshifting, moving at different speeds. The sources for "having been there" can be in your publications, in your fieldnotes, or simply stored away in your mind.

Anthropology at home

Back to Sweden, finally – and not just to time spent in front of a television screen, but in other settings, over the years. I went off to Hoosier country, to Winston Street and other places, but in between (and more and more as time passed) I was in Stockholm, and at Stockholm University, serving soon enough as professor of social anthropology.[56]

Like many European countries, Sweden long held on to an old-fashioned academic structure where most disciplines in a university would have only one full professor.[57] For a fairly long period, this was the situation I found myself in at Stockholm University. The setup had various consequences. Within the discipline, whichever it was, the single professor might leave a strong mark on teaching and training at all levels, giving priority to their own scholarly interests. It might, for one thing, have a strong influence on what dissertation projects graduate students were permitted to take on, if the professor was the only advisor available.

When I found myself in this slot, however, that did not seem like a good strategy. The spirit of the times was egalitarian. My own sense, moreover, was that the people pursuing a doctorate in anthropology often had a commitment to their particular interest that was not narrowly academic – it could be personal, moral, political. Someone coming in preoccupied with inequality in Latin American peasant society could not easily be turned around to engaging with West African kinship. So the solitary professorship became rather more of a challenge to try and be a useful interlocutor for a wide range of projects that

36 Prospectus: stops along the way

in themselves seemed practically possible. For one thing, it may have taken me to a wider range of ethnographic readings than would have been needed in a more developed division of knowledge; and an inclination to more generalized "world watching" went well with this.

It also helped that I was able to make brief visits to a number of the graduate students in their fields. This took me for example to sites in Yemen, Syria, India, Malaysia, and Colombia, as well as some places more nearby. At the time, these fields were reasonably accessible and peaceful. As several of them have since been through violent upheavals, early glimpses of their everyday life under other conditions have made their troubles come more alive and distressing to me from a distance. At the time, anyway, these quick-entry-and-exit visits seemed useful both for me and my student hosts. Later, having come to know the practices of newsmedia foreign correspondents, I have thought of these visits, again, as a kind of parachute anthropology on my part – with the graduate students as expert local "fixers." (Without one of them, how could I have gained immediate entry to a wedding feast in a Yemeni mountain town?)

The single-professor structure, however, also had implications for external relations. The professor, in the Swedish academic vocabulary of the time, was the *ämnesföreträdare*, the "discipline representative." For my part, this involved making room for anthropology in a rather tradition-bound academic landscape, with taken-for-granted disciplinary divides. Whenever you felt that your discipline had something to say that should not be ignored, or whenever someone else, in Academia or in public life, wanted an anthropologist voice to be heard, the "discipline representative" had better be awake. (The "Touring Soweto" piece was actually an example of this – a lecture to a conference of the Swedish Urban Environmental Council.) It also involved crossing discipline borders. When the death of Gunnar Myrdal was announced, I proposed that Stockholm University should institute an annual public lecture in his memory, as this had been his last academic affiliation; for some time this became one of the more successful interdisciplinary ventures among the social sciences on campus.

Another committee, in an interdisciplinary branch of a national research council exploring future-oriented research, allowed me to do some more work on my media interests. As Swedish scholarship on the media had long been mostly confined to public opinion research, the time seemed ripe to take up other possibilities in a slightly more McLuhanesque ("the medium is the message") way, and more comparatively. A resulting edited volume, interdisciplinary but with several anthropologists contributing, had chapters on Kenyan women in *purdah* watching Bollywood movies, on censorship in media in Poland under communism, and on the role of media in twentieth-century Swedish nation-building. The volume turned out to have considerable influence for some time.[58]

One slightly offbeat aspect of this demonstration of versatility was my engagement as an occasional columnist for a rather short-lived Stockholm financial daily with an ambitious page of cultural commentary. I wrote brief pieces on the growing prominence of the diaspora concept, on a reunited Berlin after the Wall had gone, on Afro-Brazilian culture in Salvador (after my visit there for Chapter 8), on "symbolic analysts," the footloose intelligentsias with supposedly only tenuous ties to any one national entity, and various other topics.[59] I enjoyed this, but there was too little time to do much of it, and after a change of editors with which I had little sympathy, I dropped out. Not so much later, the paper foiled.

Perhaps too involved in local academic entrepreneurship, I followed only somewhat distractedly (and without much urge to take sides) the factionalisms and autocritiques of U.S. anthropology that went with the political disappointments of the Reagan years, and the decline into "audit culture" of British academic life that Thatcherism brought.[60] On the other hand, Stockholm received some prominent visitors: from the Western Hemisphere ranging from Clifford Geertz to Eric Wolf and Marvin Harris; from the Eastern Hemisphere, among others, Maurice Bloch from London, Marc Augé from Paris, Archie Mafeje from Cape Town (although in exile), Shmuel Eisenstadt from Jerusalem, Satish Saberwal from New Delhi, and Chie Nakane from Tokyo. The point was to keep scholarly borders open – without too much of dominant center-periphery relationships.

In Europe, in time, the Wall crumbled in Berlin, and the Iron Curtain was no more. This happened just in time as a European Association of Social Anthropologists (EASA) was formed, with a first conference in Coimbra, Portugal. Without much funding at their disposal, anthropologists from East and Central Europe got into their cars and drove to the far end of the continent, eager to meet colleagues who had been inaccessible before. The next conference, two years later, was in Prague. I enjoyed serving as EASA president for a term in the mid-1990s. The organization has done much to create a sense of scholarly community in Europe. It has helped, at the same time, that the European Union has done much to facilitate student and faculty exchanges.

The coming of diversity

Locally, more importantly than columnist writing, there were committees and conferences. At the time, especially from the 1970s onwards, this often had to do with the fact that Swedish society was changing. Particularly from the 1960s, with Swedish industry successful and expansive, there were labor migrants, mostly from other parts of Europe. Then a little later, there were refugees, from the Balkans, the Middle East, Latin America, and Africa. In what had been a relatively homogeneous society (and where regional differences were given little official recognition) there was a new preoccupation with diversity and difference, in everyday and organizational life and in policy circles. Anthropologists were invited as experts and consultants to do field research.[61] In the offices of government and local administrations, this was largely a matter of benign curiosity about the newcomers; perhaps one of the professional inclinations of the

38 Prospectus: stops along the way

anthropologists was a bit unexpected among those seeking their advice, as these scholar-commentators tried to cast light not only on the peculiarities of the newcomers, but also on those of the host society. Swedish doctors, surprisingly to their new patients, did not behave like Turkish doctors.

For some people, even rooted in Sweden, learning how to be ethnic could be a new endeavor. Having certain connections, among colleagues and students, to both groups, I learned that representatives of a national organization of the Saami people had contacted the Jewish congregation in Stockholm to seek knowledge about such matters. Until this time, the Saami had mostly operated, in Swedish fashion, as a professional interest group of reindeer herders.

The new diversity showed in the departmental student body too. Not least for some young refugees, the university may have allowed more personal freedom to maneuver than many other Swedish settings, and an anthropology department could well offer a more open environment than most. One Brazilian undergraduate would later return home and eventually become a presidential candidate for the Green Party. Among those who stayed on as graduate students was a young Iranian refugee who had escaped from becoming cannon fodder in the 1980s Iran–Iraq War, making his way across the mountains of Central Asia to India, before flying back westward to Sweden, entering as an undocumented migrant. Later, with a doctorate, he became a colleague in the department.[62]

Again, along much of my personal journey through anthropology, I have found "culture" in the singular difficult to do without – and "cultures" in the plural recurrently an intellectual challenge, large or small. Chapter 12 is not so much specifically about Sweden, but an instance of serving more or less as a public anthropologist in the context of national self-consciousness about diversity – a lecture to an interdisciplinary elite audience, with some policy people included as well, about what to do with the culture concept. By this time, the relationship between Sweden and diversity was no longer quite so happy. Anti-immigrant sentiments were showing up; even violent xenophobia. There were reasons for my ending with a plea not to misuse academic authority to make things worse.[63]

In this chapter, although not explicitly referred to, some of the lessons from Winston Street may still be recognizable. They are there in the emphasis on a flexible, internally diverse cultural process – as opposed to a "cultural fundamentalism" making its appearance in many settings and guises, and claiming a degree of academic respectability not least with the international attention given to the political scientist Samuel Huntington's "clash of civilizations" thesis. Bringing up Huntington at this point could possibly seem a little far-fetched; yet years later, I in fact heard the leader of the newish, neo-nationalist Sweden Democrat Party referring, in an election campaign meeting, to the civilizational clash as an established historical fact.

It is true, too, that Huntington's scenario, and other global future scenarios that came together as a new Big Picture genre in the period after the end of the Cold War and then continued to develop, in Academia and in journalism,

Prospectus: stops along the way **39**

became a central interest for me from around this point on, in reading, reflecting, and writing.[64] In very large part, this was an American genre. And again, I tried to observe and scrutinize it from some distance.

September 11, 2001, Stockholm University in the afternoon: I am on my way to a committee meeting when word starts slowly spreading through campus corridors that two planes have crashed into skyscrapers in New York. In the meeting, a history professor suggests that it will all turn out to be a hoax: like in 1938, when Orson Welles' radio play of *The War of the Worlds*, about an invasion by extraterrestrial beings, was reported to have caused a panic among listeners.

And then April 7, 2017, on a Friday afternoon when the streets in central Stockholm were fairly busy, the kind of event occurred that by now had come to be expected. A stolen truck drives down a pedestrian street, the driver intending to hit as many people as possible. Fortunately, as the truck first hits some concrete obstacle which it pushes in front of the car, it makes a horrible noise, and many pedestrians hear that and get out of its way. Five people are killed, another larger number injured. The driver-assassin was apprehended later in the day. He was a middle-aged man from Uzbekistan, who had been denied political asylum and should no longer have been in Sweden. He confesses to the crime, and admits that he sympathizes with ISIS, the Islamist caliphate linked to a great many recent terrorist deeds in Europe.

In and out of Sweden: small worlds

Chapter 13 is more concretely local, focusing on a mid-century Stockholm detective story writer, Stieg Trenter, who had been a personal presence in my childhood and early youth, as a friend of my parents. Moving a little back-and-forth in time, I relate his life and work to what had become *Nordic noir*, an internationally successful body of mystery writings from the early twenty-first century, also suggesting an affinity between detective stories and urban ethnography. Trenter was inclined to model characters in his stories on people he knew, and members of my own family were occasionally among these. (I could now add that as some Trenter stories were remade, years later, in comic book form, figures I knew to have been once inspired by my father and sister also appeared there – but I, and not the artist, could know that they had not looked like that at all.)

Through my father's ear-nose-throat medical practice in Stockholm's Old Town, there are actually also links to previous chapters, and to what has already been said above. Many of his patients were very ordinary neighborhood people (at a time when the Old Town had mostly not yet begun to gentrify). But Alva Myrdal, Gunnar Myrdal's partner in life, was also an occasional patient, living a few blocks away. Another recurrent visitor, coming in from the local musical instruments shop, where he earned much of his living, was a professional jazz drummer with his origins in Surinam. But a fair number of other patients were actors and singers, locals as well as people just coming through, who often

40 Prospectus: stops along the way

urgently needed to have sore throats dealt with. And my father was remarkably ready to be there at short notice, to treat them backstage at the theater even, between exits and entrances. In this way his circle of patients over the years came to include at least one of the members of the quartet ABBA, internationally famous over a fairly extended period; and Miriam Makeba, the singer who once started her career at Sophiatown shebeens. (When I heard from my parents that Makeba, while on tour, had just needed some laryngological attention in Stockholm, I was in Washington, and could hear her hit *Pata Pata* on the radio all the time.)

I mentioned before that early on in my concern with urban anthropology, I had come to engage with network concepts. For one thing, I occasionally play with ideas of network reach – this sort of imagination was stimulated in the 1960s by the "small world" experiment of the American social psychologist Stanley Milgram, who showed that anybody in the United States could contact anybody else in the country by an average of six person-to-person links (although certainly, hardly anybody would be aware of network connections that far away).[65] The general idea was then popularized as "degrees of separation" – but one could argue that it had already been parodied in the 1920s, with a British hit tune by Herbert Farjeon: "I've danced with a man, who's danced with a girl, who's danced with the Prince of Wales."

Milgram's study stayed within the boundaries of the United States. Later, in a period when with a set of anthropologist colleagues I became engaged in a comparative study of "small countries" (with up to around 10 million inhabitants, thus including Sweden), we noted that in these, the number of links needed to reach from anyone to anyone was likely to be even smaller.[66] One prominent Swedish journalist, also devoting a column to characteristics of such countries, indeed suggested that "in a small country everybody knows everybody else" – but then quickly admitted that this is a slight exaggeration. Yet I could note that this journalist and I had indeed met on various occasions. Moreover, in my chapter for a book resulting from our "small countries" project, I could exemplify the point with my relatively recent encounter with the King of Sweden, when I could surprise him by telling him that he and I had long ago had the same physical education teacher (Hannerz 2017b).

Reflecting on my father's medical practices, I could also see that by now, one can certainly play "small world" games globally as well. Among my father's rather early patients was also the American blues singer (and political activist) Josh White. White, I have later become aware, had had his own, earlier personal contacts with the couple in the White House, Franklin and Eleanor Roosevelt. So when seeking the number of links between anybody and anybody, I am pleased to consider that retrospectively, one could reach from Miriam Makeba to the Roosevelts through three links, by way of my father's practice in Stockholm. (Of course, there could perhaps have been even shorter network paths.)

There is also an early, important article by the sociologist Mark Granovetter (1973) on "the strength of weak ties." Granovetter's point is that some personal networks form dense clusters of people who all relate directly to one another – in a few links, you may just be back at yourself. But if you really want to reach further effectively, people who have more varied contacts in their sparse networks are more useful. My father's practice seemed to suggest that. All kinds of people have everyday ear, nose, or throat illnesses, and could turn up in his waiting-room. By inclination, although without knowing it, my father seems to have been a kind of on-and-off lay-ethnographer, talking to his patients not only about their illnesses and treatments, but about one thing or other in their lives. And in his personal, away-from-the-office network, there were not so many other medical people either. Thus he got to know people of all kinds – more than many people in the academic world, who fairly often live in their intellectual and organizational silos.[67]

Finally, in Chapter 14, his son, the urban and transnational anthropologist, returns to his village roots (although as the chapter begins, I am a European anthropologist, speaking to American colleagues, in San Francisco). By the time we reach here, this village setting will not be utterly unfamiliar to a reader of this book. It has appeared in passing in earlier chapters: in a conversation with a China correspondent; with the discovery of a xenophobic leaflet in a mailbox; and with a neighbor across the road, the plumber, reading the same detective story as all those other people, elsewhere in the world.

The village is that to which my maternal great-grandparents retired, early in the twentieth century, after giving up the family farm a couple of miles away. Three of their sons had left for America, as so many young people from the area did. (Another, my grandfather, became a sea captain.) Their house has been mine for several decades now, used mostly in summers. The village may look very ordinary, but in it, or close to it, there have been some unusual people. A local entrepreneur claimed he met human-like beings coming out of a spaceship at the edge of the forest. A former bank robber was once on the global newsbeat in his own way. A retired farmer's wife turned out to be a relative of a far-away imperial dynasty. This chapter is my story about them and some others, with some final reflections on the ways the world hangs together now.

That Swedish newspaper columnist referred to above, commenting on the characteristics of small countries, also points out that small countries are superior to large countries in one way: they cannot be provincial. Someone from a small country, he argues, must always explain where he is from, learn foreign languages and customs, and accept without protest that both Shakespeare and Picasso are part of his cultural heritage. As a veteran foreign correspondent, the columnist was undoubtedly particularly aware of this, but to a degree it seems true of many of his compatriots, and other small country inhabitants.

Indeed, perhaps in terms of territory, but in any case socially or culturally, and imaginatively, you cannot go very far in such a country without stumbling across a border. My village offers examples of that. One summer as I was exploring the attic of our house, taking my time to see what might have

42 Prospectus: stops along the way

assembled in its nooks and crannies from the time when my great-grandfather moved in, I found a copy of the second Swedish edition of Harriet Beecher Stowe's *Uncle Tom's Cabin*, with an ornate binding from the 1890s. It seemed rather touching that my great-grandfather, who in those days had probably never ventured very far out of his rural neighborhood, or his wife, similarly sedentary, or at least one of those ten children of theirs who made their way to adulthood, had in their imagination entered another distant and harsher variety of farm life: that of plantation slavery in the American South.

But then again that was not the only way they came to engage with a wider world, as those three sons joined the emigration stream to America. One could wonder if impressions from the story had any part in debates within the family over the pros and cons of allowing sons and brothers to head across the Atlantic.

Notes

1 This lecture, where he dwelt on the notion of the "ancient oikoumene" – "ecumene" is the more recent form – could be seen as a pioneer attempt at a global anthropology (Kroeber 1945). Alfred Kroeber shows up again elsewhere in this book; most recently, I have also come back to him as I offer my critique of more or less current global future scenarios; see Hannerz (2016: 162–165, 183–184).

2 For one thing, there are more of these thoughts in *Anthropology's World: Life in a Twenty-first Century Discipline* (Hannerz 2010a).

3 I know of at least three anthropological books titled *Being There*: Bradburd (1998), Watson (1999) and Borneman and Hammoudi (2009).

4 I depend here on parts of my article "Confessions of a Hoosier Anthropologist" (2014), written for a section in the *American Anthropologist* devoted to drawing the attention of U.S. anthropologists to the fact that their discipline exists in other countries as well.

5 Sahlins' presentation is included in his collected papers, *Culture in Practice* (2000).

6 After a great many printings of the first edition, *Soulside* also appeared in a second edition, with another publisher, in 2004. This later edition also has a new afterword, looking back at its original context and issues emerging in the decades which followed.

7 In the first of the two volumes mentioned, there were contributors such as Sidney Mintz, active in many fields but not least in historical anthropology; the folklorist Roger Abrahams; and the editor himself, John Szwed, ethnographer-ethnomusicologist. In the other volume, contributors included the Kenyan political scientist Ali Mazrui and the South African literary scholar Ezekiel Mphahlele. That whole latter enterprise, published as *Views from Abroad* (1978), I remember was skillfully managed by the sociologist Peter I. Rose, whom I had the pleasure of meeting a number of times, in Stockholm as well in the United States.

8 A couple of lectures at conferences of the Swedish Institute for North American Studies (Hannerz 1988, 1992a) are yet further examples – presentations about American culture and its international influence to audiences mostly of non-Americans, with a special interest in American matters.

9 But the metaphor of the theme park, of course, also has connotations of spectacle and entertainment. In that later publication (in a volume named *America Observed*, with contributing non-U.S. anthropologists discussing their American field experiences) I go on to let the Geertzian concept of the theater state move from Bali to America. For one thing, I believe it shows that while the 2016 presidential campaign was in some ways unique, it also displayed some more recurrent features of American political culture (Hannerz 2017a).

Prospectus: stops along the way **43**

10 Much of this work is collected in a posthumously published volume (Herskovits 1966).

11 One was Alan Merriam, anthropologist of music and himself an accomplished jazz musician; the other was Peter Hammond, who made a great difference by recommending me for the Washington, DC job.

12 The preface of *An American Dilemma* acknowledges that Arnold Rose, one of Myrdal's closest assistants, wrote this chapter.

13 See on this Gershenhorn's (2004: 94–95) biography of Herskovits; it should be added that Gershenhorn does not really aim at a comprehensive view of Herskovits' part in American anthropology. While he is hardly much read today, he was a force outside his African and African-American field of expertise as well – writing about cultural relativism and cultural dynamics, and debating what is "economic" about economic anthropology. A memorandum he offered, with two other prominent anthropologists, on the emergent topic of "acculturation," could be seen as a forerunner of studies of globalization (Redfield et al. 1936).

14 Herskovits had to write *The Myth of the Negro Past* in a hurry, and he would have liked to do more research for it. Some of his earlier field excursions were brief, and by the standard of a later time, perhaps not of the highest quality (see on this for example Price and Price 2003). Looking back, too, it may be that his thinking, to a degree, remained inside the box of conceptualization established in American anthropology through its reconstruction of Native American cultures, as these had once been. We get a sense of his view of the changing research scene in a new preface to a later edition ([1941] 1958).

15 It was only much later that I made a brief visit to Texas Hill Country, and got a stronger sense of the modest beginnings that Lyndon Johnson came out of – the early background of his reformist streak, and his vision of a "Great Society."

16 A volume by Rainwater and Yancey (1967) discusses the controversy over the "Moynihan Report", as it was still fresh, and reprints the report as well; a retrospective study of its impact is that by Greenbaum (2015). Among the writings critically discussing the relationship between culture and poverty in the American context are also those by Valentine (1968) and Leacock (1971).

17 An aside here: when I was in Accra, Ghana, in early 1963, I made an attempt to meet with W.E.B. DuBois, who had moved there on the invitation of President Nkrumah to be the leading figure in the work on an *Encyclopedia Africana* – but at the office gate my request was declined, on the grounds that DuBois was ill. And only a few months later, DuBois died, at age 95, in Accra. The high-level gatekeeper I encountered, an associate in the encyclopedia project, was Alphaeus Hunton, another African-American radical exile who had earlier had the distinction of being jailed for "contempt of court" during the McCarthy era. A major DuBois biography by Morris (2015) describes how DuBois' pioneering work in African-American sociology was rather systematically disregarded by White mainstream scholars in the early twentieth century – including the Chicago sociologists as well as Melville Herskovits. Gunnar Myrdal, in *An American Dilemma*, mentions DuBois again and again, and even cites those "... peculiar sensation ... double-consciousness ..." lines, but treats him mostly as a Black activist. The biography by Morris, on the other hand, has virtually nothing to say about DuBois' pan-Africanist activities, or his later life.

18 I tried to offer another sketch of this complex field of research in an overview of Black ghetto research in the 1960s (Hannerz 1975).

19 In 1975, Myrdal was in fact awarded the Malinowski Award of the Society for Applied Anthropology. In receiving the award, he discussed "the unity of the social sciences," beginning his lecture by noting that he did not feel "worthy of this honor. I have not made any contribution within your discipline. The question can thus properly be raised, how I could have the audacity to accept it. I suppose the honest answer must be that I am too human and defenseless against flattery. I also looked forward with much pleasure to being together with anthropologists for a couple of

44 Prospectus: stops along the way

days. I, like all others who read books, have, of course, enjoyed occasionally following an anthropologist's adventures among primitive people even more than reading a novel" (Myrdal 1975: 327).

20 Gunnar Myrdal was awarded the Bank of Sweden Prize in Economics in Memory of Alfred Nobel in 1974, Alva Myrdal received the Nobel Peace Prize in 1982.

21 Clifford Geertz reviewed *Asian Drama* critically in the journal *Encounter* in 1969.

22 In the sociolinguistic project that I worked with in Washington, I had two women colleagues – one a native Black Washingtonian, one a White academic migrant (with Peace Corps experience from West Africa). The two became very close friends – and consequently I was amused rather than shocked when in amicable coffee room exchange, I overheard the latter address the former with the n-word, and the former responding with laughter. It was a conscious sign that they were comfortable together in a zone of Black cultural intimacy (to use a concept later coined by Michael Herzfeld). On "words in motion" generally, see Gluck and Tsing (2009).

23 Duneier (2016) provides a comprehensive overview particularly of American understandings of the ghetto, primarily in scholarship and politics.

24 The striking range of historically based variations in Black American relationships to the mainstream, and recently to African immigrants, is shown (with an autobiographical component) in Lorand Matory's *Stigma and Culture* (2015); if "ghetto" is now at the rejectionist end, one finds the assimilationist end portrayed in Margo Jefferson's *Negroland* (2015). I touch briefly on one kind of distancing dynamic between Black and White American culture in my book *Cultural Complexity* (1992a: 112–113), as I note LeRoi Jones' (aka Amiri Baraka) argument in *Blues People* (1963: 220) that Black music has been recurrently revitalized to seek its own particular forms, as its existing forms have been appropriated by White musicians.

25 It appears as such in in Blair Ruble's *Washington's U Street: A Biography* (2006), in *Chocolate City* by Chris Myers Asch and George Derek Musgrove (2017) and in Derek Hyra's *Race, Class and Politics in the Capuccino City* (2017). For Hyra, moving the ghetto concept along, my area of Northwest Washington, DC has become a "gilded ghetto."

26 Lauterbach's (2011) study of "the chitlin' circuit" dwells more on an earlier period, and on its more modest southern settings.

27 Italian-Americans in Boston have hosted two classic urban ethnographies: not only Gans' *Urban Villagers*, from the West End, but also Willam F. Whyte's *Street Corner Society* (1943), set in the old North End. I remember walking through the West End neighborhood one evening in October, 1992, after spending hours watching a meeting of Governor Bill Clinton's ultimately successful presidential campaign, and shaking hands with the candidate.

28 One earlier anthropological response to Chicago School thinking, and to the need for more comparative studies of urbanism, had been Horace Miner's *The Primitive City of Timbuctoo* ([1953] 1965), based on seven months of field work in 1940.

29 Recent writings involving network thought have included Joshua Cooper Ramo's *The Seventh Sense: Power, Fortune, and Survival in the Age of Networks* (2016), Parag Khanna's *Connectography: Mapping the Future of Global Civilization* (2016), Anne-Marie Slaughter's *The Chessboard and the Web: Strategies of Connection in a Networked World* (2017), Niall Ferguson's *The Square and the Tower: Networks, Hierarchies and the Struggle for Global Power* (2017). The original article foregrounding network thought in a local setting is that by Barnes (1954); my own first publication on networks, relating to what had been a recent exchange on the social implications of gossip, was in 1967.

30 See for example Hannerz (1992b), and what I have to say below about "small worlds," and dispersed linkages. I had a semester as a research fellow at the University of Manchester in 1976, partly engaged in working on such matters, although that was at a time when there was hardly a "Manchester School" any more.

31 This chapter was presented as a lecture in Paris, as urban anthropology was also growing in France. There is more about methodological experimentation in Kafanchan in Hannerz (1976).

32 This chapter was rather belatedly published as a journal article, after two edited volumes where it was to have been included did not materialize. That opening incident in Kingston, Jamaica, happened as I was on my way back from field work in the Cayman Islands – discussed later.

33 For some discussion of this, set in the context of the West African Sahel region, see Andersson (2016).

34 The various histories of national anthropologies, in Europe and elsewhere, involve major transnational tendencies as well as local and even personal circumstances. See on this for example the volume edited by Boskovic (2008), for which I wrote an afterword.

35 At the time, in scholarship devoted to various parts of the world, there was an interest in "populism"; see for example Ionescu and Gellner (1969). In the Cayman Islands, I discerned a shift, under changing economic conditions, from old-style patron–client relationships, to a populism where a business elite claimed to represent "common sense" and "ordinary people"; a miniature somewhat resembling what would happen in an American presidential campaign in 2016.

36 Articles by Vered Amit (1997, 2002, 2003) offer a view of later developments in Caymanian society.

37 This was the "Plural Societies" project, referring to a concept that had been coined in late colonial times in Southeast Asia (referring there particularly to plantation societies), then taken to the Caribbean and Africa by anthropologists and sociologists, before largely falling into disuse – "multiculturalism" perhaps largely taking its place. There is a little more about "plural societies" in Chapter 6; see also for example Smith (1965).

38 While Paul and Laura Bohannan wrote extensively about the Tiv in academic ethnography, perhaps what is now best remembered are the not-so-academic *Return to Laughter* (1954), published by Laura Bohannan under the pseudonym Elenore Smith Bowen, and her essay "Shakespeare in the Bush" (1966), about the Tiv critique of that British writer's poor understanding of kinship. Later, Charles Keil, taking his musical interest from urban blues in Chicago to Nigeria, wrote about *Tiv Song* (1979).

39 Certainly not all these colonial Nigerian soldiers had been Tiv: Biyi Bandele's novel *Burma Boy* (2007) portrays the young men, sometimes teenage boys, recruited from West African towns and villages to fight the Japanese enemy in Southeast Asia in World War II. Bandele's father, a Yoruba, had been among them. And as it turns out, he had told his stories to his son – in Kafanchan. So perhaps the author Bandele, born in 1967, had been among the boys playing in the streets when I was in the field? If I did not notice him, he would probably have noticed the conspicuous White stranger. Then later, he would move on to London, as a writer also active in theater.

40 A volume edited by Charles Stewart (2007) provides a very useful overview of different perspectives toward creolization. Clearly there is a divide between those like me, who find it useful to make this a traveling concept, and others who prefer to leave it as a Caribbeanist specialty. I have returned to this issue in one brief comment (Hannerz 2006a).

41 Discussing and critiquing the recent history of "flow" in anthropological thought, Rockefeller (2011: 560) suggests that "a key moment in the development of the new word came in 1984–1985, when Appadurai and Hannerz were both fellows at the Center for Advanced Study in the Behavioral Sciences." Arjun Appadurai and I first met that year in Palo Alto (having been brought together largely by chance), and we talked about a great many things, and no doubt occasionally about "flow" as well, that resulted in a very long conversation over the decades that followed. Our particular uses of "flow," it should be said, have not all been the same.

46 Prospectus: stops along the way

42 The term "Afropolitans" seems to have been first coined by the novelist Taiye Selasi, with a Ghanaian father and a Nigerian mother, and her own academic degrees from Yale and from Oxford; it has later been taken up by other commentators in different contexts. Lila Abu-Lughod acknowledges that she got the term "halfies" in a personal communication from Kirin Narayan, American anthropologist with Indian roots.

43 For some recent anthropological border research, see for example Andersson (2014) and Agier (2016). I have also considered borders, somewhat differently, in another article at about the same time (Hannerz 1997).

44 I have pointed elsewhere (Hannerz 2010a: 82–83) to the vulnerability of anthropological field commitments to political and other changes – my Nigerian situation has had diverse parallels elsewhere in the world. Nigerian forms of corruption and organized crime have been well documented, ethnographically, and historically: see Smith (2007), Ellis (2016) and Pierce (2016).

45 The work of David Price has offered the most comprehensive historical overview of this, for example in *Cold War Anthropology* (2016); the issues after 9/11 have been discussed by González (2009).

46 My first endeavor in this direction had been a paper based on readings of foreign correspondent autobiographies, later published as a chapter in *Transnational Connections* (1996).

47 In a more recent period, of course, Nicholas Kristof, at the time a relative newcomer in Japan, has gone on to be a regular columnist in the *New York Times*, with a special focus on human rights issues.

48 This was a conference on media production, organized by my friend Brian Moeran; the paper I presented there, on foreign correspondents in Japan, came out in the conference volume (2001).

49 It was Paul Rabinow who raised the question about cosmopolitanism in the Berkeley seminar; as it turned out, he had his own interest in it (Rabinow 1986).

50 For some examples of my writings on cosmopolitanism, see Hannerz (1990, 2004b, 2010b, 2016: 170–176).

51 I give some special attention to this aspect of Africa reporting out of Johannesburg in *Foreign News* (Hannerz 2004b: 132–136).

52 My Sophiatown article first appeared in the *Journal of Southern African Studies* (1994), and was then included in my *Transnational Connections*.

53 I devoted a chapter of *Cultural Complexity* to this. In a book on *The Geography of Genius* (2016), Eric Weiner later made his way to Calcutta and Vienna as well. By then, some decades later, Silicon Valley had replaced San Francisco – but the two, of course, had the Bay Area in common.

54 For a more extended discussion of "indirect rule" and the colonial management of ethnicity in Kafanchan, see Hannerz (1985).

55 In a review of how anthropologists have responded to recent events, Haugerud (2016) discusses a variety of current channels – and again, overall, there is that change in tempo: "public anthropology relies on slow ethnography and fast responses to breaking news stories."

56 My view of two decades of Swedish anthropology, 1960–1980, is in Hannerz (1982).

57 Robert Murphy (1971: 17–23) has offered a view of the implications of differences between American and British academic structures, which is now out of date but historically relevant here.

58 This book on "media and cultures" was published in Swedish – it was also a part of building a public presence of anthropology to reach a readership which was not accustomed to reading in any foreign language. I have dwelt on the language issue in academic work at some length in a chapter in *Anthropology's World* (2010a).

59 The concept "symbolic analysts" is Robert Reich's, from the book *The Work of Nations* (1991). A quarter-century later, as new populist politics became powerful in Europe as well as in the United States, Reich's analysis was obviously relevant again, although the terminology had changed. One British journalist/public intellectual,

David Goodhart (2017), drew the contrast between "anywheres" and "somewheres," where the symbolic analysts would belong to the former category.

60 The term "audit culture" was set in circulation (somewhat later) by Marilyn Strathern (2000); concepts in the same cluster would come to include bibliometrics, New Public Management, and, most generally, neoliberalism. I finally commented on such tendencies in academic governance in an *Anthropology Today* editorial, in the year of my retirement from Stockholm University (Hannerz 2007).

61 One issue of the journal *Ethnos*, on "Anthropology of Immigration in Sweden," exemplifies these research activities (Hannerz 1986).

62 Shahram Khosravi's brief book *"Illegal" Traveller* (2010) offers his account of, and reflections on, his journey. Khosravi actually shows up anonymously again, toward the end of Chapter 13: he was the student shot by the xenophobic "Laser Man."

63 In my afterword to a volume on neonationalism (Gingrich and Banks 2006), beginning with some comments on the Swedish political scene, I struck a note which later could be judged too optimistic, in suggesting that Sweden could be the first country to have reached a post-neonationalist stage (Hannerz 2006b). After some time, there would be another of those neonationalist, "right-wing populist" parties found by now, in one variety or other, in most European countries. I refer to it below.

64 Among my writings on global future scenarios are Hannerz (2003, 2008, 2015, 2016).

65 For the beginnings of "small world" research, see Milgram (1969) and Travers and Milgram (1969).

66 The book *Small Countries: Structures and Sensibilities*, discussing such matters, as well as other recurrent small-country characteristics, I edited with my Vienna colleague Andre Gingrich; we had chapter contributors on 17 countries, in most parts of the world (Gingrich and Hannerz 2017; Hannerz 2017b). The Swedish journalist referred to is Richard Swartz, with personal experience of living in three small countries (Sweden, Austria, and Croatia), and well-known in Sweden particularly for his reporting, in the Cold War era, from the countries behind the Iron Curtain.

67 On "silos" as encapsulated organizational environments, see Gillian Tett (2015), anthropologist-turned-journalist/columnist at *Financial Times*.

References

Abu-Lughod, Lila. 1991. Writing against Culture. In Richard G. Fox (ed.), *Recapturing Anthropology*. Santa Fe, NM: School of American Research Press.

Achebe, Chinua. 1958. *Things Fall Apart*. London: Heinemann.

Agier, Michel. 2016. *Borderlands*. Cambridge: Polity Press.

Amit, Vered. 1997. In Pursuit of Authenticity: Globalization and Nation Building in the Cayman Islands. *Anthropologica*, 39 (1/2): 53–63.

———. 2002. The Moving "Expert": A Study of Mobile Professionals in the Cayman Islands and North America. In Karen Fog Olwig and Nina Nyberg Sörensen (eds.), *Work and Migration*. London: Routledge.

———. 2003. A Clash of Vulnerabilities: Citizenship, Labor, and Expatriacy in the Cayman Islands. *American Ethnologist*, 28 (3): 574–594.

Andersson, Ruben. 2014. *Illegality, Inc.* Berkeley, CA: University of California Press.

———. 2016. Here Be Dragons: Mapping an Ethnography of Global Danger. *Current Anthropology*, 57 (6): 707–731.

Asch, Chris Myers, and George Derek Musgrove. 2017. *Chocolate City*. Chapel Hill, NC: University of North Carolina Press.

Bandele, Biyi. 2007. *Burma Boy*. London: Cape.

Barnes, John A. 1954. Class and Committees in a Norwegian Island Parish. *Human Relations*, 7: 39–58.

48 Prospectus: stops along the way

Bohannan, Laura. 1966. Shakespeare in the Bush. *Natural History*, 75 (7): 28–33.
Borneman, John, and Abdellah Hammoudi (eds.) 2009. *Being There*. Berkeley, CA: University of California Press.
Boskovic, Aleksandar (ed.) 2008. *Other People's Anthropologies*. New York: Berghahn.
Bradburd, Daniel. 1998. *Being There*. Washington, DC: Smithsonian Institution Press.
Clark, Kenneth B. 1965. *Dark Ghetto*. New York: Harper & Row.
DuBois, W.E.B. 1903. *The Souls of Black Folk*. Chicago: A.C. McClurg & Co.
Duneier, Mitchell. 2016. *Ghetto*. New York: Farrar, Straus and Giroux.
Ellis, Stephen. 2016. *This Present Darkness*. London: Hurst.
Ellison, Ralph. 1964. *Shadow and Act*. New York: Random House
Ferguson, Niall. 2017. *The Square and the Tower*. Milton Keynes: Allen Lane.
Fish, Stanley. 1994. *There's No Such Thing as Free Speech*. New York: Oxford University Press.
Gans, Herbert J. 1962. *The Urban Villagers*. New York: Free Press.
Geertz, Clifford. 1969. Myrdal's Mythology: "Modernism" and the Third World. *Encounter*, 30 (7): 26–34.
———. 1998. Deep Hanging Out. *New York Review of Books*, October 22.
Gershenhorn, Jerry. 2004. *Melville J. Herskovits and the Racial Politics of Knowledge*. Lincoln, NE: University of Nebraska Press.
Gingrich, Andre, and Marcus Banks (eds.) 2006. *Neo-Nationalism in Europe and Beyond*. Oxford: Berghahn.
Gingrich, Andre, and Ulf Hannerz. 2017. Exploring Small Countries. In Ulf Hannerz, and Andre Gingrich (eds.), *Small Countries: Structures and Sensibilities*. Philadelphia, PA: University of Pennsylvania Press.
Gluck, Carol, and Anna Lowenhaupt Tsing (eds.) 2009. *Words in Motion*. Durham, NC: Duke University Press.
González, Roberto J. 2009. *American Counterinsurgency*. Chicago: Prickly Paradigm Press.
Goodhart, David. 2017. *The Road to Somewhere*. London: Hurst.
Granovetter, Mark S. 1973. The Strength of Weak Ties. *American Journal of Sociology*, 78: 1360–1380.
Greenbaum, Susan D. 2015. *Blaming the Poor*. New Brunswick, NJ: Rutgers University Press.
Hannerz, Ulf. 1967. Gossip, Networks and Culture in a Black American Ghetto. *Ethnos*, 32: 35–60.
———. 1969. *Soulside*. New York: Columbia University Press.
———. 1974. *Caymanian Politics*. Stockholm Studies in Social Anthropology, 1. Stockholm: Department of Social Anthropology, Stockholm University.
———. 1975. Research in the Black Ghetto: A Review of the Sixties. In Roger D. Abrahams, and John F. Szwed (eds.), *Discovering Afro-America*. Leiden: Brill.
———. 1976. Methods in an African Urban Study. *Ethnos*, 41: 68–98.
———. 1980. *Exploring the City*. New York: Columbia University Press.
———. 1982. Twenty Years of Swedish Social Anthropology: 1960–1980. *Ethnos*, 47: 150–171.
———. 1985. Structures for Strangers: Ethnicity and Institutions in a Colonial Nigerian Town. In Aidan Southall, Peter J.M. Nas, and Ghaus Ansari (eds.), *City and Society*. Leiden: Institute of Cultural and Social Studies.
———. 1986. Anthropology of Immigration in Sweden. *Ethnos*, 51: 145–147.
———. 1988. American Culture: Creolized, Creolizing. In Erik Åsard (ed.), *American Culture: Creolized, Creolizing and other lectures from the NAAS Biennial Conference in Uppsala*, May 28–31, 1987. Uppsala: Swedish Institute for North American Studies.

———. 1990. Cosmopolitans and Locals in World Culture. In Mike Featherstone (ed.), *Global Culture*. London: Sage.

———. 1992a. Networks of Americanization. In Rolf Lundén, and Erik Åsard (eds.), *Networks of Americanization*. Uppsala: Department of English, Uppsala University.

———. 1992b. The Global Ecumene as a Network of Networks. In Adam Kuper (ed.), *Conceptualizing Society*. London: Routledge.

———. 1992c. *Cultural Complexity*. New York: Columbia University Press.

———. 1994. Sophiatown: The View from Afar. *Journal of Southern African Studies*, 20: 181–193.

———. 1996. *Transnational Connections*. London: Routledge.

———. 1997. Borders. *International Social Science Journal*, 154: 537–548.

———. 2001. Dateline Tokyo: Telling the World about Japan. In Brian Moeran (ed.), *Asian Media Productions*. London: Curzon.

———. 2003. Macro-Scenarios: Anthropology and the Debate over Contemporary and Future Worlds. *Social Anthropology*, 11: 169–187.

———. 2004a. *Soulside*. Chicago: University of Chicago Press. (Second edition.).

———. 2004b. *Foreign News*. Chicago: University of Chicago Press.

———. 2004c. Cosmopolitanism. In David Nugent, and Joan Vincent (eds.), *Companion to the Anthropology of Politics*. Oxford: Blackwell.

———. 2006a. Theorizing through the New World? Not Really. *American Ethnologist*, 33: 563–565.

———. 2006b. Afterthoughts. In Andre Gingrich, and Marcus Banks (eds.), *Neo-Nationalism in Europe and Beyond*. Oxford: Berghahn.

———. 2007. Editorial: The Neo-Liberal Culture Complex and Universities: A Case for Urgent Anthropology? *Anthropology Today*, 23 (5): 1–2.

———. 2008. Scenarios for the Twenty-First Century World. *Asian Anthropology* (Hong Kong), 7: 1–23.

———. 2010a. *Anthropology's World*. London: Pluto.

———. 2010b. Afterthoughts: World Watching. *Social Anthropology*, 18: 448–453.

———. 2014. Confessions of a Hoosier Anthropologist. *American Anthropologist*, 116: 169–172.

———. 2015. Writing Futures: An Anthropologist's View of Global Scenarios. *Current Anthropology*, 56 (6): 797–818.

———. 2016. *Writing Future Worlds*. New York: Palgrave Macmillan.

———. 2017a. American Theater State: Reflections on Political Culture. In Virginia H. Dominguez, and Jasmin Habib (eds.), *America Observed*. Oxford: Berghahn.

———. 2017b. Swedish Encounters: End Notes of a Native Son. In Ulf Hannerz, and Andre Gingrich (eds.), *Small Countries: Structures and Sensibilities*. Philadelphia: University of Pennsylvania Press.

Haugerud, Angelique. 2016. Public Anthropology in 2015: *Charlie Hebdo*, Black Lives Matter, Migrants, and More. *American Anthropologist*, 118: 585–601.

Herskovits, Melville J. [1941] 1958. *The Myth of the Negro Past*. Boston: Beacon Press.

———. 1966. *The New World Negro*. Bloomington, IN: Indiana University Press.

Hyra, Derek S. 2017. *Race, Class, and Politics in the Cappuccino City*. Chicago: University of Chicago Press.

Ionescu, Ghita, and Ernest Gellner (eds.) 1969. *Populism*. London: Weidenfeld and Nicolson.

Jefferson, Margo. 2015. *Negroland*. New York: Pantheon.

50 Prospectus: stops along the way

Jones, LeRoi. 1963. *Blues People*. New York: Morrow.

Keil, Charles. 1966. *Urban Blues*. Chicago: University of Chicago Press.

———. 1979. *Tiv Song*. Chicago: University of Chicago Press.

Khanna, Parag. 2016. *Connectography*. New York: Random House.

Khosravi, Shahram. 2010. *"Illegal" Traveller*. New York: Palgrave/Macmillan.

Kroeber, Alfred L. 1945. The Ancient *Oikoumenê* as an Historic Culture Aggregate. *Journal of the Royal Anthropological Institute*, 75: 9–20.

———. 1948. *Anthropology*. New York: Harcourt, Brace & World.

Lauterbach, Preston. 2011. *The Chitlin' Circuit and the Road to Rock'n'Roll*. New York: Norton.

Leacock, Eleanor B. (ed.) 1971. *The Culture of Poverty: A Critique*. New York: Simon & Schuster.

Mailer, Norman. 1957. *The White Negro*. San Francisco: City Lights Books. (Originally published in *Dissent*.).

Matory, J. Lorand. 2015. *Stigma and Culture*. Chicago: University of Chicago Press.

McLuhan, Marshall. 1964. *Understanding Media*. New York: McGraw-Hill.

Milgram, Stanley. 1969. Interdisciplinary Thinking and the Small World Problem. In Muzafer Sherif, and Carolyn W. Sherif (eds.), *Interdisciplinary Relationships in the Social Sciences*. Chicago: Aldine.

Miner, Horace. [1953] 1965. *The Primitive City of Timbuctoo*. Garden City, NY: Anchor Books.

Morris, Aldon D. 2015. *The Scholar Denied*. Berkeley, CA: University of California Press.

Moynihan, Daniel Patrick. 1965. *The Negro Family: The Case for National Action*. Washington, DC: United States Department of Labor.

Murphy, Robert E. 1971. *The Dialectics of Social Life*. New York: Basic Books.

Myrdal, Gunnar. 1944. *An American Dilemma*. New York: Harper & Row.

———. 1963. *Challenge to Affluence*. New York: Random House.

———. 1975. The Unity of the Social Sciences. *Human Organization*, 34: 327–331.

New York Times. 1968. Army Troops in Capital as Negroes Riot; Guards Sent into Chicago, Detroit, Boston; Johnson Asks a Joint Session of Congress. April 6, p 1.

Nzekwu, Onuora. 1962. *Blade among the Boys*. London: Hutchinson.

Pierce, Steven. 2016. *Moral Economies of Corruption*. Durham, NC: Duke University Press.

Price, David H. 2016. *Cold War Anthropology*. Durham, NC: Duke University Press.

Price, Richard, and Sally Price. 2003. *The Root of Roots*. Chicago: Prickly Paradigm Press.

Rabinow, Paul. 1986. Representations are Social Facts: Modernity and Post-Modernity in Anthropology. In James Clifford, and George E. Marcus (eds.), *Writing Culture*. Berkeley, CA: University of California Press.

Rainwater, Lee, and William L. Yancey. 1967. *The Moynihan Report and the Politics of Controversy*. Cambridge, MA: M.I.T Press.

Ramo, Joshua Cooper. 2016. *The Seventh Sense*. New York: Little, Brown.

Redfield, Robert, Ralph Linton, and Melville J. Herskovits. 1936. Memorandum on the Study of Acculturation. *American Anthropologist*, 38: 149–152.

Reich, Robert B. 1991. *The Work of Nations*. New York: Knopf.

Rockefeller, Stuart Alexander. 2011. Flow. *Current Anthropology*, 52: 557–558.

Ruble, Blair A. 2010. *Washington's U Street: A Biography*. Washington, DC: Woodrow Wilson Center Press.

Sahlins, Marshall. 2000. *Culture in Practice*. New York: Zone Books.

Slaughter, Anne-Marie. 2017. *The Chessboard and the Web*. New Haven, CT: Yale University Press.

Smith Bowen, Elenore. 1954. *Return to Laughter*. New York: Harper.

Smith, Daniel Jordan. 2007. *A Culture of Corruption*. Princeton, NJ: Princeton University Press.

Smith, M.G. 1965. *The Plural Society in the British West Indies*. Berkeley, CA: University of California Press.

Stewart, Charles (ed.) 2007. *Creolization*. Walnut Creek, CA: Left Coast Press.

Strathern, Marilyn (ed.) 2000. *Audit Culture*. London: Routledge.

Tett, Gillian. 2015. *The Silo Effect*. New York: Simon and Schuster.

Travers, Jeffrey, and Stanley Milgram. 1969. An Experimental Study of the Small World Problem. *Sociometry*, 32: 425–443.

Valentine, Charles A. 1968. *Culture and Poverty*. Chicago: University of Chicago Press.

Watson, C.W. 1999. *Being There*. London: Pluto.

Weiner, Eric. 2016. *The Geography of Genius*. New York: Simon & Schuster.

Whyte, William F. 1943. *Street Corner Society*. Chicago: University of Chicago Press.

Wirth, Louis. 1938. Urbanism as a Way of Life. *American Journal of Sociology*, 44: 1–24.

———. [1928] 1956. *The Ghetto*. Chicago: University of Chicago Press.

1
THE NOTION OF GHETTO CULTURE

For two years I have been closely involved as an anthropologist with a black ghetto neighborhood in Washington, DC.[1] In general I have acted in that anthropological tradition of fieldwork known as participant observation; that is, I have tried to be present in those situations in which ghetto dwellers carry on their everyday life among each other, and I have tried to win such confidence as a ghetto dweller may be willing to offer an outsider. This means that I have hung around at the street corners, I have taken part in the spontaneous parties which sometimes just happen, I have gone to the beer garden on Friday night, I have gathered with others to watch football games on television on Saturday afternoon, and I have taken rides with people to visit friends or just for the sake of the drive itself. I have also gone to soul music shows and to storefront church services, to the bowling alley as an alternate member of a team, and to public meetings. All in all, I have tried to get a well-rounded picture of ghetto life and the points of view of the people in the community. Of course, this still does not mean I have anything similar to the experience of the ghetto dwellers themselves. I hope it means that I have a reasonably good idea of how the black community in a big American city works, and that with some measure of empathy I can interpret certain elements of how the ghetto dwellers look at their lives. I would like to use these experiences of mine, together with the general outlook of a social anthropologist, to make some brief comments on the notion of black ghetto culture. More exactly, I want to dwell on the social bases for such a culture and on the cultural perspectives ghetto dwellers hold toward their lives.

As a point of departure for these comments, we may take a debate which has gone on for some time about what black culture is, or indeed if there is such a thing. The participants in this argument have largely been such professional observers of ghetto life as writers and social scientists but also, fortunately, some of the most politically and culturally conscious representatives of the ghetto

The notion of ghetto culture   **53**

community itself. On one point, of course, they all have to agree – there are patterns of behavior and organization which often occur among black Americans but which are absent or occur much less often in white America. The bone of contention is how to interpret these differences, and whether the culture concept, long so dear to anthropologists, is of any value in understanding what is peculiar to the ghetto.

Briefly, and perhaps with some oversimplification, one might say that there are two schools of thought with different emphases. The one which feels it might not be too useful to see behavior peculiar to the ghetto as expressions of a specific culture points out that ghetto dwellers have little choice but to act more or less the way they do. The ultimate determinant of what can or cannot be done is not some unique ghetto culture but the place assigned to ghetto dwellers in the structure of American society. If ghetto dwellers do not work, if they get into trouble with the law, and if their families break up, the major reason for all this is not that ghetto dwellers have some completely autonomous cultural values leading to such modes of action. The explanation can rather be found in such facts as shortage of employment opportunities, lack of education, poverty, and powerlessness. Those observers who take this view in its clearest form point out that most, if not all, ghetto dwellers see the way of life of the American majority as an ideal, and that when resources are made available to them, ghetto dwellers often leave ghetto styles of life behind. Thus it is felt that the actual culture of ghetto dwellers is the common American culture, that which is evident in the behavior of the white majority most of the time and which we may call mainstream culture. But ghetto dwellers are generally denied the opportunity to act according to this culture of theirs.

It is obvious that the commentators on the ghetto scene who thus most strongly emphasize the determining influence of the American social structure on the opportunities of ghetto dwellers while deemphasizing cultural factors do so to a great extent because positive policy implications emerge most clearly this way – the social and economic opportunities of ghetto dwellers must be improved. They are concerned with the danger that a discussion in terms of culture might actually have negative implications in that people might come to feel that poverty and diverse social ills are somehow built into ghetto culture and therefore are the ghetto's own responsibility, not that of the outside American society. And certainly there have been some grounds for such suspicions. The "culture of poverty" concept, developed by the anthropologist Oscar Lewis during his research on poor Mexicans and Puerto Ricans, has been applied to the ghetto situation, together with related ideas, in such a way as to suggest that poverty is self-perpetuating in the ghetto and not necessarily directly related to external conditions.[2]

However, I believe that such an emphasis in the picture of how culture works is not at all what Oscar Lewis had primarily in mind in his own "culture of poverty" studies, and to any anthropologist it probably seems quite an alien notion of culture. Anthropologists are used to seeing cultures as designs for living, adapted to the given circumstances and transmitted in communications

54 The notion of ghetto culture

between generations. Starting from this point of view, it seems natural that black people in America have evolved collective adaptations and reactions to the circumstances in which they have found themselves. Of course, to each new set of circumstances they have brought some cultural baggage from earlier conditions of existence; from West Africa by way of slavery and southern country life to the northern ghetto. But some of this baggage has also been left along the way, as new conditions have made its continuing functioning impossible or as new alternatives have been found more desirable. Thus ghetto culture today is a conglomerate of elements deriving from many sources.

It is probably already clear that this anthropological view of ghetto culture is quite compatible with an understanding of the constraining influences of the American social structure on the ghetto, influences which tend to prevent ghetto dwellers from living according to mainstream culture. The ghetto dwellers know mainstream culture but have little chance of living in line with it; they also have a culture peculiar to themselves. A man in the ghetto knows, for instance, that according to mainstream culture a man should be his family's breadwinner, he should provide it with a satisfactory status in the society's system of social ranking, and he should be a knowledgeable advisor to all its members. But as much as he thinks that all this sounds good, he cannot play the part very well when he is poorly paid or even unemployed, when his job is generally held in low esteem, and when he has little education. To this situation he responds rather realistically by sticking to alternative avenues of male expression already modeled for him by other ghetto men who have faced the same problem. He knows that he can also gain some credit by being a successful ladies' man, by demanding respect through toughness, by using his limited resources for conspicuously smart clothing, and so forth. Here is the ghetto's own cultural alternative to the mainstream male role which is so often unrealistic in the given circumstances.

This awareness of two cultures, as we may put it with some simplification, is one of the major features of the ghetto life and outlook. It is an awareness which easily leads to conflicts and contradictions even as one acts according to one model or the other. If one tries to act according to the mainstream model, the rewards may still be small because of the ghetto dweller's ascribed social position; if one accepts the ghetto model, one is aware of one's deviation from the dominant culture of American society. W.E.B. DuBois, a pioneer in the study of black life in America, put it well when he wrote in *The Souls of Black Folk*, just after the turn of the century: "One ever feels his twoness – an American, a Negro; two souls, two thoughts, two unreconciled strivings; two warring ideals in one dark body, whose dogged strength alone keeps it from being torn asunder."

Black people's awareness of the mainstream way of life that is to a great extent denied them may have become even stronger since DuBois wrote those lines. Everybody in the nation is now exposed, probably with never-equaled efficiency, to mainstream values, expectations, and standards of living. The mainstream cultural apparatus, with its authoritative definitions of what is right, proper, and normal, reaches the ghetto through schools, contacts at work,

The notion of ghetto culture **55**

social agencies, and mass media, so ghetto dwellers have no chance of going unaffected. Practically every ghetto household has a television set. Mass media critics such as Marshall McLuhan and S.I. Hayakawa have speculated that television has played a major part in bringing about the black revolution by increasing black people's awareness of and involvement with mainstream ways of life and making their expectations and demands more similar to those of other Americans.

Black people thus to a great extent share mainstream values and have made these a lively tradition in the ghetto as well. This also means that they are aware of the mainstream perspective toward many of the patterns of behavior which occur in the ghetto and that they are apt to use this framework of evaluation, consistently or now and then, in looking at the behavior of themselves and others in the ghetto community. This leads to a great deal of ambivalence but also to some synthesis of subtlety in their perspective.

I came to think of this once as I attended a meeting of sociologists and anthropologists who had come together to talk about black culture in America. A black sociologist with a ghetto background used the term "nigger culture," a concept which I think most white liberals in America, and probably most people in other countries, might find repulsive because they connect the use of the word "nigger" with prejudiced white people. But I think most of us at that meeting who were in intensive contact with the ghetto understood what he meant, provocative as the concept may seem. Ghetto dwellers themselves certainly use "nigger" as a term of abuse, but they can also give it an affectionate connotation. They know that under the abuse heaped on them and their behavior there is their shared humanity and their shared experience. They know that behind the behavior which outsiders despise and which they themselves are sometimes reluctant to condone, there are familiar motives. There are the ghetto's own varieties of sorrow and excitement, of vanity and suspicion, of anger and strategic thinking. When ghetto dwellers say "nigger," they may express disrespect and dislike, but at least some of the time they also affirm a shared perspective of understanding ghetto behavior which is unique to them and which they do not expect from an outsider. That is why black people can say "nigger," but nobody else.

Ghetto dwellers seem to see life in their community simultaneously through two pairs of eyes; those of the participant and those of the outsider. Perhaps it is because the conflict of perspectives described long ago by DuBois has become ever stronger and more obvious that the cultural self-awareness of the ghetto has become so pronounced in recent times. The focus of this self-awareness is the concept of "soul."[3] Black people are soul brothers and soul sisters. There is soul music and soul food, by black people, for black people (see Figure 1.1). To have soul is to know and appreciate the ways of walking and talking by which white people only feel confounded and threatened, to have a feeling for the food, the fashions, and the music, to know how to clap your hands correctly in church or at the concert, to have those background understandings which make it possible to enjoy the jokes about the battle of the sexes, about preachers who

FIGURE 1.1 James Brown, "Soul Brother Number One" appeared frequently at Howard Theatre, Washington, DC, in the 1960s. (Photographed here in Hamburg, 1975. © Heinrich Klaffs, CC-BY-SA 2.0)

like young women and big cars, and about the Ku Klux Klan. To know and feel these things is to have a share in ghetto culture, in the *esprit de corps* which becomes so pronounced partly because one knows so well that most people outside the ghetto community are ignorant of all this. The feeling is something like nostalgia, where one's sentiments about one's personal past are strengthened because one is able to see it in juxtaposition with one's present. But in this case, of course, it is the impressions of a certain past, a somewhat ambiguous present, and an uncertain future which are all strengthened in the contrast with that wider society of which one is also in some ways a part.

For certainly there is an awareness of more than a shared present. Ghetto dwellers know that they all got to where they are largely by the same route. They know, of course, of Africa and of slavery. But above all, they know that not long ago they were rural Southerners, at the bottom of a caste society more rigid than the one of the city. Chitterlings, black-eyed peas, collard greens, cornbread, and grits are now examples of soul food, but they are still sometimes advertised as "southern cooking" in ghetto carry-out food stores. When the ghetto movie theater on Washington's U Street shows the Sidney Poitier movie "In the Heat of the Night," and the cottonfield scene appears on the screen, the all-black audience howls and murmurs. It is true that as generations pass, ghetto dwellers retain only a more general idea of the South and know less about specific ties to southern kinsmen and towns. But there remains the notion of the South as the origin of ghetto dwellers and as a place where life was worse, in

The notion of ghetto culture **57**

spite of everything, than it is in the city. Here the mass media and the ghetto oral tradition complement and support each other.

Thus, as we have said, ghetto culture is not only a product of the ghetto and its relationship to American society today but also a product of common black social history. The culture is in continuous development, and this development goes on now as well. Ghetto dwellers are not forever transplanted rural Southerners, although new migrants continue to arrive in the big northern cities. To long-time ghetto dwellers the new arrival from "down South" often appears as a rustic. In Washington, the term for one of these newcomers who does not know how to act right, talk right, or dress right is "bama;" the term is derived from the name of the state of Alabama. Compared to these newcomers, the generations born and bred in the northern ghetto seem like sophisticated urbanites. Also, for all the trouble they experience in their depressed niches of urban society, the young generation of the ghetto has never been under the strict and almost total control of whites which the black Southerners experienced, so they have less fear and are more apt to feel that freedom and equality are their birthrights. When an internationally known Black Power leader made his appearance in the area of Washington where I worked, there was an obvious cleavage between the old, who were afraid he would cause trouble and bring the white people in, and the young, who felt they would agree with much of what he said and support it. It was no surprise, then, to find that most of those ghetto dwellers who engaged most actively in recent urban rebellions were young people who had been in these cities all their lives.

Such conflicts, of course, leave their own traces in ghetto cultures, as black people talk to each other about them, interpret them, and evaluate them, thus arriving at new shared perspectives. Watts, Newark, and Detroit have now become significant events in the tradition of the ghetto. I am not going to use my anthropological imagination here to suggest what will come out of this. I believe that a conscious black nationalism has so far been more the effect than the cause of such rebellions. All I know and all I have seen of the black ghetto in such cities suggests to me that there is a surge of attempts at organization and cultural self-definition following the rather unorganized ghetto violence.

The "soul" concept, of course, has become involved in this; to an anthropologist, it seems like the most authentic self-conscious manifestation of ghetto culture. There is also the increased interest in Africa. One may suspect that the actual African cultural heritage which has been transmitted continuously between generations of black people from the coast of West Africa to the ghetto of today is rather limited; perhaps it can be most definitely traced in such areas as language, aesthetics, and kinesics.[4] The current interest in African culture, however, is one of cultural innovation as far as the ghetto is concerned. Elements which were not there before are added to ghetto culture. The Afro hairdo, African clothes, and the interest in African languages such as Swahili are examples. This may look like fake cultural continuity to a purist, who might point out that Swahili, an East African language, was spoken by none of the

58 The notion of ghetto culture

ghetto dweller's West African ancestors. But a culture is usually very open to changes which can somehow be made to meet its bearer's desires, and as a well-known sociological theorem has it, "If men define situations as real, they are real in their consequences." If ghetto dwellers come to feel that such Africanisms are a real and significant part of their culture and identity, these may well come to spread more in the ghetto than they have so far. Perhaps they can better meet the need for a sense of cultural greatness than the humility of the soul tradition. Certainly some fragments of African history, sometimes in highly unofficial versions, are now spreading spontaneously by word of mouth in the ghetto, as a great tradition of black people.

One reason why one may doubt the possibilities of such cultural innovation spreading widely in the ghetto, however, is that ghetto dwellers seem to have very different needs when it comes to a satisfactory self-definition. As I see it, one may define a ghetto sociologically as a territory to which residents are assigned on the basis of a single characteristic of theirs which overrides all other considerations. Usually that attribute is ethnicity; so it is in the case of the black ghetto. But this may well mean that ghetto dwellers vary considerably in other attributes, and they certainly do in this case. There is no altogether typical black ghetto dweller, only at best people who are reasonably representative of one of those groups which together constitute the ghetto community. There are differences in lifestyles and points of view, for instance, between men and women, between young and old, and between those who have something in the way of status and resources and those who have almost nothing.

To some extent, ghetto dwellers' thinking about what their culture is or ought to be will reflect such variations. People who are of stable working class or even lower-middle class may prefer to isolate themselves as much as possible from other ghetto dwellers and see no need to define themselves as very different from other Americans. Since they participate very little in the activities peculiar to the ghettos, they do not necessarily develop an understanding of such behavior much different from that of other Americans outside the ghetto. In accepting the mainstream morality of most white Americans, they are prone to pass judgment on the "undesirable" behavior of other ghetto dwellers and thus commit an infraction against the solidarity of the ghetto community. In such ways, others may see them as renegades; when other ghetto dwellers occasionally call them by names such as "Uncle Tom" and "house nigger," they mean that such people align themselves morally with the dominant whites. An "Uncle Tom," of course, is one who shuffles his feet and says "yessir" to everything a white man tells him. The "house nigger" during plantation slavery was the personal servant of the white master's family; he lived a better life than the ordinary slaves, then called "field niggers."

But even those strongly mainstream-oriented ghetto dwellers, for whom such epithets may be used, can be called upon for some solidarity and identification with the black community. Certain experiences of injustice and prejudice at the

The notion of ghetto culture **59**

hands of white people, and also some shared ghetto background, seem to be quite enough as basis for a self-definition as soul brother and for using the soul vocabulary in general. Perhaps it is precisely because it is rather amorphous in definition that the soul concept can function so well as an umbrella of cultural solidarity in the ghetto. If that is so, it may be that no more exact definition of black culture and black identity may be acceptable to the entire ghetto community.

The approach to ghetto culture I have chosen here has largely been one in which that culture is seen as a set of ideas about the past and present life of ghetto dwellers. I have emphasized the self-conscious side of the ghetto dweller's culture, and since some ghetto dwellers are more self-conscious and more intellectually inclined than others, this approach does not apply to an equal degree to all members of the ghetto community. An alternative approach, to which we paid some attention at an early point, is less ideologically oriented and more concerned with how culture supplies tools for the more pragmatic domains of everyday life. Had we chosen that approach, we could have discussed what ghetto culture suggests as a design for courting, marriage, and family life, for staying out of trouble, or for meeting immediate needs. Obviously such matters of culture are also important. However, I think it may have been worthwhile to talk about Ghetto Man as a social thinker because I feel that the awareness of problems such as those discussed here has increased a great deal in the ghetto in recent years, and because this awareness has a great potential for cultural creativity and cultural development, which may have a strong influence on the future of both the ghetto community and the wider society which surrounds it.

Notes

1 The results of my study have been published in my monograph *Soulside* (1969).
2 Oscar Lewis's most accessible discussions of the culture of poverty concept are in his books *The Children of Sanchez* (1961) and *La Vida* (1966). For another discussion of the concept, see Valentine (1968).
3 I discuss the soul concept in Hannerz (1968); with special regard to music, see also Keil (1966), and Szwed (1966).
4 The classic statement on Africanisms of this kind in black American culture is that by Herskovits (1941).

References

Hannerz, Ulf. 1968. The Rhetoric of Soul: Identification in Negro Society. *Race*, 9: 453–465.
———. 1969. *Soulside*. New York, NY: Columbia University Press.
Herskovits, Melville. 1941. *The Myth of the Negro Past*. New York, NY: Harper.
Keil, Charles. 1966. *Urban Blues*. Chicago, IL: University of Chicago Press.
Lewis, Oscar. 1961. *The Children of Sanchez*. New York, NY: Random House.
———. 1966. *La Vida*. New York, NY: Random House.
Szwed, John F. 1966. Musical Style and Racial Conflict. *Phylon*, 27: 358–366.
Valentine, Charles A. 1968. *Culture and Poverty*. Chicago, IL: University of Chicago Press.

2

WASHINGTON AND KAFANCHAN

A view of urban anthropology

What is the relationship of urban anthropology, as it is nowadays practiced, to anthropology, and to urbanism? Two urban field studies of my own, in Washington, DC, and in Kafanchan, a Nigerian town, seem to lead to rather different answers. My aim here is to describe these two studies, and then sketch some of the principal issues in the development of urban anthropology as I see them, partly on the basis of these research experiences.[1]

A neighborhood in Black America

I did fieldwork in Washington in 1966–1968, in a Black ghetto neighborhood. While I was associated with a sociolinguistic research project concerned with the dialect patterns of Black Americans, my own task was defined as supplying a broad ethnographic background understanding of the culture and community life of low-income Black urban Americans, and I worked largely alone as ethnographers tend to do. The study has been fully discussed elsewhere, so I will only dwell briefly on the fieldwork itself and my most central analytical concerns.[2]

The territorial focus of my study was in one small residential neighborhood, around a short street which I have called "Winston Street", and I engaged in a rather pure form of participant observation. It had appeared to me from the very beginning that my best chance of getting the kind of access to neighborhood life which I wanted was to function, as far as possible, as an ordinary participant in its everyday activities. The fact that I was a White European in a Black American neighborhood would certainly mean that I could never be altogether unobtrusive. Yet I hoped to avoid being seen as a member of that category of White officials who were continuously present at the interface

Washington and Kafanchan **61**

between the ghetto and White America – social workers, policemen, etc. Thus I did a minimum of formal interviewing, seeking information instead through informal, more or less spontaneous conversations. Having found a small apartment a few minutes' walk from the neighborhood, I made my first contacts there by striking up a conversation with some men who were gathered at a street corner. A couple of them, I later found out, had a bad reputation, and I may not have been quite safe with them during that first encounter. Be that as it may; as I talked with them, other neighborhood people also stopped at the corner for a chat, and I made more acquaintances.

In this manner, beginning that first evening, I gradually developed my own network in the neighborhood. The fact that I was a foreigner made me something of an anomaly, a creature not directly implicated in the tensions between Black and White America: also perhaps a person of some interest as a curiosity.

While I never hid the fact that I was there as a researcher, hoping to write a book about life in Winston Street, most neighborhood inhabitants did not seem particularly concerned about this aspect of my presence. I could take part in the groups which would sit around for hours on the front stairs of houses, exchanging small talk with one another or passers-by; I could be in and out of the houses, listening to heated arguments between friends or within families, or just quietly watching television. In the back alley behind the houses I might share a bottle of wine with another group of men, or accompany them to bars and pool halls. We might drive around in a car to visit their friends and kinsmen in another part of Black Washington, and those who belonged to organized social clubs invited me to their picnics in a city park. For a period I belonged to a bowling team with some neighborhood men. I also went to services in several Black churches, and I was a frequent visitor to Howard Theatre where many of the stars of soul music – ascendant, established, or had-beens – appeared. My radio at home was usually tuned to one or other of the three Black radio stations. In this manner I had a rather wide exposure to ghetto life, and while Winston Street remained the center of my study, my network and my experiences gradually developed to take in more of the Black Washington scene.

This may possibly suffice as an indication of the nature of my fieldwork. What, then, did I actually make note of, what have been the main directions of my analysis of ghetto culture and community? Obviously my study related to the more general currents of debate over Black American life in recent times, such as that concerning "the culture of poverty." I would point to the external constraints imposed on the Black community by the wider American society, but my real emphasis was on what the Black community itself did within these constraints. As the general debate often seemed somewhat lacking in subtlety, it seemed to me that an anthropologist's contribution could well be to underline the fact that the inhabitants of the Black ghetto were neither unaffected by the constraining circumstances nor affected by them only on an individual basis. Instead, they had shaped a collective adaptation to circumstances, interacting over time to create a series of different but interconnected styles of life. Even in

62 Washington and Kafanchan

a small neighborhood like that of Winston Street, one must not underestimate the heterogeneity. Its inhabitants ranged from the more or less permanently unemployed to stable working class or even lower middle class, from "respectable people" to those inclined toward petty criminality or occasional violence. Household structures varied from nuclear families to the female-centered households recurrent in many Afro-American communities; there were of course other constellations as well. But this internal variety generated an array of expectations concerning life, modeled for everyone by people in the immediate environment, symbolically expressed for instance in soul music and streetcorner narrative. Through shared understanding of how life could turn out and through contexts serving as havens for varying personal adjustments, people in differing predicaments could still fit into the community. And although individuals could change between life styles over time, the fact that generations of low-income Blacks grew up under relatively similar circumstances appeared to contribute to a certain stability in the totality.

On the whole, I think of this as a cultural analysis; a study of the way people develop a culture as an instrument for coping with their conditions of life. My experience in the Winston Street neighborhood has been one of the bases for a long-term interest in conceptualizations of culture sophisticated enough to be useful rather than misleading in anthropological attempts to understand complex societies. In Black America, there is naturally the further complication that whatever culture its people evolve for themselves will have to co-exist in their minds with the ideas of the wider American culture from which they cannot shield themselves.

Was my study in Washington an example of urban anthropology? To this question I will return. Let me just note at this point that at the time of the study, I did not give much thought to the emergence of such a subdiscipline. As one book after another, and one journal, appeared under that label, however, and as I began to be invited to urban anthropological conferences because of my work in Washington, I was forced to consider what the expansion of anthropology into towns and cities actually meant. Of all the different things one can observe in the city, are some more urban than others, and in what way? Could an urban anthropology continue to deal with segments of city life – neighborhoods, associations, occupations, family structures – or would it have to try and deal with entire urban communities? In other words, to what extent ought anthropology to devote itself to the phenomenon of urbanism as such, and would it be able to do so? These were the kind of questions I had in mind as I found an opportunity to engage in a field study in a Nigerian town.

The complexity of Kafanchan

The site of my research, as I found it when my work there began in 1974, was an urban community of some 10,000–15,000 people (there had been no trustworthy census for a long time), close to 50 years old as a settlement, built at an important railway junction in middle Nigeria.[3] In terms of size, the town of Kafanchan seemed relatively manageable; I could still walk around it in a couple of hours, and I could get a firsthand experience of its major settings. Yet it appeared unmistakably urban. There are, of course, somewhat varying understandings of what urbanism should be taken to mean, but to me the classic definition by Louis Wirth (1938) is still useful, although not without problems; an urban community is thus characteristically large, dense and socially heterogeneous.

Kafanchan is, obviously, a town rather than a city, and Nigeria, with its old urban traditions in the north and the southwest, has long had much larger urban communities than this product of the colonial era. But it is far beyond that point, important for the shaping of social relationships, when all the people who meet in the everyday traffic of their shared space can be personally known to one another. So some contacts, at least, must become, in Wirth's words, "segmental, impersonal, and transitory" – to put it bluntly, contacts between strangers.

And what is yet more important for the type of ethnographic work I wanted to do, Kafanchan also evinces great diversity for its size. The railway corporation remains the major employer, but the town has become an important administrative and service center for its area. It has government offices, several educational institutions at different levels, a hospital, and a bank. It also has a large market place with traders of the most varied kinds. Along its streets are the shops of tailors, carpenters, watch repairers, barbers, shoemakers ... The richest people in town may be the wholesale ginger merchants and contractors. The poorest may be the water carriers, the truck pushers, and (around the many bars) the prostitutes, the shoeshiners, and the nail-cutters.

The ways of earning a living, however, provide only one of the dimensions of diversity in Kafanchan. Ethnicity is another, and also one of considerable significance. When the town was first established in the late 1920s, it attracted migrants from distant parts of Nigeria, but few of the local people in the area (known as Southern Zaria). So, for one thing, the major ethnic groups of the country, the Hausa from the north, the Yoruba from the southwest, and the Ibo from the southeast, became well represented. After some time, it was especially the Ibo who came in larger numbers, and by the 1950s they made up almost half the population. Then came the anti-Ibo riots in northern Nigeria in 1966, and the civil war which broke out in 1967, and for some years the Ibo of Kafanchan all withdrew to what was for some years the Republic of Biafra. For a while Kafanchan became almost like a ghost town. The dominant element of the population had gone, and the railway had stopped running. But gradually town life was revived. New people replaced at least some of those who had left, and it was really during this period that the peoples of the surrounding areas – the Kaje, the Kagoro, the Katab, the Jaba, the Kaninkon, the Moroa and a number of other groups – gained a real foothold inside the town. When the Ibo began, at first somewhat hesitantly, to return after the war, they found that they could not easily take up all their old positions again, however competitive they would once more turn out to be.

64 Washington and Kafanchan

Perhaps this suffices as an outline of the kind of place Kafanchan is: a place with a rather special history, and yet in many ways like countless other African towns born during the colonial period.[4] In this setting, I made it the goal of my work to develop as much of an overall view of town life as might be practically possible. To deal with urbanism per se, I believe, is for one thing to face up to its social complexity, to investigate the coherence of the differentiated structure.

Many recent anthropological studies in towns and cities, as I have implied, hardly do this. By treating various smaller units within the urban structure as well-bounded social worlds of their own, they play down analytically their major intrinsically urban dimension. If I had chosen in Kafanchan to concentrate on, say, the railway workers, I ought at least to make an effort to see how their behavior, experiences, and relationships in the work domain become embedded in town life as a whole by looking at their interrelations with domestic and neighborhood life, with ethnicity, and with the development of networks of friendship and acquaintance, and so forth. Between traditional anthropological units of study and those units in urban anthropology which are of a comparable scale, there is usually at least a difference of degree in their openness to wider structures, and this difference we ought to respect in our ethnography.

But, as I have said, I wanted to look at Kafanchan as a whole, in its entire variety. And to do this I engaged in a combination of approaches which I will briefly mention here. First of all, I would emphasize personal and, to the extent feasible, participant observation as the basis of urban ethnography. Some understandings one may not reach in any other way, and more generally it underlies the basic anthropological conceptions of society as a system of interactions and of culture as a traffic in meaning. Consequently I tried to gain the widest possible exposure to the varied scenes and activities of Kafanchan life – the market, the house yards, the workshops, the bars, the churches, the football games, the public festivals, and whatever else that offered opportunities for watching and listening (See Figure 2.1).

Participant observation, one must also recognize, however, meets with certain rather specific difficulties in a differentiated and large unit such as a town. In some smaller unit, one can often enter the social system at a single point with one or a few members of the population and make one's way through the interconnected networks so that one gradually builds up a view of the entire unit – much as I did in the Winston Street neighborhood in Washington. Such a procedure is less likely to be trustworthy when one hopes to construct a picture of a whole town. Because of the discontinuities which may exist in the structure of social relationships, it is necessary to make multiple entries into the social system, at different points, and in the long run to manage several relatively separate miniature fieldwork processes side by side. If the situation has parallels in field research elsewhere as well, its features are probably more pronounced in urban studies.

The combination of involvements can meet with various obstacles and can have somewhat different unfortunate consequences. In a more conflict-ridden

FIGURE 2.1 Conversation in a Kafanchan bar – Ben, research assistant, second from the left

community, the fieldworker's contacts with one group of people can discredit him in the eyes of others. This, however, has not been the case to any noteworthy degree during my field periods in Kafanchan. There is also the problem for the researcher of budgeting his limited time among the diverse involvements. And the ethnographer is also likely to prefer to develop with time a rather unobtrusive presence, as people become accustomed to having him there. This cumulative effect cannot be so easily reached when he keeps moving in and out of settings, introducing himself to new groups. Finally, in a case like that of Kafanchan one has to face the language problem. One can get relatively far with Hausa, the major lingua franca in the area, and with English which in pidgin or more standard-like varieties is used in a number of contexts. But some twenty Nigerian languages may be spoken with a certain frequency in intraethnic contexts, and clearly no ethnographer, and no inhabitant of the town, is linguistically competent to be a participant in all of these.

To a certain extent, I have tried to solve problems such as these by the use of local field assistants. In this way, my research in Kafanchan has been a rather larger enterprise than that in Washington. I have been not only a field researcher myself, but also a research manager. The young Nigerians who have worked with me during different periods have had quite varied tasks, but among these have been observations which I have instructed them to carry out in settings like households, ethnic association meetings, or drinking places. Ideally, of course, one should try to recruit assistants who, in their personal attributes, to same degree, reflect the diversity of the town, thereby having varying experiences and fitting into different observation contexts. Unfortunately, this may not be easy; the available and suitable individuals in Kafanchan have tended to be unevenly distributed for instance among ethnic groups. It is also a fact that it may be inconvenient to have many assistants working at the same time, if they demand much attention in terms of briefing and debriefing, interview and observation notes to be read and discussed, etc. During a period when I had three assistants working for me intensively at the same time, I found this was rather constraining on my personal field involvements. Working with assistants in this manner, then, will probably always entail compromising between different conflicting objectives, as well as between ideals and realities.

Locally recruited assistants can be useful in many ways; among other things, they can be informants on the basis of their own experiences and cultural knowledge. The next step toward extending one's overview of the complexity of town life, however – out from what to me is the core constituted by immediate personal observation – must be to select a wider panel of informants. In a more homogeneous society, anthropologists may be less concerned about the social distribution of knowledge in choosing their informants. A good general-purpose informant is experienced in community life, has a facility for introspection, and verbalizes easily; there is also the matter of personal rapport with the researcher. In Kafanchan I had some such informants as well, to whom I talked about all sorts of things. They tended, as one might expect, to be among my best friends in Kafanchan. But apart from them, I needed special-purpose informants, with expertise in particular areas of town life. These could be occupational specialists, representatives of ethnic groups and associations, people knowledgeable about local politics, or elderly residents of the town who could offer their understandings of earlier phases of its history, to give some examples. Partly I was advised on such informants by my local assistants and by the general-purpose informants, so that these also had an intermediary function.

One particular set of informants offered what I have termed "network diaries." These individuals were interviewed every day for one week about their contacts since the last interview – the general social attributes of the people they had met with, the nature of the relationship, the content of the interaction, the language used in it, and so forth. Chosen to exemplify different occupations and ethnic groups as well as both sexes, they offered information of special interest in showing how personal networks could involve different combinations and intersections of the groups and institutions we often study as separate, bounded units – in other words, this was one way of seeing how individuals contribute more or less to the coherence of the urban whole.

The network diaries were one relatively formal method of data formation. My assistants and I also used a number of other, more extensive, information gathering. We conducted an intensive survey of the Kafanchan daily market, and more limited ones of the weekly markets in surrounding villages which in various ways were connected to it. Craft occupations were also surveyed, and I devised an instrument for the study of occupational ranking which was also useful in collecting additional occupational ethnography. In a "recognition survey," we studied who were the well-known people of Kafanchan, and who was known to whom – even if many inhabitants of an urban community must be strangers to one another, there are some who are hardly strangers to anybody, and these public personae also add to its unity.

I also arranged with teachers at two secondary schools, one for boys and one for girls, to have the pupils write essays on topics of relevance to the study. And as far as written materials are concerned, I have tried to look into various existing public records and archival sources. It has seemed of great value to me to develop the historical dimension of the study of Kafanchan, not least since it is still relatively manageable (this being a young town), and because the history has been one of considerable change over time. The Nigerian National Archives in Kaduna, capital of the state in which Kafanchan is located and some 200 km away from the town, have been of great value, as they have substantial collections of documents from the colonial period. It has been especially satisfying to be able to combine information from these documents with the recollections of my elderly informants in Kafanchan, as archival and oral history have often been complementary. In this connection, I must also mention one special case of such archive/informant combinations. Having read in the archives the reports of a number of British district officers who had at one time or other been stationed in Kafanchan, I later managed to meet with a couple of them in England. Although at first they doubted that they would be able to remember much about their early postings in Nigeria, I could refresh their memories on the basis of my own fieldwork as well as their own old reports, and these interviews turned out quite interesting, with the particular perspective they could offer toward Kafanchan in the past.

Two senses of urban anthropology

What is my view of urban anthropology now, after these two field studies? I should say that it is not solely based on them but also derives from my readings in the literature of urbanism, my conversations with other anthropologists (urban and non-urban), and, not least, my own experience as an urbanite.[5]

Anyway, as far as my accounts above of these two studies are concerned, I have dwelt to a relatively great extent on matters of method, to show both how differently urban fieldwork can turn out and that even so, in my view, it can remain quite clearly anthropological in its basic approach. In Washington, participant observation was absolutely dominant. In the Nigerian study as well, participant observation was of central importance, but when taking on a larger and more complex unit, I regarded it as a both necessary and stimulating task to explore a range of methods and combine intensive and extensive data collection. In fact, part of the pleasure of the study has been the opportunity to use Kafanchan in some small way as a laboratory for urban anthropology. In both instances, however, regardless of the particular adaptations I have made to the requirements of the field situation, I have been concerned with ethnography,

68 Washington and Kafanchan

with well-rounded, primarily qualitative documentation. And to take a further step away from matters of pure field technique, this is ethnography in line with characteristic anthropological manners of conceptualization, in terms of social relationships and culture. On these grounds, I see no reason to agree with those who may still fear that anthropology in the urban milieu must become something other than anthropology.

If it can be granted that both studies are characteristically anthropological, the next question is this: are both examples of urban anthropology? I have asked the question about my Washington study already and can now return to it. As I did my work in the Winston Street neighborhood, the city was only the locus of the study, not its focus. Apart from the more general concern with cultural analysis, the more specific thematic interests which related most directly to my work were the "culture of poverty" debate, questions of ethnicity and minority relations, sex roles and socialization, and Afro-American social and cultural history. I did not pay much concentrated attention to the facts that the Winston Street people were urbanites, and the particular city they were in also contained the White House and the Capitol.

This, probably like most anthropological studies in towns and cities, should perhaps be described as urban anthropology in a loose sense of the term. In a strict sense of the term, an urban anthropology is then an anthropology of urbanism, concerned with towns and cities as social forms, and with the particular social and cultural features of these large, dense and (usually, at least) heterogeneous settlements.

From the point of view of a general, comparative anthropology, we may need more of such an urban anthropology in the strict sense than we have had hitherto. If we want to take seriously the claim of anthropology to be "the science of humanity" (as some of us may do, and others probably not), the discipline ought to include an awareness of urban life. It should not draw only on research in small, relatively uncomplicated communities, mostly in non- Western areas of the world. A special contribution of the urban part to the anthropological whole then consists of understandings of a range of social and cultural phenomena less often or never found elsewhere, to be seen against the background of human variation in general.

My study in Kafanchan I hold to be urban anthropology in the strict sense of the term, with its emphasis on complexity, heterogeneity, differentiation, and its objective of dealing with this as a whole rather than evading it by dealing only with some smaller and more homogeneous part of it. To repeat, one can hardly do justice to complexity by studying lesser units as if they were closed systems of their own: the emphasis must rather be on their embeddedness in the whole, and in the end on the relative coherence of the social order which they make up together.

There are, however, also particular phenomena in urban life which I would view as especially interesting to an anthropology of urbanism, including (as I have noted) social relationships of a certain quality. Louis Wirth, we may be reminded, described urban contacts as "segmental, impersonal, and transitory." Much criticism has been aimed at this characterization over the years. On the one hand, not all urban relationships are like this; some are even multiplex, intensely personal, and lasting. On the other hand, it is questionable whether all the relationships which fit Wirth's description can be said to be caused by urbanism in itself. In a place like Wirth's Chicago, the quick growth of a capitalist society undoubtedly also marks relationships between people.

With regard to the first of these problems, I would say that Wirth's level of generalization was clearly too high. There is a strain in his formulation toward a conception of the typical urbanite. Despite Wirth's explicit emphasis on the heterogeneity of the city, we discern an assumption of sameness. But there are many kinds of cities; each one of them has many kinds of inhabitants; and each one of these, in turn, has different kinds of relationships. This variability in itself deserves recognition and more analytical attention, but some sorts of relationships have also been more ignored than others.

What I have termed urban anthropology in the loose sense has played a part here. My own study of the Winston Street neighborhood is an example, although not extreme. Not only have lesser units of the city been treated as bounded, there has also been a strong tendency to choose units for study where relationships between people have been rather unusually intimate, closely-knit, and durable. Ethnographers have flocked to the "urban villages," in Gans' (1962) phrase, to the "peasants in cities" – in brief, to the units which in several ways most closely resemble the traditional habitats of non-urban anthropology. Surely it is easier to move into these with our accustomed forms of anthropological thought and work, but in terms of new contributions to anthropology, they may well have less to offer. Normally, we tend to think of the city, in a somewhat Wirthian manner, as a place where strangers meet, but also sometimes get to know each other; as a place of sparse networks, where mutual acquaintances may be discovered but cannot be assumed; and as a rather fluid structure, where people's life careers are not entirely predictable. The city is not only this, but neither is this only a figment of our imagination. Let us as ethnographers pay more attention to such realities.

Finally, I want us to remember that an urban anthropology in the strict sense can hardly be an urban anthropology entirely within the city limits either. Urban anthropology, as a part of a comparative anthropology, must look at the interplay between towns and cities and the societies in which they are located. It must be aware that different cultural and social systems create different forms of urbanism. Kafanchan is indeed a product of 50 years of Nigerian history, Winston Street bears the imprint of the American past and present. This, of course, has to do with the second problem of Wirth's description of urban social relationships referred to above. Cities as large, dense and heterogeneous settlements are not all alike. Their peculiar demographic characteristics interact with economic, political and cultural facts in shaping varied urban forms. Wirth's Chicago was not The City, nor is Paris or any other place we may have close at hand. I note this because there has been a tendency to think of urban anthropology as almost synonymous with doing anthropology "at home." This tendency has been quite clear in the United States and is creeping in among European anthropologists as well. It is not that I think anthropology must necessarily be exotic, non- Western: this to me is an antiquated form of inverted ethnocentrism. But we must not forget that there are towns and cities everywhere, in all countries, and we will do justice neither to urbanism nor to anthropology by developing an urban anthropology which knows all about our own cities but ignores Kathmandu, Kabul, and Kafanchan.

Notes

1 The paper is an inexact reconstruction of my presentation to the Association Française des Anthropologues in November 1981. I thank the participants in the urban anthropology session for their interest in the presentation, and especially Jacques Gutwirth for including my paper in this issue of *L'Homme*.
2 My Washington study is most completely described in Hannerz (1969).
3 Kafanchan and my research there is more fully described in Hannerz (1976, 1979); I have drawn especially on the former publication in my methodological discussion below.
4 See the description of such towns generally by Vincent (1974).
5 I have stated it much more fully in Hannerz (1980).

References

Gans, Herbert. 1962. *The Urban Villagers*. New York, NY: Free Press.
Hannerz, Ulf. 1969. *Soulside*. New York, NY: Columbia University Press.
———. 1976. Methods in an African Urban Study. *Ethnos*, 41: 68–98.
———. 1979. Town and Country on Southern Zaria: A View from Kafanchan. In Aidan Southall (ed.), *Small Urban Centers in Rural Development in Africa*. Madison, WI: African Studies Program, University of Wisconsin.
———. 1980. *Exploring the City*. New York, NY: Columbia University Press.
Vincent, Joan. 1974. The Changing Role of Small Towns in the Agrarian Structure of East Africa. *Journal of Commonwealth and Comparative Politics*, 12: 261–275.
Wirth, Louis. 1938. Urbanism as a Way of Life. *American Journal of Sociology*, 44: 1–24.

3

THE MANAGEMENT OF DANGER

A first and quite different version of this essay was presented at an urban anthropology conference in Milwaukee in June, 1970.[1] A couple of months later I was in Kingston, Jamaica, on the anniversary of Jamaica's independence. It was around noon, I had just attended a reggae concert which was part of the celebrations at a theater uptown, and I was walking along a rather lively thoroughfare down toward central Kingston to watch the afternoon events. I did not move particularly fast, but I overtook a small group of teenage boys who were even less in a hurry. Almost immediately after having passed them I sensed that it might not have been wise – I would have felt more secure being able to observe them from behind. About a block further down the road, my suspicion proved right. They surrounded me, one of them gave me a push, another had a hand in my pocket, a third cut into the side of my neck with a knife. Fortunately it was very blunt. My reaction somehow felt almost deliberate; the best I could do was to shout for help. So I did. A few people nearby who had perhaps noticed my predicament anyway came running, my attackers fled into an alley with only a few dollars out of my pocket. Knowing where I would be going that day, I had intentionally not carried more. The people who came to my aid insisted that I report the incident to the police, and one of them took me to the precinct house on his scooter, while I held a handkerchief to my shallow wound. A detective took down my report without much enthusiasm, in intervals between listening to the horse races on his radio.

So I got some further evidence concerning one phenomenon of urban life to which I had already begun to give some thought. The medieval European town was thought to be a haven from violence; its fortifications protected people from attacks from the outside, and the peace of the market place which generally prevailed inside contrasted favorably with conditions elsewhere. It is a bit

72 The management of danger

ironical, then, that one of the facts of life in many cities at present is that their inhabitants are afraid of one another. The unpredictable, violent strangers have become enemies within. The weekly magazine *New York*, probably a useful source for trends in urban imagery at least among middle-class cosmopolitans, has in recent years contained articles such as "Fear and Trembling in Black Streets," "The Pause in the Day's Occupation Known as the Mugging Hour" and "New Yorkers Fight Back: The Tilt Toward Vigilantism." It sometimes seems as if teargas pens and Your Very Own Attack Dog have become indispensable tools of urban living. While statistics generally show that city dwellers are still most likely to become the victims of violence at the hands of people whom they know well or even intimately, their idea of urban danger is rooted in fleeting relationships. From such beginnings new myths like the movie *Clockwork Orange* are created.

This essay is a sketch of an anthropological point of view toward the experience and management of urban danger – when and where danger is at hand, who is dangerous, what constitutes danger, how one copes with it. We are interested primarily in interpersonal violence between one or a few attackers and a victim, the kind of incident that may take place as an isolated event any day, rather than in collective violence such as riots. The division is somewhat artificial, for in popular consciousness the two kinds of infractions against the public order are often not kept strictly apart, and ideas about them may feed on each other. But the field as circumscribed here seems quite enough to keep us occupied for a while.

Although the popular perception may be that violence between strangers has increased greatly in the cities in recent times, it is difficult to know what is the precise difference between the present and earlier periods. Some say tendencies in official statistics are not very informative, since they may just reflect changes in the ratio between reported and unreported crime. It is also often argued that there may be political and commercial interests involved in increasing the public preoccupation with disorder, and that the growth of mass media influence has had a great deal to do with the urbanite's ideas of violence in his environment. Daniel Bell (1961: 172), whose argument in his essay "The Myth of Crime Waves" is of this type, quotes the diary of a New York lawyer for one day in 1869, stating that crimes of violence had lately been "many and audacious beyond example ... tonight's *Post* speaks of 'secret meetings of respectable citizens' and of Vigilance committees already organized and ready for action in this ward and in another." And the turbulence of other great cities in the nineteenth century took similar expressions. The historian Louis Chevalier (1973: 3), in his study of the "dangerous classes" in Paris, notes the vicomte de Launay writing in 1843 in his *Lettres parisiennes*:

> For the past month the sole topic of conversation has been the nightly assaults, hold-ups, daring robberies ... What is so terrifying about these nocturnal assaults is the assailants' noble impartiality. They attack rich and

poor alike … They kill at sight, though they may get the wrong man; but little do they care. At one time the advantage of being poor was that at least you were safe; it is so no longer. Paris is much perturbed by these sinister occurrences. A concern for self-defense greatly troubles family gatherings especially. Evening parties all end like the beginning of the fourth act of *Les Huguenots*, with the blessing of the daggers. Friends and relatives are not allowed to go home without a regular arms inspection.

It thus seems that the urban consciousness of danger is not only a contemporary phenomenon. But we will leave the rather extensive debates over decreases, increases, or fluctuations in official crime rates, and over who might benefit from manipulating that consciousness, at the fringes of our consideration of how the city dweller perceives and deals with danger on a day-to-day basis. For this a large part of our materials are set in an American context. Americans write more about their cities than most others, but cities in the United States are probably also more violent than most others. For a first major example of danger as a fact of urban life, however, we may go somewhere else.

The tsotsi paradigm

Mayer's *Townsmen or Tribesmen* (1961), with its distinction between the "Red" and "School" Xhosa in East London, South Africa, is about the closest thing there is to a classic urban ethnography. It only presents some information on danger rather incidentally, but that information, supplemented by glimpses of life in the locations of South African cities from a few other sources, may serve as a paradigm for much of our continued discussion, since it raises many of the basic questions. The other sources are Reader's (1961) and Pauw's (1963) contributions to the "Xhosa in Town" trilogy – thus also from East London – and Wilson and Mafeje's (1963) study of Langa, on the periphery of Cape Town and likewise largely Xhosa.[2]

A main social division among Africans in East London and Langa is between migrants and townspeople; the people who have come recently from the countryside and intend to return there, and the people who have long been in town, who are often born there and expect to remain there, and who have taken on most of the city ways. The "Red" Xhosa are those most committed to their rural home base and its traditions, deriving their designation from the fact that they smear body and clothes with red ochre. The typical villains among the inhabitants of these townships are the tsotsis, and these are mostly townspeople, teenage boys or young men in their early twenties. A few young migrants drift into their circles, unlike their compatriots who tend to carefully encapsulate themselves in their own groups. Tsotsis are a lumpenproletariat. They have little schooling. If they are employed at all, as many of them are not, it is usually in unskilled and temporary jobs. They are often of no fixed abode, living now with kin, next with friends or girlfriends. Frequently they come out of "broken

74 The management of danger

homes." They have a reputation for gambling, drinking and smoking dagga (hemp). Wilson and Mafeje (1963: 23) describe their language as a mixture of Afrikaans and Xhosa slang, and note that they walk differently from country people, with a shorter stride, and jerkily. The tsotsis are also fashion conscious. The Langa style is described as "widebottomed trousers without any turn-up, called *ivups*, which might be translated 'flappers'; 'skipper' shirts, sports coat, no collar or tie, and pointed shoes" (Wilson and Mafeje 1963: 22–23). In East London, it is "tight trousers, tapering toward the ankles, and jackets with heavily padded shoulders ... white shoes and white hats, and green, yellow or orange jerseys" (Mayer 1961: 189).[3] But in tastes in clothing, speech, music and manners, it is the tougher life of Johannesburg and other towns of the Reef that sets the new standards, as well as Hollywood movie stars, crooks and crooners. The tsotsi lifestyle seems very urban, and in a way cosmopolitan. For the migrants especially, however, the tsotsis are above all evil:

> Tsotsi-ism always crops up sooner or later when countryborn people talk about their impressions of town. It is the feature of town life that has come through most clearly to their consciousness, and has been absorbed into their own folklore. The tsotsi idea has become, even in the countryside, a kind of power rivalling that of the witch myth, and with definite parallels: for both tsotsi and witch embody the same basic concept – the reversal of "ordinary decent" human values. Like the witch, the tsotsi is both terribly dangerous and terribly unpredictable, so that nobody knows who the next innocent victim may be.
>
> *(Mayer 1961: 73–74)*

The tsotsis are the violent strangers in the street, without scruples, capable of doing anything to anyone. They rob drinkers in the shebeens or attack people in the street with knives, stones, bicycle chains or sharpened bicycle spokes. They rape women. This is the categorical image held by migrants, as well as by some townspeople, and not without substantiating evidence.

The danger, however, is not evenly distributed within the matrix of space and time. Security is at least somewhat greater in one's own neighborhood, and certain other areas are judged as particularly difficult. This seems most marked in Johannesburg townships, where boys and young men follow only defined routes walking to or from shops or the bus stop. If they were to stray they would get into territories known to be dominated by violent groups. Langa has long been regarded as a quieter place, comparatively speaking, with a high proportion of the African middle class. Its inhabitants have been reluctant to visit other communities with a poorer reputation in the Cape Town area, such as Kensington or Windermere. But with increasing restrictions on the admittance of families, Langa is getting a growing proportion of young single men, and the difference between it and neighboring African settlements thus diminishes. Pressures are such that people take whatever housing they can get. As Wilson and Mafeje

The management of danger **75**

(1963: 7) note, a clergyman may live next door to a beer brewer. With regard to time, danger is naturally enough assumed to be greater after dark. Apart from this, tsotsis are expected to be particularly active in periods when there is more money about. On the last day of the month they will be waiting at the railway station to rob domestic servants on their way home of their wages, and before Christmas when people carry unusual amounts of spending money the tsotsis are also thought to be ready to seize the opportunity. At the beginning of the Christmas season in 1958 the location people of East London felt sufficiently provoked to take action against the tsotsis, and since the ensuing events occurred during Mayer's period of field work he has been able to give a relatively detailed account of it. A widow's son had been murdered, and location talk dwelt on the tsotsi perpetrator's alleged boast that this would be neither his first nor his last victim. Tsotsis had also taken to sticking up bills in the streets, threatening people to be indoors by nine in the evening or face the consequences. Finally, a young man was attacked by a gang as he left a beer drink in the early evening – but this time other men carrying sticks came to his rescue, and while most of the attackers fled, one of them was caught and given a thorough beating before he was taken to the police. The gang threatened vengeance, but among the men who had beaten off their first attack was one with good connections in the location through his activities both in commerce and ward affairs, and through his network, mobilization occurred. A large crowd met and agreed that since the police was incapable of dealing with the tsotsi menace, they themselves would join forces to beat up gang members in the streets. This clean-up movement was fundamentally a migrants' affair. For a few days, youths were unsafe as migrant men brandishing sticks went around and increasingly indiscriminately attacked such young men as they came across.

Townspeople, to begin with rather passive in the situation, watched the events with growing resentment as they saw that not only tsotsis but other youths as well were made to suffer. For much the larger number of youths in town were their sons, not those of the migrants, who would rarely leave the rural areas until after initiation. The townspeople, in the first place, were more likely to have some sort of personal connection to actual tsotsis, and were therefore less likely to see them quite so unqualifiedly as evil as the migrants did. But furthermore, the migrants, thinking in the age grade terms of rural society, felt all youths needed to be taught a lesson. The authority of seniors must be reasserted. The campaign could have turned into a serious open conflict between townspeople and migrants if the government had not in the end intervened.

Street wisdom I: the dangerous encounter

A characteristic form of urban social life, I have suggested elsewhere, is the traffic relationship – in Goffmanian terms, an unfocused co-presence, on the borderline of being a relationship at all. Traffic relationships are what you have with the people you pass on the sidewalk, sit next to in a movie theater, or

76 The management of danger

stand behind in a queue (cf. Hannerz 1980: 105). The use or threat of violence by strangers in the more or less public spaces of a city may often be thought of as a traffic relationship gone awry. This is the case when the ordinary "man in the street" is involved as a victim. For some occupational categories – policemen, prostitutes, and taxi drivers, for example – it may be a routine business contact turning into something quite different. In most cases, such as muggings or rapes, the interaction becomes a focused one, with participants more or less equally observable to one another. These are the situations with which we will be more concerned. But once in a while, there is a heightening of public consciousness of other forms of anonymous violence. Sniping and bombing are instances of this.

Our emphasis here will be on people as consumers of danger, as potential or actual victims, and on their responses to danger in thought and action. This is in some contrast to much of the research centering or touching on violence in the city, by criminologists or by sociologists of deviance and juvenile delinquency, which has focused on the producers of violence, trying to explain their conduct. But we should be aware that the contrast is sometimes difficult to maintain. It would be a little too simplistic to assume that the city consists on the one hand of consumers, whose management of danger consistently aims at minimizing it, and on the other hand of producers trying to maximize it – for others. Masochists possibly apart, it is perhaps true that nobody really strives to get hurt. Yet people sometimes knowingly court danger. Some do it occupationally, like the policeman dressed up to look like an old and fragile lady, conspicuously carrying a handbag, a decoy intended to attract muggers. For others, danger is an end in itself, a mode of leisure. This is part of the "subterranean tradition" which Matza and Sykes (1961) have written about; although its values may be publicly condemned, there is widespread cultural ambivalence of a more or less private sort. From Nietzsche by way of Ruth Benedict, we may appropriate "Apollonian" and "Dionysian" as convenient descriptive labels for the tendencies involved. It is Apollonian to avoid danger. It is Dionysian to seek out thrills such as intoxicants (some at least), fast motor vehicles, and the potential of violence.[4] "Slumming" is a popular form for the occasional pursuit of Dionysianism in the city, by people whose lives may by and large be Apollonian. Others may seek Dionysian experiences more regularly. Here the consumer–producer distinction may become blurred; the management of danger can turn into a form of brinkmanship, and only the outcome may show who is what. This qualification stated, let us assume for the time being that most of the time, most urbanites are Apollonians, trying to stay away from danger. The violent or potentially violent encounter is one of the few cases of a traffic relationship which urbanites show much concern about. Most of the strangers they pass by in their everyday moving about are of no greater concern to them than so many trees in the forest would be to members of a band of hunters. The dangerous ones, on the other hand, are Very Important Persons. Preoccupation with the theme varies between groups of city dwellers and over time, of course, as we have seen in the case of the reaction to tsotsis. But where consciousness is heightened, the urbanite can feel almost continuously vulnerable. He cannot easily avoid spending a great deal of his time in the presence of strangers but may be unable to determine which one poses a threat to him. Or he may identify certain kinds of people as the sources of danger but still cannot avoid facing them time and time again. Information reaches him about the dangerous ones having been in action in nearby familiar places, or about individuals personally known to him who have become their victims.

Finally, he may have his own direct experience. Like other Very Important Persons, these will be worth talking about repeatedly and at some length. Lejeune and Alex (1973: 280), in a paper on mugging victims, describe them as creating afterwards "little cultures that give character, texture, and context to their plight." The networks in which such information is passed around, pooled and analyzed, include both people with a personal experience of violent encounters and people without firsthand experience, with the former in a position of expertise, a kind of star quality.

Such cultural constructs may show a higher or lower degree of correspondence with realities. Being "street wise" – a particular form of urban cultural competence – is in part a matter of having a realistic assessment of the amount of danger in one's environment, and instead of seeing the mass of strangers as just a forest, being able to pick out which trees are important for one's wellbeing. At times, people come into an environment where they would urgently need street wisdom they do not have. Perhaps the middle-class suburban background of many hippies was a poor preparation for life in Haight-Ashbury of San Francisco or on the Lower East Side of New York; the "flower children" might not even have tried to keep their traffic relationships with some of the more hardened inhabitants of these areas to that minimal definition of contact, but saw them as openings to sociability instead. Dionysian values without competence. This could have been a cause of some of the well-known tragic events in hippie communities, and may have contributed to their demise. (Which is not to say that the hippies may not have been exposed to trouble in other ways as well, or that their troubles may not have been more publicized than those of other people in the same neighborhoods.)

When I myself began field work in a black ghetto neighborhood in Washington, DC, in the mid-1960s, I was struck by the concern of its inhabitants with the dangers in their surroundings, and more particularly with their opinion that I was especially vulnerable, not only because I was a conspicuous stranger but at least as much because of my ignorance. This, naturally enough, was when I began taking an interest in the management of danger. They for their part had rather detailed ideas on the subject, and although they were not necessarily successful in avoiding becoming the victims of violence altogether (this was in part where their ideas came from), they tried to some extent or other to let these ideas guide their actions. A few of them could obviously derive some of their knowledge of the circumstances of danger from familiarity with the characteristic

78 The management of danger

viewpoint of producers. If they had never been dangerous ones themselves, at least they could glean something about how these work from within their own networks. But even people with no immediate access to such insights, and with strong claims to "respectability," had considerable funds of street wisdom. I would expect the same to have been true among the middle-class inhabitants of Langa in their mixed neighborhoods. This is one of the ways in which the cultural repertoires of middle-class people in ghettos and suburbs are likely to be different.

There are several components to the way in which a city dweller may look at danger and try to deal with it. We may note what goes on when he is actually in the presence of somebody he perceives as dangerous. It may be possible to avoid the attention of the other person, or those other persons – to avoid transforming, in a traffic relationship, what from the latter's point of view is unfocused co-presence into an encounter. This would have been my advantage, walking down the street in Kingston, had I not overtaken that group of youths but stayed behind them. If one is clearly observable to the dangerous one, it is likely that one still tries to be inconspicuous. But this may not be so easy, at least if the dangerous one is in full control of his senses (unlike for instance a disorderly drunkard). The impression one gets from evidence from the other side, such as Willwerth's (1976) "portrait of a mugger," is that the dangerous one is often himself street-wise enough not to let an interesting object pass by unattended if the situation is otherwise right. One is perhaps better off posing as a counter-danger, a conspicuously uninspiring candidate for attack. More about this later.

If mutually focused interaction has come about, what does one do? Fight? Shout for help? Try to break loose and run away? Submit? Who is likely to react in which way? Undoubtedly the choice – if that is the right term – is in large part due to personality and situational factors; possibly there are cultural variations as well. More intensive inquiries into kinesics, proxemics and the ethnography of speech could perhaps reveal ways in which one can place oneself favorably in order to handle aggression, or messages which serve to lessen a threatening person's propensity for violence. Course work in the "martial arts" like judo and karate is one way in which some members of the general urban population acquire skills of this kind. Otherwise such microcultural tricks of the trade are perhaps given more thought and articulation, and may therefore be most readily discernible, in groups with an unusually high degree of exposure to acute danger, including the occupational groups mentioned above whose business relationships may turn into violent encounters. Banton (1964: 112), writing of police work in a city in the American South, notes that officers regarded even the motorist whom they had stopped for a routine check as potentially dangerous. Even if it might seem more courteous of a driver who has been stopped to get out of his car, they preferred that he remained inside so that they could come up to his window from behind and he would have to turn his head to speak to them. Thus they would be better able to watch him, and he could not so easily point a gun at them. Somewhat similarly, Henslin (1968: 149–150), in a study of St. Louis taxi drivers, describes their discomfort with single passengers who choose the seat just behind the driver, where they are least observable to him. Such a passenger could be setting him up for robbery; since he cannot very well ask the passenger to move, he may think of other reasons why this seat was chosen, and if none is readily available he may be rather more on guard than usual.

Street wisdom II: mapping danger

Ethnographic accounts may thus be produced of specific forms of dangerous encounters, although they are often likely to be of limited scope. For many urbanites, however, even getting into a dangerous situation is in a way a failure in danger management, as knowledge and effort may primarily be involved in avoiding it altogether. Like in the South African location dweller's day-to-day handling of the tsotsi threat, this is in large part a matter of thinking in terms of times and places. The people in my neighborhood in Washington had rather definite ideas about where the territories of dangerous categories of people were located, and one of their ways of minimizing trouble was simply to avoid these places whenever possible, or at least not to go there alone. In their general area of black ghetto Washington the corners of 14th and U streets and 7th and T streets were the most widely recognized trouble spots, with several disreputable bars nearby. Around them one might run into both rather slick young street bandits and older, unpredictably violent alcoholics. In the more immediate vicinity, one should avoid, at least after dark, a street a few blocks away as well as a nearby playground, since there were teenagers and young men around there with a criminal reputation. The middle-aged men who had a hangout at a nearby street corner, on the other hand, were considered more dangerous to each other than to anyone else. Among the bars, some were known to be frequented by people who tended to get into fights, others by gamblers or homosexuals. These facts of life were rather often referred to or alluded to in conversations, and neighborhood residents could hardly avoid being aware of them. The word soon spread when a new gang of teenage boys from another part of town had been causing trouble in the area, and there was general consensus that the streets were more dangerous before Christmas (as in South Africa), because there was money around, some people who did not have any were desperate to get it, and dusk also came early (cf. Hannerz 1969: 20–23).[5]

This is a variety of what has been called vernacular culture, "culture-as-it-is-lived appropriate to well defined places and situations" (Lantis 1960: 203), and it occurs in varied forms in many urban milieux. La Fontaine (1970: 204–205), offering another example, points out that gangs of *la jeunesse bandite* in Kinshasa were regarded as such a menace by the inhabitants of some squatter areas there that few would go outside after dark. These criminal gangs were also known to be particularly active at the middle and the end of the month when employees were paid. In London, people became more cautious and observant in public places during a period of IRA bomb scares in early 1976; a number of bombs

80 The management of danger

were thus discovered before detonation. In Stockholm, people are somewhat wary about certain subway stations where young people while away their leisure hours and are assumed liable, especially when intoxicated, to behave in unpredictable ways. There is some fear of the subway trains themselves, especially late at night, as one could get trapped in a car with a threatening co-passenger without a chance to get away. An apparently mythical version has it that if one takes one of the seats where one can have someone else sitting next to oneself but where there are no seats opposite, one may be attacked with an injection needle by a stranger in the adjoining seat, unnoticed by anybody else. Variations of the "danger in the subway" theme recur in other large cities as well. In the study of reactions of mugging by Lejeune and Alex (1973: 274–275) referred to above, we learn also of someone attacked in an elevator who refuses to ride in it alone with a stranger again, or even to be alone in its somewhat secluded waiting area.

We can see here that in the mapping of danger in urban space, people's considerations can be of two different tendencies: some places are dangerous because dangerous people are known or believed to spend their time there habitually, others because their physical characteristics make them particularly unsuitable settings for encounters with danger. (It is of course possible for the two to combine, if the dangerous ones intentionally or by chance make such settings their meeting places with potential victims.) This kind of concern with features of physical layout clearly plays some part in the small-scale management of danger of individual urbanites. On another level, we have seen how there has been an increasing interest in the subject especially in American urban planning in more recent times. The best-known example may be Jane Jacobs' (1961) espousal of the sort of neighborhood where a hundred pairs of eyes are watching the street scene, and her suggestions of ways to make many kinds of people use the same public spaces, with varying schedules so that they never become deserted and thereby dangerous. Newman's *Defensible Space* (1973), with its more immediate emphasis on the physical features of architecture – the design of lobbies and staircases, lighting, barriers to visibility and so forth – is another instance. Certainly new designs continue to appear, however, which seem almost to maximize the potential of danger even in social contexts where one might predict that this will be an issue of concern to users. Low-cost mass housing projects in high-crime areas in many countries provide sufficient evidence.

And some, indeed most, of the urban milieux where physical features do seem to contribute to safety have emerged spontaneously, without anybody giving conscious systematic thought to this factor. Jacobs shows this well; she also shows that the ingredients which make for a safe habitat may not be immediately obvious, and that its physical attributes often should not be considered in isolation from the daily round of its inhabitants. Different local economies, for example, create different street uses, and different timings for street use. There seem to be interesting implications here for the comparative study of urban danger.

Dangerous appearances

In the last analysis, however, times and places are not in themselves dangerous; only people are. So urbanites are also likely to form ideas of the enemy himself, apart from questions of "Where?" and "When?".

When the dangerous person is a stranger, one does not have – or at least is not aware of – any indirect network link to him through an intermediary. Two consequences of this seem important. One does not beforehand have access to personal information about him as a unique individual from other sources. Moreover, should violence occur, it may well be impossible afterwards to track him down and hold him accountable.

People who are aware of danger in their occupational relationships sometimes establish ways of dealing, more or less successfully, with these problems. Merry (1980), in a study of prostitutes in a city in the northeastern United States, found that they were more willing to trust regular customers, whose hangouts or places of work they may know. With an unknown single-stand trick they would be more hesitant to enter high-risk situations, such as going along with him to his home. One technique of dealing with such danger was to have him leave his driver's licence or ID card with somebody known to the woman until he brought her back. The prostitute, on the other hand, might herself plan to rob the customer, in which case she would not take him to her own place, and would not appear again in the street the same night, or only in disguise. In his research on police work on Skid Row, Bittner (1967) noted that the patrolmen tended to deny inhabitants the right to anonymity and privacy. Charged with keeping the peace in an area where traffic relationships are understood frequently to turn into predatory encounters, and where people's movements over time are not very predictable on the basis of roles, a policeman would insist on breaking through to personal information which would allow him to judge whether an individual was dangerous or exposed himself to danger.

For most people who do not have such licence to demand individualized information in fleeting relationships, it becomes necessary to estimate the danger potential of strangers on the basis of their appearance and overt behavior in the co-presence. In a way, the most dangerous person then is the one who cannot be spotted before the show of violence. No doubt at least some of those who are occupationally engaged in violence, or the threat of violence, consciously try not to signal their intentions in any way. Willwerth's (1976: 158–160) mugger goes into the bank and feigns writing out a withdrawal slip while picking a suitable victim (to be followed outside) among the people around him, looking at least to his own mind like an ordinary workingman. If he is successful in this, one might say that he is an absolutely unpredictable attacker from the victim's point of view. And the mugging victims interviewed by Lejeune and Alex (1973: 270–271) indeed asserted that the appearances of their attackers had been deceptive – in the words of one, "He looked so wonderful, so proper and conservative and square and clean."

82 The management of danger

Some people, on the other hand, are predicted to be unpredictable. A person has a heightened sense of danger in their presence, because they can be identified in categorical terms. As far as the ordinary role-discriminatory attributes (cf. Hannerz 1980: 151 ff.) are concerned, sex, age, and ethnicity, a male is likely to be perceived as more dangerous than a woman, a youth as more dangerous than an old person, and in American cities at present, some ethnic groups as more dangerous than others. Not that most people are likely to worry about every male they meet, or every young person. It is rather that in particular circumstances, these criteria will contribute to an intensified awareness of danger – as they did for me, although a little too late, in Kingston.

Social typing, identification by behavioral style, also involves the categorical signaling of danger. Britain has seen the teddy boys, the rockers, and the skinheads; Sweden the *raggare*, mostly defined by their old American cars; South Africa its tsotsis; and the United States its street people and various motorcycle outlaw groups such as the Hell's Angels. There are others, and there may be something to be gained by some special attention to types like these. Here categorization focuses on a consciously elaborated style; those who display it are held to be dangerous. But one may quickly sense that the relationship between the public perception of danger and any actual tendency to violence needs to be problematized. For types which are understood to be dangerous are not actually equally violent. The tsotsis have indeed been depicted by most commentators as a general menace. The skinheads specialize in "Paki bashing" – attacks on Asian immigrants – and engage in fights with others of more or less their own kind and in material destruction, often in the context of acting out their support for rival soccer teams. Yet their notoriety is more diffuse.[6] The early hippies were with few exceptions peaceful, while undoubtedly they were regarded as dangerous by many people.

Although the propensity for violence may vary, the categorical relationships between the individuals thus typed and the wider public seem to have one thing in common. There is among the public a reaction against style, against what may be termed symbolic threats. Through appearance and demeanor, the people belonging to certain types may announce to other people – as the latter understand the message – that they cannot be relied upon to play the game even of a traffic relationship by the normal rules. Sometimes it is obvious enough what cues are used. Just about all the social types we are concerned with here entail conspicuous clothing. We know the tsotsi concern with dress. The skinheads, apart from closely cropped hair, have colored or patterned shirts with button-down collars (the top button undone and the cuffs of the sleeves turned up once), sleeveless pullover, denim jeans a size too large around the waist and held up by brightly colored braces, also with the legs turned up to give emphasis to a pair of heavy, cherry red industrial working boots (Daniel and McGuire 1972: 11). Such or comparable ensembles are not in line with conventional taste. They may not always play with precision on symbolic overtones of color or texture, as one could perhaps with a heavy dose of black leather. Even without

The management of danger **83**

that, the wearer may have himself defined as bizarre, unreliable, an affront to the moral and intellectual order of society. And as anthropologists are aware, not least after the work of Mary Douglas (1966), it is a common fact that such disorder equals danger.

The discomfort a city dweller registers from his impressions of strangers like these thus seems to be channeled, in ways which he is unlikely to be aware of himself, into a vague fear of outright attack. The symbolic threat is reinterpreted as a physical threat, which may or may not be there also as something more tangible. The danger concept becomes one, diffuse and comprehensive.

We should perhaps return here to Mayer's parallel between the tsotsi and the witch – both the reversal of ordinary values, utterly unpredictable, the image of evil incarnate. A more or less similar symbolic load is apparently carried by various other social types as well, in different parts of the urban world. It may be possible to pursue the analogy a bit further.[7] In the system of witchcraft belief and anti-witchcraft action of small-scale society, one may discern a gap between the witch as a thought-of being, the unreservedly evil creature of collective fantasy, with nonhuman habits and capabilities, and the witch suspect, a real person of flesh and blood who may have personality quirks but who has been experienced by others in the many dimensions of daily life, and probably often as a quite ordinary human being. The trick of successful witchcraft accusation, if one may generalize, is to close the gap by assimilating the idea of the suspect as a person into the realm of witchcraft ideas, a rather dramatic example of the labeling process. A frequent result is the rupture of relations, in some manner or other, whereby everyday interaction between witch and accusers is no longer necessary or possible.

One could think of the tsotsi, or the English rocker or an American motorcycle outlaw, as located similarly somewhere along a stretch between a city dweller's firsthand experience and a received collective image. But in this case the stretch may be a short one, with little dissonance between the two. Relatively fewer people have a rounded view of the life of the supposedly dangerous one; these, however, may have the expectable difficulty in seeing him as the personification of evil. We have seen that the townspeople of the South African locations, to whom the tsotsis tended to have their personal links, could not take quite so unqualifiedly a negative view of them as did the migrants. In the segmental, fleeting relationships, however, which most people have to individuals of the social types concerned, there is little room for qualification or contradictory information. The attribution of evil nature or intent to such individuals tends to entail no practical problem, not changing any important enduring relationship, and for the interpretation of what they see, people in this situation are likely to become more dependent on the received image. The dangerous stranger, to a greater extent than the witch suspect, would seem to be from the very beginning a one-dimensional man.

It may be asked what is the source of the received image. In part, no doubt, it comes through informal channels of word-of-mouth communication. People

84 The management of danger

in enduring relationships to another, but mostly in fleeting contact with hippies, skinheads, or whatever type may be concerned, pool their impressions. There may be some bias toward emphasizing the aberrant here already. But this is one place where one may well take note also of the mass media impact under conditions of modern urbanism; what some British sociologists have referred to as the "amplification of deviance" (cf. Young 1971a, 1971b: 174 ff.; Cohen 1973). City dwellers rely on the information brokers in newspapers and magazines, radio and television for knowledge about what goes on outside their personal networks of enduring relationships. Before the rise of mass media, such information could be scarce. Now there is, in a McLuhanesque phrase, a "knowledge implosion" whereby people who are not in intensive contact still impinge on each other's consciousness. The consumers of media information tend to assume that it is reliable. Sometimes, however, it may be above all newsworthy. The students of British social typing suggest that the media formula is to "select events which are *atypical*, present them in a *stereotypical* fashion and contrast them against a backcloth of normality which is *overtypical*." Young (1971a: 35–36) quotes an item from a popular newspaper as an example:

> HIPPIE THUGS – THE SORDID TRUTH: Drugtaking, couples making love while others look on, rule by a heavy mob armed with iron bars, foul language, filth and stench, THAT is the scene inside the hippies' Fortress in London's Piccadilly. These are not rumours but facts – sordid facts which will shock ordinary decent family loving people.
>
> *(The People, September 21, 1969)*

Thus the difference between the ordinary and the more or less unusual is amplified, the boundary between them more sharply drawn, the reaction of the "man in the street" to the threat intensified. When there is a sudden and dramatic buildup of such news, a moral panic may be released, as Cohen (1973) shows in his study of the rise to fame of the mods and the rockers. For some people, subject to the same media implosion at country farms or in small towns, this hippie thug will only be like the witch as a thought-of being, fitting comfortably perhaps into a more general notion of the distant evil city. It is for the urbanite to have this information in mind concerning the very real people sharing his environment.

The analogy between witches and certain urban social types should not be overdrawn. People like tsotsis and skinheads can, in palpable ways, be physically dangerous to all people or to some people who cross their paths, while we may have our doubts about witches in this regard. The point remains that as we note what people are identified in the city as dangerous, it may be useful to inquire into the ways in which the contours of a social type are drawn and filled in within the network of social relationships, and necessary to take a wider view of the sense of threat within the framework of culturally defined normality. As discontinuity between networks of enduring relationships, and the maintenance

The management of danger **85**

and elaboration of sectional cultures, characterize urban life, one can only expect that many encounters with strangers may involve symbolic threats, even where no physical danger is involved. Sometimes a perception of such danger may be a crystallization of some more or less clear notion of broader economic or political conflict, as between classes or ethnic groups, and the sense of threat perhaps cannot even be linked to any particular overt act at all. The *Rumour in Orleans* documented by Edgar Morin (1971) – and reminding us perhaps of the Stockholm subway rumor – about Jewish boutique owners in a French town giving drug injections to female customers in fitting booths and then selling them into white slavery, was evidently this kind of fabrication. At other times, in his fleeting relationships, the urbanite will run into others who deviate overtly from his ideas of the natural order of things. Not all will reject these as consciously and as blatantly as the people of some of the social types discussed above. We have noticed clothing which almost amounts to uniforms; but a person may seem threatening even if he only wears his hat tilted at a particular angle. He may reach the same effect by being noisy, or with a facial expression, or with his movements of body and limbs, since miniature variations in behavior are often irritatingly sensed rather than understood. The tsotsi does not walk like other people. Between the cultures of ethnic groups there may be differences of the same kind, and people may react to them with unease. Suttles (1968: 66–67) has noted in the multiethnic neighborhood he studied in Chicago how the Italians were upset when the blacks averted their eyes, while one black exclaimed about the Italians, "dammit, why they gotta eyeball everybody walk past?". It is not a sign of street wisdom, even on the part of people who otherwise may have a great deal of it, to mistake a cultural difference for a real danger, while at the same time perhaps being unable to read any signs of the latter. But such mixups seem to occur with some regularity in the heterogeneity of the city.

Danger as put-on

It would clearly be mistaken, however, to see all the symbolic threats issued in urban fleeting relationships as existing only in the eye of the beholder, without being so intended by the individual thus categorized as dangerous. In the case of several of the social types mentioned here, appearance and demeanor obviously constitute elaborate purposive statements. But why should anybody bother to scare somebody else, particularly a stranger? If a physical attack were really planned, to adumbrate it in this manner would be dysfunctional to the perpetrator.

One possible answer would be that the threat is basically defensive. If one expects to come into the presence of dangerous others, it may be better to signal "don't mess with me" loud and clear than to try avoiding attention at all, which may well fail. Suttles (1968: 127), again, interprets much of the appearance of black ghetto youths as intended to show that the individual is too powerful to be treated as fair game – a way of walking, certain clothes, and not

86 The management of danger

least the "rag," originally used to protect processed hair but more recently above all a sign of toughness. Since in traffic relationships one's messages tend to be literally broadcast rather than channeled to specific recipients, it may be inevitable that some will see the sender as a possible attacker rather than as himself simply an unsuitable victim.

It seems very likely, however, that such impression management is frequently not purely defensive. The example of ghetto youths leads us back from Apollonianism to Dionysianism, and this is where many of the urban social types belong as well. Walter (1970: 41–42), reporting on the Warlocks, a motorcycle outlaw gang active around Philadelphia, points out that the "1%" patch they wear on their denim jackets is a flippant reference to a statement by the American Motorcycle Association that "99% of all motorcyclists are decent, law-abiding citizens." The main theme in Warlock public behavior is to be "righteous," to be interpreted as spectacular. It is righteous to urinate in the middle of a busy street, or to pull down one's pants on a crowded dance floor – "because it blows the citizens' minds, baby." This is danger as a put-on, a purely symbolic, provocative presentation of evil. In order to see in a general way how this Dionysianism fits into our conception of the urban structure of social relations, we will make one quick foray into the interpretation of danger production, even though it must be recognized that numerous writers have subjected it to much more intensive analysis.

The urban role structure, with its tendency to variable role constellations and substitutability of role incumbents, might generate a rather intense concern with the idea of the self (cf. Hannerz 1980: 115, 221 ff.). Modular, highly routinized work roles could be unsatisfactory for an anchoring of the sense of individuality, and individuals might seek for alternative points of anchorage in other domains of life, not least in leisure. It would only.be the general common sense of symbolic interactionism to assume that this self would be constructed in interaction validated by significant others. But under urban circumstances the achievement of recognition from others may require special effort. Rivière (1967: 577–578) has pointed this out in his reanalysis, in terms of "honor and shame," of Oscar Lewis' *The Children of Sanchez*. In a small community, honor may be ascriptive, as networks are dense and one has a share in the collective reputation of one's family. In the city, one's background may not be known to others, and so honor must be earned anew. Its characteristic urban form in Mexico, Rivière concludes, is *machismo*.

The argument apparently corresponds well to the realities surrounding Dionysian social types. Hunter Thompson (1967: 197), in his celebrated account of the Hell's Angels, the Warlocks' more famous California counterpart, depicts the outlaws as drifting between various unengaging jobs, and emphasizes that he never met an Angel who claimed a home town in the ordinary sense of the word. Many had lost contact with their families, had spent their lives in total mobility, and now related entirely to "the present, the moment, the action." One could see also why Dionysianism is often an urban youth phenomenon – young people do not just hit harder and run faster than their elders, thus being better able to get away with thrill seeking, they are also at a point in their life careers where whatever networks they have had are undergoing radical reconstruction and they must catch the attention of new significant others.

Skinheads, teddy boys, *raggare*, motorcycle outlaws and others thus respectively come together to formulate solutions to shared problems. What this does not quite explain is why they have to be specifically Dionysian solutions, a sensation of the self reached through the outrage of others. Why not some nice, wholesome, consensual manner the way other people seem to do it? Perhaps in these cases the desire for a more sharply delineated self is paired with a more general orientation toward agonistic categorical relationships, rooted in ethnic, class or generational experience. So there is a denial of communitas. Anyway, the social typing here is not only other-typing but self-typing as well. One chooses a cluster of attributes by which one wants to be recognized. The greater the public recognition given to the cluster, the more standardized will it probably become as a successful type. Much of the recognition may be played out inside the group formed around it, and as involvement in the common task of reputation building may crystallize into notions of rights and obligations within the group, types may even turn into something like roles. But individually or collectively, with a concentration of effort or as a side event to some other activity, members also demand the attention of others outside. The form of the claim to recognition is a threat, and its acknowledgment by a victim is the validation of the self – immediate or mediated through the appreciation of the group. Actual physical violence may or may not be used to back up the claim if necessary. Yet since it is a matter of a symbolic interaction, just appearing evil, unpredictable and dangerous, just inspiring fear and loathing among the public, may be effective enough.

Organizing against danger

Hitherto, we have depicted the individual as acting more or less singly on his perceptions of the distribution of danger in his environment (however socially constructed these perceptions may be), and the dangerous encounter has similarly been seen largely as dyadic in nature. But the urbanite does not always face danger alone. The prostitute in the American city who might ask for a customer's ID card to put away in safe storage before going off with him for a rendezvous in an unknown place could alternatively insist on taking a friend along (Merry 1980). The black youth who wears the "rag" over his hair may communicate not only individual toughness but also membership in a gang which may be called upon to deal collectively with an attacker. In my own predicament of being mugged in Kingston, I called for help from others in the street, rather than trying to handle the situation alone.

Just as there may be a plurality of predators, then, those who find themselves exposed to danger may form alliances to ward it off. One variety is where the dangerous encounter itself gives rise to immediate spontaneous organization. We

88 The management of danger

tend to assume that an attack may never take place, or is less likely to be successful, when there are other people present who can intervene. Thus we have the ideas of planners like Jacobs and Newman, who for safety's sake prefer lively public places, under continuous although casual surveillance, to the more or less deserted settings toward which the view is obstructed. But one cannot quite take for granted that people, even when they have some awareness of what is going on, will come to the aid of the victim. "Bystander apathy" became a watchword in thinking about big-city life not least after that notorious 1964 New York murder case when Kitty Genovese was murdered in the street late one night while 38 of her neighbors, awakened by her screams, looked out through their windows. Such passivity has since been the subject of much speculation as well as some social-psychological experimenting; there have also been claims of a recent swing toward greater activism among New Yorkers as observers of street crime.[8]

In any case, it would seem that some specification of the quality of the relationships between the people present may give a better idea of whether bystanders will become actively involved. One might think of the attacker and his intended victim, as well as all the people who through sight or sound are notified of that ongoing confrontation, as constituting together a momentary social network where the content of each link may play a part in determining the outcome of the incident. The archetypical situation is that where only traffic relationships exist between the people in the network, apart from that between victim and aggressor. Bystander apathy in its most clearcut form may be identified here with the possibility that each one of these others maintained his own commitment to the norm of traffic relationships – the less involvement, the better. Experimental evidence shows, however, that passivity could have another basis. Each bystander may try to check the overt reaction of the others before deciding whether it is appropriate to become involved. Even if they are personally concerned, they may not communicate this effectively to each other, since they are all strangers. And so their involvement may remain intense but covert. A lone observer might more readily have taken action, not being constrained by the urge to share in an apparently prevailing definition of the situation. What would be needed here is a rapid "cultural process," where consensus on the desirability of intervention could be quickly established. A further complicating factor may be if the observers find the relationship between attacker and victim ambiguous. Is it a traffic relationship misused, which would warrant involvement, or is it a private relationship which has just spilled over into the public arena? A fight between a man and a woman may turn out to be a marital quarrel; perhaps this is something one should not meddle with. When children get mugged by others just a few years their senior, they may be ignored by adult passers-by who view children's fights as an ordinary fact of life and none of their concern (cf. Lamont 1975: 59 ff.).

Reactions may be different, naturally, when the people present are not all to the same extent strangers to each other, or to the public setting where the

The management of danger **89**

dangerous encounter occurs. Where a sense of neighborhood exists, neighbors would probably at least be apt to come to one another's assistance should one of them be attacked in that setting by a stranger. (Such a sense may have been lacking on Kitty Genovese's block.) But would these people intervene if one stranger assaulted another there, on grounds of a concern with the peace of the neighborhood, and on the basis of their more effective contacts with each other as co-observers? Or if one of their own were to attack a stranger in the neighborhood, could the latter expect any sympathy from bystanders? It is difficult to deal in general terms with such questions. They probably become more manageable when more informed with sociocultural detail, concerning for instance the nature of categorical relationships between the people involved. It could be, anyway, that people in their evaluation of more or less dangerous places sometimes also take their potential for counteractive organization into account, and that places with a relatively high ratio of neighbor relationships are sensed to be safer, even to a stranger.

Organizing against danger, however, is not only of an instantaneous, fleeting kind. City dwellers may also consciously form or expand enduring relationships to cope with threats in their shared space. The police, of course, is in part a highly specialized organization of this sort emerging in something like the present professional form from the tumult of the great cities of the nineteenth century, but we will not take it into much account here. (For some people, of course, like South African township people and some American urban minorities, the police have become more like a threateningly unpredictable social type, with uniform and all.) Our concern is rather with vigilantism, once a frontier phenomenon in America but in the twentieth century an urban one, since it is now in the city one finds the unsettled conditions giving rise to it.[9] In a simple definition, vigilantism involves "taking the law into one's own hands." It operates outside an existing centralized governmental apparatus of law enforcement, yet assumes its own legitimacy as an agent of justice. In its typical form, however, it does not counterpose its own principles of justice to those of established authority; it is not revolutionary. One might think of it rather as a "parallel structure" – but as with many phenomena so labeled, it is something of a misnomer, insofar as it may interwine with the official structure and stretch and twist its aims and procedures.

Vigilante organizations tend to come into existence when there is a heightened concern with public disorder, and growing doubts about the ability or willingness of established agencies to keep it under control. The reaction against the tsotsis in East London could be seen as a short-term vigilante movement; there were suggestions of vigilante action in some British seaside resorts after the mods' and rockers' incidents in the mid-1960s; and in urban America the appearance of such groups as the Maccabees of Brooklyn, New York, and Anthony Imperiale's North Ward Citizens' Committee in Newark, New Jersey, at about the same time, were part of an upsurge of preoccupation with "law and order." The specifically urban aspect of vigilantism in the city is that it aims at the control of

90 The management of danger

intensively used public space. And here its concepts of legitimacy may be on a collision course with the law. In most contemporary cities, according to the latter, there is only the rather simple distinction between public and private space, and to the former there is universal access. Present-day exceptions exist, as for example in societies with rigid racial regimes, and in the preindustrial cities with their enclosed quarters, there was some gradation of access; the gates to these quarters may at least have swung shut during the night. Even where equal access is the law, the law enforcement agents themselves may have less formal notions of "people out of place," as Blacks walking in a White neighborhood have often been made to understand. But the restriction of access has often been a vigilante impulse. Urban vigilantism is part of a striving for a turf, to use the term favored by Jacobs (1961: 47 ff.), or a "defended neighborhood," in Suttles' (1972: 21 ff.) phrasing. Through residential segregation of one kind or other, neighbor relationships are denied to undesirables. Vigilantism comprises the next one or two steps, a surveillance of strangers entering the area or even the attempt to keep them out altogether, a denial of traffic relationships to at least some people within a given space.

If vigilantism is limited to surveillance, its relationship to the law need not be problematic. Where suspicions arise, they could conceivably be reported to the police, which would then take whatever action necessary. An exception here would be the Black Panther Party for Self Defense, originally formed in Oakland as a sort of vigilante organization for which the police were the dangerous strangers to be controlled. But it is particularly when vigilantes begin to enforce laws, even rules which are only of their own making, that this parallel structure is hardly parallel any longer. No strangers are allowed at all onto certain public space, or enter it only at the risk of harassment. Or access is differentiated, on the basis of a categorization of strangers – in particular, people of certain ethnic groups or certain social types may be kept out. It could be that such measures, putatively designed to prevent dangerous encounters, are grounded in some more or less realistic assessment of the propensity for violence of these people. Yet it is also possible that such vigilantism is a reaction against the symbolic threats of others, threats which as we have seen may or may not be intentional. Where this is the case, the connection between vigilante action and the legal order would seem to become even more tenuous. Whether vigilante groups are rare or common in cities is in part a matter of definition. The more purely defensive groups, composed largely of adults and committed fairly unambiguously to a minimization of danger in the area, taking action against strangers relatively sparingly and in an instrumental manner, are perhaps after all relatively few. It is worth considering, however, to what extent big-city youth gangs also have a vigilante streak. Already Thrasher (1927) noted the territorial basis of gang formation in one of the early Chicago studies, and a more recent study such as Keiser's *The Vice Lords* (1969) is quite clear on the way gangland is a congeries of protected neighborhoods. Expressed through the *West Side Story* motif, this would make vigilantism a time-honored and widespread approach to

The management of danger **91**

the uncertainties of life in shared urban space, at least in the United States. Ware (1965: 130) has described the clashes between Irish and Italian gangs from different blocks in her study of Greenwich Village, New York, in the 1920s, Padilla (1958: 226 ff.) portrays the fighting gangs of Puerto Rican youths in the same city a quarter of a century later. Outside America, gangs and gang territories figure less prominently in the urban popular consciousness; but Clarke (1975: 101), at least, notes that the British skinhead "mobs" took to marking off their territories with painted warnings on house walls – "Quinton mob rules here."

Gangs of this kind, like other vigilante groups, often seem to make their appearance where and when a redistribution of urban space is going on, so that new people are likely to come into contact in neighbor as well as traffic relationships, and in part they may be a reaction against pressures arising in these situations. If one is still reluctant to think of these gangs as vigilante groups, however, it is because their commitment to the reduction of danger does not appear wholehearted. They tend, after all, to Dionysianism, to the expressive production of at least the symbolism of danger. Although they may try to protect their own members from attacks by others, it often seems less certain that the same protection is extended to other neighborhood people. Or if neighbors are accorded immunity while strangers in traffic relationships are subjected to Dionysian threats, this is hardly more than a vigilantism by default. Naturally, it is highly questionable whether the gangs actually help keep down the net amount of danger in the city (however that may be measured). It is at least as likely that what is protection to one is threat to others, and that there is an escalation of danger. But this may be a possibility with other vigilante groups as well.

Who becomes a vigilante? One may try to reply in psychological terms, delineating a vigilante personality.[10] More in line with our perspective here is to do it in terms of social relations. Vigilantism, one may speculate, is born in a network of potential co-vigilantes, dangerous strangers, and relatively disinterested others. Given that people in a neighborhood perceive that their environment is dangerous, they can respond in different ways. They may regard their neighborhood as a "community of limited liability" (Janowitz 1952), pack up and move out. They may stay on and deal with it individually as best they can. Or they may get together and try to do something about it, vigilante fashion. The latter would seem most probable where there is already a pre-existing network of strong enduring relationships between people.[11] Since pure neighbor relationships are not necessarily particularly strong, it may be that vigilantism grows most readily where there are multiplex relationships among neighbors. If everybody cannot be linked with everybody else this way, perhaps at least one or a few people may be able to reach out effectively this way, to mobilize others.

One might also hypothesize that outside the neighborhood, on the other hand, vigilantes have fewer contacts. This would seem probable both because they have (according to the above) invested heavily in neighborhood contacts and because they have not been tempted to move off. But close contacts with others who are not involved in the situation and who might take another and more tempered

92 The management of danger

view of it could dilute the potential vigilante's intellectual and emotional commitment to his solution, developed in interaction with others in the neighborhood. Finally, this commitment may depend on a discontinuity in the network of enduring links between the vigilante and those perceived as dangerous. This is to repeat what has already been pointed out above; if one can reach a person through common acquaintances, if one has a relatively full picture of him as an individual, and if one can even appreciate his style as a cultural variety instead of feeling threatened by it, one may be less concerned to organize against him.

In the absence of much significant ethnography of urban vigilantism, this argument is at best plausible. Some of the best-known examples, it may be added, do indeed involve groups which may tend somewhat to encapsulation and who are probably partly motivated by ethnic stereotypes. But the line of reasoning is mostly intended to show that the tools of an anthropologist's trade are perhaps well suited for investigating vigilante organization, just as they have been useful in analyzing other "parallel structures" elsewhere in the world.

The danger complex

The concern with danger in the city has turned out to be a thing of many parts, an entire danger complex. Some urbanites may take too little notice of it for their own good, others are more preoccupied with it than necessary. Some know where danger is, others look for it in the wrong places. At times mythologies are created around it, at other times organizations. Both the peculiar social fabric of the city and its cultural diversity contribute to the formation of the sense of danger. Clearly, one cannot disregard the conditions under which physical violence is actually produced by some city dwellers. But to understand the quality of life among urbanites generally, one cannot ignore either the way they feel about danger, as potential or actual victims. It may even be held that the production of violence cannot be dealt with realistically without a grasp of the consumers' perspective. In recent years, it has occasionally been proposed that crime statistics should be computed to take this more systematically into account (cf. Wilson 1966: 33; Wolfgang 1970: 292 ff.). Some suspect that this may throw new light on a multi-faceted situation. The facts about danger, however, are not only statistical but relational and cultural as well. Perhaps these notes can suffice to show that some understanding of this sort may result if we sometimes think about the danger complex with an urban anthropologist's hat on.

Notes

1 The first version was at different times intended for publication in two different collections of papers, neither of which were in the end published. The present version was written in early 1977, and I then expected to include it in the volume which eventually became *Exploring the City* (Hannerz, 1980). In the end, I decided not to, but meanwhile, the versions have been circulated fairly widely in mimeographed form, and have occasionally been cited in print. Apparently the essay is of some

The management of danger **93**

interest; hardly because of new ethnography, of which there is very little, but as an attempt to take an anthropological view of a novel but not unimportant topic. I have therefore decided that I may as well let this version get into print, with minimal updating. The most significant events in the development of an ethnography of danger since it was written, undoubtedly, are the publications of a couple of studies by Merry (1980, 1981).

2 Field work for these studies was conducted in the late 1950s and early 1960s. While the ethnographic present is used here, it is obviously worth noting that the conditions of South African urban life continue to change under the impact of *apartheid* policies of settlement for Africans. As elsewhere on the continent, the urban imagery of African writers provides useful additional insights. On tsotsis, see e.g. Can Themba's (1972: 68–71) story "Terror in the trains."

3 For another comment on tsotsi fashions see Pauw (1963: 58).

4 Gans' (1962:28 ff.) "action seekers" and "routine seekers" are thus Dionysians and Apollonians.

5 For a more general conceptualization of fear among low-income black urbanites in the United States see the well-known paper by Rainwater (1966).

6 Some readings on the skinheads: Daniel and McGuire (1972), Clarke (1975) and Taylor and Wall (1976).

7 I must beg forbearance if in doing so I do violence to variations and finer points in documented witchcraft systems.

8 For one of several available accounts of the Genovese affair see Seedman and Hellman (1974); for an experimental inquiry into the psychology of bystander apathy see Latané and Darley (1969); for a report of New Yorkers "fighting back" see Claiborne (1973).

9 For overviews of American vigilantism generally and in cities specifically see Brown (1969) and Marx and Archer (1976).

10 As Kreml (1976) has done.

11 A further factor influencing the choice between fighting and quitting, of course, is the highly tangible one of financial loss. A property owner in a neighborhood of declining values cannot easily leave for a more expensive area.

References

Banton, Michael. 1964. *The Policeman in the Community*. London: Tavistock.

Bell, Daniel. 1961. *The End of Ideology*. New York, NY: Collier.

Bittner, Egon. 1967. The Police on Skid-Row: A Study of Peace Keeping. *American Sociological Review*, 32: 699–715.

Brown, Richard Maxwell. 1969. The American Vigilante Tradition. In Hugh Davis Graham, and Ted Robert Gurr (eds.), *Violence in America*. Washington, DC: U.S. Government Printing Office.

Chevalier, Louis. 1973. *Labouring Classes and Dangerous Classes*. London: Routledge & Kegan Paul.

Claiborne, William L. 1973. New Yorkers Fight Back: The Tilt toward Vigilantism. *New York*, 6 (42): 49–53.

Clarke, Johan. 1975. The Skinheads and the Magical Recovery of Community. In *Working Papers in Cultural Studies*. Birmingham: Centre for Contemporary Cultural Studies, 7–8.

Cohen, Stanley. 1973. *Folk Devils and Moral Panics*. London: Paladin.

Daniel, Susie, and Pete McGuire. 1972. *The Paint House*. Harmondsworth, UK: Penguin.

Douglas, Mary. 1966. *Purity and Danger*. London: Routledge & Kegan Paul.

Gans, Herbert J. 1962. *The Urban Villagers*. New York, NY: Free Press.

Hannerz, Ulf. 1969. *Soulside*. New York, NY: Columbia University Press.

———. 1980. *Exploring the City*. New York, NY: Columbia University Press.

94 The management of danger

Henslin, James M. 1968. Trust and the Cab Driver. In Marcello Truzzi (ed.), *Sociology and Everyday Life*. Englewood Cliffs, NJ: Prentice-Hall.

Jacobs, Jane. 1961. *The Death and Life of Great American Cities*. New York, NY: Random House.

Janowitz, Morris. 1952. *The Community Press in an Urban Setting*. Chicago, IL: University of Chicago Press.

Keiser, R. Lincoln. 1969. *The Vice Lords*. New York, NY: Holt, Rinehart and Winston.

Kreml, William P. 1976. The Vigilante Personality. In H. Jon Rosenbaum, and Peter C. Sederberg (eds.), *Vigilante Politics*. Philadelphia, PA: University of Pennsylvania Press.

La Fontaine, Joan S. 1970. Two Types of Youth Group in Kinshasa (Léopoldville). In Philip Mayer (ed.), *Socialization: The Approach from Anthropology (ASA 8)*. London: Tavistock.

Lamont, Barbara. 1975. *City People*. New York, NY: Macmillan.

Lantis, Margaret. 1960. Vernacular Culture. *American Anthropologist*, 62: 202–216.

Latané, Bibb, and John M. Darley 1969. Bystander "Apathy." *American Scientist*, 57: 244–268.

Lejeune, Robert, and Nicholas Alex 1973. On Being Mugged: The Event and Its Aftermath. *Urban Life and Culture*, 2: 259–287.

Marx, Gary T., and Dane Archer 1976. Community Police Patrols and Vigilantism. In H. Jon Rosenbaum, and Peter C. Sederberg (eds.), *Vigilante Politics*. Philadelphia, PA: University of Pennsylvania Press.

Matza, David, and Gresham H. Sykes. 1961. Juvenile Delinquency and Subterranean Values. *American Sociological Review*, 26: 712–719.

Mayer, Philip. 1961. *Townsmen or Tribesmen*. Cape Town: Oxford University Press.

Merry, Sally E. 1980. Manipulating Anonymity: Streetwalkers' Strategies for Safety in the City. *Ethnos*, 45: 157–175.

———. 1981. *Urban Danger*. Philadelphia, PA: Temple University Press.

Morin, Edgar. 1971. *Rumour in Orléans*. New York, NY: Pantheon.

Newman, Oscar. 1973. *Defensible Space*. New York, NY: Collier.

Padilla, Elena. 1958. *Up from Puerto Rico*. New York, NY: Columbia University Press.

Pauw, B. A. 1963. *The Second Generation*. Cape Town: Oxford University Press.

Rainwater, Lee. 1966. Fear and the House-as-Haven in the Lower Class. *Journal of the American Institute of Planners*, 32: 23–31.

Reader, D. H. 1961. *The Black Man's Portion*. Cape Town: Oxford University Press.

Rivière, Peter. G. 1967. The Honour of Sánchez. *Man*, 2: 569–583.

Seedman, Albert A., and Peter Hellman 1974. Why Kitty Genovese Haunts New York: The Untold Story. *New York*, 7 (30): 32–41.

Suttles, Gerald D. 1968. *The Social Order of the Slum*. Chicago, IL: University of Chicago Press.

———. 1972. *The Social Construction of Communities*. Chicago, IL: University of Chicago Press..

Taylor, Ian, and David Wall 1976. Beyond the Skinheads: Comments on the Emergence and Significance of the Glamrock Cult. In Geoff Mungham, and Geoff Pearson (eds.), *Working Class Youth Culture*. London: Routledge & Kegan Paul.

Themba, Can. 1972. *The Will to Die*. London: Heinemann.

Thompson, Hunter S. 1967. *Hell's Angels*. New York, NY: Ballantine.

Thrasher, Frederic M. 1927. *The Gang*. Chicago, IL: University of Chicago Press.

Walter, Greg. 1970. The Warlocks Are Coming! In Alan Halpern (ed.), *The Improper Philadelphians*. New York, NY: Weybright and Talley.

Ware, Caroline F. 1965. *Greenwich Village 1920–1930*. New York, NY: Harper & Row.
Willwerth, James. 1976. *Jones: Portrait of a Mugger*. Greenwich, CN: Fawcett.
Wilson, James Q. 1966. Crime in the Streets. *The Public Interest*, 5: 26–35.
Wilson, Monica, and Archie Mafeje. 1963. *Langa*. Cape Town: Oxford University Press.
Wolfgang, Marvin E. 1970. Urban Crime. In James Q. Wilson (ed.), *The Metropolitan Enigma*. Garden City, NY: Anchor.
Young, Jock. 1971a. The Role of the Police as Amplifiers of Deviancy, Negotiators of Reality and Translators of Fantasy. In Stanley Cohen (ed.), *Images of Deviance*. Harmondsworth, UK: Penguin.
———. 1971b. *The Drugtakers*. London: Paladin.

4

MARGINAL ENTREPRENEURSHIP AND ECONOMIC CHANGE IN THE CAYMAN ISLANDS

In recent years, international tourism has expanded into a rising number of territories outside or on the periphery of the western world where practically all the travelers originate, leading to changes in social and economic structure. One territory thus affected is the Cayman Islands, a small British colony in the western Caribbean. This short note will set three case histories of individuals engaged in new small business enterprises in the context of ongoing changes in island society, to throw some light on one sector of the emerging economy, directly as well as indirectly influenced by the growth of tourism.[1]

The Cayman Islands – Grand Cayman, Cayman Brac, and Little Cayman – were never a plantation society of the familiar Caribbean kind. Their permanent settlement appears to date from the early eighteenth century, when settlers came over from Jamaica, the larger territory with which the Cayman Islands have had their most intimate links. Some of these settlers were white; they also brought slaves, but not in very large numbers. Consequently, there is still a significant proportion of native whites in the population, about 25%, and the greater proportion of the remainder is colored rather than black. Of the current population of about 10,000, some 90% live on the largest island, Grand Cayman, while Little Cayman has only a handful of inhabitants. Thus the district of the Lesser Islands is in practice almost synonymous with Cayman Brac.

Until the last couple of decades, most Caymanians earned their livelihood from some combination of small-scale agriculture, fishing, turtling, and seamanship. Only rather small areas could be cultivated, since the low-lying land is often swampy and since rock formations are close to the surface. Agriculture was thus often of a subsistence variety only.[2]

On the other hand, turtling was long an important activity among the islanders – around their own islands as well as south of Cuba in an early period, and outside

Central America (particularly Nicaragua) in this century. This took the men involved away from the islands for prolonged periods and also made them experienced seamen. As such they also engaged in carrying goods between Caribbean ports, on schooners and sloops built in the islands. Fishing, on the other hand, was largely of an offshore kind for which smaller boats or canoes were used.

To be a Caymanian has thus frequently meant to be involved in a number of different pursuits, a kind of occupational multiplicity which is also encountered elsewhere in the Caribbean outside the centers of the plantation economy (cf. Comitas 1964). Even the members of the small business elite, mostly white, have usually had no single focus for their activities. A leading merchant house in the period before that of recent changes could thus be engaged in running not only a general store but also turtling and transport vessels as well as brokerage, insurance, and other agencies for metropolitan companies, and it was likely to be constantly looking for new opportunities along yet other lines. But perhaps this should not be considered true occupational multiplicity, as the activities of the merchants could all be seen as entailing a rather similar kind of managerial involvement. Yet even many of them had spent periods as seamen, and they could also maintain an interest in agriculture.

Despite this readiness to avail themselves of all opportunities, however, Caymanians often found it hard to make an acceptable living on their islands, and consequently there has been considerable emigration, to Central America in the nineteenth century, and mostly to the United States in the twentieth century. Increasingly often, too, Caymanian seamen joined American shipping lines, with the result that they stayed away for even longer periods from the territory, in some cases leading to the attenuation of their ties to it. At the same time, of course, the Caymanian sailship fleet was gradually taken out of traffic. Thus by the middle of the twentieth century, at any one time, a considerable proportion of the adult male population would be away from the islands. Agriculture declined, and the territory became dependent on remittances as well as foodstuffs from abroad.

The development of the tourist industry

A new era began in the Cayman Islands with the construction of an airport on Grand Cayman in 1953. One consequence of the new communication facilities was that Caymanian seamen could more easily reach the foreign ports where they joined their ships. More important in the long run, however, was the fact that the attractions of the islands became more accessible to foreigners, especially North Americans. Miami was now only about an hour away. Some businessmen, as well as one or two of the colonial administrators sent out from Britain, had long been aware of the potential for tourism, but with the poor communications it had remained largely unrealized. Now the possibilities were greater, even if there was no real boom until the 1960s.

98 Economic change in the Cayman Islands

In this most recent period much land has changed hands, activity in the construction industry has been intensive (so that even with many seamen returning home there has been a labor shortage), and some of its efforts have involved the construction of a series of new beach hotels. Furthermore, apart from the growth of tourism, the status of the territory as a tax haven has drawn wide international attention. The changes which have resulted are most visible on Grand Cayman, particularly in the capital George Town and along the splendid beach stretching out north of it. They are noticeable elsewhere on the main island as well, however, and since the island is small its population serves as one single labor force which can fairly easily reach any place of employment. On Little Cayman, an establishment catering to foreign visitors now dominates the island with its minuscule permanent population; Cayman Brac, on the other hand, has not been very strongly affected by the tourist industry. Although there are now air connections between Grand Cayman and the smaller islands, they have not been of a sufficient quality to help spread changes more evenly over the territory. One consequence of this has been some migration of people from Cayman Brac to Grand Cayman, where they hope to find employment.

Who does what in the new structure of economic activities in the territory? As one might expect, no longer are only Caymanians involved. The hotel industry is a major sphere of expatriate control. By 1970, only one of the ten beach hotels on Grand Cayman was owned and operated by Caymanians, although the owner-managers of several of the others could with time become naturalized. With few exceptions, individual Caymanian businessmen apparently did not have the financial resources nor the know-how for operations on this scale, although by international standards these establishments would not be considered very large. A further step toward foreign influence in the hotel industry was taken with the more recent opening of a Holiday Inn on Grand Cayman, the first international hotel chain to become represented in the territory. At the other end of the spectrum, there are a couple of more modest Caymanian-run guest houses as well as a larger number of self-service cottages for rent, a form of tourist accommodation requiring less in terms of financial investments and management skills on the part of the proprietors.

In the real estate business there are some Caymanians as well as several expatriates. Certainly, many islanders have had some income from selling land previously of little value to visitors intending to build second homes in the territory. Yet much of the profit has been reaped by relatively few people who have speculated in rising land values and who have subdivided larger tracts to considerable advantage. In the construction industry, a greater part of the enterprises are Caymanian, and this, as we have already noted, is also a major area of employment for wage-earning islanders. In this respect it is at present more important than the hotel industry, but while one may assume that the latter could at least maintain its current level of employment over time, it would seem likely that the construction industry must at some time in the future face a decline when only less attractive properties remain undeveloped.

Economic activities have certainly expanded also in other areas than those mentioned above, involving both Caymanians and foreign newcomers. One must be aware in this context of the fact that the new business climate in the territory does not only involve catering to the desires of the new arrivals from abroad; the Caymanians themselves also earn more money and can afford new services and consumer goods. To a considerable extent, however, new lines have been assimilated into the enterprises of the old merchant elite, operating either alone or in partnership with foreign interests. While the Cayman Islands have obviously never had a strong self-sufficient economy, ties of this latter kind in particular have meant that Caymanian businessmen in the contemporary era tend to constitute what Schneider et al. (1972) have called a "dependence elite," its personal welfare being directly linked to foreign influences.

Yet even if the old business elite has done well for itself under the new circumstances, there has been some diversification of commercial activity among other Caymanians as well. Some individuals or families have risen to prominence from more modest ranks, and at the periphery of economic growth spheres another number of small enterprises have emerged which draw their strength from a skillful juggling of limited resources.

After this overview of the current situation as a whole, we will now turn to case histories of some such marginal entrepreneurs, in order to arrive at some understanding of what economic strategies are available in the current situation to ordinary Caymanians going into business for themselves.[3]

Case history 1: Melville Bodden

West Bay is the northwesterly settlement on Grand Cayman, at the northern end of the best stretch of beach in the territory. This is the home of Melville Bodden, more often referred to as "Captain Melville," a businessman with a direct tie to the tourist trade. Melville Bodden went to sea for a few years as a young man and then came back to join what was at that time a very minimal Caymanian police force. After several years there, he became one of the few taxi drivers in the late 1940s. (In more recent years, their numbers have increased considerably.) In this period before good air communications, he only got occasional tourists as customers, some of them just coming ashore briefly before their ships would proceed on their routes. As he took them on rides around the island, however, he gradually became more of a guide, learning what kinds of things visitors would enjoy. He also began to bring lobsters to cook on the beach for his guests. The next step was to start taking out tourists in a small boat for snorkeling, spearfishing, and other offshore pleasures. In this line of activity he was alone for several years, but more recently a number of other Caymanians have taken it up. For Melville Bodden it has remained a great success, however, particularly since he built a larger boat which could take guests on more extended tours. Meanwhile, he has continued to take occasional taxi jobs when time has permitted. For some time he was in the car-rental business

100 Economic change in the Cayman Islands

on a small scale, but he left it as it turned out to demand considerable investments if he were to remain competitive. By and large, this is a family enterprise. At times when he takes clients out on longer tours – such as to the Bay Islands, off the coast of Honduras – he assembles a crew of up to four persons, hired on a day-to-day basis, but for shorter day tours of the more ordinary kind, he only needs his wife or adolescent son to assist him. His wife and his mother-in-law also participate in the tourist business in another way, by weaving straw from the thatch palm into hats, baskets, and other items. Most of these products can be sold directly to tourists, many of whom are Melville Bodden's customers and learn of their availability through him. Selling them through hotels or George Town shops is obviously less profitable.

The Bodden family also has some self-service cottages for rent, and while Melville Bodden has little land of his own, he handles some real estate on a brokerage basis; local people know that he is in a strategic position to contact prospective customers. He gets much of his tour business through the hotels but also by distributing business cards personally in the commercial center of George Town and through word of mouth from satisfied customers. He has also had favorable publicity in a number of American newspapers and magazines.

Case history 2: Evelyn Watler

By 1970, Evelyn Watler was a little over thirty years old; her entire adult life thus coincides with the period of economic change. Her father, now retired, owns a George Town bar (mostly with working-class clientele), and she thus grew up in a business-oriented family. As a school girl she started doing hairdressing, mostly for other girls who made small payments for it. When she was in her late teens she left the territory for New York, where she entered a hairdressing school while at the same time working at a hospital during nights. Having completed her training as a hair stylist she went into a dressmaking school; later on her sister also went through a hairdressing institute. During this period Evelyn Watler also took missionary courses run by a fundamentalist sect resembling the denominations playing a significant part in Caymanian religious life.

Although she lived in the United States for several years, she made a number of visits home. While she was away her mother wrote that a small house with a shop was for sale, and Evelyn Watler arranged to buy it. During return trips home she had additions to the house built, much in the way that Caymanian seamen have continuously added to their homes between periods at sea. In the early 1960s, finally, she came home to settle. Her hairdressing salon got its clientele through her old network of friends and neighbors and on the basis of a growing reputation, but also through advertisements in the telephone directory and in the newspapers as these began to appear in the territory. Only one person, an American lady, had previously been in the beauty business on Grand Cayman. Evelyn Watler also made dresses to order, and for a while she also kept wigs in stock. This proved too costly, however, so that more lately she has only put through orders from customers who make deposits. Recently she has also turned one part of the ground floor of her house into a café.

These are the major facets of Evelyn Watler's enterprise, but it has also included other activities, sometimes on a short-term basis. Before the downstairs area became a café, she ran a mission there for some time, with some weeknight meetings and a Sunday school for children. Many neighborhood children used to come, and girl friends helped take collections. The church in Miami which had promised to support the mission did little to help her, however, and some of her neighbors were critical of the venture, so it was closed down. Other involvements have ranged from retaining her old car, to be rented to visitors, after buying a new one from Miami, to buying whole watermelons and selling slices to neighborhood children. Not all of them have been profitable, but their variety marks Evelyn Watler's readiness to try new openings.

We have noted how Evelyn Watler's personal network has played a part in building a clientele for her enterprise. It may be added that it has also been a resource on the personnel side. In her hairdressing salon, she has been able to call on the help of two sisters as the need has arisen. In her café, girl friends who are otherwise employed elsewhere have come in to help her during "big nights." Before opening it, she heard from one friend that she could pick up furniture cheaply from a bar which had lost its lease, and another friend could help her with construction work.

Case history 3: Bertram Wood

Close to the shoreline, in Bodden Town on the south coast of Grand Cayman stands another leisure establishment, a restaurant and bar where the latter's business usually dominates. It is run by Bertram Wood, a former seaman who returned ashore to stay in the mid-1960s. The place is most lively at night when people come to drink and play cards and dominoes. Meals are prepared, also on a carry-out basis, by the owner's wife. Now and then Bertram Wood arranges dances with one of the new Caymanian dance bands, which are fairly expensive, and he might then also hire a couple of extra helpers, but his wife and sons also assist. During the daytime, on the other hand, there is normally little business, since most people with money to spend are then at their jobs in the George Town area. Consequently Wood can close down during these hours if he is busy with other things, or his wife can come over from their home across the road should any business come up. This makes it possible for Bertram Wood also to engage in other activities. He started an extermination business even before he built the bar and restaurant, doing most jobs himself but hiring assistants occasionally for bigger tasks. Among his customers are some private individuals, but many are hotels and other larger business – establishments which have expanded considerably in recent years. Wood also takes on construction work on a small scale, mostly alone or with two or three temporarily hired men – "where I can see my profit," as he puts it.

102 Economic change in the Cayman Islands

Both extermination and construction work relate well to his catering business. The bar functions as an information exchange, and he can readily find out who is available when extra laborers are needed for his other lines of activity. And as we have seen, they tend not to make conflicting demands on his time.

Conclusions: entrepreneurship on a shoestring

What are the common themes in the stories of Melville Bodden, Evelyn Watler, and Bertram Wood? One is that of simultaneous involvement in several different lines of activity which on inspection turn out either to support each other (as in the case of the Bodden family's various relationships to tourism) or at least to be complementary in the sense of not usually making contradictory demands on the person in question (as in the case of Evelyn Watler's hairdressing work, mostly in the daytime, and café, open later in the day and evening). Certainly such combinations could be held as no more than rational, particularly as the alternative may be underemployment coupled with even greater economic marginality.

One might speculate, however, over the possibility that this kind of adaptation to the opportunity structure is facilitated by the Caymanian entrepreneurial tradition of consistently reaching out for new openings. This tradition itself has certainly developed under conditions when there were hardly any non-marginal Caymanian businessmen; but it may have played a part in creating a business atmosphere where even successful and secure businessmen are ever ready to dabble in new areas peripheral to their established concerns. It may be apropos here to note the amusement of one young woman of Caymanian background, on a visit from Jamaica where she had her home, as she noted one example of this tendency in a relative of hers – a man who has obviously achieved a measure of affluence by running a major car-rental agency as well as dealing in real estate and dairy products, who is also a director of one of the international banks in George Town, but whom she could yet discover standing in the harbor selling fish which he had caught from his new speedboat.

Another theme is the substitution of social for economic resources. The people we have encountered seldom have the opportunity to make large financial investments in their businesses. In economic terms, they operate on shoestring budgets. Instead they are able to use their social contacts, to pick up information, to build up clienteles, and to get assistance in their work when this is needed. Extra employees are hired only rarely and on a temporary basis. Friends are asked to help who do not calculate their rewards purely in financial terms, and above all the use of family members gives a staff which is both loyal and flexible. At the periphery of growth sectors of the Caymanian economy we thus find "Mom and Pop"-type enterprises, although the kinship links are more varied than this. As Burton Benedict (1968) has pointed out, the family firm, at some stages of development at least, can be a quite efficient structure; and the Caymanian enterprises we have dealt with seem to remain at this stage. We may be reminded also of Eric Wolf's (1966: 7–8) comment that the family, since it can perform multiple tasks in small units of output and in rapid succession, with a relatively low cost and overhead, is both maximally efficient and maximally adaptive to changes defining and circumscribing its existence. This, Wolf notes, may be particularly important for families with meager resources, where labor can be increased to meet changing demands without other expenses than the exploitation of self. In the cases of Caymanian enterprises such as those we have discussed, the business itself is integrated into this kind of husbanding of resources.

Finally, we may note that of the people in our three case histories, only Melville Bodden is centrally involved in the tourist industry, while the two others draw some of their business directly from it but probably benefit to a higher degree from the improved finances of Caymanian wage-earners. Without claiming that they are representative in this respect, we may consider the possibility that enterprises with modest bases of this kind will more often tend to have this largely indirect advantage of the development of a tourist industry, as they can best use their assets in relationships to a local clientele. Melville Bodden, with his fishing, swimming, and sightseeing tours, also has a particular kind of non-economic resource in the form of "knowing the territory"; he is in a business where having grown up in the islands, knowing the sea around them and its creatures, has a value in quite rational terms, and where, besides, tourists expect some local cultural flavor.

Apart from this kind of enterprise, however, it seems that ordinary Caymanians cannot easily benefit directly from the development of tourism in their islands by going into business for themselves. To the extent that participation in the tourist industry requires great financial assets and cosmopolitan expertise (and to the extent that it remains based on private enterprise) it seems rather likely to come under strong foreign influence and/or maintain or even increase existing inequalities in the local society. Even such forms of self-employment as arranging tours, driving a taxi cab, or renting some cottages are vulnerable, as larger hotels and other organizations often tend to encapsulate visitors in the variety of their own arrangements, placing them out of reach for minor entrepreneurs in the host society. While this has not yet happened on a large scale in the Cayman Islands, there have been signs such as a conflict between the taxi drivers and the larger car-rental firms, where the former have felt increasingly squeezed out of a reasonable share of the transportation market, due to the expansive marketing techniques of the latter. In a way, this may be seen as little more than a new version of a problem which faced the small businessmen in the Cayman Islands already before the current period – the danger that any line of activity which showed enough potential of development would be appropriated by a larger concern which could substitute greater financial investments for the flexible use of social resources. Thus the growth of an enterprise beyond a certain point could meet with obstacles, then as now, in the form of an increased competition from other resource arrangements.

The relationship between tourism and local culture and social structure anywhere is obviously a thing with many facets. This note is merely an attempt to

104 Economic change in the Cayman Islands

show how a few small businesses, of a kind with which we have become familiar in many other contexts, have developed in the interstices of the changing economy of one West Indian territory. There are changes in other areas of the socioeconomic opportunity structure as well, and in this as in other societies affected by tourism, inquiries could also be directed to changes in access to natural as well as social amenities, to new influences on race and other group relations, and to the kind of changes of ideals and expectations resulting from the general exposure to new styles of life. If we could have a series of examinations of such topics, perhaps an anthropology of tourism can at some time play a part in an informed appraisal of the advantages and disadvantages to local people of the travels for pleasure originating in the affluent countries of the world.

Notes

1 This research note is a by-product of a larger study of Caymanian political change. Field work in the Cayman Islands was carried out between April and August, 1970, on a grant from the Swedish Research Council for the Humanities.
2 For a brief study of agriculture at East End village, Grand Cayman, see Buchler (1963).
3 Names have been altered.

References

Benedict, Burton. 1968. Family Firms and Economic Development. *Southwestern Journal of Anthropology*, 24: 1–19.
Buchler, I. R. 1963. Shifting Cultivation in the Cayman Islands. *Anthropologica*, 12: 1–5.
Comitas, Lambros. 1964. Occupational Multiplicity in Rural Jamaica. In *Symposium on Community Studies in Anthropology*. Seattle, Washington.
Schneider, Peter, Jane Schneider, and Edward Hansen. 1972. Modernization and Development: The Role of Regional Elites and Non-Corporate Groups in the European Mediterranean. *Comparative Studies in Society and History*, 14: 328–350.
Wolf, Eric R. 1966. Kinship, Friendship, and Patron-Client Relations in Complex Societies. In Michael Banton (ed.), *The Social Anthropology of Complex Societies (ASA 4)*. London: Tavistock.

5

TOOLS OF IDENTITY AND IMAGINATION

I begin with a scene from Kafanchan, a town in central Nigeria. Magajiya Street, wide and quite muddy toward the end of the wet season, is the home of the Hausa butchers. At the end of the Muslim holiday of Id-el-Fitr, the youth of pastoralist Fulani communities in the area come there to stage the *sharo*, a series of ritual battles between young men. (The young women watch the proceedings, admiringly, critically, or amusedly, as does a crowd of townspeople.) Magajiya Street seems to be the natural setting for this event, since the Fulani have long-standing relationships with the butchers, to whom they sell their cattle.

The climactic event of these rather unorganized and long-drawn-out gatherings is a kind of duel, in which a young man stands absolutely still, bare to the waist, and takes the beatings which his opponent delivers with a long stick. (At a later stage, he gets an opportunity to reciprocate.) In the version of the *sharo* which I saw in Kafanchan, he holds a mirror in front of his face and gazes into it as the blows hit his body. A brave young Fulani is not supposed to move his face at all to betray the terrible pain he must feel.

In the published descriptions of the *sharo* which I have come across, I have not found any mention of the mirror. As an element of a "traditional" African ritual, it may seem out of place. But what difference does it make? More generally, how do human lives with mirrors compare with those without? People like us are used to mirrors just about everywhere, in homes and in public places. When there is no mirror, we may steal a glance at our reflections in a shop window. And so mirrors have become trustworthy, ubiquitous tools of identity, keeping us informed in one way of who we are.

There is perhaps no other equally conspicuous example of the relationship between identity and the material world. But this is the wider topic I want to bring up. How are people's understandings of who they are, and who other people are, affected by resources in the man-made environment?

FIGURE 5.1 The *sharo* duel

In a way, it is Fulani ethnography that prompts me to raise the issue, not only by way of my observation of the *sharo* in Kafanchan. In Paul Riesman's (1977: 161–162) study of a Fulani group in Upper Volta, he has a brief but provocative passage about how the conception of "society" of these pastoralists may differ from ours; the one we may have in our everyday lives, anyway, when we do not have our scholarly thinking-caps on. To us, at least, society not only consists of people and practices but is embodied in "houses, offices, churches, uniforms, vehicles, roads, telephones, walls, towns, villages." The daily impression which Fulani society makes on the individual, on the other hand, involves few such embodiments in man-made objects, and what there is of this is fragile rather than permanent. "Society," if there is such a notion at all among the Fulani with whom Riesman stayed, is "the people one is with." If the products of technology can have this impact on the way we understand "society," what do they do to our ideas of identity? The answer to this question I would not claim to know, but I have some working notes on it. And, in raising the issue, I find some comfort in those varied currents in the analysis of human consciousness which emphasize the connections between thought and externalities. "Thinking as an overt, public act, involving the purposeful manipulation of objective materials, is probably fundamental to human beings," Clifford Geertz (1973:76) writes, and in anthropology there is also Jack Goody (1968, 1977) on writing as a technology of the intellect.

On the whole, however, understandings of identity and the processes involving it do not usually seem to move far in this direction. In most cases, the technology of identity is simply ignored. Conceptualized as a construction in the mind, identity already slips away from the world of things. And as they consider what sources of external impulses are significant, the scholars of the human sciences will first, like Paul Riesman's Fulani, think of "the people one is with." There is even, in popular psychology, a readiness to oppose identity to the material world. The idea of the individual who "has everything" but is still, or actually because of that, "in search of an identity" is by now an irony which has become a cliché.

There is another tendency, in the pop sociology of western society, as well as in the anthropology of other societies, to think of material objects only as vehicles of declarations about identity. Here we have the loose talk about "status symbols" (Mercedes cars, furs, videograms or what not), and the passing ethnographic comment on how, at a quick glance, tribe X can be distinguished from tribe Y, aristocrats from commoners, or married women from unmarried. Certainly, material attributes can be significant in this way in categorical relationships, but perhaps things do not relate to identities only as simple sorting devices.

A view of identity

Of course, it would be foolish to try and deal with the technology of identity in isolation. My inclination is rather to look at the everyday interplay between technology and the structure of social relationships in shaping ideas of identity. As far as the concept of identity itself is concerned, my way of looking at it is quite simple and has much to do with the ordering of social contacts. Identity is a matter of information about people – about oneself, as well as about others. The information may consist of fact or fantasy. What information we have, and what we do with it, can vary a great deal. It is very obvious, although less so to specialists in the field than to other people, that we have a lot of information about ourselves; indeed, that we are experts on ourselves and that we may choose to share or not to share this information with others. It may be slightly less obvious that there are things about ourselves that we do not necessarily know but which we may be informed about by others. All this information about self or other may be given away or withheld, with or without intention. It may be abundant or scarce. To be information at all, finally, it must not be absolutely self-evident. We must have some awareness that things could be different. With regard to the information we call identity, this means that we must have some understanding that we could be different and, in particular, that there are people who are different. In other words, identity information is contrastive.

108 Tools of identity and imagination

The fact that I have two eyes, two ears and a nose is, in this context, usually of little interest, because so do most people. These contrasts could set me against you or even simply against an imagined non-me, at an individual level. Or they could emphasize how we differ from them, at a collective level. Obviously, the term "personal identity" and "cultural identity" are often used to describe these two different instances. This is a usage with which I am not entirely comfortable, since I would expect all human identities to be fashioned in cultural terms. That is to say, the information involved is culturally coded. Anyway, what I am concerned with here is mostly personal identity, information pertaining to individuals.

This is obviously a minimal and quite artless notion of identity. I take nothing for granted about which information about oneself or others should be regarded as the most important, nor about the form or amount of patterning of the information. I am sure identities may have their critical moments – probably, for a Fulani youth, the sharo battle may be one of them – but we need not for that reason ignore all that routine identity-handling in which people keep up, modify, or check their identities without giving much thought to what is going on. And whether all people, everywhere and at all times, have been concerned in the same way and to the same degree with the coherence of identity information is, I suppose, at the very least an open question.

This view, I hope, will serve my purposes in thinking about how ideas concerning identity are generated in different kinds of social order and in different material worlds. There is clearly a considerable amount of contemporary and classical thinking about societies which suggests that there are structurally based differences among them in the ways in which information about self and other is sought, offered or generally handled as a day-to-day concern. Let us look at some of the tendencies in this thinking.[1] According to what we may describe as an "alienation perspective," a society like ours tends to deprive people of opportunities to develop satisfactory information about themselves, by placing them in the constraining circumstances of industrialism and bureaucracy. They are forced to become modular men. A possibly necessary difference between I and non-I gets blurred. But when this sort of information does not become available as a matter of course, people become preoccupied with finding it, and set up particular situations and relationships for the purpose. In this manner, it is suggested, public and private life become differentiated, and role and self part company.

From another point of view, the constraining characteristics of particular roles may seem less important than the ways in which roles and relationships fit together. Where people encounter others who are different from them, they are likely to begin to think about who or what they are themselves. There is an awareness of alternatives. The more varied people are, the more probable it is that individuals will come to think of themselves as unique. Social arrangements are not all that enters into this, but obviously, if a society has a great many different types of situations and activities, and if people's involvements and combinations of involvements in these are varied, then it is also more likely that they will vary as individuals.

With its fragmentation of contacts, the same kind of social order will also tend to offer its participants only a rather limited direct view of many others. Often enough, they probably could not care less about this, as they do not need or want full information about everybody they run into. Yet there are times when there is some recognition of an information gap. And people may maneuver in order to fill it in various ways.

We may refer to a related characteristic of many of the same social structures as their "fluidity." People may move in and out of roles and relationships. This may add to the set of contrastive understandings of identity – in particular, the sense of the present self as different from past or future selves. Identities, to put it differently, may be sharpened in careers. (This idea has become connected in my mind with an old Frank Sinatra song: "I've been a puppet, a poet, a pauper, a pawn, and a king. I've been up and down and all around ...") Furthermore, the fluidity consists, in great measure, of achieved, as opposed to ascribed, relationships. One must create one's own contacts, and to put it brutally, identity becomes currency in the exchanges involved. In one way or other, the question may arise whether a self is attractive enough for success in social life.[2]

Books, portraits and movies: the artifacts of identity

It is fairly obvious that most interpretations of the development of a concern with personal identity point more or less in the same direction, toward a conception of a Great Divide of the kind to which anthropologists are forever coming back, although probably each time a little more wary of the difficulties it entails. It is, these lines of interpretation suggest, people like "Us," in modern society, who have an awareness of personal identity – sometimes perhaps as a problem, in another way more continuously as an obvious fact. People like "Them," in small-scale, more simply organized, traditional societies, for better or for worse, do not go through the experiences which shape that awareness.

To repeat, it may be wise to remain somewhat sceptical of this or any other variety of the Great Divide. Although some actual differences may be there, it is hard to imagine that any existing designs for living can manage to exclude all experiences of contrast, all frustrations or whatever else may cause some sense of individuality. On the whole, our real knowledge of things like this appears limited, since sophisticated and intensive studies of such subtle matters as indigenous notions of person, self or identity in other societies have actually only arisen as an important ethnographic genre rather recently.

I will, however, accept that there may be at least a difference of degree in the extent to which various conditions of social life foster concerns with personal identity, and also that the sorts of circumstances already sketched contribute to it in one way or other in our society. It is with the use of material tools of identity in this context that I shall mostly be occupied here. But let us proceed in a slightly roundabout way.

110 Tools of identity and imagination

The sense of individuality, Jacob Burckhardt has told us in *The Civilization of the Renaissance*, developed in early modern Europe, more especially in Italy. Other historians, like Colin Morris (1973), suggest somewhat earlier beginnings in eleventh- and twelfth-century medieval society and may not have precisely the same idea about the location. Such minor differences need hardly detain us here. On the whole, they often seem to think similarly in terms of their own versions of a Great Divide, and the reasons they offer for the emergence of individuality are rather reminiscent of the kinds of conditions we have just noted here. Morris notes the growth of a new urbanism in western Europe in the Middle Ages. There was a flow of new ideas, and shifts in social structure and economy to which people had to respond partly in individual ways. Burckhardt attaches particular significance to the unstable political order of the Italian city-states. True Renaissance men had to operate delicately in their personal alliances, develop a sophisticated eye for the qualities of persons who could be partners or adversaries, and might still have careers containing dramatic rises and sudden falls. Migration and exile became common experiences. Agnes Heller, in her more recent interpretation of *Renaissance Man* (1981), points out the new relationship between people and their work. In feudal society, a man was what he had been born to be. In the emerging division of labor, one could shift between roles, barber-writer-condottiere, and still remain the same self. But this new individuality, the same authors tell us, was not merely some kind of intangible sensibility. It was connected with specific, external forms. There were, in literature, new standards for writing about people's lives. According to Burckhart [1860] 1960: 241):

> Much of what, till the close of the Middle Ages, passed for biography, is actually nothing but contemporary narrative, written without any sense of what is individual in the subject of the memoir. Among the Italians, on the contrary, the search for the characteristic features of remarkable men was a prevailing tendency; and it is this that separates them from the other Western peoples, among whom the same thing happens only accidentally, and in exceptional cases. This keen eye for individuality belongs only to those who have emerged from the race and become individuals.

Even more remarkably, there was autobiography, a genre which in its fully developed form had hardly existed before, except for the single instance of Saint Augustine's *Confessions*. The peculiarity of autobiography, Heller notes, lies in its reflecting the unique interaction between the world and the individual's development. In this period, internal and external experience could be mediated through craft or calling in a way that they had never been before. There was also satire, depending, to quote Burckhardt again, on the appearance of its natural victim, a developed individual with personal pretensions. In art, there was portraiture, showing more of personal characteristics, not just social attributes. And alongside these, there occurred the characteristic forms of speech, relationship, and feeling – confessions, friendship, and romantic love.

Tools of identity and imagination **111**

In principle, it would seem, any "special relationship" between an individual or group and any other thing can be relevant to identity, insofar as it contrasts with other individuals or groups. From this point of view, the possibilities of considering the material world in relation to identity may be practically limitless; especially so, one might think, in societies of technological abundance. But what Burckhardt and the other historians emphasize is that some artifacts of human life may, like the mirror, express better than others the peculiar characteristics of individuals, and that an involvement with such artifacts – kinds of books, kinds of pictures – thus betrays a concern with identity.

Return with me now to Kafanchan, the Nigerian town. It has struck me that, in a perhaps rather twisted way, there are similarities between the present situation there and the one in which, according to the historians, the sense of individuality developed in Europe. During my stays in Kafanchan, I have come to know especially a number of young people, usually more fully engaged in urban living than the young Fulani in the sharo. Many of them are of the first generation to go to school; the Christian missions reached many of the villages in this part of Nigeria rather late. They are also often of the first generation to try to find permanent employment in some other occupation than farming. They may have served apprenticeships with a photographer, tailor, or carpenter – in Kafanchan or some other town. Now they want a shop of their own. Or they try, with whatever formal, educational qualifications they may have, to find a place behind a desk in an office. Or they still hope to further their education, by getting into secondary school, a teacher-training college or even the university. But some are also occupied in trying to make ends meet by doing odd jobs and have one foot in urban life and the other still in the country. The Fulani youth who comes in for the sharo this year may shine your shoes in a Kafanchan bar the next.

The aspirations, uncertainties, satisfactions and disappointments of such lives tend to be of a more or less individualizing kind, and so one may expect some sort of concern with personal identity. Do we then find, in contemporary Nigerian urban life, any external forms to carry the kind of meanings involved, at least roughly comparable to those of Renaissance culture? In a modest but nonetheless conspicuous way, they do seem to be there.

The development of a popular literature in Nigeria is commonly connected with the chapbooks from Onitsha, one of the major market centers of West Africa (see, for example, Obiechina 1973). Here, since the 1940s at least, a multitude of small and rather antiquated printing-presses have issued large numbers of pamphlets which, through the small-scale networks of Nigerian commerce, have spread over the country. One often finds a selection of them with the stationery sellers outside post offices. Among these pamphlets are political plays, etiquette manuals, moral and religious tracts, and educational self-help materials. But there is also simple fiction, preoccupied with the themes of love and success in a modern Nigerian setting. The plots may be simple and yet get mixed up, and the writing, like the printing, is far from faultless. Certainly there

112 Tools of identity and imagination

is little of the balancing of internal and external experience said to characterize the outstanding autobiographies of the Renaissance. The popular literature of Nigeria today is, more often than not, action-packed. Even so, it does hold up to its readers an imagery in which the paths through life of the central characters may be lined with conservative kinsmen, corrupt politicians or false friends who turn out to be bandits, but in which, in the end, the situations of the characters are seen to be of their own making. The idea is conveyed of the individual who must rely on his or her own inner resources. And this seems still to be the case, as popular fiction in more recent years has graduated from the Onitsha printing-presses to a growing Nigerian publishing industry, offering the short novels of a body of young authors increasingly sophisticated in the arts of both living and writing.[3]

But not everybody reads novels, in Kafanchan or anywhere else. The young adults of Nigerian towns depend for the facts and fantasies of a modern way of life to a yet greater extent on the popular press, national or foreign, which offers whatever passes for news about celebrities in music, films, or sports, with photo-novels, advice columns, and comic strips. And at the outdoor cinema, there are the Indian, Hongkong, or Hollywood films, which offer long hours of action and adventure, as well as encounters between the sexes varying from prim romanticism to soft pornography.

In what ways, then, do these new cultural forms noticeably affect the ways in which young people in Kafanchan go about handling matters of identity? I say noticeably, because I have so far not had an occasion to dig much below the surface. But a few things are noticeable. Naming, it has often been pointed out, is intimately connected with identity.[4] Real names may be serious things. Nick-names, however, can be playful and imaginative. In Kafanchan, they are frequently a way of assimilating something of the cosmopolitanism of mass culture. The hawkers, shoeshiners, or perpetual job applicants can call themselves Django or Albeela after foreign movie heroes; other nicknames come from English or American magazines, or from records. Often they are selfchosen: Mighty Sparrow, Prince Love, Alabama City, Baby Uhuru. (A clever way of introducing one's new nickname to the world, I have been told, is to offer a handful of peanuts to small children in exchange for a promise that they will henceforth call the person in question by the new name. Since children tend to call out names to greet people "a mile away," a great many people will soon know the new nickname.)

But some names are given by others. Chinese Goalkeeper in Kafanchan is a popular football player, whose agile movements of body and limbs once reminded a spectator of the ballet which is claimed to be fighting in Hongkong movies. Ringo Star, the Kafanchan tailor, does not actually know what is the origin of his name (and consequently misspells it on his signboard). It was given to him by the master to whom he was once apprenticed. It seems commercially useful, however, in attracting young men who come to have their bell-bottom trousers sewn by him.

Many young people in Kafanchan also have photo albums. If portraiture was a sign of new understandings of identity some centuries ago in Europe, we may wonder what photography does to the sense of identity in our own times. There are not many private cameras in Kafanchan, but there are a fair number of commercial photographers, who are in demand for special events, as well as for portraits in which the facial expressions, postures, and props are clearly borrowed from record albums, movies, and magazines. To pose for a picture together in a photographer's studio is a way in which people can bear witness to the tie between them. In the personal albums, pictures of friends of both sexes, family members, and other acquaintances may be combined with cutouts from newspapers of sports or movie stars, luxury cars, and intimate scenes. Again, personal identity is connected in play with glamor and abundance. All photographs, however, are not kept. They are also given away or exchanged within the personal network. Possibly, one will be sent to a pen pal. Letter-writing has become quite popular as a pleasure in itself and is clearly another form of expression in which the formulation of an identity is a particular concern. Columns in which prospective pen pals can advertise themselves and their interests, often with a photograph, occur regularly in the Nigerian popular press.

Assertions and experiments

There may be some similarities between the life situations of Renaissance men and those of the people in present-day Kafanchan and, in both cases, people seem to have found material forms appropriate to their personal-identity work. But is their relationship to these forms the same? I must now try to specify the relationships between people and those artifacts which we find relevant to identity; what people do with the things, what the things do to people. What we have noted about Kafanchan may be useful here, and also what I have said about the history of early modern Europe. But let us also keep in mind what we see in everyday life in our own society.

In our received picture of the Renaissance, we see the Renaissance men above all as the producers of, among other things, the art and literature of identity. The young men and women of Kafanchan, in contrast, seem mostly to be the consumers of the comparable forms. There are hardly any Leonardo da Vincis or Cellinis walking the streets of Kafanchan (although it may be added that some of the intellectuals in larger Nigerian centers like Lagos or Ibadan are notably versatile).

As producers, historians such as Jacob Burckhardt tell us, the great men of the Renaissance were concerned with fame. In exchange for the recognition which they must ultimately seek from others, they offered access to their finished work. On the basis of the latter, they wanted to be defined in terms of excellence, and they wanted such information to spread widely. In a way, obviously, they were different from the tribespeople, who stake a claim to a particular identity through their facial scars, or from married people, who do so with their

114 Tools of identity and imagination

wedding rings. While these claim membership of a category, the Renaissance men claimed uniqueness. But in another way, one might see a similar dramaturgy of self involved in each case. Assertive statements are made, supported by particular attributes. To put it simply, these people are all claiming to know who they are and are concerned to tell others. This is one kind of identity work.

Yet it is not really what matters most to us here. In so far as the Renaissance masters were only producing advertisements for themselves, any skills cultivated to the same degree of acknowledged superiority might have been equally useful. But some of the particular forms they developed – portraiture, biography, autobiography, satire – do not just lend themselves to a presentation of self in terms of craftsmanship. They can be used also in the construction of self; finding, developing and assembling information about oneself for oneself, rather than offering it to others.

Through these forms, the masters could match and even enhance a sensibility which many shared. For the artists themselves, as well as for their contemporaries, the less well-known consumers of the Renaissance, they were part of the equipment needed to deal with the individuating experiences of the age. They could be good to think with at several levels. Such artifacts were a mnemonic of the idea of individuality itself; people are indeed different. They could identify dimensions along which the characteristics of self or others could be analyzed. More specifically, they could even be an identikit, an inventory of elements that one might use in putting together an identity of one's own.

Such externalities seem to be tools of both identity and imagination. They serve an expansive sense of what an individual may be or can become. Clearly, one can expect experimental identity work of this nature to occur more readily with regard to individual identities than collective identities (which would be one reason why anthropologists have given it less attention). Experimentations with style can then be less constrained by considerations of membership. An identity can be symbolically offensive to others and yet not an obvious case of intrusion or betrayal, of the kind which could lead to more immediate reprisals.

The young in Kafanchan who pick their nicknames from international mass culture are using these tools in one way. There are other, more subtle ways of using them to sharpen one's states of consciousness or feeling. Jerome Bruner (1968: 31–57) has dwelt on this in a couple of essays discussing the relationship between identity myths and the novel. Myth, he suggests (and the general idea is, of course, fairly familiar to us), responds to the human preference for coping with events which are outside rather than inside. The human plight is embodied and represented in its plots and characters. But there are no longer any great unifying myths, fully shared, taking the form of drama and serving simultaneously as proto-science, proto-religion and proto-literature. With their decline, men have had to turn more inward to deal with personal experience and consciousness. And the rise of the novel as an art form, and especially the subjectification of the novel after the nineteenth century, in Bruner's view, is a sign of a search for some form of external guidance in the attempt to deal the question of identity, as it is now posed.

We may look at autobiography, one of the genres of the Renaissance, in a similar way. Real autobiography, we have been told, involves an interplay between internal and external experience. One may see an autobiography as a presentation of self, but, to complicate things a little, it is in these terms a presentation of the construction of self, an account of a process rather than a mere exhibition of a product. And it may speak to the reader's matching awareness of his own experiences and responses.

How great is the influence of such imaginative instruments on our identities? There are those who think that in these times, in a society like ours, they can be very important. I have in mind particularly the psychohistorian Robert Jay Lifton (1970) and his conception of "self-process," entailing an idea of flow and blurred boundaries. Our image of personal identity, Lifton suggests, is derived from the vision of a culture in which men's relationship to institutions and symbols is still relatively intact, and it is therefore characterized by inner stability and sameness. But the image is increasingly misleading. Lifton sees a "protean man" emerging, named after the shape-shifting figure of Greek mythology. This kind of individual is continually trying on and discarding identities. His greatest difficulty is in trying to commit himself to any one of them. The prevalent spirit is one of absurdity and mockery. Two general developments, Lifton says, are especially fundamental to the creation of protean man. One is a historical dislocation. The sense of connection is broken with the vital symbols of family, religion, idea systems and a predictable lifecycle. The other major development is "the flooding of imagery," the extraordinary quantity of new cultural influences carried by the mass media:

> The images they convey cross over all boundaries, local and national, and permit each individual everywhere to be touched by everything, but at the same time often cause him to be overwhelmed by superficial messages and undigested cultural elements, by headlines and by endless partial alternatives in every sphere of life. In other words, as an individual one can maintain no clear boundaries. And the alternatives contained in the endless flow of images are universally shared, if not as causes of action, at least in the form of significant inner possibilities.
>
> *(Lifton 1970: 43–44)*

Checking and recording

There are, however, also other tools of identity, which we use with quite different consequences. You or I may have fantasies about being all kinds of people we have read about or seen in the movies, and we may even begin to believe that there is something to it, but we are brought to our senses when we look in

116 Tools of identity and imagination

the mirror. Like the young man in the sharo, we can use it to check our real character. And there are in fact a whole series of tools which we use at different to get down-to-earth, factual information about ourselves: the mirror to determine how we look, the measuring rod to show how tall we are, the scales to tell us what we weigh, the tape recorder which may surprise us with the sound of our voice, even the thermometer to show if we have a fever.

Perhaps we are unwilling to regard these ways of measuring our physical states as particularly relevant to our most central sense of identity. Whatever that may be, I do not think that we should underestimate the importance of ongoing, sometimes even intense involvement with these tools. In front of the mirror, we say "I look OK," "Snow White looks better than I do," or "I'm old." Checking our height, when we are young, "Wow! Am I growing!" On the scales, "I've lost five pounds." There can be close monitoring here, in which even minor changes, neither noticed nor commented on by people, become reasons for pride, happiness, embarrassment, or worry, as well as for further action.

I would suggest, at least half-seriously, that the existence of technical devices such as these may help to make the physical features involved more significant to the sense of identity than they might otherwise have been. Individuality must have some form, and as social scientists we are certainly familiar with the assumption that what can be measured must be important. But we may also think of other possible implications of these checks on aspects of the self. The resulting information, we have noted, can be used to compare oneself with others. More often, however, the comparison may be between the present and an earlier version. The information is not necessarily instantly received and instantly forgotten. In at least a minimal way, it can become instead a record. Variations which, in an imprecise form, may pass without notice or be assimilated in memory to a dominant understanding of sameness and stability are by those means made to show up and demand attention, however fleeting and minute.

The time factor thus requires consideration, but the mirror is obviously an exception here. The information it offers may be as exact as any, but it is ephemeral, not in itself easily inserted into a lasting record. Instead, however, we have pictures: paintings, drawings, photographs. These are instruments of both identity experimentation and recording. We can use the pictures of others to stimulate imagination and we can try new poses, as the young people in Kafanchan do in their photo albums, but as the picture is made, the information is fixed for all time to come as to what we have been or have pretended to be.

There is much to be said about the relationship between identity and photography. Susan Sontag has touched on some of its facets, and on photography as a cultural phenomenon generally, in her book *On Photography* (1979). She notes that photography, like portraiture in painting, is not absolutely truthful: "The news that the camera could lie made getting photographed much more popular" (1979: 86). But, in another way, photography is very different from painting.

The eighteenth- or nineteenth-century bourgeois would be painted only once. The purpose of this portrait was to confirm an ideal image of the sitter. Photographs today come in large numbers, the more varied, the better. Which is not to say that there are no preferred contexts. In our society, Sontag points out, photography goes with tourism and with the family. Not to take pictures of one's small children would be a sign of parental indifference, and "a family's photograph album is generally about the extended family – and, often, is all that remains of it" (Sontag 1979: 9). But this may vary between societies, individuals, and albums. As I have said, photography in Kafanchan seems very often to be about friendship.

As I sketched my conception of identity as a matter of information, I noted that I made no assumption about its patterning. To this issue I now return. Surely we have a tendency to think of identity as involving some measure of continuity and coherence. In different situations, as well as over time, people are expected to be in some way the same. To what extent they really are depends primarily, I think, on whether the social order allows them to be. Some societies require more than others in terms of situational shifting. I do not take it for granted that one can easily sort out a substantive self from fluctuating constraints and opportunities.

Secondarily, however, the possibilities of a sense of overall consistency would also seem to be affected by the external recording devices which I have just dwelt on. (Along with others that I have not discussed: old diaries, collected letters, home movies, etc.) In principle, these allow the selves of all times and all situations to be present simultaneously. The evidence remains there of what we have been or have wanted to be. If there is a strain toward a single, uniform identity, this evidence may be an obstacle. Yet it is also possible that, in the face of the diversity of opportunities and experiences, some people at least will take pride in their ability to show many faces, and the same evidence may then appear as a resource. With its own tough-minded approach to reality, the technology of measurement and recording may make its own contribution to the sense of a protean identity.

Different equations

So, in summary, what difference do mirrors, films, photographs, books, tape recorders, bathroom scales, letters, and thermometers make? When novels replace myths, does it matter that myths, as anthropologists think of them, are told by real people with voices and gestures, while novels are printed and bound sheets of paper?

Equipment like this, it seems, may make it easier for us to become preoccupied with our selves, like Narcissus, when he encountered one of nature's own mirrors. The artifacts may indeed in same ways become alternatives to other people. Man's dependence on the immediate circle of face-to-face contacts for personal models is lessened, as he can find these in print or on the screen

118 Tools of identity and imagination

instead. And the fact that the objects require no immediate response, no clear commitment, can be an advantage in scanning and experimentation.

But again, let us not only see a dyad between individual and thing. People may use these devices in the routines or crises of their identity work, but this does not turn them into hermits, and the uses need by no means be antisocial. What is more fruitful for a comparative anthropology of society, culture, and identity is to consider the varying equations between self and others and the material tools of identity and imagination. The young man in the *sharo* does not only measure his bravery by the mirror; there are also praise-singers and an audience around him as he faces his opponent in Magajiya Street. Other young people in Kafanchan, indulging in some degree of proteanism inspired by the foreign magazines, will also have to seek its validation among their peers, for in the end only real people can be the significant others who inform us whether a chosen identity is credible and acceptable. And, unlike their parents, perhaps, who may have known most people in their villages since childhood and who have seen them all in most situations, these young people, like modern urbanites everywhere, may find that they know many of their contemporaries only in fragments. They may see them only in particular contexts of life, and they may not have seen them at all in their past. In such cases, the road to an understanding of the identity of the other, and thus to a closer relationship, may pass through the childhood scenes and the revelations of family, networks and travel contained in a photo album.

Notes

1 What is said here I have covered a little more fully elsewhere (Hannerz, 1980: 221 ff.)
2 For an example of this view, see Rainwater (1966).
3 I do not have in mind the more academic Nigerian authors, oriented to a more cosmopolitan circle of readers; these authors often deal with quite other themes.
4 See for instance Strauss (1959: 15 ff.) and Morgan et al. (1979).

References

Bruner, Jerome S. 1968. *On Knowing*. New York, NY: Atheneum.
Burckhart, Jacob. [1860] 1960. *The Civilization of the Renaissance in Italy*. New York, NY: New American Library.
Geertz, Clifford. 1973. *The Interpretation of Cultures*. New York, NY: Basic Books.
Goody, Jack (ed.). 1968. *Literacy in Traditional Societies*. Cambridge: Cambridge University Press.
———. 1977. *The Domestication of the Savage Mind*. Cambridge: Cambridge University Press.
Hannerz, Ulf. 1980. *Exploring the City*. New York, NY: Columbia University Press.
Heller, Agnes. 1981. *Renaissance Man*. New York, NY: Schocken.
Lifton, Robert Jay. 1970. *Boundaries*. New York, NY: Random House.
Morgan, Jane, Christopher O'Neill, and Rom Harre. 1979. *Nicknames*. London: Routledge & Kegan Paul.

Morris, Colin. 1973. *The Discovery of the Individual 1050–1200*. New York, NY: Harper & Row.

Obiechina, Emmanuel. 1973. *An African Popular Literature*. Cambridge: Cambridge University Press.

Rainwater, Lee. 1966. Work and Identity in the Lower Class. In Sam Bass Warner, Jr. (ed.), *Planning for a Nation of Cities*. Cambridge, MA: MIT Press.

Riesman, Paul. 1977. *Freedom in Fulani Social Life*. Chicago, IL: University of Chicago Press.

Sontag, Susan. 1979. *On Photography*. Harmondsworth: Penguin.

Strauss, Anselm L. 1959. *Mirrors and Masks*. Glencoe, IL: Free Press.

6

THE WORLD IN CREOLIZATION

A people is judged by history according to its contribution to the culture of other peoples flourishing at the same time and according to its contribution to the cultures which arise afterwards.

(T. S. Eliot (1948) 1962: 56)

I'd given myself a nickname just for fun: 'Simon Templar'. But before that I'd called myself 'El Paso Kid', a real colonial nickname. Then one day I changed it to 'Simon Templar'. You see, at this time I had read this novel – *The Saint* – whose main character was named Simon Templar. This guy was very, very clever. In fact, he impressed me as being so clever that one day I went into the classroom, straight to the blackboard and wrote, 'Don't call me El Paso Kid any more. I'm now Simon Templar,' Ohhhhh, can you imagine how stupid I was then, man?

(Fela Anikulapo-Kuti, in Moore (1982): 48)

From the time when I first became entangled with the Third World, in the late 1950s and early 1960s, I have been fascinated by those contemporary ways of life and thought which keep growing out of the interplay between imported and indigenous cultures.[1] They are the cultures on display in market places, shanty towns, beer halls, night clubs, missionary book stores, railway waiting rooms, boarding schools, newspapers and television stations. Nigeria, the country I have been most closely in touch with in an on-and-off way for some time, because of its large size, perhaps, offers particular scope for such cultural development, with several very large cities and hundreds if not thousands of small and middle-size towns. It has a lively if rather erratic press, a popular music scene dominated at different times by such genres as highlife, juju and Afro-beat, about as many universities as breweries (approximately one to every state in the federal republic), dozens of authors published at home and abroad, schoolhouses in just about every village, and an enormous fleet of interurban taxicabs which with great speed can convey you practically from anywhere to anywhere, at some risk to your life.

During my stays in Kafanchan, a multi-ethnic, polyglot town close to the geographical center of Nigeria, I have often found myself somewhat irritated and embarrassed as various townspeople have seen me as a possible resource in implausible schemes for going abroad or getting into some lucrative import-export business (often import rather than export, really). To begin with, I only saw this as a distraction from my purpose of finding out what town life was actually like. With time, I came to realize that these schemes were indeed one part of what it was all about. Such hunches about the good life belonged with the popular tunes about the life styles of the rich and famous, with the hole-in-the-wall commercial school where adolescents may pick up typing, book-keeping and other skills designed to take them from the village to the city, and with the star system of urban folklore, the tales told in beer bars in which politicians, high military officers and business tycoons become the new tricksters and hero figures.

Contemporary Nigerian culture may seem almost overwhelmingly rich and varied in its manifestations. Even so, it is of a kind that practically every anthropologist who has been working in the Third World is well acquainted with. Most of us, on the other hand, seem to choose not to write about it; not about the kinds of phenomena I have just enumerated. Or at least not in cultural terms.

A considerable number of anthropologists, of course, have indeed become preoccupied with the fact that many people in Africa, Asia, Oceania and South America are nowadays not hunters and gatherers or swidden cultivators but work on plantations or in mines or microelectronic assembly plants, or eke out a living in some urban "informal sector." In the last two decades or so, anthropologists with such interests have focused on issues of development and underdevelopment, metropolis-satellite relations, dependence and the contemporary world system. But, on the whole, they have been more concerned with bodies than with souls. There has been more of an economic and political anthropology here than an anthropology of structures of meaning.[2] Meanwhile, many of the anthropologists concerned with ideas-and-symbols, with culture in the stricter sense of the term, have tended to retreat deeper into the hinterland, to the villages and the forest dwellers – as far from 59th Street as you can get. Their anthropology is sharply defined as a study of the Other, an Other as different as possible from a modern, urban, post-industrial, capitalist self.

Consequently the kinds of things I exemplified from Nigeria have been mostly neglected. There is surprisingly little of a post-colonial ethnography of how Third World people see themselves and their society, its past, present and future, and its place in the world; a cultural analysis of their fantasies and of what they know for a fact. A major historical change has been taking place here, beginning long ago, for sure, but proceeding with particular intensity in the twentieth century; Third World cultures have been radically changed, and more

122 The world in creolization

than ever they must be seen as involved in an intercontinental traffic in meaning. "Galton's problem" keeps getting more difficult to solve.

T. S. Eliot, Fanon, Naipaul and Said have addressed themselves to the problems of this new cultural order, in their different ways. Yet as anthropologists we seem to have made no great progress even in developing a vocabulary for talking about such things in an acceptably subtle, well informed way. So, when called upon to say something about them, we may speak piously of living in an interconnected world or even a global village, or we may lapse (with or without embarrassment) into the simple rhetoric of denouncing cultural imperialism, or we come up with one more improvisation on the "between two cultures" theme; all of which, we probably realize, are rather limited intellectual resources for actually making much sense of these things. A macro-anthropology of culture is apparently required, to provide us with an improved overall understanding of how ideas and their public manifestations are organized, in those social structures of considerable scale and complexity which now encompass Third World lives just as certainly as they encompass our own. And it is required also because no entirely coherent and credible macro-oriented perspective in cultural studies seems to have developed anywhere else in the human sciences, either.

To begin with, two contrasting pictures of Nigerian society and culture may give an idea of what shape such a macro-anthropology could take – Nigeria will serve generally to provide my ethnographic corpus. I will just sketch one of these pictures very briefly, and develop the other more fully. When "serious journalism" in North American and Western Europe is called upon to provide a background to the tumultuous events of Nigerian politics, it draws the picture of an entity made up of some 250 tribes, with about as many languages. Nigeria comes across as an artefact of British colonialism, with inevitable conflicts among its heterogeneous population. A similar view seems to be reflected in the conventional format for writing Nigerian anthropology, the monograph about some particular ethnic group – Yoruba or Hausa, Nupe or Tiv. Where there is no cultural homogeneity, no shared indigenous language, it may appear that there is no such thing as a Nigerian culture to study.

Yet Nigeria is a reality, of a certain kind. Countries like it are the results of the expansion of the present world system into non-Western, non-northern areas, and they have developed cumulatively through interactions within the world system, in its political and economic as well as its cultural dimensions. Their emerging social structures have provided the matrices within which an international flow of culture has continuously entered into varying combinations and syntheses with local culture. In this manner pre-colonial cultures have turned into colonial cultures, and colonial cultures into post-colonial cultures. The entire process must be viewed in historical terms, where the present is also part of history.

The second view of Nigerian culture, and others more or less like it, then, places it in a world system framework, and its emphases are rather different from that of the ethnic mosaic. First of all, it is true that as they moved into Africa a hundred years ago or more, the colonial powers may have drawn boundaries which were at the time entirely arbitrary from the point of view of local life. And countries like Nigeria may have inherited some of the arbitrariness at independence. It is also a fact, however, that, these days, the creation of a State tends, to some degree at least, to be a self-fulfilling prophecy of the development of a nation. Even if it has been an uphill struggle in many cases, including that of Nigeria, and in the end an unsuccessful one in some of them, the former colonies have continuously accumulated more common history, and each one of them now has an overarching apparatus of administration, education and media power. Gradually, if still quite incompletely, they have become more nation-like, and at least some of the varied currents of meaning flowing through their social structures, and hardly insignificant ones, can now well be described as national, rather than local, regional or ethnic in their circumscription. One could only ignore this by bracketing a century or more of history.

At the same time, from the very beginning and continuously since, these national cultures have been parts of a wider whole. The world system as an international order, according to the view which came to the forefront in the social sciences in the 1960s and 1970s, is integrated through largely asymmetrical links between centers and peripheries, with Third World countries like Nigeria at the peripheries. And the system of centers and peripheries also continues into the national society, to order it internally. In broad terms, the national culture becomes similarly organized. It may in fact seem to begin already outside the national boundaries, with the migratory flux between metropolitan and Third World countries. Asians, Africans, Latin Americans and West Indians in Europe and North America are usually considered in social science research only as immigrants to the metropoles. Simultaneously, however, they form extensions of their home societies, of which they often remain active members. In this way London, Paris, Brussels and Miami are among the major Third World cities, and a varied cultural flow passes from them through the networks of migrant workers, students, exiles, international petty entrepreneurs and tourists. In the late colonial period the "been-to," who had been to England, became a conspicuous social type in Nigeria, portrayed, for example, in Cyprian Ekwensi's novel *Jagua Nana* (1961). By now the passenger load capacity of air traffic between, say, Western Europe and Lagos in a week would probably be large enough to hold several entire highland New Guinea ethnic groups. And a rather large part of media production specifically for the Third World, such as books and news magazines, to no small extent created by Third Worlders, is also based in London and Paris.

Looking at things within the territorial boundaries in simple spatial terms, there is a cultural spectrum where the capital, and perhaps some small number of other large cities, are at one end; in Nigeria places like Lagos or Ibadan, Kano or Kaduna. The concentration of certain entities within the institutional and occupational structures in these centers turn them into bridgeheads for the penetration of metropolitan cultural influences into Third World national cultures. I have in mind here, for example, the occupational subcultures as well as

124 The world in creolization

the general life styles of certain groups of peoples who are at home in metropolitan culture as any European or American, who may have spent a considerable part of their lives abroad, and who may continue to constitute the national jet set. (And who, furthermore, may potentially be a part of the brain drain from the Third World to metropolitan countries.) Academics belong here, as do people in the professions and the media, and management staff in large, often transnational, enterprises (see, e.g., Sauvant 1976; Golding 1977). On the national scene they may serve as cultural models of metropolitanism, manifested in their styles of housing, food and drink, clothing, cars and other consumption patterns, as well as − at least in some contexts − in their modes of speech.

At the other end of the cultural spectrum we may find a remote rural village. If international cultural influences reach at least some of the people in the large city quite massively and directly, they perhaps make their way to that village in fragments, and indirectly. But between the city and the village a relatively open network of relationships is stretched out, including, for instance, such provincial towns as Kafanchan. Meanings are made available in one way or another not only within small, self-encapsulating segments of society, and not only intentionally. So people can develop a certain awareness of, and familiarity with, cultural forms which are not primarily theirs, at least not at the given moment; even if these forms are out of reach, not quite relevant to one's present situation, or not actually well understood. One stands to lose many insights into the dynamic of this totality by looking at only one of its parts. As the people of different communities and regions become more entangled with one another, what were previously more self-contained cultures (not least in the eyes of ethnographers) turn increasingly into subcultures within the national culture. And at the same time, the national culture is much more than a mosaic of such subcultures; for the flow of meaning and the construction of perspectives within it organize themselves in such a way as to create much cross-cutting and overlap between clusters of meaning of varied derivation and salience.

The two pictures of what sort of entity Nigeria is should of course not just be placed side by side; they should be merged. An analysis of Nigeria which leaves out ethnicity and ethnic cultures cannot make much sense. The emphasis on a developing, internally diverse national culture, with some cohesion of its own and at the same time a part of world culture, on the other hand contributes a great deal to an understanding of what Nigeria is now, and of the way Nigerians in Kafanchan and elsewhere look at life. But here, and for the purpose of synthesizing the two views, a reconsideration of our assumptions about culture seems necessary. Some of what I have to say about this relates to anthropological thinking about culture generally, while some of it has more to do with what kinds of understandings we can evolve about the working of the world system.

What most of our textbooks say about culture in their opening pages does not help us much in the study of complex societies and their cultures. This should not lead us to ignore the realities but to re-examine our conceptual conventions. "A culture" need not be homogeneous, or even particularly coherent.

The world in creolization   **125**

Instead of assuming far-reaching cultural sharing, a "replication of uniformity," we should take a distributive view of cultures as systems of meaning.[3] The social organization of culture always depends both on the communicative flow and on the differentiation of experiences and interests in society. In the complex society, the latter differentiation is by definition considerable. It also tends to have a more uneven communicative flow – that is, different messages reach different people. The combined effect of both the uneven flow of communications and the diversity of experiences and interests is a differentiation of perspectives among the members of the society. Here and there these can be collectivized into subcultures, so that cultural sharing recurs at a lower level of organization. But in a differentiated society people are also to some extent in contact with (or at least aware of) others whose perspectives they do not share, and know they do not share. In other words, there are perspectives towards perspectives; and one may indeed see the social organization of a complex culture as a network of perspectives. I would also argue that we need to see cultures generally, but perhaps especially complex cultures, in more processual terms. There is a "management of meaning" by which culture is generated and maintained, transmitted and received, applied, exhibited, remembered, scrutinized and experimented with. Often this is something much more than just a routine maintenance of culture. Where there is strain between received meanings on the one hand and personal experiences and interests on the other, and where diverse perspectives confront one another, cultures can perhaps never be completely worked out as stable, coherent systems; they are forever cultural "work in progress."[4]

So much for fairly general considerations of cultural analysis. A little more specifically, with what intellectual tools may we best be able to grasp the nature of cultural organization and process under circumstances like those of present-day Nigeria? Over the years anthropologists and their neighbors in related disciplines have tried different approaches to complexity and change in the Third World. At one time – let us say, between the 1930s and 1950s – a great many anthropologists, especially in the USA, were doing acculturation studies. One problem with these was that they usually involved a rather weak sense of social structure, of the overwhelming power of Western expansion and of the material bases of change. They were also inclined to conceptualize situations of culture contact as if they were new or at least recent. It is questionable whether this was often realistic then; certainly there are not too many such situations around now. A little later, in the 1950s and early 1960s, "modernization" was a key concept, although anthropologists were probably never quite as enthusiastic about it as some other social scientists. The overtones of ethnocentrism and unilinearism were, after all, fairly noticeable.

For our purposes, furthermore, it is noteworthy that modernization theorists often dwelt on social psychology and patterns of social organization, stripping culture away. A very different framework was that dealing with the notion of plural societies, drawing especially on research experience in colonial plantation societies with conspicuously heterogeneous populations in South East Asia and

126 The world in creolization

the Caribbean. Here the emphasis was strongly on institutionalized cultural separateness, an ethnic or racial division of labor, and the dominance of a single group in the polity. This remains one of the few macro-anthropological approaches to the overall organization of cultural complexity, but at the present stage there are probably in most Third World countries considerably wider areas of the social structure which are relatively open, not the restricted territory of any particular group. There is also usually a more developed overarching cultural apparatus, forcefully breaking down some of the barriers to a society-wide flow of meaning. Such tendencies create rather different conditions for the development of more intricately organized national cultures.

I may have left out one or two other formulae, frameworks or orientations dealing with similar problems. Clearly enough, however, it is not that we have no past of attempting to understand large-scale cultural systems and their change. It is rather that much of this past does not now seem very usable.

So cultural studies could well benefit from a fresh start in this area, one that sees the world as it is in the late twentieth century. Scattered here and there in anthropology recently, there have been intimations that this world of movement and mixture is a world in creolization; that a concept of Creole culture with its congeners may be our most promising root metaphor. Moving from the social and cultural history of particular colonial societies (where they have tended to apply especially to particular racial or ethnic categories) to the discourse of linguists, Creole concepts have become more general in their applications.[5] And it is with a usage along such lines that they are now being retrieved. Drummond (1980; see also 1978) thus moves from a consideration of internal variability and change in the symbolic processes of ethnicity in Guyana to a general view that there are now no distinct cultures, only intersystemically connected, creolizing Culture. Fabian (1978: 317) suggests that the colonial system in Africa – "frequently disjointed, hastily thrown together for the purpose of establishing political footholds" – produced pidgin contact cultures. In the following period there was creolization, the emergence of viable new syntheses. In Zaire he finds this represented in popular painting, such as in the *mamba muntu* genre of mermaid images; in the Jamaa religious movement, based on a Belgian missionary's interpretation of Bantu philosophy; and in Congo jazz. Graburn (1984: 402 ff.) sees new Creole art forms, anchored in the reformulated consciousness of Third and Fourth World peoples, expanding beyond the restricted codes of tourist art.

Current creolist linguistics probably has enough theoretical diversity and controversy to allow for rather varied borrowings into cultural theory. As I see it myself, creole cultures like Creole languages are those which draw in some way on two or more historical sources, often originally widely different. They have had some time to develop and integrate, and to become elaborate and pervasive. People are formed from birth by these systems of meaning and largely live their lives in contexts shaped by them. There is that sense of a continuous spectrum of interacting forms, in which the various contributing sources of the culture are

The world in creolization **127**

differentially visible and active. And, in relation to this, there is a built-in political economy of culture, as social power and material resources are matched with the spectrum of cultural forms. A number of important points seem to come together here. If the "Standard," the officially approved language of the metropolis, stands at one end of the creole continuum of language, metropolitan culture in some prestige variant occupies the corresponding position on the cultural spectrum. But what are the mechanisms which place it there, on the range of variations of a national culture, and how do the members of the society come to be arranged in some fashion along that range on the basis of their personal cultural repertoires? I sketched such a spectrum above in spatial terms, from city to village, but this tends not to explain much in itself. If we should look for the mechanisms which are more directly involved in the distributive ordering of culture, we must note first of all that in Third World societies, as elsewhere, the division of labor now plays a major part in generating cultural complexity. Anthropological thinking about culture seems too often to disregard this fact. On the one hand, the division of labor entails a division of knowledge, bringing people into interaction precisely because they do not share all understandings. By not sharing, of course, they can increase their collective cultural inventory. On the other hand, as people are differently placed within the division of labor, they develop varied perspectives going beyond that knowledge which is in some sense commoditized, involved in material transactions.

Within the division of labor one set of specializations make up what, with a term from C. Wright Mills (1963: 405 ff.), we may describe as the cultural apparatus, where a relative few control a largely asymmetrical flow of meanings to a great many more people. The cultural apparatus encompasses, for example, formal education, the mass media, the arts, spectator sports, organized religion and a large part of secular ritual life. Some segments of the cultural apparatus reach out to everybody in society. Others have more differentiated audiences.

This cultural apparatus contributes a great deal to the center-periphery organization of national cultures, and to the channeling of the international cultural flow into them. The role of education is particularly significant here. Education is cultural process, an organized way of giving individuals cultural shape. At the same time, in much of the Third World, the growth of formal education is a facet of its penetration by the world system (see, e.g., Ramirez and Meyer 1980). Many Third World societies have also become intensely meritocratic; their critics suggest that they are afflicted with a "diploma disease" (see Dore 1976).

I would like to insert some Nigerian evidence here. Those at all aware of the political history of Nigeria know that it has been intensely ethnicized, with a major divide between the north and the south of the country. This may seem to fit the notion of Nigeria as a collection of tribes, united mostly in conflict. A major political figure in the years around independence was Ahmadu Bello, Sardauna of Sokoto, premier of the Northern region, and leader of the dominant political party. The image of Ahmadu Bello, among politicized southern

128 The world in creolization

Nigerians and among many expatriate observers, was that of a Muslim feudal aristocrat, an emirate man, a spokesman of the old order. Yet a recent biography by the political scientist John Paden (1986) presents a rather different picture. Ahmadu Bello was indeed a northerner and a Muslim, but at least as much an intense modernizer, deeply concerned with the problem of bringing the people of his region into the emergent national structure on acceptable terms. So one of his major fields of activity was the rapid expansion of northern Nigerian education, including crash programs to establish northerners in the new meritocracy.

Relate this to an inside account of that first military *putsch* in 1966 in which Ahmadu Bello was killed. The author, Captain Ben Gbulie (1981: 12–19), was one of the young southern officers engaged in the conspiracy. It turns out that, apart from everything else that was going wrong in Nigeria in the mid-1960s, one of the things they found most scandalous was the rapid promotion of northern officers. The northerners had been sent to what Gbulie and his friends saw as inferior British training institutions:

> the implications were quite clear – and most disturbing. Not only had these Northerners become commissioned officers before we were half-way through our first year at Sandhurst, they had all risen to the enviable rank of Captain before we could even appear at the sovereign's parade which served essentially as a pre-requisite for our passing out as Second Lieutenants ... A *coup d'état*, then, I was fully convinced, would go a long way to remedy the whole situation.

The conclusion, it would seem, is that the emphasis on ethnicity in analyzing Nigerian national society contains no more than half the story. Contests may repeatedly be defined in ethnic terms; but the prizes are defined in terms of the new, world system-oriented national culture and the social structure predicated on it.

Education, to reiterate, becomes a key factor in sorting people into the division of labor and determining their life situations, and thereby both directly and indirectly their perspectives – Peel (1978, 1983) and Berry (1985: 30 ff.) have recently written perceptively about local understandings of this among the southwestern Nigerian Yoruba. I believe anthropologists would do well to take more interest in education in the Third World, as a part of the endeavor of understanding the social organization of culture.[6] Not least is this important because schools tend to impart something more than the knowledge and skills they are officially expected to teach. The notion of a "hidden curriculum" is now common currency in debates over education in the metropolitan countries. It is hardly any less relevant for an understanding of Third World education and its place in national cultures. And this hidden curriculum often appears to involve, centrally, one orientation or other to metropolitan cultural influences. More classroom ethnography, of a type hitherto carried out mostly in the metropolitan countries, would allow us to examine not only what is formally taught and learned but also the workings of the hidden curriculum. My Nigerian experience suggests that not least boarding schools at the secondary level have often been virtual hothouses for the development of metropolitan orientations (see also Masemann 1974). At one end of the national cultural spectrum we thus usually find the people with a greater degree of formal education, which has also probably served them as a passport to social power and material affluence. Occupational and status group subcultures are constructed around their perspectives. Further along the spectrum other groups and subcultures come into being, again to a greater or lesser extent on the basis of shared levels of educational capital. Observers of many Third World societies are familiar with "the problem of school leavers," mostly young people who may have finished primary schooling, or who have not quite completed it, or who have dropped out at a fairly early point in secondary schooling. They also often form distinct subcultures – at times, of a disreputable sort: they are the "rascals," or "sons of the wind." That formal cultural capital they have acquired does not take them very far. At the same time they may have been strongly influenced by the hidden curriculum; the modeling of consumption patterns by school teachers, attitudes to manual work, to rural life, and so forth.

With the school leavers the world system in its cultural dimensions may reach the remote village; in their sunglasses and ragged t-shirts they are at its tail end, as it were. But they are also pioneer consumers of the products of another part of the cultural apparatus – popular culture. We have already seen that at least in Nigeria it is all there: music, fashion, television, a popular press. It has intense reflexive qualities, telling us how producers as well as consumers see themselves, and the directions in which they would like their lives to move. Clearly it also helps order the continuum of Creole culture. And, like education, it has mostly been ignored in the anthropology of the Third World.[7]

Much of the popular culture of the Third World is certainly in some way dependent on international influences. Its technology, its symbolic modalities and its genres are often not entirely indigenous. We may even think of the concept of popular culture itself as an import to Third World studies from a metropolitan vocabulary. As we cannot be sure that it is easily transplanted, it may require some critical examination.

In the analysis of contemporary metropolitan cultures we contrast popular culture especially with some more refined "high culture," produced and largely consumed within a cultural elite. Such a contrast may have some relevance in many Third World contexts as well. It is also important to recognize, however, that the involvement with popular culture often seems to be less precisely a cultural expression of a system of social stratification, and more directly a reflection of the center–periphery relationships in the world system of culture. In Nigeria popular culture appears above all to be a manifestation of a metropolis-oriented sophistication and modernity, contrasting not so much with "high culture" as with "bush," the derogatory term for anything rustic, uncouth, at least by implication connected with the idiocy of rural life. In some ways popular culture here may even be more like what it was in early modern Europe, as described by the historian Peter Burke (1978); a field of activity more or less uniting elites and masses in shared pastimes and pleasures.

130 The world in creolization

Popular culture engages people in fantasy and play; but to whom do the games belong? Especially in the debate over the impact of the media, the view is often strongly expressed that through radio and television, mass journalism and advertising, and other related information technologies and cultural forms, the cultures of North America and Western Europe threaten other cultures in the world with extinction, a sort of deadly diffusion.[8] Indeed, it is true that *Dallas* and *Charlie's Angels* may be seen on Nigerian television, and that hawkers in Kafanchan sell pirate tapes of metropolitan pop music from the back of their bikes. But the more popular sit-coms are made in Nigeria (see Oreh 1985). And Michael Jackson, Abba and Jimmy Cliff have certainly not destroyed the popular music market for Fela Anikulapo-Kuti, Sunny Ade or Victor Uwaifo.

I believe there is room for a more optimistic view of the vitality of popular expressive forms in the Third World, at least if the Nigerian example is anything at all to go by. But, of course, these forms are by no means pure traditional Nigerian culture. The world system, rather than creating massive cultural homogeneity on a global scale, is replacing one diversity with another; and the new diversity is based relatively more on interrelations and less on autonomy. Yet meanings and modes of expressing them can be born in the interrelations. We must be aware that openness to foreign cultural influences need not involve only an impoverishment of local and national culture. It may give people access to technological and symbolic resources for dealing with their own ideas, managing their own culture, in new ways. Very briefly, what is needed to understand the transforming power of media technology, from print to electronics, on cultures generally is a subtle understanding of the interplay between ideas, symbolic modalities with their varied potentialities, and the ability of the media to create new social relationships and contexts (as well as to alter old ones). Of that subtle understanding there is as yet little in the anthropology of complex cultures, at least in any systematic form. Along the entire creolizing spectrum, from First World metropolis to Third World village, through education and popular culture, by way of missionaries, consultants, critical intellectuals and small-town storytellers, a conversation between cultures goes on. One of the advantages of a creolist view of contemporary Third World cultural organization, it seems to me, is that it suggests that the different cultural streams engaging one another in creolization may all be actively involved in shaping the resultant forms; and that the merger of quite different streams can create a particular intensity in cultural processes. The active handling of meanings of various local and foreign derivations can allow them to work as commentaries on one another, through never-ending intermingling and counterpoint. Fela Anikulapo-Kuti, or Fela for short, the creator of Afro-beat music, political radical and hero of Nigerian popular culture, tells his biographer that he was Africanized by a black American girlfriend in California who gave him a consciousness-raising working-over (Moore 1982: 85). Third World intellectuals generally – writers, artists or academics – may be close to the point of entry of the international flow of meaning into national cultures, but, like intellectuals in most places, they are to some extent counter-cultural, carriers of an adversary culture. While far from immune to the charms of the metropolis, they respond to them critically as well, self-consciously making themselves the spokesmen and guardians of

Third World cultures (at least some of the time). What they may broadcast about metropolitan culture through the channels of communication reaching into their society, then, is not necessarily that culture itself, in either a pure or a somehow diluted form. It is their report on the dialogue between the metropolitan culture and themselves – as they have heard it. Back in the provincial town a schoolteacher may speak admiringly of the classic ethnography of his people, from the heyday of colonialism, although he may be critical at points on the basis of the oral history he has collected himself. Receding into the past, the "serial polyandry" of their forefathers and foremothers now seems as titillating to the sophisticates in Kafanchan as Mormon polygamy may be to many Americans. They cannot take the subject as seriously as the missionaries and the first generation of Christian converts did.

The dominant varieties of world system thought which have developed in recent times seem mostly to leave anthropologists uninterested, ambivalent or hostile. This may in part be due to the tradition of anthropological practice, with its preference for the small-scale, the face-to-face, the authentically alien. Another reason, however, would seem to be our distrust of approaches which seem too determined not to let small facts get in the way of large issues, too sure that the dominant is totally dominant, too little concerned with what the peripheries do both for themselves and to the center. World system thought sometimes indeed breeds its own rhetorical oversimplifications, its own vulgarities. It seems a little too ready to forget that the influences of any one center on the peripheries may not be wholly monolithic, but may be varied, uncoordinated and possibly contradictory. In its typical figures of speech there may be no room for recognizing that there may be several centers, conflicting or complementary, and that certain of them may not be the products of colonial or post-colonial periods. (For Ahmadu Bello, the northern Nigerian politician, the real Mecca was not London; Mecca was Mecca.) And, last but not least, too often in world system thinking there simply seems to be no room for culture.[9]

A macro-anthropology of culture which takes into account the world system and its center-periphery relations appears to be well served by a creolist point of view. It could even be the most distinctive contribution anthropology can make to world system studies. It identifies diversity itself as a source of cultural vitality; it demands of us that we see complexity and fluidity as an intellectual challenge rather than as something to escape from.

It should point us to ways of looking at systems of meaning which do not hide their connections with the facts of power and material life. We can perhaps benefit from it, too, because an understanding of the world system in cultural terms can be enlightening not only in Third World studies but also as we try to make of anthropology a truly general and comparative study of culture. Creole cultures are not necessarily only colonial and post-colonial cultures. I spend most of my time in a small country which for the last half-millennium or so has been nobody's colony, at least not as far as politics goes. Yet we are also drawn into the world system and its center-periphery relations, and the terms of debate in these 1980s seem to be those of creolization. What is really Swedish culture?

132 The world in creolization

In an era of population movements and communication satellites will it survive, or will it be enriched? And the questions are perhaps just slightly changed in the real centers of the world. What would life be like there without swamis and without reggae, without Olympic Games and "the Japanese model?" In the end, it seems, we are all being creolized.

Notes

1 This article was first presented in the Centennial Lecture series of the Department of Anthropology, University of Pennsylvania, in March 1986. Parts of it have been adapted from a paper presented in colloquia in the Departments of Anthropology of the University of California, Berkeley, Stanford University and the University of California, Santa Cruz, April and May 1985. I am grateful for comments made on those occasions. I have also benefited from discussions with my colleagues in the World System of Culture project in the Department of Social Anthropology, Stockholm University, Stefan Molund, Helena Wulff, and C. Bawa Yamba.
2 Nash (1981) has reviewed this body of anthropology, using the notion of a world system.
3 My interest in distributive models of culture has been inspired by the writings in this area of Wallace (1961: 26 ff.), Goodenough (1971) and Schwartz (1978a, 1978b), although it has taken a rather different direction. Sperber's (1985) notion of an "epidemiology of representations" is another recent expression of a concern with the distribution of culture.
4 Although most of Eric Wolf's *Europe and the People without History* is not directly concerned with cultural analysis in a stricter sense, his "Afterword" in its own way offers this kind of more processual understanding of culture (Wolf 1982: 387–391).
5 For discussions of regionally restricted conceptions of creolism, in the New World context, see, e.g. Adams (1959) and Brathwaite (1971: xiii ff.).
6 Cf. Eickelman (1978: 485): "the study of education can be to complex societies what the study of religion has been to societies variously characterized by anthropologists as 'simple', 'cold' or 'elementary'."
7 On the neglect of popular culture in African anthropology see Fabian (1978: 315) and Hart (1985: 254–255). For one brief comment on Nigerian popular culture see Rubenstein (1978).
8 Schiller (1971) and Hamelink (1983) exemplify writings in this vein.
9 In the work of Immanuel Wallerstein, with whom the world system concept is at present most closely associated, attention to culture is very limited, as some commentators have pointed out (e.g. Collins 1981: 45 ff.; Chirot and Hall 1982). To the extent that he does discuss the topic, he sees the differentiation of national cultures largely as the outcome of ideological maneuvering on the part of dominant strata in both the core countries of the world system and the peripheral areas (Wallerstein 1974: 349 ff., 1984: 170 ff.).

References

Adams, Richard N. 1959. On the Relation between Plantation and "Creole Cultures". In *Plantation Systems of the New World*. Washington, DC: Pan American Union.
Berry, Sara S. 1985. *Fathers Work for Their Sons*. Berkeley and Los Angeles, TYS: University of California Press.
Brathwaite, Edward. 1971. *The Development of Creole Society in Jamaica, 1770–1820*. London: Oxford University Press.
Burke, Peter. 1978. *Popular Culture in Early Modem Europe*. New York, NY: Harper & Row.
Chirot, Daniel, and Thomas D. Hall 1982. World-System Theory. *Annual Review of Sociology*, 8: 81–106.

The world in creolization **133**

Collins, Randall. 1981. *Sociology since Midcentury*. New York, NY: Academic Press.

Dore, Ronald. 1976. *The Diploma Disease*. Berkeley and Los Angeles, TYS: University of California Press.

Drummond, Lee. 1978. The Transatlantic Nanny: Notes on a Comparative Semiotics of the Family in English-Speaking Societies. *American Ethnologist*, 5: 30–43.

———. 1980. The Cultural Continuum: A Theory of Inter-Systems. *Man*, 15: 352–374.

Eickelman, Dale F. 1978. The Art of Memory: Islamic Education and Its Social Reproduction. *Comparative Studies in Society and History*, 20: 485–516.

Ekwensi, Cyprian. 1961. *Jagua Nana*. London: Hutchinson.

Eliot, T. S. (1948) 1962. *Notes Towards the Definition of Culture*. London: Faber.

Fabian, Johannes. 1978. Popular Culture in Africa: Findings and Conjectures. *Africa*, 48: 315–334.

Gbulie, Ben. 1981. *Nigeria's Five Majors*. Onitsha: Africana Educational Publishers.

Golding, Peter. 1977. Media Professionalism in the Third World: The Transfer of an Ideology. In James Curran, Michael Gurevitch, and Janet Woollacott (eds.), *Mass Communication and Society*. London: Edward Arnold.

Goodenough, Ward H. 1971. *Culture, Language, and Society*. Reading, MA: Addison-Wesley.

Graburn, Nelson H. H. 1984. The Evolution of Tourist Arts. *Annals of Tourism Research*, 11: 393–419.

Hamelink, Cees T. 1983. *Cultural Autonomy and Global Communications*. New York, NY: Longman.

Hart, Keith. 1985. The Social Anthropology of West Africa. *Annual Review of Anthropology*, 14: 243–272.

Masemann, Vandra. 1974. The "Hidden Curriculum" of a West African Girls' Boarding School. *Canadian Journal of African Studies*, 8: 479–494.

Mills, C. Wright. 1963. *Power, Politics, and People*. New York, NY: Ballantine.

Moore, Carlos. 1982. *Fela, Fela: This Bitch of a Life*. London: Allison & Busby.

Nash, June. 1981. Ethnographic Aspects of the World Capitalist System. *Annual Review of Anthropology*, 10: 393–423.

Oreh, O. O. 1985. *Masquerade* and Other Plays on Nigerian Television. In Frank Okwu Ugboajah (ed.), *Mass Communication, Culture and Society in West Africa*. Munich: Hans Zell/K. G. Saur.

Paden, John N. 1986. *Ahmadu Bello, Sardauna of Sokoto*. London: Hodder & Stoughton.

Peel, J. D. Y. 1978. *Olaju*: A Yoruba Concept of Development. *Journal of Developmental Studies*, 14: 135–165.

———. 1983. *Ijeshas and Nigerians*. Cambridge: Cambridge University Press.

Ramirez, Francisco O., and John W. Meyer 1980. Comparative Education: The Social Construction of the Modern World System. *Annual Review of Sociology*, 6: 369–399.

Rubenstein, Joseph. 1978. On Nigerian Pop Culture. *Dialectical Anthropology*, 3: 261–267.

Sauvant, Karl P. 1976. The Potential of Multinational Enterprises as Vehicles for the Transmission of Business Culture. In Karl P. Sauvant, and Farid G. Lavipour (eds.), *Controlling Multinational Enterprises*. Boulder, CO: Westview Press.

Schiller, Herbert L. 1971. *Mass Communications and American Empire*. Boston, MA: Beacon.

Schwartz, Theodore. 1978a. Where Is the Culture? Personality as the Distributive Locus of Culture. In George D. Spindler (ed.), *The Making of Psychological Anthropology*. Berkeley and Los Angeles. TYS: University of California Press.

———. 1978b. The Size and Shape of a Culture. In Fredrik Barth (ed.), *Scale and Social Organisation*. Oslo: Universitetsforlaget.

134 The world in creolization

Sperber, Dan. 1985. Anthropology and Psychology: Towards an Epidemiology of Representations. *Man*, 20: 73–89.

Wallace, Anthony F. C. 1961. *Culture and Personality*. New York, NY: Random House.

Wallerstein, Immanuel. 1974. *The Modem World System*. New York, NY: Academic Press.

———. 1984. *The Politics of the World Economy*. Cambridge: Cambridge University Press.

Wolf, Eric R. 1982. *Europe and the People without History*. Berkeley and Los Angeles, TYS: University of California Press.

7

FLOWS, BOUNDARIES AND HYBRIDS

Keywords in transnational anthropology

In Jorge Amado's novel *Tent of Miracles* (1971), that self-taught, streetwise ethnographer of Bahia life, Pedro Archanjo, is breakfasting on yams and couscous when he happens to come across a blue-eyed, wheat-blonde girl, Kirsi, who has just come ashore from a Swedish cargo ship.[1] The ship toots for its lost passenger, then leaves without her, and Archanjo tells her that if the two of them make a man-child together, he will be the smartest and bravest man there ever was; either king of Scandinavia or president of Brazil. If the child would be a girl, on the other hand, there would be nobody to match her for beauty and grace (see Figure 7.1).

We do not find out very much more about the girl Kirsi, who leaves six months later on another boat, and it is certainly purely coincidental that years after Amado's novel appeared, there would in fact be a Queen of Sweden with a partially Brazilian background. But of Pedro Archanjo we learn that he spent his early years traveling, and was in a way the son of Exú, mythical trickster and lord of the crossroads. The encounter between Kirsi and Pedro is an encounter of individuals as well as of races, continents, and cultures.

"In the neighborhood of Pelourinho," begins *Tent of Miracles*, "in the heart of Bahia, the whole world teaches and learns ..." One should perhaps be a bit wary here, because the novel also very entertainingly, and quite devastatingly, portrays another encounter, that of local knowledge with international academic traveling theory. But it is true that in Jorge Amado's Bahia, anthropologists seem to find much of what they now often look for, in life and in ethnography.[2]

These days, rather than seeking out the comfortable intimacy of village life, we debate the cultural distance between ship and shore, and the ways of traversing that distance. Flux, mobility, recombination and emergence have become favored themes as globalization and transnationality frequently offer the contexts

FIGURE 7.1 Jorge Amado, Salvador writer

for our thinking about culture. We now look for test sites of theory where some, at least, of the inhabitants are creoles, cosmopolitans, or cyborgs, where communities are diasporas, and where boundaries do not really contain, but are more often interestingly crossed. Borderlands are often where the action is, and hybridity and collage are among our preferred words for characterizing qualities in people and their products.

But then the question arises: what of this is actually new? I do not really want to engage here with any argument as to whether globalization is in itself a recent thing or not. The ancient Greeks certainly had their ideas of an ecumene, stretching from Atlantic Europe to distant East Asia; and the notion of an increasingly interconnected world has followed us fairly continuously from Prince Henry the Navigator to Marshall McLuhan, and beyond. Only this is hardly all just the same globalization; it needs, for one thing, to be periodized.[3]

What I will be more immediately concerned with here is the place of globalization in the history of anthropological ideas. In her inaugural lecture at Cambridge not so long ago, Marilyn Strathern (1995: 24) noted that as another *fin-de-siècle* approaches, "it sometimes feels that we are closer to the beginning of the century than to the middle of it" – anthropologists have come back to questions of material culture and technology, and by way of the interest in globalization, they have also after a fashion returned to diffusion.

Perhaps the discontinuity of concerns is more real in the case of technology. With regard to cultural interconnections in space, and the ongoing reorganization of cultural diversity in the world, it may be true that they were not given much attention in that major current of the discipline inclined to depict cultures as stable or bounded. Yet I think it may be argued that they have never been durably absent from the concerns of anthropology, even if they have appeared in varied conceptual guises. The preoccupation with cultural diffusion which Strathern mentions as a characteristic of the beginning twentieth century was at least not long gone when American anthropologists got involved in a debate over whether "acculturation" was a fit object of study. Many decided it was, and so particularly from the 1930s to the 1950s this offered a somewhat ramshackle framework for a great deal of research activity. (And indeed Salvador – also known as Bahia – was one of the places acculturation theorists like Melville Herskovits found good to think with, some 60 years ago.) Meanwhile across the Atlantic, the Malinowskians, after having defeated the diffusionists in academic battle, somewhat half-heartedly concocted their own guidelines for studying "culture contact."[4] The modernization and dependency theories of a slightly later postwar period were hardly really congenial for someone concerned with culture in its variations, nor was 1970s world system theory, but they, too, offered some stimulation for whoever might be inclined toward an anthropology of interconnectedness. And then again, in the last decade or so, globalization and transnationality have become a new research focus.

The way we talk now about culture in flux, about the zones where cultures meet, and about the agents and products of cultural mixing is certainly in some respects different from the anthropology of even 10 years ago. Yet perhaps we can hear in it some echoes from this rather stop-go, on-and-off history of earlier anthropologies of interconnectedness, partly disconnected from one another over time. The changing language of anthropology may show some of what we remember, some of what is half-forgotten, and some of what has been reinvented.

Let me shift, then, from *Tent of Miracles* to another book. In 1976, Raymond Williams, British literary theorist and cultural critic, published a small volume named *Keywords*, with the subtitle *A Vocabulary of Culture and Society*. In it, Williams explored a little over a hundred of the most central concepts of twentieth century discourse, in their historically accumulated complexity. It is interesting that a couple of decades ago, "globalization" was not among these keywords. Perhaps among Williams' choices, we could make our approaches toward it for example by way of "civilization," "imperialism," "humanity," "media" and "tradition." But had he lived to revise his book now, Williams might have thought that "globalization" belonged among his keywords.

In some small way, what I want to do here may remind of Raymond Williams' book, in that it is an inquiry into our vocabulary, an attempt to bring together some of the ideas and imageries it may evoke; experiences, visions and problem definitions which have become linked to it and which still have implications for our intellectual agenda. I will pick out a mere handful of those words anthropologists now find themselves using, not "globalization" itself, but words which tend to appear in one or other connection with it. The keywords of transnational anthropology on which I will concentrate my comments are "flows," "boundaries," and "hybrids."

138 Flows, boundaries and hybrids

Like much of the recent vocabulary we are engaging with here, these are metaphorical, somewhat tentative notions, perhaps in a slightly longer run imprecise or ambiguous, and thus open to contestation. Such words may appeal to us as we try to take a fresh look at the world around us, because they seem to offer an immediate grasp of some central quality of whatever we are referring to. The metaphors may have little to do with any "native's point of view" (although some natives may like them when they come across them, and others may not). Above all, they speak to our own previous experience, turning it into a provisional conceptual tool kit. But we may need to get beyond them, to elaborate on the points they make and to identify their ambiguities. I am reminded of Gregory Bateson's (1972: 73 ff.) classic essay on thinking about ethnological materials, where he suggested that in a first phase of reflecting on the Iatmul of New Guinea, he had found it useful to contrast, rather wildly, societies structured like jellyfish or sea anemones with those structured like earthworms or lobsters. From this hunch, he had then been able to move on to other more intellectually domesticated formulations. Perhaps in thinking about globalization, we are still in a phase of rather untamed words.

Flows, boundaries and hybrids, then; a few comments on their past and present places in our shifting habitats of meaning, sometimes in the history of anthropology, at other times in an interdisciplinary conceptual landscape. But then these three turn out to have in their immediate vicinity a number of other concepts of a similar nature, which may also require a passing remark.

Flows

It is not only anthropologists who talk about "flows" these days. Rather, the term has become transdisciplinary, a way of referring to things not staying in their places, to mobility and expansion of many kinds, to globalization along many dimensions. Scott Lash and John Urry (1994: 4, 12), social theorists, suggest that late twentieth-century societies are characterized by flows of capital, labor, commodities, information, and images. Thus economists, demographers, media researchers, geographers and others can all engage with flows.[5]

No doubt the rise to prominence of notions of flow in anthropology draws inspiration from such convergent usage elsewhere in the social sciences. When the new journal *Public Culture*, interdisciplinary but perhaps with anthropology at its center of gravity, appeared in 1988, the editors could declare that they wanted "to create an intellectual forum for interaction among those concerned with global cultural flows." And as one of them, Arjun Appadurai, proposed that one could see the "global cultural economy" as involving the five dimensions of ethnoscapes, mediascapes, technoscapes, finanscapes and ideoscapes, one senses the parallels with comprehensive formulations such as that of Lash and Urry (Appadurai 1990; see also, 1995). "Flow," like several of the other keywords in question here, thus points toward a macro-anthropology, a reasonably comprehensive view of the (relative) coherence and the dynamics of. larger social and territorial entities than those which the discipline have conventionally dealt with.

In anthropology's past there may never have been any very systematic use of a notion of flows, but neither is it a novelty of the last few years.[6] Let me offer two quotes from Alfred Kroeber, an ancestral figure who was not afraid to think about culture on a large scale. In this context, he would berate Spengler for neglecting "the interflow of cultural material between civilizations" (Kroeber 1952: 154). And he also noted that one should examine civilizations "not as static objects but as limited processes of flow in time" (Kroeber 1952: 404).

The reason why I juxtapose these two Kroeber quotes is that they demonstrate how the flow notion can really be used in two ways. It is the first of them that seems in line with the more conspicuous current usage, referring to the shift of something over time from one location to another, a territorial redistribution. This would indeed seem to be a way of bringing the idea of diffusion back in, without having to resort to the apparently still unfashionable term. The second is primarily temporal, with no necessary spatial implication.[7]

That double sense is really still with us. Some years ago, as I myself gave the flow concept a conspicuous part in my book *Cultural Complexity* (1992), I was actually primarily concerned with the time dimension, with the processual understanding of culture. I wanted to emphasize that only by being constantly in motion, forever being recreated, can meanings and meaningful forms become durable. Taking process seriously can at the same time be seen as keeping people in the picture. To keep culture going, people as actors and networks of actors have to invent culture, reflect on it, experiment with it, remember it (or store it in some other way), debate it, and pass it on.

It was clearly this processual emphasis Johannes Fabian (1978: 329) also had in mind when he wrote playfully of "a liquidation, literally speaking, of the concept of culture" – more recently, it is true, some anthropologists have thought of liquidating the culture concept in a quite different sense.[8] And Fredrik Barth (1984: 80–82), working out an understanding of cultural pluralism in a town in Oman, was likewise engaging with culture in processual terms as he followed Firth in viewing culture as something that people "inherit, employ, transmute, add to, and transmit," and drew attention to conceptions of co-existing traditions in the work of Redfield and Marriott. Such concepts, he argued,

> should serve to emphasize properties both of separability and interpenetration, suggested perhaps by an imagery of streams, or currents within a river: distinctly there, powerful in transporting objects and creating whirlpools, yet only relative in their distinctness and ephemeral in their unity.

But Barth approached the spatial sense of flow as well, in noting that the separability, coherence and contents of co-traditions could be explored in terms of their geographical distribution as well as social organization, history, and prospects. And certainly, as I devoted the last chapter of my *Cultural Complexity* to emergent concerns with global cultural interconnectedness, I too shifted partially

140 Flows, boundaries and hybrids

to a view of flows as occurring in space – at one point referring to an imagined "global cultural flow chart" (Hannerz 1992: 221).

To what kinds of questions, then, does a notion of cultural flows draw our attention? I will point here to two kinds. As far as the spatial dimension is concerned, let us consider that flow chart. One fundamental fact about flows must be that they have directions. In the case of cultural flows, it is true, what is gained in one place need not be lost at the source. But there is a reorganization of culture in space.

Once upon a time, in anthropology, a handful of British diffusionists were inclined to view ancient Egypt as the source of much of world culture – an utterly extreme view, most commentators have since felt, of global center-periphery relationships. At present, in one global scenario of flows, perhaps a similarly dominant position may be taken up, figuratively speaking, by some combination of New York, Hollywood, and the headquarters of the World Bank. Here would be where flows originate. And if they reach everywhere, global cultural uniformity would be the final outcome.

For quite a long time now, certainly, such images of dominant centers have met with little sympathy among anthropologists. The group of American scholars (Broom et al. 1954) who met in the 1953 Social Science Research Council "Summer Seminar on Acculturation" commented, for their part, that anthropologists, "in a sense of fairness and moral indignation," have been forever delighted to find evidence of cultural influence by the weak on the strong. A book title from 1937, *The Savage Hits Back*, by the German ethnologist Julius Lips, suggests that the roots of this enduring preoccupation within the discipline go further back yet. And from about the same time, there is Ralph Linton's (1936: 326–327) classic, "100% American." A "solid American citizen" goes through his morning routines, and as Linton follows him around, it turns out that hardly an object he uses is actually of American origin as a cultural invention; it is from India, Germany, China, the near East, and so forth. Yet as he considers the accounts of foreign troubles in his morning newspaper, the man thanks "a Hebrew deity in an Indo-European language that he is 100% American."

Many decades later, the theme is still easily recognizable. We are inclined to pay close attention not only to the active handling of cultural flows at the receiving end, but also to the multicentricity of flows, to crisscrossing flows, and to counterflows. As I read Amado's *Tent of Miracles*, I am attracted to its depiction of the continuing influence of old West African cultural currents from across the South Atlantic on the folk culture of Bahia. By now the theme resonates with more or less postmodernist perspectives in other disciplines as well, where the conception of the world is increasingly one of decenteredness (cf. Lash and Urry 1994: 4). Along related lines, Appadurai (1990: 6) goes as far as to argue that the new global organization of culture cannot be understood in terms of existing center-periphery models, even those which allow for multiple centers and peripheries.

I would still suggest some rather unexciting caution here. Howell (1995), in an essay celebrating counterflow, has no difficulty finding a variety of instances. On a visit to London she finds exotic *bric-à-brac* in Camden market and sees an exhibition of contemporary African artists; at home in Oslo she finds encounter therapy groups drawing on Malayan techniques of dream interpretation.[9] I am not surprised – the kinds of examples of counterflow are already getting a bit predictable – but I think our credibility as commentators on contemporary human life will suffer unless we maintain some sense of the relative weight of things. Some net asymmetries of flow during the last century or so seem to me undeniable, involving for example the spread of some of those fundamental skills and central institutional forms which we refer to collectively as modernity; say, western–origin types of basic and higher education, administrative practices, or biomedicine (even when these are adopted in forms which are not exact copies of the original).

It is true that history accumulates currents of cultural flow into shifting patterns. This complex of asymmetries took shape in Europe centuries ago and, in accelerating in this century, has also in itself created some of the conditions for those later cultural counterflows and crisscross flows in space which by now we find so striking. I doubt, however, that we are at a point when it has become entirely impossible to tell centers and peripheries apart.

With regard to my other kind of questions about flows, I will return to my concern with time and process. Once I had started thinking in flow terms here, it occurred to me as I continued to look at variations in the organization of culture that this worked rather well as a root metaphor, in the sense of leading on to further elaborations. Not only does the idea of flow stand in opposition to static thought. It implies, moreover, that we may think of mighty rivers and tiny rivulets, separate currents as well as confluences, "whirlpools" (according to Barth, above), even leaks and viscosity in the flow of meaning.

Yet as I have said somewhere else, when you take an intellectual ride on a metaphor, it is important that you know where to get off. If for some purposes you find it useful to think about culture as flow, then, no need to believe it is a substance you can pour into bottles. But perhaps there is another, more real risk in the imagery of flow that we must hurry to identify. Some have objected that it may make cultural process seem too easy, too smooth. Certainly we must not just understand it as a matter of simple transportation, simple transmission, of tangible forms loaded with intrinsic meanings. It is rather to be seen as entailing an infinite series of shifts, in time and sometimes in changing space as well, between external forms available to the senses, interpretations, and then external forms again; a series continuously fraught with uncertainty, allowing misunderstandings and losses as well as innovation. What the flow metaphor presents us with is the task of problematizing culture in processual terms, not the licence to deproblematize it, by abstracting away the complications. One chapter in my book *Cultural Complexity* is indeed titled "Unfree flow."

Boundaries (borders, frontiers, beaches)

What I have in mind may become clearer as I turn to my second keyword. If "flow" suggests some sort of continuity and passage, after all, "boundaries" have to do with

142 Flows, boundaries and hybrids

discontinuity and obstacles. I take a boundary to be a quite sharp line of demarcation. Something is either in or out. But what? Let me refer to Fredrik Barth again. The formulation of cultural pluralism in terms of co-occurrent streams which I quoted above was a critical reaction to a tendency he had discerned in anthropology to recast discussions of cultural pluralism in terms of ethnicity; this Barth (1984: 80) saw as "an abdication and counsel of despair."

Barth was himself one of the major theorists of ethnicity in anthropology, and I believe the word "boundaries" actually came into more frequent use in anthropology after the publication of his *Ethnic Groups and Boundaries* (Barth 1969). In that volume, maintaining the analytical distinction between the social and the cultural – referring to people and their relationships, on the one hand, and meanings and meaningful forms, on the other – Barth emphasized that ethnicity is best seen as a matter of social organization, and suggested that there is no simple relationship between ethnic group membership and the distribution of cultural items among populations. In the normal case, ethnic group membership, as a matter of social identity, would be either one or the other; in or out. Here the boundary would be clearly demarcated. In large part this would involve selected cultural forms, dichotomously distributed and understood as emblematic of membership.[10] Yet it is important to realize that far from all cultural distributions among people and relationships need to follow the same lines.

I think Barth's 1960s work did much to make us think of boundaries as something *across* which contacts and interactions take place; they may have an impact on the form and extent of these contacts, but they do not *contain* natural isolates. And the distinction between the social and the cultural was made so that the relationship between the two could be problematized.

It is instructive to compare Barth's view with that of the acculturation theorists of the Social Science Research Council seminar (Broom et al. 1954: 974 ff.) 15 years earlier. In their formulations about "autonomous cultural systems" the distinction between the social and the cultural was mostly blurred. When they turned to "boundary-maintaining mechanisms," these were defined as "the techniques and ideologies by means of which a system limits its participation in the culture to a well-recognized group." Here they seem to take much the same view as Barth would later, of boundaries as something channeling participation in social relationships. But the cultural systems talk of the 1950s turned group boundaries into boundaries of cultures without anyone giving it much thought.

This history may now be repeating itself. As the culture concept becomes increasingly popular in wider circles, there is again a tendency to focus attention on culture only as a group marker. In "identity politics," in debates over multiculturalism, and in many contexts of "cultural studies," it becomes primarily a basis of group formation and mobilization, involving ascriptive memberships. Or, on the other hand, it turns into a tool of social exclusion, on the part of dominant majorities. There may be a preoccupation with cultural autonomy and the defense of a cultural heritage for its own sake, yet frequently this rhetoric of culture is closely linked to power and material resources.

Flows, boundaries and hybrids **143**

We must be attentive to this particular strategy of linking the cultural to the social, to culture as "totemic capital," as Kearney (1991: 59) has aptly put it. Lash and Urry (1994: 4) argue that in our times, the economy is increasingly an economy of signs. Signs, not material objects, tend to become the major products. Yet we have not only an economy of signs, in that case, but also a lively politics of signs, a politics of culture.[11] Our interest in culture, however, need not be limited to those distributions of meanings and meaningful form which are emblematic, involving clear group distinctions. And thus the question is raised, in what other terms could one possibly think of cultural boundaries?

Turn back to our ethnographic miniature in *Tent of Miracles*. Amado has Pedro Archanjo and that girl Kirsi mostly gesturing to each other to begin with, and trying to guess what they are saying in their respective languages. Still they seem in a way to understand each other quite well. And while Kirsi was still in Bahia, it would seem she learned some of its dances rather successfully. Perhaps by the time she left, she was better at doing the *lundu* than at Portuguese.

We could argue that when the cultural flow has somehow stopped somewhere, where there is a discontinuity in the distribution of meanings and/or meaningful forms among individuals and social relationships, then we have identified a cultural boundary. But where would it be with respect to Kirsi and Pedro Archanjo? Now you see it, now you don't. Think of it, perhaps, as a zigzag or a dotted line. Perhaps this is where we should just get off this particular metaphor. Alternatively, we might think about what are the units in terms of which we discern discontinuities, along the social as well as the cultural dimension.

Consider some history again. In 1954, the acculturation theorists of the SSRC seminar took a hard line against construing the culture concept at any other than a "broadly inclusive level" such as the "society." Otherwise, they warned, the analyst might ultimately be reduced to dealing with such particularized cultures as those of families and even individuals (Broom et al. 1954: 974). Even some twenty years earlier, commenting on a first American memorandum on principles for acculturation research (by Redfield, Linton and Herskovits 1936), Gregory Bateson ([1935] 1972: 61 ff.) had actually taken a more flexible position. Bateson suggested that a notion of "culture contact" could be fruitfully extended to contacts for example between the sexes, between the old and the young, between aristocracy and plebs; even to include "those processes whereby a child is moulded and trained to fit the culture into which he was born."

If Bateson was thus in favor of considering smaller units along the social dimension, he was on the other hand critical of the tendency to disaggregate units along the cultural dimension; arguing, that is, in favor of the Malinowskian celebration of integrated wholes, against the breakdown into "traits" which at least the early American writers on acculturation seemed to have inherited from diffusionism.

By now my inclination would be not to take larger units for granted, along either the social or the cultural dimension; to disaggregate first, before moving back (possibly) to larger-scale formulations. In the late twentieth century phase

144 Flows, boundaries and hybrids

of globalization, many people have increasing experiential access to flows of cultural form which used to be localized elsewhere, as well as to whatever we think of as belonging to their own locality. And some currents of culture are perhaps hardly identifiable as belonging to any particular place at all. As they engage with these varied currents of culture present in their habitats, individuals as cultural beings are probably now shaped, and shape themselves, to an increasing degree by peculiarities of autobiography, taste, and the cultivation of competences. Ascriptive group identities need not be all-important.

Cultural flows over distances are also getting increasingly polymorphous. Remember again Pedro Archanjo and Kirsi gesturing to one another, without knowing one another's languages, and Kirsi learning the dances of Bahia. As culture moves through such more specific currents as migrant flow, commodity flow and media flow, or combinations of these, a range of perceptual and communicative modalities are involved which probably differ importantly in the way they shape their discontinuous distributions over people and relationships. In part, they may entail alien languages, or whatever else is like them – mere exposure is not at all the same as understanding, appreciation, or any other sort of appropriation. But in other instances, a gesture, a tune, a shape, whether carried through electronic media by way of communication satellites or by a stranger who has come ashore, could be somehow immediately grasped, so that a distribution is changed, a boundary transcended, promptly and with ease. To borrow a term from Dan Sperber (1985), different "epidemiologies" seem to be involved, and this would tend to dissolve "cultures" as distributional units. Different cultural forms make different passages.

What we may want to reach for here, for one thing (to get beyond metaphor and striking anecdote), is a more general understanding of cultural acquisition as a continuously ongoing process; an understanding which is pluralistic enough to take the variations in cultural form into account. And here, to return to a concern I expressed earlier, it hardly seems necessary to look at cultural flow in space (which is of course, more precisely, both in space and time), and its discontinuities, as sharply different from more localized flow in time. Whatever we may have learnt about the acquisition of culture more generally, along cognitive, motivational, situational, institutional and other dimensions, could be brought to bear on the study of passages of meanings and meaningful forms over greater distances, as diffusion is understood to be merely a matter of cultural acquisition spatially rearranged.

Not that this kind of understanding of cultural process is fully developed, or without its own current controversies, even in the more conventionally delimited local contexts.[12] But it was hardly available at all to those old-style diffusionists of seventy, eighty or a hundred years ago, who were engaged in historical reconstructions and could only inspect the enigmatic traces of past cultural passages.

On the question of boundaries, and the flows which shape them or dissolve them, one more comment should perhaps be made here. To the old diffusionists, cultures were, as one of them put it, "things of shreds and patches" (Lowie 1920: 441). Perhaps in this era of striking juxtapositions, we may seem to be approaching such a view again, only with a better understanding of how, and in what exact sense, they get to be that way. Now some might think that detailing diffusion, whether as a process or in its outcome, is an obscure academic game, even if our skills in playing are improved. It matters not at all if spaghetti came from China to Italy, or if the pajamas of Linton's "100% American" originated in India. What matters, such an argument goes, are local interpretations, local frameworks of meaning.

Now obviously, for some purposes, the local frameworks are important, although perhaps no longer to everybody to quite the same extent (and the category of "local" must not in itself remain unexamined). Yet if we are now unhappy with more fundamentalist and exclusivist forms of culturespeak, it may not be a bad idea to insert other understandings of culture into the public conversation, making even local frameworks less parochial. I do not think Linton intended his vignette of the "100% American" only as a curiosity. There is a sense of irony, a cultural critique here. In what was another period of some xenophobia and striving toward cultural closure, a view from a little further afar which drew attention to the continued flux and reorganization of the cultural inventory of all humanity, to crisscrossing commonalities, and to our forgetfulness of such things, need not just have been a plaything of the ivory tower. Neither is it necessarily so now.[13]

Anyway, we may recognize some of the difficulties with the notion of a boundary, a sharp and more or less continuous demarcation line, when applied to the realities of cultural diversity, not least in the present. Perhaps it is partly due to these difficulties that alternative terms of discontinuity now seem at least as attractive in mapping culture, terms I can hardly ignore here. In a small bundle of geographical metaphors, "boundary" would seem to belong with "frontier," and with "borderland." These latter, however, are terms not for sharp lines, but for zones where one thing gradually shifts into something else, where there is blurring, ambiguity and uncertainty.[14]

I will say something about the frontier concept first. The American historian Frederick Jackson Turner's (Turner [1893] 1961) writings a hundred years ago set in motion a small, mostly North American, but for some time also transnational and comparative academic industry.[15] For Turner, the moving frontier had been a region of opportunity – forever more wilderness turning into free land, where pioneers were self-reliant but could also join together without the constraints of the traditions and inequalities they had left behind, without the burden of a heritage:

> The frontier is the line of most rapid and effective Americanization. The wilderness masters the colonist. It finds him a European in dress, industries, tools, modes of travel, and thought. It takes him from the railroad car and puts him in the birch canoe. It strips off the garments of civilization and arrays him in the hunting shirt and the moccasin.
>
> *(Turner [1893] 1961: 39)*

Later critics have pointed out that Turner's frontier history could serve as an American myth, even as a symbolic tool of domestic cultural debate between the established East and the changing West. No doubt, from Turner to John F. Kennedy's

146 Flows, boundaries and hybrids

1960s "New Frontier," the idea of the frontier has had largely favorable connotations in American culture, pointing toward the future, suggesting an environment of progress and opportunity which committed and able human beings can shape for themselves.

In the sense which Turner put into scholarly circulation, however, the frontier has at the same time stood for a particular historical form of globalization: the expansion and settlement of Europeans in other parts of the world. Inside Europe, Turner noted, a frontier would be "a fortified boundary line running through dense populations."[16] In South America, in Australia and in Southern Africa, just as in North America, the frontier was between what counted and what did not count; wilderness. If there were indigenous inhabitants there, to the extent that they entered into frontier imagery, they too were wild. Indeed, as Turner suggests, "the wilderness masters the colonist" as well. He is stripped of the superfluous baggage of civilization. The frontier, in this view, becomes primarily an ecological zone, rather more than one of a confluence of cultural streams.

When as scholars we face the "frontiers of knowledge," it is also this sense of the frontier as next to wilderness that takes hold of our imagination. On this side, the cultivated fields. On the other, the great unknown. And the sense of wilderness is still there as the idea of the frontier in the popular imagination now often shifts its locus, to urban life, to streets and alleys which seem beyond the reach of the organized centers of society. In other words, the urban frontier is an urban jungle. Other people one encounters there may really be beasts, and the law of the jungle is the survival of the fittest. (Pelourinho, Pedro Archanjo's neighborhood in Salvador, seems for a while to have been a little like such an urban frontier, before its recent revival as a World Heritage site and tourist attraction.)

But anthropology has also developed other understandings of the frontier. In his work on the highlands of Burma, Edmund Leach (1960), problematizing the conventional notion of political frontiers, described a zone in which cultures interpenetrated dynamically, through varied political, ecological, economic and kinship frameworks. And more recently, in a volume on *The African Frontier* (1987), the editor Igor Kopytoff has delineated a Subsaharan landscape where innumerable microfrontiers keep developing, not just at the outskirts of established societies but precisely in the interstices *between* them (and "interstices" is another recurrent term in this vocabulary of betweenness); where small groups of people meet to form the beginnings of a new society, having left their respective earlier homes for example after succession disputes or witchcraft accusations. In a pattern where centers and peripheries keep changing places, Kopytoff argues, frontiers in Africa have kept resynthesizing cultures, although the main tendency in this case has been conservative, involving variations on enduring themes within a single ecumene.

Kopytoff takes Turner's frontier thesis as his point of departure, and he draws on classical Africanist ethnography while at the same time subverting its assumptions of

Flows, boundaries and hybrids **147**

stability and timelessness. But his emphasis on the meeting and mingling of people, in territories in-between, brings him, like Leach before him, closer to those colleagues in anthropology who have recently, in rather less conventional ethnographic settings, been more inclined to speak of borderlands. So let me turn to these.

Alvarez (1995: 451), reviewing the anthropology of the Mexico–United States border recently, has remarked that this has become "the model of border studies and borderland genre throughout the world"; a striking parallel, it seems, to the status of the American frontier as the somehow exemplary frontier. One observer of that border is Renato Rosaldo (1988), another is Michael Kearney (1991). It is interesting to compare them, for although the borderlands they write of are more or less the same, their emphases are different. Kearney's border is rather more that "real," political border, and around it is mostly a grim region, of predators and victims, one which fairly well matches that updated frontier imagery of the wilderness of cities. If it is not really under anyone's control, there is more of terror, and evasion. The key people are the "coyotes," who arrange the passage of illegal migrants from south to north. And Kearney reminds us that *El Coyote* is also, in indigenous Mexico and North America, a "supremely ambiguous and contradictory trickster and culture hero."

In Rosaldo's border zone, defined more by the poets than by the police (and consequently more metaphorical), the small-time hero is El Louie, a lumpenproletarian from the streets, playing with fashions and Hollywood images. The inhabitants here as well are typically migrants, minorities, the "undocumented." Yet he draws our attention not so much to the battle for survival, but to the border as a cultural zone "between stable places" – to its freedom, to people playing, to a dance of life. The border becomes a ludic space. Or, to remind ourselves of yet another current of anthropological thought, and moving between Turners, from Frederick Jackson Turner to Victor Turner (e.g. 1974), an area of liminality.

Again, it seems, "the savage hits back"; or if not quite the savage, at least someone who stands at some remove from the dominant center. We have indeed encountered the type in a number of memorable ethnographic portrayals over the years.[17] Eric Wolf's (1959: 238–241) mestizo, in *Sons of the Shaking Earth*, had to jettison much of whatever of the Spanish heritage might have reached Central American lands. For in the erratic rhythm of his life, "his chances of survival lay neither in accumulating cultural furniture nor in cleaving to cultural norms, but in an ability to change, to adapt, to improvise." He had to seem both more or less than what he was, and to be both more and less than what he seemed. Language could turn into a strategy where explicit meanings disguised implicit messages, and where speaking two contradictory tongues would be a way of confusing the uninitiated. And he enjoyed the play of fantasy because standing on the edge of society, he had also placed himself on the edge of reality. The mestizo's favorite, says Wolf, would be the great clown Cantínflas, "who in an eternal round of wish fulfilment steps nimbly around the traps of life with fancy footwork and hilarious doubletalk, traveling lightly through the social corridors."[18]

148 Flows, boundaries and hybrids

There is one more contact zone metaphor that I should not ignore here. In his remarkable book on the ethnohistory of the Marquesas, in Polynesia, Dening (1980) develops an imagery of cultural "islands", and the "beaches" constituted around them through definitions of "we" and "they."[19] These are not beaches like present-day Copacabana, then, but rather those of Pedro Cabral or James Cook, more like borderlands. And one might compare Dening's portrayal of "beachcombers" – "whatever they did on the beach, they had to carve out a new world for themselves" – with Frederick Jackson Turner's of the frontiersman. Yet there is a difference in that Dening gives full recognition to the fact that as they crossed the beach, they arrived not in a wilderness, but in "other worlds that were well-established and self-sufficient."

To sum up, then, the landscapes of the interstitial zones seem lively but not entirely safe. If you survive and even prosper there, it is thanks to your own cultural, perhaps even physical, agility. Part of this, some of our guides suggest, may be a matter of deculturating: stripping oneself of a cultural overload to achieve a greater freedom of movement. Yet deculturating too much, you risk becoming dehumanized, a dangerous beast. The freedom of the border zone is more creatively exploited by situational shifts and innovative combinations, putting its resources together in new ways, experimenting. In the borderlands, there is much scope for agency in the handling of culture.

Hybrids, and other terms of mixture

On that note, we may turn to our third keyword: hybrids. But only after looking back, momentarily, to earlier years again. Consider these lines:

> It is a peculiar sensation, this double-consciousness, this sense of always looking at one's self through the eyes of others, of measuring one's soul by the tape of a world that looks on in amused contempt and pity. One ever feels his twoness – an American, a Negro; two souls, two thoughts, two unreconciled strivings; two warring ideals in one dark body, whose dogged strength keeps it from being torn asunder.

This is from that pioneer Afro-American intellectual, W.E.B. DuBois' *The Souls of Black Folk* ([1903] 1961: 16–17). There may be a feeling for agency here, but if so, it mostly concerns strength in the face of adversity. The dominant mood seems to be tragic. Something of this mood obviously continued as a theme for at least the first half of the twentieth century in much social and cultural commentary. In American sociology, a body of writing grew around the new concept of "the marginal man." The originator of the concept, Robert E. Park ([1928] 1964: 356), ancestral figure of Chicago sociology and more concerned than most other academics at the time with what we might now term a sociology of globalization, wrote 25 years after DuBois that "it is in the mind of the marginal man that the moral turmoil which new cultural contacts occasion, manifests itself in the most obvious forms."

"Margins" obviously go with the vocabulary of borders, frontiers, and interstices, and the marginal man is also a part of the intellectual genealogy of contemporary understandings of cultural recombinations.[20] But something has clearly happened between his time and ours. Compare DuBois and Park to Salman Rushdie (1991: 394), commenting in a well-known passage on his famous and controversial novel:

> The Satanic Verses celebrates hybridity, impurity, intermingling, the transformation that comes of new and unexpected combinations of human beings, cultures, ideas, politics, movies, songs. It rejoices in mongrelization and fears the absolutism of the pure. Mélange, hotchpotch, a bit of this and a bit of that is how newness enters the world.

There has been a shift of ethos, away from quiet pain or compassion, toward assertiveness and, indeed, celebration. Impurity and intermingling now offer not only an escape from DuBois' "twoness", a possibility of reconciliation. It is a source – perhaps the most important source – of desirable cultural renewal.

The shift clearly took place earlier in the Brazilian world of scholarship and letters than in most places, and perhaps one could argue that this is where it was pioneered. Pedro Archanjo, from Tent of Miracles, and through him Jorge Amado, is surely a Rushdie forerunner. In the annals of artistic hybridity, it seems, Bahia comes before Bombay. And Gilberto Freyre's (1946, 1959) writings on Brazil as a meeting place of Portuguese, Amerindians and Africans, must surely be central to an intellectual and cultural history of hybridity – especially for its bold attempt to delineate not only a character type, or a mode of artistic production, but an entire new civilization, a level of macro-anthropological ambition paralleled perhaps most closely here by Frederick Jackson Turner on the frontier. We should note, too, that while the "marginal man" was mostly a sociological creature, anthropology already at mid-century (rather predictably) tended to take another view. "The conjunction of differences in culture contact," wrote the members of the SSRC acculturation seminar in 1954, "provides a kind of catalyst for cultural creativity" (Broom et al. 1954: 985). And in their somewhat laborious systems language, they concerned themselves with the conditions for the emergence, in contact situations, of "a genuine third sociocultural system through a process of fusion."

Anyway, here we are now, with hybridity, collage, mélange, hotchpotch, montage, synergy, bricolage, creolization, mestizaje, mongrelization, syncretism, transculturation, third cultures and what have you; some terms used perhaps only in passing as summary metaphors, others with claims to more analytical status, and others again with more regional or thematic strongholds. Mostly they seem to suggest a concern with cultural form, cultural products (and conspicuously often, they relate to domains

150 Flows, boundaries and hybrids

of fairly tangible cultural materials, such as language, music, art, ritual, or cuisine). Some appear more concerned with process than others.

It seems hybridity is at present the more favored general term; no doubt drawing strength, like "flow," from easy mobility between disciplines (but then several of the other terms are also fairly footloose). Despite its biologistic flavor, it has a strength not least in literary scholarship, due in large part to its presence in the work of Mikhail Bakhtin (1968). For Bakhtin, I take it, hybridity was above all the coexistence of two languages, two linguistic consciousnesses, even within a single utterance; commenting on one another, unmasking each other, entailing contradiction, ambiguity, irony. Again, the trickster theme may seem not far away. As Homi Bhabha (1994) takes the notion into the cultural critique of colonialism, it comes to draw attention to the subversion, the destabilization, of colonial cultural authority. But as different commentators, from a range of disciplines, have taken it in different directions, with varied analytical objectives, hybridity is by now itself a term which is far from unambiguous.[21]

Let us have a quick look at some of the other words for mixture. "Synergy" may not have much of a past in anthropology. It has been pointed out that the concept shows up in some of Ruth Benedict's lecture notes, from 1941 (Maslow and Honigmann 1970). But Benedict used it for situations understood as internal to cultures, where an "act or skill that advantages the individual at the same time advantages the group." At present, too, the term seems less popular in anthropology than among professionals in the growing field of intercultural communication, who use it to refer to the dynamic advantages of contacts and mergers between cultures. And of course, these interculturalists themselves often move in the borderlands of the world of business, where the idea of synergy tends to lend an attractive aura to mergers and takeovers. "Synergy," that is to say, has distinctly celebratory overtones built into it.

Going back about equally far in anthropology is "transculturation," a term coined by the Cuban social historian Fernando Ortiz in his book *Cuban Counterpoint* (1947). Bronislaw Malinowski, who met Ortiz in Havana in 1939, wrote an introduction (dated 1940) to the book, stating that he had promised the author to "appropriate the new expression for/his/own use, acknowledging its paternity, and use it constantly and loyally." It was, Malinowski felt, a term much preferable to acculturation, which he thought fell upon the ear in an unpleasant way – "sounds like a cross between a hiccup and a belch" – and which, as he understood it, suggested a more one-sided cultural change. Transculturation, he agreed with Ortiz, was a system of give and take, "a process from which a new reality emerges, transformed and complex, a reality that is not a mechanical agglomeration of traits, nor even a mosaic, but a new phenomenon, original and independent." It hardly seems that at least some of Malinowski's American colleagues actually understood "acculturation" very differently. In recent times, "transculturation" may have been made more popular again especially by Pratt's (1992) use of it in her study of travel writing. And in post-colonial times, one of the attractions of this concept may be that it is in itself an example of counterflow, from periphery to center.

Perhaps, despite their somewhat different histories and emphases, it does not matter much which of these concepts one chooses, but that to which I have been most strongly drawn myself, primarily on the basis of my field experience in Nigeria, is "creolization."[22] While I believe that the others mostly denote cultural mixture as such, and although "creolization" is no doubt sometimes also so used, I think this concept can be used in a more precise, and at the same time restricted, way.

The origins of the idea of "creole" people and cultural phenomena are in the particular culture-historical context of New World plantation societies, and some might feel that the notion should be left there. One could have a debate over this, much like those over other concepts which have been taken out of particular areas to be used for more comparative purposes (caste, totem, taboo ...).[23] In any case, the more expansive use has been an established fact for some time, particularly in sociolinguistics, and in analogy with creolist understandings there, I would argue that a creolist view is particularly applicable to processes of cultural confluence within a more or less open continuum of diversity, stretched out along a structure of center-periphery relationships which may well extend transnationally, and which is characterized also by inequality in power, prestige and material resource terms. Along such lines, it appears to me possible to integrate cultural with social analysis, in a way not equally clearly suggested by many of the other concepts in this cluster, and thus also to pursue a more macro-anthropological vision.[24] But again, this also means that creolization becomes a less general term, by referring to a more elaborated type of sociocultural order – a social landscape which is rather more structured, not so much a frontier or a borderland.

The identification of creole cultures draws attention to the fact that some cultures are very conspicuously *not* "bounded," "pure," "homogeneous," and "timeless," as in the anthropological tradition cultures have often been made to seem, and to the extent that the celebratory stance toward hybridity recurs here as well, it is also suggested that these cultures draw some of their vitality and creativity precisely from the dynamics of mixture (although the celebration here may be somewhat tempered by the recognition that the cultures are also built around structures of inequality). One objection occasionally raised against the creolization concept – and other related notions may be confronted with it as well – is that such an identification of creole cultures as a particular category might simply push those features of essentialism a step back, implying that the cultural currents joined through creolization were pure, bounded, and so forth, until they were thus joined.

I do not find this implication inevitable. Drawing on the linguistic parallel again, there are a number of English-based creole languages in the world, but nobody would seriously argue that the English language is historically pure – remember 1066, and all that. The claim need only be that in one particular period, some cultures are more creole than others; to the extent that the cultural streams coming together, under the given conditions and with more or less dramatic results, are historically distinct from another, even as they themselves may have resulted from other confluences. At some point or other, with some duration, we or our forefathers may all have been creolized, but we are not forever engaged in it to the same degree.

152 Flows, boundaries and hybrids

Finally, syncretism; again an old idea, although perhaps not a continuously highly visible one, used in and out of anthropology, but especially in the field of comparative religion, for example in the study of how, in Afro-American cultures, West African deities have merged with Catholic saints.[25] Recently there appears to have been some revival of interest, coupled with an interest in "anti-syncretism" – in a world where academics study non-academic lives and non-academics read academic texts, the leaders and adherents of some of the faiths involved are not particularly pleased with scholarship which appears to deny the authenticity and purity of their beliefs and practices (cf. Stewart and Shaw 1994; Palmié 1995).

Conclusion: the words and the world

And that leads to a concluding comment. I began with three keywords of an emergent transnational anthropology, but I have ended up touching on rather more of them, out of the present and the past: acculturation, the frontier, the marginal man, diffusion ... This is a vocabulary which spans the twentieth century and moves into the next, and which also connects continents. At the same time, however, it brings globalization down to earth, and can help show its human face. It suggests that the world is not necessarily becoming all the same. There is struggle but also play. Tricksters thrive in the borderlands.

We need these words ourselves, and more of them, and sometimes new and more exact words, to map the changes. We should also remember old keywords and the past comments on them, to know from where we have come, and to sense if we have moved much forward. But they will not always be only our words; words known only to us. The present world is also one of increasing reflexivity, which for one thing means that lay people, "natives," take note of what scholars say about them, and sometimes speak back.

"Syncretism" is certainly not the only item in the vocabulary exemplified here on which the people somehow or other reported on might have opinions. We had better give some thought to how we relate to this fact. If people do not think of culture as "flowing," or if for that matter they prefer to think of their ways of life and thought as pure, stable, and timeless, it could hardly be that they should be allowed to veto those of our analytical, or at least proto-analytical, notions which suggest otherwise. These latter notions are not necessarily either validated or invalidated by coinciding or not coinciding with ordinary, everyday, "native" usage.

We need to have a sense of which words, and ideas, and interests, are ours, and which are "theirs." But then our vocabulary does not inhabit a separate world of its own either. For following in the steps of Raymond Williams and Pedro Archanjo, each a public intellectual in his own way, in no small part it must be by sharing their keywords with others, and arguing over their implications with these others, that those who make a vocation of the study of culture in an interconnected world can help bring about an informed public scrutiny of that world. There is more work to be done here.

Notes

1 This chapter was first published in Portuguese as "Fluxos, fronteiras, híbridos: palavras-chave da antropologia transnacional", *Mana* (Rio de Janeiro), 3(1): 7–39, 1997. In an earlier version it was presented in an earlier version as a plenary lecture at the twentieth biennial meeting of the Associacao Brasileira de Antropologia at Salvador de Bahia, April 14–17, 1996. I am grateful to the Association for the invitation and for its hospitality during the conference. The paper was written within the framework of the project on "National and Transnational Cultural Processes", based at the Department of Social Anthropology, Stockholm University, and the Department of Ethnology, University of Lund, and supported by the Swedish Research Council for the Humanities and Social Sciences. For publication in this book it has been slightly edited and updated.

2 I am, of course, not the first anthropologist to draw inspiration from Amado; see DaMatta (1982).

3 For one important such effort, see Robertson (1992: 57–60).

4 Vincent (1990: 125), in her history of the anthropological study of politics, has noted that "what was distinctive about diffusionists such as Rivers, Hocart, Wheeler, Perry and Elliot Smith was their uncompromising insistence that anthropology study not only primitive or savage peoples but the whole world, ancient and modern, in its historical complexity." In the collection of papers on the study of culture contact in Africa resulting from 1930s work at the London School of Economics, Malinowski (1938: vii) – the "presiding genius," in the words of the editor, Lucy Mair (1938: v) – noted that

> anthropology, which used to be the study of beings and things retarded, gradual, and backward, is now faced with the difficult task of recording how the "savage" becomes an active participant in modern civilization, how the African and the Asiatic are being rapidly drawn into partnership with the European in world-wide co-operation and conflict.

Much of the American work on acculturation occurred in the period between two major conceptual and theoretical statements, that by Redfield et al. (1936) and that by Broom et al. (1954). For one early and one late critique, see Bateson (1972: 61 ff., first published in 1935) and Murphy (1964).

5 See also for instance the leading urban sociologist Manuel Castells' (1989: 126 ff.) notion of a "space of flows," referring to the handling of information within and between dispersed organizations. Czikszentmihalyi (e.g. 1990) has at the same time popularized a quite different flow concept, referring to the experience of optimally rewarding activity. In anthropology, Victor Turner (e.g. 1982: 55 ff.) has related this latter understanding of flow to communitas and liminality, thus approaching some of our other concerns here – see the discussion of borderlands below.

6 For examples of varied uses, see Watson's (1970) and Vincent's (1977) conception of "society as organized flow," or Adams'(1975: 114 ff.) comments in the context of a discussion of energy. The brief formulation by Mintz and Price (1992: 32 ff.) on the flow of culture in the early formation of African-American culture, within the plantation context, is somewhat reminiscent of Barth's as discussed below, not least in its program of close attention to both culture and social relationships.

7 In an instance of a more elaborated use of the temporal metaphor of flow, Kroeber (1952: 405) also remarks that

> our Dark Ages are not really a reversal, a retracing, of a current of flow. They mark the cessation of flow of one civilization; a consequent slack water and hesitation of confused fluctuating drift; and then the gradual and slowly increasing flow of a new Western civilization – new precisely because the set of its current is in a new direction.

154 Flows, boundaries and hybrids

8 See e.g. Abu-Lughod (1991) and Ingold (1993).

9 Perhaps I may add that Howell (1995: 172), after quoting me in a somewhat jumbled fashion, seems to suggest that I disregard the continued significance of a flow of meaning in face-to-face relationships. Such an interpretation of any of my work is entirely fallacious; see for instance some other pages in that article which Howell quotes in her own way (Hannerz 1991: 113–114).

10 Cohen (e.g., 1986, 1994), another prominent writer on "boundaries," is also concerned primarily with the symbolic demarcation of social identities.

11 More recently, Barth (1995: 65; see also Barth 1994) has commented on current discourses on cultural identity that they

> provide an extremely fertile field for political entrepreneurship; they allow leaders and spokesmen to claim that they are speaking on behalf of others; they allow the manipulation of media access; and they encourage the strategic construction of polarizing debates that translate into battles of influence. Such battles create hegemony and reduce options; they disempower followers and reduce the diversity of voices.

It is interesting to note Verdery's (1994: 56) comment here –

> from the point of view of anthropology in the field of disciplines, a Barthian critique of multiculturalism is risky. To see identity politics as misguided and resting on unacceptably essentialist foundations could serve to marginalize anthropology, as its message is seen to obstruct developments that are backed by powerful forces in the world economy. In an era when disciplinary identities and boundaries (and their associated resources) have become as evanescent as in the most fluid ethnic systems, such marginalization should not be considered lightly.

See also e.g. Terence Turner (1993) on multiculturalism, mostly in the American context, and Stolcke (1995) on cultural fundamentalism in Europe; and Robertson's (1992: 83) comment that the growth of the field of "cultural studies" seems entirely in line with Wallerstein's (1990) view of culture as an ideological battleground of the world system.

12 I would imagine that a view of diffusion (and related cultural processes with a spatial dimension) as cultural acquisition could draw inspiration in different ways for example from Bloch's (e.g. 1992) explorations of connectionist theory, Lave and Wenger (1991) on situated learning, Schudson's (1989) discussion, drawing on media studies, of cultural efficacy, Urban's (1993: 220 ff.) contrast between lateral and vertical culture, or Turner's (1994) critique of the notion of shared practices.

13 Interestingly, Raymond Williams (1985: 177) has a perhaps quite independently invented version of a "100% British" which carries such an antiparochialist message.

14 It is true that not every language allows these distinctions, but in American English the words carry different historical and symbolic loads; and such is its power as a world language that these are often understood elsewhere as well. See also some comments by Cohen (1994: 62–63).

15 See for example Leyburn (1935), Hofstadter and Lipset (1968), Hennessy (1978) and Velho (1979).

16 For a recent discussion focusing rather more on such frontiers, and largely in political terms, see Anderson (1996).

17 Apart from Wolf's mestizo, as another example from the history and ethnography of cultural borderlands, take Christopher Waterman's study of jùjú, a West African popular music emerging in the eras of colonialism and early postcolonialism. Popular cultural styles in Africa, argues Waterman (1990: 8–9), "have rarely trickled down from the Western-educated elites or bubbled up from an autochthonous wellspring";

Flows, boundaries and hybrids **155**

they are more often pioneered by an intermediate, cosmopolitan layer of artisans, laborers, sailors, railway workers, drivers, teachers and clerks. These are the people who are "characteristically adept at interpreting multiple languages, cultural codes, and value systems, skills which enable them to construct styles that express shifting patterns of urban identity." And among them, then, are the musicians – "highly mobile and positioned at important interstices in heterogeneous urban societies, they forge new styles and communities of taste, negotiating cultural differences through the musical manipulation of symbolic associations."

18 For a consideration of the anthropological notion of "islands," see also Eriksen (1993).

19 For a few examples from a generation of writings on marginality, see Stonequist (1937), Green (1947), Riesman (1951) and Golovensky (1952).

20 For attempts at overview of the idea of hybridity, see Nederveen Pieterse (1994), Young (1995) and Papastergiadis (1995); and for a discussion of Bhabha's understanding of hybridity, see Purdom (1995). For a recent critical discussion of the idea of mestizaje, see Klor de Alva (1995). The notion of "third cultures," apparently appearing first in an attempt to conceptualize interactions between expatriate Americans and postcolonial Indians (Useem 1963), has since then appeared with some regularity in the field of intercultural communication studies, and occasionally elsewhere (e.g. Featherstone 1995: 90–91).

21 For some of the discussions of creolization in culture which I have found useful, see e.g. Fabian (1978: 317), Drummond (1980), Jackson (1989) and Barber and Waterman (1995). Hannerz (1987) is reprinted in this volume.

22 Perhaps Mintz (1996: 300–303) would prefer the more limited usage, although I find his argument a little ambivalent. I find quite puzzling his conclusion that "creolization" in its current, not exclusively Caribbeanist, usage somehow refers to "the end of culture," or simply to modernization. At least in my own writings, to which Mintz refers, this is surely not the case.

23 As Mintz (1996: 309) finds my analogy between linguistic and cultural dimensions in creolization at the level of cultural form "insouciant" – as it may be in the sense that the particular passage he quotes is a very general statement – he disregards the central fact that I find much of my inspiration in creolist thought in its attention to the social dimension. This should be clear in earlier writings as well, but I have tried to make it especially clear in Hannerz (1996: 65 ff).

24 For a recent discussion of conceptions of syncretism from a current anthropological perspective, see Droogers (1989).

25 An interesting twist to the debate is contributed by that expansive policy of the Roman Catholic Church which, by way of a concept of "inculturation," favors the indigenization of its eternal, transcendent message through openness to local cultural forms (Angrosino 1994).

References

Abu-Lughod, Lila. 1991. Writing against Culture. In Richard G. Fox (ed.), *Recapturing Anthropology*. Santa Fe, NM: School of American Research Press.

Adams, Richard N. 1975. *Energy and Structure*. Austin, TX: University of Texas Press.

Alvarez, Jr., Robert R. 1995. The Mexican–US Border: The Making of an Anthropology of Borderlands. *Annual Review of Anthropology*, 24: 447–470. Palo Alto, CA: Annual Reviews.

Amado, Jorge. 1971. *Tent of Miracles*. New York, NY: Knopf.

Anderson, Malcolm. 1996. *Frontiers*. Cambridge: Polity.

Angrosino, Michael V. 1994. The Culture Concept and the Mission of the Roman Catholic Church. *American Anthropologist*, 96: 824–832.

156 Flows, boundaries and hybrids

Appadurai, Arjun. 1990. Disjuncture and Difference in the Global Cultural Economy. *Public Culture*, 2 (2): 1–24.

———. 1995. The Production of Locality. In Richard Fardon (ed.), *Counterworks*. London: Routledge.

Bakhtin, Mikhail. 1968. *Rabelais and His World*. Cambridge, MA: MIT Press.

Barber, Karin, and Christopher Waterman. 1995. Traversing the Global and the Local: Fújì Music and Praise Poetry in the Production of Contemporary Yorùbá Popular Culture. In Daniel Miller (ed.), *Worlds Apart*. London: Routledge.

Barth, Fredrik (ed.) 1969. *Ethnic Groups and Boundaries*. Oslo: Universitetsforlaget.

———. 1984. Problems in Conceptualizing Cultural Pluralism, with Illustrations from Somar, Oman. In David Maybury-Lewis (ed.), *The Prospects for Plural Societies*. Washington, DC: American Ethnological Society.

———. 1994. Enduring and Emerging Issues in the Analysis of Ethnicity. In Hans Vermeulen and Cora Govers (eds.), *The Anthropology of Ethnicity*. Amsterdam: Het Spinhuis.

——— (ed.) 1995. Other Knowledge and Other Ways of Knowing. *Journal of Anthropological Research*, 51: 65–68.

Bateson, Gregory. [1935] 1972. *Steps to an Ecology of Mind*. New York, NY: Ballantine.

Bhabha, Homi. 1994. *The Location of Culture*. London: Routledge.

Bloch, Maurice. 1992. What Goes without Saying: The Conceptualization of Zafimaniry Society. In Adam Kuper (ed.), *Conceptualizing Society*. London: Routledge.

Broom, Leonard, Bernard J. Siegel, Evon Z. Vogt, and James B. Watson. 1954. Acculturation: An Exploratory Formulation. *American Anthropologist*, 56: 973–1000.

Castells, Manuel. 1989. *The Informational City*. Oxford: Blackwell.

Cohen, Anthony P. (ed.) 1986. *Symbolising Boundaries*. Manchester: Manchester University Press.

———. 1994. Boundaries of Consciousness, Consciousness of Boundaries: Critical Questions for Anthropology. In Hans Vermeulen and Cora Govers (eds.), *The Anthropology of Ethnicity*. Amsterdam: Het Spinhuis.

Csikszentmihalyi, Mihaly. 1990. *Flow*. New York, NY: Harper & Row.

DaMatta, Roberto. 1982. Dona Flor e seus dois maridos: A Relational Novel. *Social Science Information*, 21: 19–46.

Dening, Greg. 1980. *Islands and Beaches*. Chicago, IL: Dorsey.

Droogers, André. 1989. Syncretism: The Problem of Definition, the Definition of the Problem. In Jerald Gort, Hendrik Vroom, Rein Fernhout, and Anton Wessels (eds.), *Dialogue and Syncretism*. Grand Rapids, MI: Eerdmans.

Drummond, Lee. 1980. The Cultural Continuum: A Theory of Intersystems. *Man*, 15: 352–374.

DuBois, W.E. Burghardt. [1903] 1961. *The Souls of Black Folk*. Greenwich, CT Fawcett.

Eriksen, Thomas Hylland. 1993. In Which Sense Do Cultural Islands Exist? *Social Anthropology*, 1: 133–147.

Fabian, Johannes. 1978. Popular Culture in Africa: Findings and Conjectures. *Africa*, 48: 315–334.

Featherstone, Mike. 1995. *Undoing Culture*. London: Sage.

Freyre, Gilberto. 1946. *The Masters and the Slaves*. New York, NY: Knopf.

———. 1959. *New World in the Tropics*. New York, NY: Knopf.

Golovensky, David I. 1952. The Marginal Man Concept: An Analysis and Critique. *Social Forces*, 30: 333–339.

Green, Arnold W. 1947. A Re-Examination of the Marginal Man Concept. *Social Forces*, 26: 167–171.

Hannerz, Ulf. 1987. The World in Creolisation. *Africa*, 57: 546–559.

———. 1991. Scenarios for Peripheral Cultures. In Anthony D. King (ed.), *Culture, Globalization and the World-System*. London: Macmillan.

———. 1992. *Cultural Complexity*. New York, NY: Columbia University Press.

———. 1996. *Transnational Connections*. London: Routledge.

Hennessy, Alistair. 1978. *The Frontier in Latin American History*. Albuquerque, NM: University of New Mexico Press.

Hofstadter, Richard, and Seymour Martin Lipset (eds.) 1968. *Turner and the Sociology of the Frontier*. New York, NY: Basic Books.

Howell, Signe. 1995. Whose Knowledge and Whose Power? A New Perspective on Cultural Diffusion. In Richard Fardon (ed.), *Counterworks*. London: Routledge.

Ingold, Tim. 1993. The Art of Translation in a Continuous World. In Gísli Pálsson (ed.), *Beyond Boundaries*. London: Berg.

Jackson, Jean. 1989. Is There a Way of Talking about Culture without Making Enemies? *Dialectical Anthropology*, 14: 127–143.

Kearney, Michael. 1991. Borders and Boundaries of State and Self at the End of Empire. *Journal of Historical Sociology*, 4: 52–74.

Klor de Alva, J. Jorge. 1995. The Postcolonization of the (Latin) American Experience: A Reconsideration of "Colonialism," "Postcolonialism," and "Mestizaje". In Gyan Prakash (ed.), *After Colonialism*. Princeton, NJ: Princeton University Press.

Kopytoff, Igor (ed.) 1987. *The African Frontier*. Bloomington, IN: Indiana University Press.

Kroeber, A.L. 1952. *The Nature of Culture*. Chicago, IL: University of Chicago Press.

Lash, Scott, and John Urry 1994. *Economies of Signs and Space*. London: Sage.

Lave, Jean, and Etienne Wenger. 1991. *Situated Learning*. Cambridge: Cambridge University Press.

Leach, Edmund R. 1960. The Frontiers of "Burma". *Comparative Studies in Society and History*, 3: 49–68.

Leyburn, James G. 1935. *Frontier Folkways*. New Haven, CT: Yale University Press.

Linton, Ralph. 1936. *The Study of Man*. New York, NY: Appleton-Century-Crofts.

Lips, Julius. 1937. *The Savage Hits Back*. New Haven, CT: Yale University Press.

Lowie, Robert. 1920. *Primitive Society*. New York, NY: Liveright.

Mair, Lucy P. (ed.) 1938. *Methods of Study of Culture Contact in Africa*. International African Institute, Memorandum XV. London: Oxford University Press.

Maslow, Abraham H., and John J. Honigmann. 1970. Synergy: Some Notes of Ruth Benedict. *American Anthropologist*, 72: 320–333.

Mintz, Sidney W. 1996. Enduring Substances, Trying Theories: The Caribbean Region as *Oikoumenê. Journal of the Royal Anthropological Institute*, 2: 289–311.

———, and Richard Price. 1992. *The Birth of African-American Culture*. Boston, MA: Beacon Press.

Murphy, Robert F. 1964. Social Change and Acculturation. *Transactions of the New York Academy of Sciences*, ser. II, 26: 845–854.

Ortiz, Fernando. 1947. *Cuban Counterpoint*. New York, NY: Knopf.

Palmié, Stephan. 1995. Against Syncretism: "Africanizing" and "Cubanizing" Discourses in North American Òrìsà Worship. In Richard Fardon (ed.), *Counterworks*. London: Routledge.

Papastergiadis, Nikos. 1995. Restless Hybrids. *Third Text*, 32: 9–18.

Park, Robert E. [1928] 1964. *Race and Culture*. New York, NY: Free Press.

Pieterse, Nederveen. Jan. 1994. Globalisation as Hybridisation. *International Sociology*, 9: 161–184.

158 Flows, boundaries and hybrids

Pratt, Mary Louise. 1992. *Imperial Eyes*. London: Routledge.

Purdom, Judy. 1995. Mapping Difference. *Third Text*, 32: 19–32.

Redfield, Robert, Ralph Linton, and Melville J. Herskovits. 1936. Memorandum for the Study of Acculturation. *American Anthropologist*, 38: 149–152.

Riesman, David. 1951. Some Observations Concerning Marginality. *Phylon*, 12: 113–127.

Robertson, Roland. 1992. *Globalization*. London: Sage.

Rosaldo, Renato. 1988. Ideology, Place, and People without Culture. *Cultural Anthropology*, 3: 77–87.

Rushdie, Salman. 1991. *Imaginary Homelands*. London: Granta.

Schudson, Michael. 1989. How Culture Works: Perspectives from Media Studies on the Efficacy of Symbols. *Theory and Society*, 18: 153–180.

Sperber, Dan. 1985. Anthropology and Psychology: Towards an Epidemiology of Representations. *Man*, 20: 73–89.

Stewart, Charles, and Rosalind Shaw (eds.) 1994. *Syncretism/Anti-Syncretism*. London: Routledge.

Stolcke, Verena. 1995. Talking Culture: New Boundaries, New Rhetorics of Exclusion in Europe. *Current Anthropology*, 36: 1–24.

Stonequist, Everett. 1937. *The Marginal Man*. New York, NY: Scribner's.

Strathern, Marilyn. 1995. *The Relation*. Cambridge: Prickly Pear Press.

Turner, Frederick Jackson. [1893] 1961. The Significance of the Frontier in American History. In Ray A. Billington (ed.), *Frontier and Section*. Englewood Cliffs, NJ: Prentice-Hall.

Turner, Stephen. 1994. *The Social Theory of Practices*. Chicago, IL: University of Chicago Press.

Turner, Terence. 1993. Anthropology and Multiculturalism: What Is Anthropology that Multiculturalism Should Be Mindful of It? *Cultural Anthropology*, 8: 411–429.

Turner, Victor. 1974. *Dramas, Fields, and Metaphors*. Ithaca, NY: Cornell University Press.

———. 1982. *From Ritual to Theatre*. New York, NY: Performing Arts Journal Publications.

Urban, Greg. 1993. Culture's Public Face. *Public Culture*, 5: 213–238.

Useem, John. 1963. The Community of Man: A Study in the Third Culture. *Centennial Review*, 7: 481–498.

Velho, Otávio G. 1979. The State and the Frontier. In Neuma Aguiar (ed.), *The Structure of Brazilian Development*. New Brunswick, NJ: Transaction Books.

Verdery, Katherine. 1994. Ethnicity, Nationalism, and State-Making – *Ethnic Groups and Boundaries*: Past and Future. In Hans Vermeulen, and Cora Govers (eds.), *The Anthropology of Ethnicity*. Amsterdam: Het Spinhuis.

Vincent, Joan. 1977. Agrarian Society as Organized Flow: Processes of Development Past and Present. *Peasant Studies*, 6: 56–65.

———. 1990. *Anthropology and Politics*. Tucson, AZ: University of Arizona Press.

Wallerstein, Immanuel. 1990. Culture as the Ideological Battleground of the Modern World-System. In Mike Featherstone (ed.), *Global Culture*. London: Sage.

Waterman, Christopher A. 1990. *Jùjú*. Chicago, IL: University of Chicago Press.

Watson, James B. 1970. Society as Organized Flow: The Tairora Case. *Southwestern Journal of Anthropology*, 26: 107–124.

Williams, Raymond. 1976. *Keywords*. London: Fontana.

———. 1985. *Towards 2000*. Harmondsworth, UK: Penguin.

Wolf, Eric. 1959. *Sons of the Shaking Earth*. Chicago, IL: University of Chicago Press.

Young, Robert J.C. 1995. *Colonial Desire*. London: Routledge.

8

OTHER TRANSNATIONALS

Perspectives gained from studying sideways

In the twentieth century, more people know something about parts of the world further away, or at least have ideas about distant lands and people.[1] For some of them, horizons have widened by way of firsthand experience, but on the whole, this is not some global village where everybody is in direct touch. In very large part, such knowledge or ideas depend on intermediaries. A number of occupations make it their business, centrally or tangentially, to report from some parts of the world to others: missionaries, spies, journalists, the travel industry, the interculturalists of what I have called the culture shock prevention industry ... and, of course, anthropologists.

We are still somewhat inclined to assume that we, as anthropologists, move, and our Others stay put. A favored genre in anthropological studies in the contemporary global ecumene has consequently been that of "the global and the local" – showing how outside, transnational forces reach people in a place, affecting them but, in one recurrent motif, meeting with resistance. Yet there are also those Others who are themselves transnational in their operations, more or less mobile, hardly rootless but themselves multilocal, in large part as an integral part of their occupations (professions, vocations). Globalization at work is indeed often globalization in the work place, and the work place is then often in more than one place.

In a well-known essay from more than twenty years ago, Laura Nader (1972) argued that anthropologists have mostly engaged in studying people less powerful and prosperous than themselves, that is, studying down – now the time had come to study up. What I have in mind here is rather more a question of studying sideways: looking at others who are, like anthropologists, in a transnational contact zone, and engaged there in managing meaning across distances, although perhaps with different interests, under other constraints.[2]

160 Other transnationals

Indeed, I think we have again and again been made somewhat irritatedly aware of the presence of these other kinds of transnational practitioners in our habitat, and of the affinities between their lines of work and ours, even as we frequently dispose of that irritation with a shrug or a sneer. Mostly, it is clear, we have tended not to approach them as allies in the pursuit of knowledge and the enlightenment of publics, but rather we quietly keep our distance, holding our own efforts to be either intellectually or morally superior (or both).[3] Or we may protest vehemently when boundaries are blurred, where identities are mistaken or even brazenly manipulated. At times, strong fences make at least slightly better neighbors. Yet we occasionally also regret that at least some of these others do not seek our advice.

Some of these ambiguous or discordant relationships of ours have already generated bodies of commentary. To take one example, whether visible or hidden away from view in ethnographies, missionaries have been present from the very beginning in the classic field sites of anthropology.[4] Often, ethnographers may have been dependent in large or small ways on missionaries for practical favors, and at times, they may even have conducted their work out of the mission compound. Nonetheless, argues Clifford (1992: 126), within the context of "a restless Western desire for encountering and incorporating others, whether by conversion or comprehension," anthropologists and missionaries have emerged as rivals:

> The social scientist, seen from the missionary's point of view, has little deep concern for the people he or she investigates. A godless person and a moral relativist, the fieldworker is usually a transient. The ethnographer has even harsher opinions of the evangelist, who appears as an enemy of science, ethnocentric, and unscrupulous in fomenting cultural chaos for the sake of questionable religious alterations.

All the same, a fair number of missionaries have been, or have become, anthropologists – Clifford's remarks are in his biography of Maurice Leenhardt, who left his pastoral work in Melanesia to succeed Marcel Mauss at the Ecole Pratique des Hautes Etudes (and to be in turn succeeded in the same chair by Claude Lévi-Strauss).

Or for another example, take spies. Probably, they are less often really present in the locations where anthropologists are at work. But in the postcolonial and cold war era, at least, it is no small number of anthropologists whose tales from the field have included suspicions and allegations, fleetingly or with more serious consequences, that they have themselves engaged in espionage. In the history of American anthropology, too, major controversies over the relationship between anthropology and intelligence work have arisen at least twice: in 1919, when Franz Boas, in a letter to *The Nation*, accused certain anthropologists working in Central America of having "prostituted science by using it as a cover for their activities as spies" for the United States government, and half a century later, when Eric Wolf and Joseph Jorgensen (1970), in *The New York Review of Books*, found "Anthropology on the Warpath in Thailand."[5] And at other times, it seems, after returning from field work in foreign lands, anthropologists have heard from the intelligence services of their own countries, expressing an interest in debriefing them.

Others, and others' others

What, then, might we get out of attending more closely to the work of these particular other workers in the transnational contact zones? Certainly they are important enough to learn something about, and reflect on. Again, they have more or less important parts in creating the global and transnational as a meaningful space. They form a part of what would be, in C. Wright Mills' (1963: 405 ff.) useful term, the transnational "cultural apparatus." And as the particular kinds of knowledge and images they can offer are evidently in demand somewhere, they indicate the organizing of knowledge of the world in terms of an array of different interests, different interpretive communities.

Another outcome of looking at missionaries, spies, journalists and others of those I just mentioned, however, is that it may sharpen our sense of our own practices, and our own moral and intellectual assumptions – they may be good to think with, about ourselves and our own work (even if, as is perhaps especially likely in the case of spies, we may never really get around to doing the ethnography). It is not simply that we can take them as "Others." Like us, they are engaged in othering. Moreover, somewhat complicatedly so: for as intermediaries, they are typically depicting one Other to anOther. Contrasting what they do with what we do ourselves, then (seriously or maybe at times facetiously), we may better understand what are the characteristics of each instance. We can inspect a series of different Others, emerging under different conditions of construction and for different purposes.

In recent times, anthropologists have been more given to self-scrutiny. The following, I think, are some features we tend to see, or would like to see, in the mirror. We are inclined to think about our relationships to those whom we describe as preferably consensual and harmonious, and there is some inclination now to think of ethnography as a collaborative enterprise between us and the locals. While we may be aware of the difficulties inherent in the idea, we probably still want to try to grasp "the native's point of view." And we would claim – despite the missionaries' opinion of us as transients, as suggested by Clifford in the quote above – that we are willing to take our time in trying to get it, and our other facts, right. A year or more in a field is considered normal, and if one of us stays there much longer, or returns again and again, it is more likely to be considered heroic than a sign of stupidity. We have become increasingly self-conscious about the fact that we have been doing our reporting on others mostly in writing, with its own stylistic devices but also with the attendant problems of trying to render in written language that whole range of experiences we have through all our senses (some of which we may simply have been to apt to disregard).[6]

162 Other transnationals

Remarkably, we are largely our own audience. Our stories about the Other we tell mostly to one another. There is a familiar ethical problem in this itself – should we not try harder to get out of the ivory tower, pass on our knowledge, even make more of it practically useful? But on the other hand, we are also likely to become ethically concerned about taking that knowledge to the outside, in ways which may harm the people we write about, making them individually or collectively vulnerable, allowing others to manipulate or dominate them.

In principle, we allow ourselves to concern ourselves with anything social and/or cultural. Yet the bias may have been toward emphasizing precisely what is otherness and difference – a bias which at present some among us also find worrisome.[7]

There are some themes here, and a quick glance at the different groups of othering others allows us to discern variations on these themes; looking sideways, we find ourselves in a hall of mirrors. Recently I have begun taking a particular interest in one of these groups – that of journalists, specifically foreign correspondents. I will have more to say about them below, but for a few quick thumbnail sketches of some of the range of variations, allow me simply to draw in large part on our stock of common knowledge, unreliable and given to stereotyping or even caricature as it may be.

The main thing about spies, from our point of view, would seem to be their involvement in adversary relationships, and consequently in secrecy; very unlike the relationships anthropologists idealize. The Other is the enemy, but usually cannot be treated as such to his face. The information spies seek is not freely and willingly given, but must be won through theft, false pretenses, or through cooperation with renegades. Spies have a special place among the practitioners we discuss here in that they may claim the identity of at least some of the others, but none of the others will claim theirs – that is, nobody who is really a missionary or an anthropologist will pretend to be a spy. (Of course, there are also some people who function as spies more or less openly, such as some officials in diplomatic service.) The information gathered by the spy focuses on strengths and weaknesses relevant to the adversary relationship, and it is made available to very restricted circles of recipients. Usually the information flow in which spies engage is highly asymmetrical, except in the case of double agents.

Indeed, spies may often be rather marginal to our concerns here. Much of the time, they are seeking out technical data, rather than doing any depiction of the thought and conduct of any human Other. Yet as these instances suggest where the borderline between anthropology and espionage has seemed to risk being blurred, there are times when social structures, values and beliefs become topics of intelligence work. The 1940s efforts by Margaret Mead, Ruth Benedict and others at "studying culture at a distance" were linked to the United States war effort, and the post-war political situation emerging soon after (Mead and Métraux 1953). Richelson (1995: 205), in his chronicle of twentieth century espionage, notes of this period that "anthropologists studied Japanese films."

Turning to missionaries, one may argue that their main task, strictly speaking, is not reporting about other people, across the surface of the earth, either. Their vocation is centrally a different one. But vertical and horizontal messages become somewhat difficult to disentangle, insofar as heaven may borrow some of the features of home. Villagers in Papua New Guinea, notes Kulick (1992: 22), see lands such as *Indonesia, Saina, Pilipin, Soutamerika, Rusia, Aprika* and *Urop* strung out in a line outwards from themselves, and ending in Belgium, which is the *namba wan kantri* – at least that is the impression they received from their Belgian missionary. On the other hand, there will be some traffic in images of the Other in the opposite direction as well, as missionaries report back to where they came from, not least to their supporting congregations at home.[8] More two-way flow, then, than among spies or anthropologists.

The context of the missionary representations of otherness would seem to be not so much one of conflict as of hope: of conversion, actual or potential. It may therefore have a before-and-after quality: greater difference between "us" and "them" before, more resemblance, unity and human fellowship afterwards. And the topics of reporting may be especially those where changes are to occur through conversion: beliefs, ritual practices, forms of family life. Or more generally, well-being and uplift.

Of the interculturalists there have been a rapidly increasing number in recent years.[9] They may occasionally praise cultural diversity in general terms, but they are really rather more in the business as problem-solving technicians, involved in the piecemeal cultural engineering of encounters with the Other. On the one hand, this may lead them to try and identify particular friction points in these encounters, such as in body language, or concepts of time, or the ritual micro-politics of politeness. On the other hand, they may just try to increase general sensitivity to the possibility of difference, without even describing any particular culture at all (apart from, implicitly at least, the client's own). As a relatively recently begun professionalization process continues, the interculturalists are gradually forming a community with an internal structure, but in large part, they engage with their outside clients, in fairly short-term relationships, through courses, lectures, and consultancies. And their clients are typically people who are, or will be, directly engaged in contacts with otherness, through transnational business, development work, or counseling transnational migrants. Whatever time it may have taken them to acquire their understandings of cultural difference themselves, the interculturalists take it upon themselves to impart such knowledge to their audiences quite quickly. They describe the Others and how to deal with them in large part through videos, diagrams, checklists, and simulation games. Writing prose is rather less important.

Anthropologists, it appears, often find the interculturalists superficial – if not in their own knowledge, at least in the way they communicate it to clients. In another way, the anthropologists and the interculturalists might have something in common: the tendency to emphasize cultural diversity. Roland Robertson (1992: 172), who sees the emergence of the interculturalist profession as an aspect of recent globalization, suggests that its representatives "have a vested

164   Other transnationals

professional interest in accentuating difference, at least in the middle run; for if there occurs an attenuation of the perception of difference their *raison d'être* is in doubt." Yet perhaps they are in the end more like the missionaries, insofar as there is again the before-and-after conception of their practical activity. They try actively to deal with, and get beyond, difference.

Primarily, the travel industry is in the business of selling transportation and accommodation, and the depiction of distant places and peoples is incidental to this purpose. More than most of the lines of work considered here, the travel industry tries to reach out to a very wide audience (although it has a developed sense of the latter's internal differentiation). The built-in bias in its imagery is toward the experience of pleasure. It may be that people do not always figure prominently here, compared to beaches or famous buildings. Where an Other is present, however, there is a qualified emphasis on enjoyable difference; readily accessible, more or less on show, no unsettling culture shock. You are not advised to go and see your interculturalist before you embark on your trip. The travel industry is inclined toward evocative imagery. Not too much wordage, many pictures, some music, "the sights and sounds of ..." At times, the travel industry does not only depict the Other, but actively recruits and trains natives to conform to tourist expectations of pleasurable diversity. If there are no crafts which can be turned into souvenirs, no local cuisine, no folk dances, they may have to be invented.[10]

Otherness in the news: routines and emphases

I have one group of practitioners left, the foreign correspondents; those with whom I have recently been more directly concerned.[11] They are, of course, an internally diverse group. They are of many nationalities, although certainly more from the West than from the rest. They work for newspapers, agencies, radio and television, and for publications of varying periodicity. And they report to quite different publics. Let me just note that I cannot go into all the implications of this diversity here.

Are there particular consistent biases in these newspeople's depictions of their Others as well? How do the foreign correspondents relate to the people on whom they report, do their characteristic working conditions in any way shape their constructs? Certainly they might be reluctant to see anything resembling the tendencies I have suggested above with regard to other transnational lines of work. Their others are not necessarily enemies, or heathens to be saved, or interesting only if exotic. In news work, it is sometimes said, there is a "cult of objectivity." If anything, people are whatever they are that makes them newsworthy.

This simple conclusion, however, may point toward certain lines of further inquiry. I will briefly pursue a couple of them, in a comparison of what newspeople and anthropologists do. One of them relates to the time dimension of work; the other has to do with what kinds of events, activities and conditions are more likely to translate into news. When they run into people like anthropologists, foreign correspondents are quick to point to the difference between the hurried pace of their own work and the leisurely publication schedule of the academics. They are concerned with events, datelines and deadlines. Another bias of foreign newswork is that it is in considerable part concerned with trouble: war, coups, disasters. Where other people may be more inclined to try to flee, foreign correspondents are trying hard to get in. How, then, might these peculiarities affect the handling of otherness?

In some ways, the practice of foreign correspondence may rather point away from any more intense concern with, or celebration of, difference. Much of the reporting, to begin with, is from areas of the social landscape where transnational cultural similarities are considerable, due to a global diffusion of institutional forms. Political reporting, not least, involves elites and structures of a modern sector where it may at least appear that little cultural translation is required.

Yet even as they leave that modern sector, foreign correspondents, especially as they operate under great time pressure, may apply rules of thumb which allow limited room for the culturally alien. Gaye Tuchman (1973), an American sociologist, has identified "routinizing the unexpected" as a major aspect of newswork, and while her ethnographic study was concerned largely with American domestic journalism, it would seem that in some ways, that principle also extends to foreign news coverage.

"Every story is a local story," the international editor of one New York newspaper (himself a former Asia correspondent) said to me. And as he interpreted the point, it meant that stories in the same genre would be basically like each other anywhere. A fire is a fire, a murder is a murder, an industrial accident is an industrial accident. At his paper and many others, foreign correspondents would primarily be people who had served their apprenticeship on local beats, at that paper, or a small-town paper, or a suburban paper. And so when they arrived in a strange environment on some other continent (even as "parachutists," a term they would sometimes use to emphasize their most hurried movements and styles of practice), with perhaps a few hours to get together their story, they knew habitually what should be the routine even in what for them was a very non-routine place – what categories of information to include, what kinds of sources to look up. No doubt, under the circumstances, the availability of such frames could be what made reporting possible at all. You may be in a state of stress or even shock, but the good journalist should still be able to follow established procedure. The former Asia correspondent had been beaten up by police in India, and had on another occasion arrived at a scene of mass murder in that country, seeing the corpses, then going on to interview the people who were obviously the killers. There were stories, he said, which emotionally he would find it difficult to talk about, even much later, but he had been able to write about them.

From the comfortable position of the academic second-guessing commentator, we could speculate about what might be left out when this kind of "every story a local story" approach guides correspondent work. Perhaps much of what is really locally specific, culturally different? Yet it should be said that the "routinization of the unexpected" need not work in only this way. A book by another correspondent, about another contemporary news beat, complicates the picture. The Jerusalem-based radio reporter Jim Lederman's book *Battlelines: The American Media and the*

166 Other transnationals

Intifada (1993) is a remarkably revealing critical scrutiny of newspeople's practices and working conditions. For one thing, Lederman draws attention to the continuous importance of that construct described as a "story line."

The Palestinian *intifada*, Lederman argues, took the foreign correspondents covering Israel and the occupied territories by surprise. And this was in large part because they were stuck with a story line which did not alert them to the kind of situation that had been developing in Gaza and on the West Bank. A story line, says Lederman (1993: 12), is what gives reporting its sense of continuity:

> The story line is a frame into which a journalist can place seemingly random events and give them coherence. It simplifies the narrative thread, reducing it to manageable dimensions by using a single overarching theme so that each dramatic incident can be highlighted as it occurs and each "chapter" of the ongoing story can be slotted in easily and given a context.

The story line with respect to the occupied territories, and Israeli-Arab conflict generally, had long been "violent conflict over possession of land." It had worked well enough for a long time. Many kinds of stories could be hooked onto it. A report on Christmas in Bethlehem would emphasize security issues rather than the religious experience; or you could write about higher education, turning soon enough to the fact that students would go off on reserve army duty now and then. The trouble is that an entrenched story line stops people from noticing things that do not fit. When the *intifada* began, claims Lederman (1993: 6) in a formulation which will no doubt strike anthropologists as dramatic, "in only a few days, the social structure of Gaza had changed beyond recognition." And the reason was that a generational conflict had been building up within the occupied territories which reporting along the story line had disregarded.

What might be the more general implications of such a notion of story lines for an understanding of foreign correspondence? To begin with, we could note that story lines would seem to work in a somewhat different direction from that routinization procedure we identified before – "a fire is a fire, a murder is a murder …" A story line could allow a bit more attention to the peculiarity of that place, and yet also be of help in simplifying work. But then again it is also a routinization procedure, and it constrains at the same time as it supports. In fact, it shows some affinity with what have become identified in anthropology as "gatekeeping concepts": concepts that "limit anthropological theorizing about the place in question, and that define the quintessential and dominant questions of interest in the region" (Appadurai 1986: 357) – be they caste in India, honor and shame around the Mediterranean, or filial piety in China. To put it differently, story lines may construct somewhat one-dimensional Others.

The other peculiarity of foreign news work which I identified above is that correspondents are often, as I have described it elsewhere, "on the trouble trail" (Hannerz 1996: 117). The first reaction to this fact on the part of anthropologists may well be that journalists will get, and pass on to their audiences, a somewhat

Other transnationals **167**

peculiar view of the human condition, if they mostly show up at times of wars, upheavals, and disasters, and are already long gone when things begin to return to normal. Possibly we should be a little wary of this reaction, as it may just be that we exhibit the opposite bias here, presenting mostly views of peace and stability in varied localities. These are the conditions we have tended to prefer for field work, and perhaps we have tended to underestimate tendencies toward conflict and violence as historically recurrent aspects of social life in some regions once they are not under the *Pax Britannica*, or the *Pax Sovietica*.

Another aspect of the focus on trouble could be that it is particularly in the crisis situations that ordinary people become newsworthy; but then often as victims. It may be that one consequence of the relentless portrayal of disasters, wars and revolutions in the media is that the ordinary consumer comes to understand the world as a dangerous place. Yet as I have argued elsewhere, especially in television news, there can also be a sense of direct encounters with the faces and bodies of people far away (Hannerz 1996: 121). In a very special kind of representation of the Other, the sight of starving children, or of the suffering after a bombing, just possibly brings about a kind of "electronic empathy," a view where notions of shared human nature may weigh more heavily than ideas of cultural difference.[12]

Earthquake in Kobe

Yet rather than speaking only in general terms of tendencies, and dwelling mostly on what are likely to be differences in the ways anthropologists and foreign correspondents describe the world, let us also look at one particular instance of foreign news coverage. I want to dwell for a moment on one set of stories, published in January and February, 1995, in the *New York Times*. And here we will perhaps discern that if there are important differences, one may at times find convergences as well between anthropologists' and newspeople's reporting.

The earthquake struck Kobe, one of Japan's commercial and industrial centers, with one of the busiest ports in the world, in the early morning of January 17, 1995. More than five thousand people died, there was major physical destruction, and life in the city was severely disrupted. It was the kind of event foreign correspondents flock to. By my count, the *New York Times* had at least six journalists reporting on it from Japan (mostly from Kobe, but since it could not quite be considered only a local story, from Tokyo as well), apart from drawing to some rather minor extent on news agency coverage. There were also related articles from elsewhere, such as on the Japanese bookstore in Manhattan which came to function as a disaster information center for the Japanese in New York itself. My very rough estimate would be that in quantitative terms, the entire *New York Times* coverage of the earthquake and its aftermath, over a period of several weeks, would have equalled a small book-length ethnography.

While most foreign journalists probably came to Kobe as quickly as they could after the earthquake and left quite soon afterwards, the main *New York Times* correspondent in Japan, Nicholas D. Kristof, continued reporting from

168 Other transnationals

there into the middle of February. Kristof has been in Asia for this newspaper since 1986, based previously in Hong Kong and Beijing.[13] In the early days of reporting from Kobe, the physical facts of death and destruction dominated. In a front-page story on January 22, we encounter a survivor:

> It's not the thousands of deaths that trouble her most, or the loss of her home, or the paralyzing fear of the ground swaying again. It's the screams.
>
> The veterinarian around the corner was pinned in his house after it collapsed in the earthquake, but he shouted that he was all right. And so Shizuko Hirajima shouted back and told him he would be okay, and she worked frantically to rescue other neighbors who seemed to be in greater need. When the fire erupted, there was not enough time to go back and dig the vet out of his home, so they stood at the edge of the blistering heat and listened as he burned to death.
>
> "We could hear him call out," she said, shivering, "'Help me,' he shouted. 'Help me.' But we couldn't do a thing. We just had to stand there."
>
> *(Kristof 1995a)*

And further into the same article:

> The eeriest time to be in Kobe is at night, when the back alleys are dark and silent and the only sound is endless sirens in the distance. The alleys are strewn with bricks and beams, and here and there a building leans so far over that it is difficult to squeeze by it. On the sides are the hulking shadows of abandoned, damaged houses, and the open spaces where homes collapsed into piles of debris – some of which still contain bodies, or even perhaps a person still alive but now struggling at the limits of endurance.

As time passed, however, the reporting gradually changed character. In a "Week in Review" article on the same day, named "Japan's Nature: A People Tremble in Harmony with the Land," Kristof began with a quick portrait of what kind of place Kobe had been – "with its neon lights and heated toilet seats and cellular faxes, the great trading city of Kobe a week ago seemed a citadel of modernity and affluence and internationalism, an antipodean New York with more sushi" – but went on to spell out what, it became increasingly clear, was a continuing assumption underlying his reporting, and to a degree that of other *New York Times* correspondents in Kobe:

> It is of course risky to generalize too much about differences in foreign cultures. A century ago one of the first Japanese to travel to the United States wrote back, "In America, unmarried women are called Jones, and married women are called Johnson."
>
> Yet differences can be real, and sometimes the way people or nations react to disasters can open a window on their souls. The catastrophe in

western Japan, and its orderly aftermath, with hardly a looter to be found, may offer some insights into life and society in Japan.

To a degree, then, Kristof's writings from Kobe could be viewed as a rapid ethnography of a city and a nation, their culture and social relationships, as seen through a physical disaster.

Japan, he remarks, sometimes seems torn between two perceptions of itself; on the one hand as an "irepressible, unstoppable powerhouse, whose secret weapon is its own special characteristics," and on the other hand as "the poor island archipelago with few natural resources ... always living on the edge of one disaster or another." As Japan holds a mirror to itself after the earthquake, it is the second image that appears again. "One of the phrases the Japanese have used in describing themselves is 'gaman,' a term that has no equivalent in English but that roughly means a kind of stoical perseverence." Kristof notes the old contrast between guilt-based and shame-based societies, comments that the theory can be taken too far, yet points to the possibility that "this sense of personal honor and dignity, and fear of being shamed, may be one reason why the Japanese in Kobe are ideal disaster victims." In another article, by Sheryl WuDunn, also a *New York Times* correspondent (and Kristof's wife), we get some "studying up," relating to the allegedly slow response of the Japanese government to the catastrophe. A political science professor at Tokyo University is quoted as explaining that this shows a weakness in the Japanese political system; the consensus style of management became unworkable as communication lines between bureaucracies and ministries broke down, and officials seemed reluctant to act decisively on their own. And Kristof reports, on February 5, that whereas normally "it is Western businessmen who gripe about bureaucratic stonewalling as they try to penetrate the Japanese market," after the earthquake, Japanese officials seem to have been just as unwilling to accept foreign disaster assistance, arguing for example that the medical supplies offered might not be appropriate for Japanese bodies. Yet back at the grassroots again, with Kristof, we find order and generalized reciprocity. Rumors of looting turn out to be almost always only rumors, and in the one case when a store clerk actually claims to have seen looters, he asserts that they were foreigners (Kristof 1995a). Generosity, however, can be troublesome as well:

> Narumi Nakagawa has plenty of problems, like a house that collapsed in last week's earthquake, but as she sits on a futon in a refugee shelter, she is fretting about another painful quandary.
>
> Friends have brought her so many apples and rice balls and other gifts that she can never get through them all. That creates a risk of an aftershock of terrible embarrassment: what if a friend returned and found a gift moldering in a corner?
>
> *(Kristof 1995d)*

About a week or so after the catastrophe, the army set up tents containing public baths, and these, Kristof (1995e) notes, "in a nation where cleanliness is

170 Other transnationals

almost a fetish and drug stores sell disposable underwear," were greeted with much satisfaction:

> "I'm so excited I can have a real bath now," said Toshika Hakenaka, a 66-year old woman who stumbled across the army-established baths this afternoon. "I've been cleaning myself with wet tissues, but now I can have a real bath. I'm going to dash home and get my friends and get some clean underwear, and then I'll be back."

And thus we get a view of the Kobe disaster as refracted through the experiences of the homeless, the shop attendants, the mail carriers who cannot deliver the mail, the undertakers, the visitors to the temporary bath houses, and the woman who heard a neighbor die. Kristof and his colleagues draw our attention, as well, to the diversity and inequalities of contemporary Japanese society. In a wealthy neighborhood in the hills above Kobe, a surgeon's wife sees little damage to her home, although some porcelain was broken and an aquarium tipped over. It is mostly the older wooden houses down below, with heavy tile roofs, that have been destroyed, and their inhabitants are mostly among the (by Japanese standards) relatively poor (Kristof 1995f). A gritty industrial ward, inhabited in large part by Koreans and the discriminated minority of burakumin, suffered among the worst damage and worst fires, reports Kristof's colleague James Sterngold (1995a), who also notes that a yakuza (gangster) syndicate, the Yamaguchi-gumi, is offering free food, water and diapers to earthquake victims in its turf (Sterngold 1995b). But unlike in the great earthquake in Tokyo in 1923, after which thousands of Koreans were killed in riots, there has been no real tension between Koreans and Japanese in Kobe in 1995. And in Kobe's Chinatown, its modern brick buildings not much damaged, business is thriving (Kristof 1995g). Meanwhile, some 40 miles away in ancient Kyoto, there is also some worry about what Kobe's troubles will do to particular local enterprises.

> "We're very concerned," said Miss Takada, 17, a maiko, or apprentice geisha. "The earthquake was on the 17th, and that night all of our banquets were canceled. We had many customers in Kobe, so we're very alarmed about our business. I hear there are lots of cancellations, and I wonder what will happen."
>
> Miss Takada paused and delicately adjusted her red and purple silk kimono, and a hint of anxiety showed through the layers of white makeup on her face.
>
> *(Kristof 1995h)*

Geishas and looting

What sort of Japanese Other is constituted in the *New York Times* coverage from Kobe? How does it compare to what we may tend to do as anthropologists? What constraints, assumptions and values can we at least guess at (and one could surely get further, by talking to Kristof and his colleagues) behind the reporting?

Other transnationals **171**

The Japanese, to begin with, are more than an abstract collectivity here. Shizuko Hirajima mourning her neighbor, the veterinarian; Narumi Nakagawa, embarrassed by too many gifts; Toshika Hakenaka, who cannot wait to get into the bath; and Miss Takada, the apprentice geisha – all real people. Encountering them, hearing their voices however briefly, may resonate with the current desire in anthropology to portray individual fates, and let cultures, if there are such entities, be represented by polyphonies.

There is also, in Kristof's reporting and that of many of his colleagues, an openness to a wider range of senses and feelings. The eery walk through night-time Kobe, Miss Takada with anxiety showing through the makeup as she adjusts her kimono – this is again the kind of detail about self and other which some anthropologists now complain has tended to be left out of a too sanitized, scientizing ethnography. There is yet more of it in the brief portrayal of Mrs. Hirajima, the veterinarian's neighbor:

> ...she is dealing with the screams that haunt her by going deaf; she has lost much of her hearing since the quake struck on Tuesday. The veterinarian's shouts no longer echo in her head, but she cannot hear much else, either.
>
> The reaction of Mrs. Hirajima, a graying woman of 61 years who wrings her hands endlessly, is unusual ...
>
> *(Kristof 1995a)*

Even so, the attention to individuals in the Kobe coverage may not be quite of the kind anthropologists have in mind. Mostly, it seems to me, these vignettes and voices do not serve to give a view of variations within structures, because the structures hardly come into view themselves. They are rather stylistic devices, livening up stories, suggesting immediacy and presence, and beyond that a means of persuading the reader that common humanity can be recognized across great distances. Anxiety, coquetry, happiness, pride: all appear visible by way of small but unmistakable signs.

Kristof, however, is otherwise hardly inclined to avoid showing how Japan is different. Perhaps a Japan specialist would see other things in the *New York Times* reporting from Kobe than I do, but the mix of topics in the articles reminds me at least of what seem to be recurrent themes in the anthropological study of Japan, with a somewhat similar balance between unity and diversity. On the one hand the concern with honor, dignity and appearance, the orderli-ness of social life, the somewhat decentered, fluid nature of Japanese govern-ment; on the other hand the problematic presence of outsiders (burakumin, Koreans and Chinese).

On the whole, my sense is that Kristof's Kobe reporting has rather stronger affinities with ethnographic writing than much foreign correspondence does, even as differences are also apparent. There may be several reasons why it has worked out this way. One is perhaps that over the somewhat extended period of reporting, time constraints came to matter somewhat less. It is true that

172 Other transnationals

Kristof and colleagues filed a great many stories, day after day after day, but the fact that they could go on doing so for some time allowed them to pursue more angles according to their own choice. Apart from that, not least Kristof himself obviously came to the task with a grasp of things Japanese, past and present, which a more or less parachutist correspondent would most likely not have had.

The fact that the *New York Times* gave so much space over several weeks to the Kobe earthquake and its consequences is of course also noteworthy. One background fact is certainly this publication's claim to an intellectual niche as a paper for the "informed citizen," and a paper of more general coverage. Other papers halted their coverage earlier, a more specialized paper such as the *Wall Street Journal* concentrated more of its Kobe reporting on the implications of the disaster for business.

At the same time, the coverage undoubtedly had much to do with the special place of Japan in the contemporary American view of the world. It was not only that Kobe was a strategic site in the world economy. At least as importantly, the country was recognized as a place of sometimes admirable, sometimes irritating otherness, a place which it was always relevant to compare to the United States. The orderliness and the lack of looting contrasted with recent disasters and unrest in American cities. To those who had long been hearing of, or directly experiencing, the difficulties of breaking into Japanese markets, it may have brought some consolation, or amusement, that even gifts to disaster victims seemed to be set on obstacle courses. And a detour to Kyoto, to get a geisha's point of view, would seem to be a sure way to dramatize the Japaneseness of an event.

Conclusion: crises, changes, opportunities

The occupations within the transnational cultural apparatus have varying reach, and in combination they will give a fragmented and contradictory view of the world. Some pious people may yet get their ideas about distant lands mostly from the missionaries; some get theirs from a combination of newspapers, television news, and travel agencies; rather few from us anthropologists; a restricted circle have spies added to their other sources. Combinations shift, horizons vary. Some thus become "the man (or woman) in the street," others informed citizens, others again specialists.

Are we all getting ever more world-wise, better informed, as globalization proceeds? One would perhaps think so, but looking sideways at the other transnationals, one may discern a rather more complicated state of flux. Certain of these lines of work may be in decline, others may be in a phase of mushrooming growth, others again are perhaps undergoing restructuring.

"Maybe I'm like a monk in the age of Gutenberg," said one of the correspondents I have talked to; "I just like to write." Foreign correspondents, particularly those of the print media, and not least the Americans, feel that they live through uncertain times. The news business is a business, and keeping correspondents abroad is expensive. When the management wants to cut costs, foreign news coverage may lose out.

Other transnationals **173**

There is the major factor of communication technology. Television works faster than the print media, and as film footage comes in from almost everywhere, one need only add a local voice. If one wants a reporter of one's own where a major story is on, one may fly out an anchorperson with a familiar face, who by his presence defines the importance of the event, even if his knowledge of it is not exactly deep. For American correspondents especially, too, reporting to a public with a somewhat limited tolerance for foreign news, the end of the Cold War has meant the loss of a major framing device, a global story line. It used to be that the first question about any Other was whether he was "theirs" or "ours" – "now how do you get people interested in the Hutu and the Tutsi?"

Foreign correspondents, then, may be going through a crisis period. Or at least the craft seems to need some rethinking, within a changing division of labor. One might think missionaries, forerunners in the transnational contact zone, would now be in a declining occupation, but some of their organizations seem to be turning into successful transnational NGOs, with new niches where state apparatuses are weak. After the Cold War, again, spies may be retooling; or perhaps more exactly, old spies retire, and new kinds of intelligence work emerge. The travel industry seems to do well enough, and interculturalists, almost non-existent as a group only a couple of decades ago, are apparently multiplying fast. Perhaps some new light can be cast on the changes, and the crises, and the new opportunities, in our anthropological enterprise by setting them in the context of those shifting conditions for other transnationals?

Notes

1 This chapter was first published in *Paideuma* (Frankfurt am Main), 44: 109–123, 1998, after being presented at the conference on "The Question of the Other in Anthropology," Jagdschloss Niederwald, Rüdesheim am Rhein, April 30–May 5, 1995. I am grateful to the conference organizers, Professor Karl-Heinz Kohl and Professor Tullio Maranhao, and to other participants for their comments. The paper was written in the framework of the project on "National and Transnational Cultural Processes," based at the Department of Social Anthropology, Stockholm University, and the Department of Ethnology, University of Lund, and supported by the Swedish Research Council for the Humanities and Social Sciences. For my earlier work in the project, some of it directly relevant to the present paper, see especially Hannerz (1996).

2 I should perhaps point out that this "sideways" is not, as in Nader's case, a matter of power but rather of a similarity in task. See also Hannerz (1993).

3 Cf. Pratt (1986: 27), commenting on a remark by Malinowski:

> The statement is symptomatic of a well-established habit among ethnographers of defining ethnographic writing over and against older, less specialized genres, such as travel books, personal memoirs, journalism, and accounts by missionaries, settlers, colonial officials, and the like. Although it will not supplant these genres altogether, professional ethnography, it is understood, will usurp their authority and correct their abuses.

4 On anthropologists and missionaries, see also for example Johansson (1992), Stipe (1980), and Van der Geest (1990).

5 Boas was censured by the American Anthropological Association for the letter to *The Nation*; for an account of the affair, see Stocking (1982: 273 ff.).

174 Other transnationals

6 On such matters, see for example Bloch (1992) and Stoller (1989).
7 See for example Keesing (1989), Abu-Lughod (1991) and Wikan (1992); and for some comment, Hannerz (1996: 30 ff.).
8 See for example Comaroff and Comaroff (1992: 35) on the writings of South African evangelists in an earlier period, with their awareness of audiences:

> They differed a good deal in their intent and formality: The ambiguities, agonies, and self-doubts aired in letters to kin were not exposed to morally vigilant mission overseers, for example; nor to philanthropists, who were more responsive to evocative accounts of savagery; nor to the churchgoing masses, with their strong taste for Christian heroics.

9 My understanding of the practices of the interculturalists has benefited greatly from the work of Tommy Dahlén, of the Department of Social Anthropology, Stockholm University, who has recently published a study of this transnational occupational community (Dahlén 1997).
10 The Swedish ethnologist Orvar Löfgren's (1999) studies of the travel industry deal with such tendencies.
11 What follows draws mostly on a series of interviews with American journalists, resident in New York, about their experiences as foreign correspondents, and attention to news coverage in the media. I have also found the many autobiographies by foreign correspondents quite useful (cf. Hannerz 1996: 112 ff.).
12 This might be the more optimistic view of what media can do; for a more sceptical diagnosis, see Kleinman and Kleinman (1996).
13 See on this Kristof and WuDunn (1994).

References

Abu-Lughod, Lila. 1991. Writing against Culture. In Richard G. Fox (ed.), *Recapturing Anthropology*. Santa Fe, NM: School of American Research Press.

Appadurai, Arjun. 1986. Theory in Anthropology: Center and Periphery. *Comparative Studies in Society and History*, 28: 356–361.

Bloch, Maurice. 1992. What Goes without Saying: The Conceptualization of Zafimaniry Society. In Adam Kuper (ed.), *Conceptualizing Society*. London: Routledge.

Clifford, James. 1992. *Person and Myth*. Durham, NC: Duke University Press.

Comaroff, John, and Jean Comaroff. 1992. *Ethnography and the Historical Imagination*. Boulder, CO: Westview.

Dahlén, Tommy. 1997. *Among the Interculturalists*. Stockholm Studies in Social Anthropology, 38. Stockholm: Almqvist & Wiksell International.

Hannerz, Ulf. 1993. Mediations in the Global Ecumene. In Gísli Pálsson (ed.), *Beyond Boundaries*. London: Berg.

———. 1996. *Transnational Connections*. London: Routledge.

Johansson, Göran. 1992. *More Blessed to Give*. Stockholm Studies in Social Anthropology, 30. Stockholm: Almqvist & Wiksell International.

Keesing, Roger M. 1989. Exotic Readings of Cultural Texts. *Current Anthropology*, 30: 459–479.

Kleinman, Arthur, and Joan Kleinman. 1996. The Appeal of Experience; The Dismay of Images: Cultural Appropriations of Suffering in Our Times. *Daedalus*, 125: 1–23.

Kristof, Nicholas D. 1995a. Kobe's Survivors Try to Adjust: Hand-Wringing, Relief, Laughter. *New York Times*, January 22.

Other transnationals **175**

————. 1995b. Japan's Nature: A People Tremble in Harmony with the Land. *New York Times*, January 22.

————. 1995c. Japan Reluctant to Accept Help from Abroad for Quake Victims. *New York Times*, February 5.

————. 1995d. Kobe's Best Problem: Too Many Gifts. *New York Times*, January 28.

————. 1995e. As Kobe Comes Back to Life, Happiness Is a Bath. *New York Times*, January 26.

————. 1995f. Fault Lines and Class Lines in Japan. *New York Times*, January 25.

————. 1995g. Kobe Chinatown Booms as Post-Quake Market. *New York Times*, February 11.

————. 1995h. An Ancient City Hopes to Reassure Tourists that It Is Safe to Visit. *New York Times*, January 24, 1995.

————, and Sheryl WuDunn. 1994. *China Wakes*. New York, NY: Times Books/Random House.

Kulick, Don. 1992. "Coming Up" in Gapun: Conceptions of Development and Their Effect on Language in a Papua New Guinean Village. In Gudrun Dahl and Annika Rabo (eds.), *Kam-Ap or Take-Off: Local Notions of Development*. Stockholm Studies in Social Anthropology, 29. Stockholm: Almqvist & Wiksell International.

Lederman, Jim. 1993. *Battlelines: The American Media and the Intifada*. Boulder, CO: Westview.

Löfgren, Orvar. 1999. *On Holiday*. Berkeley, CA: University of California Press.

Mead, Margaret, and Rhoda Métraux (eds.) 1953. *The Study of Culture at a Distance*. Chicago, IL: University of Chicago Press.

Mills, C. Wright. 1963. *Power, Politics and People*. New York, NY: Ballantine Books.

Nader, Laura. 1972. Up the Anthropologist – Perspectives Gained from Studying Up. In Dell Hymes (ed.), *Reinventing Anthropology*. New York, NY: Pantheon.

Pratt, Mary Louise. 1986. Fieldwork in Common Places. In James Clifford, and George E. Marcus (eds.), *Writing Culture*. Berkeley, CA: University of California Press.

Richelson, Jeffrey T. 1995. *A Century of Spies*. New York, NY: Oxford University Press.

Robertson, Roland. 1992. *Globalization*. London: Sage.

Sterngold, James. 1995a. Minorities in Gritty Part of Quake City Bear Big Loss. *New York Times*, January 24.

————. 1995b. Gang in Kobe Organizes Aid for People in Quake. *New York Times*, January 22.

Stipe, Claude E. 1980. Anthropologists versus Missionaries: The Influence of Presuppositions. *Current Anthropology*, 21: 165–179.

Stocking, Jr., George W. 1982. *Race, Culture, and Evolution*. Chicago, IL: University of Chicago Press.

Stoller, Paul. 1989. *The Taste of Ethnographic Things*. Philadelphia, PA: University of Pennsylvania Press.

Tuchman, Gaye. 1973. Making News by Doing Work: Routinizing the Unexpected. *American Journal of Sociology*, 79: 110–131.

Van der Geest, Sjaak. 1990. Anthropologists and Missionaries: Brothers under the Skin. *Man*, 25: 588–601.

Wikan, Unni. 1992. Beyond the Words: The Power of Resonance. *American Ethnologist*, 19: 460–482.

Wolf, Eric R., and Joseph G. Jorgensen. 1970. Anthropology on the Warpath in Thailand. *New York Review of Books*, 15 (9): 26–35.

9

BEING THERE ... AND THERE ... AND THERE!

Reflections on multi-site ethnography

In 1950, Professor Edward Evans-Pritchard, not yet "Sir" but certainly a central figure in mid-century anthropology, gave a radio lecture on the *BBC Third Programme* where he outlined what an Oxford man (no doubt here about gender) would properly do to become an accomplished field worker in social anthropology. Having prepared himself meticulously for a couple of years, and if fortunate enough to get a research grant, the anthropologist-to-be would proceed to his chosen primitive society to spend there usually two years, preferably divided into two expeditions with a few months in between, if possible in a university department where he could think about his materials. In the field, Evans-Pritchard's anthropologist would throughout be in close contact with the people among whom he was working, he must communicate with them solely through their own language, and he must study their "entire culture and social life." For one thing, the long period in the field would allow observations to be made in every season of the year. Having returned home, it would take the anthropologist at least another five years to publish the results of his research, so the study of a single society could be reckoned to require ten years. And then, Evans-Pritchard concluded, a study of a second society was desirable – lest the anthropologist would think for the rest of his life in terms of a particular type of society (Evans-Pritchard 1951: 64ff).

The idea of such a thorough, formative, exclusive engagement with a single field is of course at the base of the enduring power in anthropology of the prospect, or experience, or memory, or simply collectively both celebrated and mystified notion, of "being there."[1] Something much like Evans-Pritchard's prescription has very long remained more or less the only fully publicly acknowledged model for field work, and for becoming and being a real anthropologist. Perhaps it works with full force especially in the continued instruction of newcomers in the discipline – in many ways I conformed to it myself in my first field study, in an African American neighborhood in Washington, DC, although that was something quite different from Evans-Pritchard's classic "primitive society." Yet the hegemony of the model seems remarkable since it is fairly clear that a great many anthropologists, especially those no longer in the first phase of their careers, have long, but perhaps a bit more discreetly, been engaging in a greater variety of spatial and temporal practices as they have gone about their research. It may have been only Gupta and Ferguson's *Anthropological Locations* (1997) that really brought this variety entirely into the open. (I realize, certainly, that the power of the model has not been as strong among the ethnographically inclined in other disciplines, not so fully exposed to it, and obviously working under other conditions.)

So it may be, then, that when the conception of multi-site field work – being there … and there … and there! – propagated most consistently by George Marcus (e.g., 1986, 1995), first gained wider recognition in anthropology in the later years of the twentieth century, it was not really so entirely innovative. For one thing, in studies of migration, it was already becoming an established ideal to "be there" at both points of departure and points of arrival (see e.g., Watson 1977), thus working at least bilocally. Nor should we disregard the fact that the real pioneer of intensive anthropological field work, Malinowski, was already going multilocal when he followed the Trobrianders along the Kula ring. Yet the very fact that this style of doing ethnography was given a label, and prominently advocated, and exemplified (if in large part by borrowing a case from journalism), and that this occurred much at the same time as ideas of place and the local were coming under increasing scrutiny in and out of anthropology, no doubt helped accelerate its recent spread, as a practice or as a topic of argument.

Whether due to convergent interests or mutual inspiration, a number of my colleagues in Stockholm and I were among those who fairly quickly saw possibilities in configuring our projects along multilocal lines. One of us studied the organizational culture of Apple Computer in Silicon Valley, at the European headquarters in Paris, and at the Stockholm regional office; another studied the occupational world of ballet dancers in New York, London, Frankfurt and Stockholm; a third connected to the Armenian diaspora across several continents; a fourth explored the emergent profession of interculturalists, what I have elsewhere a little facetiously referred to as the "culture shock prevention industry"; and so on. We debated the characteristics of multilocal field studies fairly intensely among ourselves and with other colleagues, and a book some ten of us put together on our projects and experiences, particularly for teaching purposes, may have been the first more extended treatment of the topic (Hannerz 2001a). As far as I am concerned myself, perhaps lagging a little behind my more quickly moving colleagues and graduate students, my involvement with multi-site work has been primarily through a study of the work of newsmedia foreign correspondents which I will draw on here.[2]

Among the foreign correspondents

The general background was that some 20–25 years ago I rather serendipitously drifted into the area which later came to be known as "globalization" through a

178 Being there ... and there ... and there!

local study of a West African town, and then spent some time in large part thinking about the anthropology of the global ecumene in more conceptual and programmatic terms. By the time my itch to return to field work combined with an actual opportunity to do so, several of us in Stockholm were concerned with "globalization at work" – that is, responding to the fact that a large proportion of existing or emergent transnational connections are set up in occupational life. (This meant that we could also find food for thought in occupational ethnography outside anthropology, not least in the Chicago sociological tradition of Everett Hughes, Howard Becker and others.) More specifically, my own project could draw on the fact that I am a lifetime news addict, and assumed as I began to think about it that if globalization was also a matter of becoming more aware of the world, and having more elaborated understandings of the world, "foreign news" would be a central source of such understandings.[3] Perhaps most concretely, my curiosity fastened on some of the reporting I was habitually exposed to, for example when listening to the morning news program on the radio while having breakfast, and trying to wake up. There – this would have been in the mid-1990s – a familiar voice would report on street riots in Karachi, or the latest triumph of the expanding Taliban ... and then sign off from Hong Kong.

There are people, then, such as "Asia correspondents," or "Africa correspondents." These are also people, clearly, engaged in an occupational practice of "being there ... and there ... and there" – and sometimes possibly even appearing to be where they are not, if for example they can make a Karachi street scene come alive in their reporting even when they quite clearly are at a desk thousands of miles away from it. But just how do they do it?

I should say that as I was becoming seriously attracted to the idea of doing something like an ethnography of the social world of foreign correspondents, I was still a bit ambivalent. I found that on my shelves I already had some number of the kind of autobiographies some correspondents do, usually probably as their careers begin approaching an end; and I had seen most of those movies which over the years have turned the foreign correspondent into a kind of popular culture hero. As the saying goes, "anthropologists value studying what they like and liking what they study" (Nader 1972: 303) – and I wondered whether I would find foreign correspondents unapproachable, or perhaps arrogant prima donnas, or just possibly too suspicious of an academic whom they might fear would always be inclined to carping criticisms of their work.

As it turned out, I need not really have worried. I did a series of pilot interviews in New York during a period when I found myself there as the field spouse of another multi-site ethnographer, and the journalists I talked to there, having made first contacts through anthropologist mutual acquaintances, were very hospitable and encouraging. (The only thing I found a bit funny was that so many of them were Pulitzer Prize winners.) And that is how it continued to be. In the following years I engaged in a series of conversations with foreign correspondents and, sometimes, strictly speaking, ex-correspondents, mostly in Jerusalem, Johannesburg and Tokyo, but also in some number of other places including New York and Los Angeles, where I seized on the opportunity which some other kind of trip provided, to add another handful of interviews. Altogether, I talked to some 70 correspondents, and a few foreign news editors offering the perspective from headquarters.

As I see it, an ethnography of foreign news work of my kind can attempt to fill a noteworthy gap between two sets of representations of international news. At least since the 1970s, when a critical awareness grew of the communication imbalances in the world, it has been recurrently noted that the apparatus of global news flow is in large part controlled by what we have described as either "the West" or "the North" – the obvious examples of such dominance have been major news agencies such as Reuters or the Associated Press, with CNN more recently added as another key symbol of the apparatus. The other set of representations I have in mind consists of those memoirs by the newspeople themselves which I just referred to. These tend to be quite individual-centered, focusing on the authors as men and women of action, facing all kinds of dangers as they struggle to file their reports from the trouble spots of the world.

The gap, then, is one between foreign correspondents represented as puppets and as heroes. In the heavily macro-oriented views of media imperialism, the individuals who would be its flesh-and-blood representatives at the outer reaches of the newshandling apparatus are hardly seen as anything other than anonymous, exchangeable tools. In the autobiographical genre, in contrast, the individuals tend to be strong, the wider structure of news reporting not so noticeable.

Certainly my study of the foreign correspondents reflects the asymmetry in the global landscape of news. I deal mostly with Europeans and Americans, reporting from parts of the world which do not send out a comparable number of correspondents of their own to report from other places. In large part, this obviously matches the classic asymmetry of anthropology; and my choice of Jerusalem, Johannesburg and Tokyo as main field sites also reflects an interest in the way foreign correspondents, on a parallel track to ours, deal with issues of "translating culture," of "representing the other." Apart from that, however, we face here once more the problem of striking a balance between structure and agency. What I have attempted to do in my study is to portray the networks of relationships more immediately surrounding the foreign correspondents, locally or translocally; the patterns of collaboration, competition and division of labor which organize their daily activities, formally or informally; and not least their room for maneuver and personal preferences in reporting. I have been curious about the partnerships which evolve between correspondents who prefer each other as company when going on reporting trips, and about the relationships between correspondents and local "fixers," reminding me of the multifaceted links between anthropologists and their field assistants.

I have explored, too, the often obscure passages of news in roundabout ways between news agencies, electronic media and print media, which sometimes offer convenient shortcuts in correspondent work but which also generate tensions and now and then backstage satirical comment about recycling and plagiarism. And not

180 Being there ... and there ... and there!

least have I been concerned with the implications of career patterns and with the spatial organization of foreign correspondence. How might it matter to reporting that some correspondents spend most of a lifetime in a single posting, while others are rotated every three years or so, between countries and continents? When large parts of the world get only brief visits by correspondents, described on such occasions as "parachutists" or "firemen," and only when there is a crisis to cover, how does this shape their and our view of these lands?

I am not going to devote my space here to any great extent, however, to discuss the specifics of my own project. I will rather try, against the background of this experience and that of some of my colleagues, to spell out a few of the issues which characteristically arise in multi-site ethnography, and ways in which it is likely to differ from the established model of anthropological field study, as I have let the latter be represented above by Evans-Pritchard and his half-century old formulation. For I believe that in arguments over the worth of multilocal work, it is not always made entirely transparent how it relates to the assumptions based on classic understandings of "being there."

Constituting the multi-site field

In a way, one might argue, the term "multilocal" is a little misleading, for what current multilocal projects have in common is that they draw on some problem, some formulation of a topic, which is significantly *trans*local, not to be confined within some single place. The sites are connected with one another in such ways that the relationships between them are as important for this formulation as the relationships within them; the fields are not some mere collection of local units. One must establish the translocal linkages, and the interconnections between those and whatever local bundles of relationships which are also part of the study.[4] In my foreign correspondent study, a major such linkage was obviously between the correspondents abroad and the editors at home. But then there was also the fact that the correspondents looked sideways, toward other news sites and postings, and sometimes moved on to these. They often knew colleagues in some number of other such sites, having been stationed in the same place some time earlier, or by meeting somewhere on one or more of those "fireman" excursions which are a celebrated part of the public imagery of foreign correspondence, or by working for the same organization. In some loose sense, there is a world-wide "community" of foreign correspondents, connected through local and long-distance ties.

These linkages make the multi-site study something different from a mere comparative study of localities (which in one classical mode of anthropological comparison was based precisely on the assumption that such linkages did not exist). Yet certainly comparisons are often built into multisite research. My colleague Christina Garsten (1994), in her study of three sites within the transnational organization of Apple, was interested in comparing center and periphery within the corporation, as well as the way company culture in the offices was influenced by national cultures. As Helena Wulff (1998) studied the transnational ballet world she was similarly interested in national dance styles, but also in the differences between those companies in large part supported by the state and those working more entirely in the market. In my own study I could note the differences in foreign correspondent work between Jerusalem, where close at hand there was an almost constant stream of events commanding world attention; Tokyo, where it was a certain problem for correspondents that much of the time nothing really newsworthy seemed to happen; and Johannesburg, where designated "Africa correspondents" based there would mostly travel to other parts of the continent when there was a war or a disaster to report on.

If we could make use of the possibilities for comparison, however, neither I nor my colleagues could claim to have an ethnographic grasp of the entire "fields" which our chosen research topics may have seemed to suggest – and this tends to be in the nature of multi-site ethnography. It may be that in a migration study where all the migrants leave the same village and then turn up in the same proletarian neighborhood in a distant city, the potential and the actual combinations of sites are the same. On the other hand, a multinational corporation has many branches, ballet companies exist in a great many cities, a diaspora like that of the Armenians is widely dispersed, and foreign correspondents are based in major clusters in some 20–25 places around the world (disregarding here those temporary concentrations which result when the "firemen" descend on a remote and otherwise mostly neglected locus of hard news). Consequently, multi-site ethnography almost always entails a selection of sites from among those many which could potentially be included. Evans-Pritchard may not actually have been everywhere in Azandeland or Nuer country, but this would hardly be as immediately obvious as the selectiveness, or incompleteness, of the multi-site study, where potential sites are clearly separate from one another.

The actual combination of sites included in a study may certainly have much to do with a research design which focuses on particular problems, or which seeks out particular opportunities for comparison. When I chose the somewhat exotic sites of Jerusalem, Johannesburg and Tokyo, it was because I was interested in reporting over cultural distances – I would have been less attracted by reporting between, say, Brussels and Stockholm, or between London and New York. Yet I wonder if it is not a recurrent characteristic of multi-site ethnography that site selections are to an extent made gradually and cumulatively, as new insights develop, as opportunities come into sight, and to some extent by chance. I had originally had in mind including India in my study, but then the first time I was planning to go a national election was called there, and while that could have been an attractive field experience, I suspected it would be a time when correspondents would have little time for me. Then the second time an ailment of my own made the streets of Delhi seem a less appealing prospect. To begin with, I had not expected to include Tokyo in my study, although it turned out to be a very good choice. But in no small part I went there because I had an invitation to a research workshop in Japan at a time when I could also stay on for some research.

182 Being there ... and there ... and there!

Questions of breadth and relationships

Evans-Pritchard's anthropologist, again, would study the "entire culture and social life" of the people assigned to him. Being around for at least a year, he could make observations during all seasons, and he would work in the local language (although it would probably be true that it was a language which in large part he had to learn during that year). And then, having spent, everything included, a decade of his life on that study, one could hope that there would also be time left for getting to know another people.

This is the kind of image of "real" field work which tends to worry current practitioners of, and commentators on, multi-site studies in anthropology. Compared to such standards, are these studies inevitably of dubious quality? If you are involved with two, three or even more places in much the same time span that classical anthropology would allow for one, which for various practical reasons may now be the case, what can you actually do? I do not want to assert that no problems of depth and breadth arise, that no dilemmas are inevitably there to be faced. Yet it is important that we realize how one site in a multi-site study now differs from the single site of that mid-twentieth century anthropologist.

I was in Jerusalem and Johannesburg and Tokyo, and more marginally in several other places, but I was clearly not trying to study the "entire culture and social life" of these three cities. I was merely trying to get to know some number of the foreign newspeople stationed in them, and the local ecology of their activities. In fact, I was not trying hard to get to know these individuals particularly intimately either; what mattered to me about their childhood or family lives or personal interests was how these might affect their foreign correspondent work.

Anthropologists often take a rather romantic view of their fields and their relationships to people there. They find it difficult to describe their informants as informants because they would rather see them as friends, and they may be proud to announce that they have been adopted into families and kin groups – not only because it suggests something about their skills as field workers, but also because it carries a moral value. They have surrendered to the field, and have been in a way absorbed by it. (Evans-Pritchard [1951: 79] shared similar sentiments: "An anthropologist has failed unless, when he says goodbye to the natives, there is on both sides the sorrow of parting.") Perhaps it is for similar reasons that I much prefer describing my encounters with correspondents as conversations, suggesting a more personal quality, rather than as interviews, although I certainly also want to convey the idea of only rather mildly structured exchanges, with room for spontaneous flow and unexpected turns.

There is no doubt a time factor involved in how relationships evolve. Yet I believe most multi-site studies really also have built-in assumptions about segmented lives, where some aspect (work, ethnicity or something else) is most central to the line of inquiry, and other aspects are less so. The ethnographer may be interested in the embeddedness of a particular line of belief or activity in a wider set of circumstances, but this hardly amounts to some holistic ambition.

It is a pleasure if one discovers a kindred soul, but one keeps hardnosedly in mind what more precisely one is after, and what sorts of relationships are characteristic of the field itself, as one delineates it. To some extent personalizing encounters in the modern, multi-site field comes not so much from deepening particular interactions as from the identification of common acquaintances – from placing the ethnographer in the translocal network of relationships. Meeting with foreign correspondents, I have sensed that it is often appreciated when it turns out that I have also talked to friends and colleagues of theirs in some other part of the world; perhaps more recently than they have. Or even to their editor at home. As I have tried to include informants from the same news organization in different postings, to develop my understanding of its operations and as a kind of triangulation, such connections can be discovered fairly often and easily. It is a matter of establishing personal credentials.

Site temporalities

Anthropology's classic image of field work also includes an assumption about the durability of fields, and the involvement of "natives" in them, relative to the length of the ethnographer's field stay. At least implicitly there is the notion that the ethnographer, alone a transient, has to develop in that year or two the understandings which match what the locals assemble during a lifetime. That year, moreover, covers the most predictable variation that one finds in local life: that of seasons.

Obviously the people we are concerned with in present day field studies tend mostly to be less dependent on seasons and their cycles of activity – on planting and harvesting, or on moving herds to greener pastures. But in addition, these people themselves often have other kinds of relationships to the site than that of real "natives." In Evans-Pritchard's time, the Azande and the Nuer among whom he mostly worked were pedestrians – in a lifetime they did not go all that far away. There may be some such people in Jerusalem, Johannesburg and Tokyo as well, but hardly among the foreign correspondents. And generally the people on whom we focus in multi-site field studies tend to be the more mobile ones, those who contribute most to turning the combinations of sites into coherent fields, and who also make the sites themselves, at least for the purposes of the studies, more like "translocalities" (Appadurai 1996). Some of the sites may even in themselves be short-lived phenomena. My Stockholm colleague Tommy Dahlén (1997), studying the making of the new interculturalist profession, found international conferences, including ritual events, workshops, exhibits and parties, central to his ethnography. And by the time his study was over, he had surely attended more of these conferences than most interculturalists. Such temporary sites – conferences, courses, festivals – are obviously important in much contemporary ethnography.

In some sites now, this goes to say, there are no real natives, or at any rate fewer of them, sharing a lifetime's localized experience and collectivized understandings. There are more people who are, like the anthropologist, more like strangers. I find

184 Being there ... and there ... and there!

thought-provoking James Ferguson's (1999: 208) comment on what ethnography on the urban Zambian Copperbelt was like toward the end of the twentieth century:

> Here there is much to be understood, but none of the participants in the scene can claim to understand it all or even take it all in. Everyone is a little confused (some more than others, to be sure), and everyone finds some things that seem clear and others that are unintelligible or only partially intelligible .... Anthropological understanding must take on a different character when to understand things like the natives is to miss most of what is going on.

This can be as true in single-site as in multi-site studies, but it problematizes the relationship between "native" and ethnographer knowledge. Do things become easier for field workers if their informants also find the world opaque, or more difficult as they have to understand not only the structure of knowledge such as it is, but also the nature and social organization of ignorance and misunderstandings? In any case, we sense that we have moved away from the classic field work model.

Materials: interviews, observations, etc.

Again, in my foreign correspondent project, interviews, be they long, informal and loosely ordered, were a large part of my field materials. I did sit in on a daily staff meeting of the foreign desk at one newspaper, and went on a reporting trip to the Palestinian West Bank with one correspondent. More materials of these and other kinds would no doubt have been of value, but for practical reasons I did not pursue some such possibilities, using the time at my disposal rather to ensure diversity through the interviews. (I tried to include different kinds of media, although with an emphasis on print correspondents, and I wanted to include a reasonably broad range of nationalities.) Also, in Jerusalem, Johannesburg and Tokyo, and to a more limited extent in a couple of other places, I met with correspondents as they were immersed in the activities of a particular beat, and so the interviews could be detailed and concrete.

Probably the time factor has a part in making many multi-site studies rather more dependent on interviews than single-site studies. If the researchers have to handle more places in the time classic field work would devote to one, they may be more in a hurry. Language skills also probably play a part. In interviews, it is more likely that you can manage in one or two languages. My conversations with foreign correspondents were in English, except for those with fellow Scandinavians. In those sites, for many of the correspondents – particularly those who were expatriates, rotating between assignments – English was their working language as well. George Marcus (1995: 101) concludes that most multi-sited field studies so far have been carried out in monolingual, mostly English-speaking

Being there ... and there ... and there! **185**

settings. This is surely not to say that multi-site ethnography must rely entirely on interviewing and informant work (in which case some might even feel that in the field phase, it is less than fully ethnographic – the ethnographic tendency may become more obvious in the style of writing); this still depends on the nature of research topics. Studying ballet companies, Helena Wulff could view perform-ances and sit in on endless rehearsals. Although she could not very well "partici-pate" in the public performances, her own dance background meant that she still had a particular empathetic insight into the more practical, bodily aspects of dan-cing lives.

But then if pure observation, or participant observation, has a more limited part in some multi-site studies than in the classic model of anthropological field work, it may not have so much to do with sheer multi-sitedness as with the fact that they tend to involve settings of modernity. There are surely a great many activities where it is worthwhile to be immediately present, even actively engaged, but also others which may be monotonous, isolated, and difficult to access. What do you do when "your people" spend hours alone at a desk, perhaps concentrating on a computer screen?

At the same time, whatever you may now do along more classic ethnographic lines can be, often must be, combined with other kinds of sources and materials. Hugh Gusterson (1997: 116), moving on personally from an ethnography of one California nuclear weapons laboratory to a study of the entire American "nuclear weapons community," and looking intermittently at the counterpart Russian community as well, describes contemporary ethnography as a matter of "polymorphous engagements" – interacting with informants across a number of dispersed sites, but also doing field work by telephone and email, collecting data eclectically in many different ways from a disparate array of sources, attending carefully to popular culture, and reading newspapers and official documents. Skills of synthesis may become more important than ever. Certainly it is in considerable part relationships which are not, or at least not always, of a face-to-face nature which make the multi-site field cohere.

Media, personal or impersonal, seem to leave their mark on most multi-site studies. Ulf Björklund (2001: 100), my colleague engaged in studying the Arme-nian diaspora, quotes an editor explaining that "wherever in the world there are two dozen Armenians, they publish some kind of paper." Helena Wulff describes the varied ways in which dance videos are used in the transnational dance community, including instruction as well as marketing. In my foreign cor-respondent study, the correspondents' reporting itself naturally makes up a large part of my materials, interweaving with my interviews. In the end, too, this means that Evans-Pritchard's words about the "sorrow of parting" seem just a little less to the point. Just as their reporting could allow me to know at least something about them before meeting them in the flesh, so I could also to a degree keep track of them thereafter by following their reporting, from the sites where I met them or from elsewhere in the world, as I was back in Stockholm.

186 Being there ... and there ... and there!

An art of the possible: fitting field work into lives

The pilot interviews apart, I began field studies for my foreign correspondent project in late 1996, and did the last interview in early 2000. In a way, then, I could seem to come close to Evans-Pritchard's five-year norm for a project, but that did not really include my preparatory work, nor time for writing up. On the other hand, I was not at all working full time on the project. In between, I was back in Stockholm engaged in teaching and administration, and also had a couple of brief but gratifying research fellowships elsewhere. But all the time, of course, I was following the reporting of foreign news.

Whether it is single-site or multi-site, I am convinced that much ethnographic work is now organized rather like that. Professional or domestic obligations make the possibility of simply taking off for a field for a continuous stretch of another year or two appear rather remote. For some that means never going to the field again, so there is no "second society" experience of the kind which would supposedly broaden your intellectual horizons. But then ethnography is an art of the possible, and it may be better to have some of it than none at all. And so we do it now and then, fitting it into our lives when we have a chance.

Often, no doubt, this will be a matter of being there – and again! And again! – returning to one known although probably changing scene. Multi-site ethnography, however, may fit particularly well into that more drawn-out, off-and-on kind of scheduling, as the latter does not only allow us to think during times in between about the materials we have, but also about where to go next. It could just be rather impractical to move hurriedly directly from one field site to the next, according to a plan allowing for little alteration along the way.

Concluding one of his contributions to a recent British volume on anthropological field work – Oxford-based, and thus also in a way updating the classic Evans-Pritchard model – detailing his own enduring East African commitment, David Parkin (2000: 107) notes that practical circumstances such as the growing number of anthropologists, and governmental financial restrictions on purely academic research, are factors which probably matter more to changes in styles of doing research than does intellectual debate; and he suggests that if more ethnographers now actually spread their field work over many shorter periods than do it in the classic way of larger blocks of time, that is one such change. That sounds very likely, for again, ethnography is an art of the possible. Yet this is not to say that intellectual argument over changes and variations in the conduct of ethnography is useless. Perhaps these notes on experiences of multi-site field work can contribute to such debate.

Notes

1 This chapter was first published in article form in *Ethnography*, 4: 201–216, 2003, after presentation at the "Ethnografeast" Conference held at the University of California, Berkeley, September 12–14, 2002. I am grateful for comments by the participants, and to my colleagues in the Department of Social Anthropology, Stockholm University,

especially those on whose work I have also drawn here: Ulf Björklund, Tommy Dahlén, Christina Garsten and Helena Wulff. "Being there" is, for one thing, the title of the first chapter in Clifford Geertz' (1988) study of anthropological writing, where another chapter is indeed devoted to Evans-Pritchard. It is also the title of another British anthropologist, C.W. Watson's (1999) collection of accounts of field work, half a century after Evans-Pritchard's statement. Paul Willis reminds me, moreover, that it is the title of a Peter Sellers movie.

2 The project has had the support of the Bank of Sweden Tercentenary Foundation. Previous writings resulting from it include Hannerz (1998a, 1998b, 1999, 2001b, 2002). The project was discussed in the Lewis Henry Morgan Lectures at the University of Rochester in November 2000, and a book will result from these lectures (Hannerz 2004). I will also draw to a certain extent here on my discussion of multi-site ethnography in a more general handbook chapter on transnational research (Hannerz 1998c).

3 As I soon learned, that was not self-evident – foreign correspondents have recently been inclined to think that international news reporting is under great pressure, perhaps particularly in the United States. As I write this, I come upon an item in what amounts to the gossip column of the *International Herald Tribune* (August 28, 2002), according to which Dan Rather, CBS anchorman, tells *TV Guide* in an interview that less than a year after September 11, 2001, there is a new lack of emphasis on such reporting. "The public has lost interest," Rather says. "They'd much rather hear about the Robert Blake murder case or what is happening on Wall Street. A feeling is creeping back in that if you lead foreign, you die."

4 Marcus (1995), in his discussion of this matter, has seen it in large part as a matter of choosing between, or making some combination among, six strategies: follow the people; follow the thing; follow the metaphor; follow the plot, story, or allegory; follow the life or biography; or follow the conflict.

References

Akhil, Gupta, and James Ferguson (eds.) 1997. *Anthropological Locations*. Berkeley, CA: University of California Press.

Appadurai, Arjun. 1996. *Modernity at Large*. Minneapolis, MN: University of Minnesota Press.

Björklund, Ulf. 2001. Att studera en diaspora: den armeniska förskingringen som fält. In Ulf Hannerz (ed.), *Flera fält i ett*. Stockholm: Carlssons.

Evans-Pritchard, E.E. 1951. *Social Anthropology*. London: Cohen & West.

Ferguson, James. 1999. *Expectations of Modernity*. Berkeley, CA: University of California Press.

Garsten, Christina. 1994. *Apple World*. Stockholm Studies in Social Anthropology 33. Stockholm: Almqvist and Wiksell International.

Geertz, Clifford. 1988. *Works and Lives*. Stanford, CA: Stanford University Press.

Hannerz, Ulf. 1998a. Of Correspondents and Collages. *Anthropological Journal on European Cultures*, 7: 91–109.

———. 1998b. Reporting from Jerusalem. *Cultural Anthropology*, 13: 548–574.

———. 1998c. Transnational Research. In H. Russell Bernard (ed.), *Handbook of Methods in Anthropology*. Walnut Creek, CA: Altamira Press.

———. 1999. Studying Townspeople, Studying Foreign Correspondents: Experiences of Two Approaches to Africa. In H.P. Hahn and G. Spittler (eds.), *Afrika Und Die Globalisierung*. Hamburg: LIT Verlag.

——— (ed.) 2001a. *Flera fält i ett*. Stockholm: Carlssons.

188   Being there ... and there ... and there!

———. 2001b. Dateline Tokyo: Telling the World about Japan. In Brian Moeran (ed.), *Asian Media Productions*. London: Curzon.

———. 2002. Among the Foreign Correspondents: Reflections on Anthropological Styles and Audiences. *Ethnos*, 67: 57–74.

———. 2004. *Foreign News*. Chicago, IL: University of Chicago Press.

Gusterson, Hugh. 1997. Studying Up Revisited. *Political and Legal Anthropology Review*, 20 (1): 114–119.

Marcus, George E. 1986. Contemporary Problems of Ethnography in the Modern World System. In James Clifford and George E. Marcus (eds.), *Writing Culture*. Berkeley, CA: University of California Press.

———. 1995. Ethnography In/Of the World System: The Emergence of Multi-Sited Ethnography. *Annual Review of Anthropology*, 24: 95–117.

Nader, Laura. 1972. Up the Anthropologist – Perspectives Gained from Studying Up. In Dell Hymes (ed.), *Reinventing Anthropology*. New York, NY: Pantheon.

Parkin, David. 2000. Templates, Evocations and the Long-Term Fieldworker. In Paul Dresch, Wendy James and David Parkin (eds.), *Anthropologists in a Wider World*. Oxford: Berghahn.

Dahlén, Tommy. 1997. *Among the Interculturalists*. Stockholm Studies in Social Anthropology 38. Stockholm: Almqvist and Wiksell International.

Watson, C.W. (ed.) 1999. *Being There*. London: Pluto.

Watson, James L. (ed.) 1977. *Between Two Cultures*. Oxford: Blackwell.

Wulff, Helena 1998. *Ballet across Borders*. Oxford: Berg.

10

FOREIGN CORRESPONDENTS AND THE VARIETIES OF COSMOPOLITANISM

I met Rowan Callick, China correspondent of the *Australian Financial Review*, at the Foreign Correspondents Club in Hong Kong – a climb up the hillside, in the old thick-walled Ice House from the colonial days, white and brick with "FCC" in large black letters over the entrance door. Perhaps this is the most famous foreign correspondent club anywhere. John le Carré (1977), for one, depicted it, in a previous location, and primarily as a watering hole, in his novel *The Honourable Schoolboy*. The club had come into being when Mao Tse-tung's revolutionary army was gaining control over mainland China, and it became clear that, for the foreseeable future, Hong Kong would be the main site for China watching (see Figure 10.1).

Callick was, I believe, the only Australian correspondent I met with in my late-1990s study of newsmedia foreign correspondents – but then he was not really Australian either.[1] He had started out as a journalist at a provincial paper in northern England. Wanting to move on, he had thought the choice was between London, which he did not like, and going abroad. So he went to Port Moresby, in Papua New Guinea, beginning as a stringer and working his way into the *Australian Financial Review*. As a "Pacific Correspondent," he was actually in a small specialty. At the time, there seemed to be only six or seven people engaged in serious reporting on Oceania for the outside world: one or two New Zealanders, three or four Australians and one American. In Hong Kong, the foreign correspondent community was obviously much larger, although after the crown colony had been handed over to the People's Republic, it was possibly no longer so clear why, or on what, correspondents should report from there in the future.

Among his Hong Kong colleagues, anyway, Callick thought he could distinguish basically between three kinds. There were the Sinophiles, who wanted to be in China and had become correspondents as a way of supporting themselves

FIGURE 10.1 Foreign Correspondents Club, Lower Albert Road, Hong Kong © *Smuconlaw CC BY-SA 4.0*

there; there were the correspondents who had arrived on this beat somewhat unsuspectingly but had then become entirely committed to it, "falling in love with China"; and then there were those like Callick himself, journalists with a more generalized curiosity, who were in principle mobile, and saw Hong Kong mostly as another step in their careers. Some years ago, then, Port Moresby – and another few years ahead, who knows?

Foreign correspondents are perhaps among the most celebrated transnational migrants of our times, sometime heroes and heroines in print and on the screen, present as witnesses whenever something dramatic happens in the world; ready, as some of them like to say, to offer "the first draft of history." Yet everyday life does not always, or not even mostly, conform to the occupational mythology. There are less striking topics, too, and there are office routines. When Rowan Callick was a "Pacific Correspondent" in Port Moresby, he reported mostly on business, in large part on the mining and logging industries of Papua New Guinea. A contemporary of his in Hong Kong, Keith Richburg, of the *Washington Post* and President of the Foreign Correspondents Club, wrote in the club magazine about the changing content of reporting – and about the garb of the reporter (Richburg 1998). He reminisced about spending his career mostly as a political reporter, which often meant dealing with coup attempts, insurgencies, guerrilla wars and military crackdowns. This had been a time for the safari jacket, and the photographer's vest with lots of pockets. Yet now, he wrote, it seemed the safari jacket was out, and pinstripes were in: "Instead of romping through the bush with armies, we're conducting interviews in brokerage houses and corporate board rooms."

I was drawn to a study of the work and lives of foreign correspondents not least by a curiosity about their spatial practices. In a way, foreign correspondents are like anthropologists: they report from one part of the world to another, often over great geographical as well as cultural distances. But then their relationships to their beats must be different from that of anthropologists to their fields, at least as we have usually thought of it. If you are an "Africa Correspondent," or a "South-East Asia correspondent" as Keith Richburg was in Hong Kong, or for that matter, again, a "Pacific Correspondent," just how do you go about it? More generally, I wanted to get a sense of the daily life of a transnational occupation, the role of personal backgrounds and career patterns, the networks of colleagues, competitors, helpers, sources, and adversaries which surround the correspondents in their far-flung habitats of work, and the room for maneuver and choice they have in shaping their own reporting.

Then there is another set of relationships of foreign correspondents which must not be forgotten: those to their audiences – readers, viewers, listeners. If one aspect of globalization is a globalization of consciousness, a growing sense of "the world as a single place" (Robertson 1992), foreign correspondents, through these relationships, must be among its more significant agents.

While I was engaged in my foreign correspondent study, I gradually also came to return to a concept and a topic on which I had commented rather off-handedly several years earlier: that of cosmopolitanism (Hannerz 1990). Multifaceted as the concept is, it fits in at least two ways in a study of foreign correspondents and their reporting. On the one hand, the correspondents themselves may be seen as cosmopolitans: world-wise travelers, familiar with many places, connoisseurs of diversity. Here the emphasis is more cultural and experiential (along the lines I sketched cosmopolitanism in the context of world culture). On the other hand, in recent years, notions of cosmopolitanism have returned on the intellectual scene with a stronger political and ideological load than they have had for some time. In an increasingly interconnected world, and not least in one where market forces, personified by these men in pinstripes, often seem dominant, it is felt that a more developed sense of global civic responsibility is needed. Even if it is not exactly preoccupied with the construction of cosmopolis, a world society, as some sort of politically integrated entity, the cosmopolitan impulse tends to favor more inclusive arrangements of compassion, human rights, risk management, solidarity, and peacefulness.[2]

How, then, do people – some people, at least – possibly arrive at such a stance? No doubt in varied ways, but in part at least it is presumably a matter of being an informed citizen. And perhaps not just well-informed within some narrow sector of knowledge either. If, as the phrasing now often goes, being a cosmopolitan involves feeling "at home in the world," it may be as much a question of breadth as of warmth – it may entail having a similar range of experiences out there, of others and of oneself, as one has closer at hand, in a local community or in a nation. Yet even if the world is turning into a single place, most people do not have personal experiences of very much of it. Rather than having been everywhere and seen, heard, smelled, tasted, and touched everything for themselves, people depend on the representations provided by

192 Foreign correspondents and cosmopolitanism

various agencies of information brokerage, and here the news media have a central part. Foreign correspondents, that is to say, could be cosmopolitans themselves, but they may also do something to cultivate cosmopolitanism in their audiences.

I will be concerned with cosmopolitanism in both senses in these comments on the work of foreign correspondents in this paper.[3] I should note here that Hong Kong was not really a major site of my study. Apart from close attention to reporting as a product, with a certain emphasis on newspapers and the printed word, and to connected materials such as correspondent autobiographies, my main materials are a series of extended conversations with foreign correspondents, most of which took place in Jerusalem, Johannesburg, and Tokyo. Some other conversations were scattered over a number of other places, when further opportunities arose to add to the number and variety of my informants, and Hong Kong was only one of these places. Nonetheless, it so happens that Rowan Callick's categorization of his local colleagues in the Hong Kong foreign press corps, and my own encounters with a couple of them, can begin to help me sketch some of the main variations in foreign correspondent lives, and also show some of the complexity of the relationship between foreign correspondence and cosmopolitanism.

Spiralists and long-timers

Rowan Callick of the *Australian Financial Review* saw himself as rather loosely and temporarily attached to Hong Kong. With Keith Richburg, of the *Washington Post*, this was clearly likewise true. Richburg, an African-American, had already done one tour as a South-East Asia correspondent, but then he had been stationed in Manila, at a time when more hard news was coming out of the Philippines. Then he had been in Nairobi as East Africa correspondent for a period – we will come back to that. After Hong Kong, as it later turned out, he moved to the Paris bureau of his paper, and wrote from here and there in Europe. While still in Asia, however, he covered the riots in Jakarta leading to President Suharto's fall, and the conflict in East Timor as it broke away from Indonesia. Momentarily, it seems, he was back in the safari jacket.

In Jakarta and East Timor, Richburg was what is known in the trade as a "fireman" or "parachutist," coming in rather briefly to cover hard news in a place otherwise only seldom reported from, often under difficult conditions; the kind of practice and experience much foreign correspondent mythology is made of. But in his more gradual, step-by-step mobility from Manila to Nairobi to Hong Kong to Paris, perhaps 3–5 years in each posting and after that quite likely back to an editorial position in Washington, he was in the rather typical career of a successful correspondent working for a prosperous newsmedia organization. It is the career of a "spiralist," to borrow a term from the classic Manchester School in social anthropology, coined by William Watson (1964: 147) to refer to the way social mobility within the hierarchy of an organization can be coordinated with geographical mobility.

Foreign correspondents and cosmopolitanism **193**

The other Hong Kong correspondent I want to present briefly here is one whom I did not actually meet in Hong Kong. Göran Leijonhufvud is someone whose reporting I have followed over a long time, since he has been writing from China for my home-town (Stockholm) newspaper *Dagens Nyheter* since the early 1970s. In a way he fits into Rowan Callick's second category, as he arrived in China when he was already a journalist, but then became what I would describe as a long-timer, with a strong commitment to his beat. Since he had already travelled in China with a student group in the 1960s, at the time when the Cultural Revolution was just beginning, and had studied Chinese at Stockholm University, he probably had the beginnings of that commitment already much earlier.

I missed seeing Leijonhufvud when I was in Hong Kong, as he was travelling in southern China at the time. But then it turned out a few months later that he was on vacation close to where I have my summer house in southern Sweden, and I had the chance to spend a quiet afternoon with him at the edge of the forest, talking about his experiences in reporting from China over a quarter of a century. He had first been stationed in Beijing, when his paper had been allowed to open a bureau there. In the early 1970s, there had been altogether about 30 foreign correspondents in the city, all living in a foreign quarter surrounded by walls, where Chinese people were allowed only by special permission. Correspondents were not allowed to make contacts on their own, and their access to Chinese publications was also restricted (two dailies and a magazine). So they had each other to turn to, for company and to practice the local counterpart of Kremlinology. When a major annual military parade had suddenly been cancelled, they all wondered why – not accepting the official claim that it was just a matter of saving money. Somehow word came out that Lin Piao, Minister of Defence and Mao Tse-tung's likely successor, was in disfavor, and a Yugoslav correspondent, with a developed habit of interpreting signs in a totalitarian society, wondered what would happen to the "Little Red Book" which Lin Piao had compiled. Leijonhufvud went out to look for it in the shops – and indeed, it was no longer on the shelves.

Beijing in the 1970s, he reminisced, had still had the rhythm of a peasant society. You could hardly get a meal in a restaurant after 7.30 pm, and just a little later most lights would be out in the city. Stories had to be sent home in roundabout ways using the primitive telecommunication technologies of the time, there were very few air connections out of the country, and if one travelled to Hong Kong, it was by way of a domestic flight to Canton, with one intermediate stop where everyone got off to have a leisurely lunch. The train from Canton to Hong Kong then left the next morning, and was perhaps most noted for its drinks. Leijonhufvud had been back in Sweden for some time in the 1980s, doing a PhD in Sinology with a thesis on wall posters as a means of public expression in the Chinese tradition. Since then he had mostly found it more convenient to operate out of Hong Kong, although spending about half his time in Beijing and other parts of China. While earlier he had

194 Foreign correspondents and cosmopolitanism

reported more on South-East Asia as well, he now limits this to occasional trips to Indonesia – he prefers to be more strictly a China correspondent.[4]

Routes and roots

Categorizations like Rowan Callick's, or at any rate a rough distinction between spiralists and long-timers, do not fit only Hong Kong or China correspondents, but work more or less well in many foreign correspondent postings. The relative preponderance of each may depend on the centrality of particular beats in the global landscape of news, and the economics of the news business but, as in the Hong Kong case, it also has to do with the aggregate of personal inclinations among correspondents.

In terms of lifestyle and experience, then, are foreign correspondents cosmopolitans? It would seem to depend on circumstances, and also what we mean by the term "cosmopolitans." But the spiralist/long-timer distinction could appear to have something to do with it. Marked by interest in, familiarity with, or knowledge and appreciation of many parts of the world; not provincial, local, limited, or restricted by the attitudes, interests or loyalties of a single region, section, or sphere of activity; worldwide rather than regional, parochial, or narrow is one of the definitions of "cosmopolitan" offered by *Webster's Third New International Dictionary of the English Language* (1981). That might seem to fit better, in sheer quantitative terms, with spiralists of Richburg's kind, moving about between "many parts of the world." The long-timers, spending perhaps their entire professional lives, and a large part of their lives as a whole, on a single beat could seem, meanwhile, to become more marked by their commitments to "single regions." Along the lines of the classical contrast of Archilochus by way of Isaiah Berlin, the spiralists would be like foxes and the longtimers like hedgehogs; foxes know lots of things, and hedgehogs one big thing.

Yet if there is something to that, it still makes our view of the relative cosmopolitanism of varieties of foreign correspondents too simple. One problem is that the quick passages of spiralists – not to mention the yet more rapid movements foreign correspondents must cope with when they operate as parachutists – may not allow them to develop so much familiarity with, or knowledge and appreciation of, each place where they find themselves. Time itself is clearly a factor here; when outside observers, and not least anthropologists, frequently express their doubts about the quality of local knowledge of foreign correspondents, they often have particularly parachutist practices in mind. But the characteristics of the beat are also important. If familiarity is in no small part a matter of access, it does not help if correspondents, as in Göran Leijonhufvud's first period in Beijing, are confined to a foreigner's ghetto, allowed to speak only to their domestic staff and selected other locals. That case may have been among the most extreme, but it is true that correspondents find places variably approachable, and variably constraining as far as local explorations are concerned. An

American correspondent in Johannesburg found South African society, in the transition years after the fall of apartheid, still extremely segmented, sorted into little boxes by race and class, with few personal contacts in between – "Afrikaners, English-speakers, Indians, Zulu ..." That affected her freedom of movement as well, and that of other correspondents.

Under such conditions particularly, some spiralists may tend to become rather less cosmopolitan in a stricter sense, and more like what we are perhaps inclined to label "expatriates": people not strongly rooted in the territory where they reside for a period, often more affluent than the locals, engaging in a lifestyle and a pattern of social contacts which somehow does not quite belong there, in large part in the company of others of more or less their own kind. (Not that it is entirely impossible for a long-timer to remain an expatriate in such a sense, too.) And it becomes a mark of the commitment and skill of the individual correspondent to move off the verandah, as it were, and cultivate a more intimate acquaintance with the beat. That kind of familiarity with the character of one beat will more probably go with the long-timer way of foreign correspondence. We should remember here, too, that if you are an "Africa correspondent" or for that matter a "China correspondent," and remain in that posting, this is in itself something far beyond a local or parochial experience.

Most importantly, however, foreign correspondence is itself by definition something other than a confinement to a single region, in the sense that you are stationed in one place, and reporting to another. In history, the term "cosmopolitan" has often been turned into the epithet "rootless cosmopolitan" – not least by state apparatuses wishing to render suspect the loyalties of one group or other. But then, more recently, the point has been made recurrently that it is entirely possible to be a rooted cosmopolitan as well, to combine cultural and civic expansiveness with a strong sense of personal linkage to a particular locality or nation (see e.g. Appiah 1996). As far as foreign correspondents are concerned, such a rooting surely comes in most cases with a sense of audience; and if ever one seems to forget it, one may be reminded of it by the editor at headquarters. There are some newspeople who report to a more widely and vaguely defined audience. Ted Turner, founder of CNN, is rumored to have banned the use of the word "foreign" from broadcasts. No CNN viewer should ever feel "othered" by finding that his or her part of the world was covered by a "foreign correspondent," and so CNN has "international correspondents" instead. Yet most correspondents expect that their readers, listeners, or viewers are in a particular town or country, very likely the one they come from themselves, and this provides foreign correspondence with its own kind of rootedness, its notion of "at home." (Although it happens occasionally, of course, as in the case of Rowan Callick, northern English but reporting to Australians, that the construct becomes a bit artificial.)

In this condition of being in one place and reporting from there to people who are elsewhere, and who cannot be assumed to know much about that place, at least a degree of cosmopolitanism, a sensitivity to difference and a concern with

196 Foreign correspondents and cosmopolitanism

how to report on it, may be more or less a professional requirement. Admittedly it may be less important if you report between places much like each other, or on internationally fairly standardized matters. I should emphasize here that, in my own study, I have focused on those correspondents who would seem to have greater cultural distances to cover, and who thus face more complex tasks of cultural translation or representation.

A sense of wonder, and the baggage from home

The need to relate to the audience at home has some part in the way foreign correspondents and their organizations think about the advantages and disadvantages of spiralists and long-timers. The latter may indeed become very knowledgeable. They may have a longer-term perspective on stories, remembering what led up to them, and they may have wide and varied local networks which can be important resources in their reporting. Quite possibly they may be considerably more skilled in using a local language.[5]

The assumption behind a preference for spiralists, and a quicker rotation, however, is that "going stale" is a significant occupational hazard. The correspondents might start taking things in their surroundings for granted, instead of seeing stories in them. They get bored when they have to do basically the same story the second or third or umpteenth time. A spiralist correspondent for a major American newspaper whom I met in Tokyo, which has a similar range of types of correspondents to that described by Rowan Callick for Hong Kong, commented that certain long-timers were really walking advertisements for the value of not staying too long: they were world-weary and jaded in their views, and if they absolutely must stay in Japan, they really ought to turn to some other line of work.

At least to a degree, then, there is virtue in innocence. The ideal correspondent, according to this view, has a fresh eye for the peculiarities of a beat – "a sense of wonder." And it helps not to lose touch with the audience at home; to retain a sense of its interests, experiences, and assumptions. For such reasons, some news organizations prefer not to have their spiralists take just one foreign assignment after another, but to bring them back home once in a while to remind them of how things are there.

Yet then one may find that what the newcomer on a beat, or someone who does not stay there very long, brings to it may not be only that fresh perspective, but a certain more specific baggage of ideas from home. In Japan, where hard news stories fit for foreign correspondence are fairly few and far between, "otherness" itself tends to become a major theme in reporting, and correspondents – and probably no less, their editors at home – are often drawn to classic, and stereotypical, Western notions of what is Japanese: geishas, samurais, harakiri, and kamikaze. Africa undoubtedly has more than its fair share of conflicts and disasters but, as much of the continent is covered mostly through parachutist reporting, such stories become even more dominant in international news coverage. Nonetheless, some other stories are also conspicuously present. Wildlife stories are popular. Foreign correspondence from this continent probably has the highest animal/human ratio in the world: meet the chimpanzees, gorillas, lions, elephants, rhinos, hippos, giraffes, crocodiles. A remarkable number of Africa correspondents, too, sooner or later make it to Timbouctou. One may wonder why, but perhaps it is because there are two or three Timbouctous: the real but perhaps least significant one, in Mali, and one or two in the more or less popular Northern imagination. For some, as the *New York Times* foreign affairs columnist Thomas Friedman (1998) notes, the city is "a synonym for the most obscure spot on earth." For others, it stands as a symbol of a glorious African past of empire, trade, and learning. And for some again, it may be both at the same time, or at slightly different times. Looking back on his own Timbouctou trip, one *Los Angeles Times* correspondent told me this was the first place in Africa he ever heard of when he was a child.

It is not entirely surprising if some of the reporting from distant places is in fact making a kind of return trip, catering to ideas, even stereotypes, which are in fact already well-established at home. Partly, this is because correspondents arrive in their postings carrying these ideas with them, and may not really have the time and opportunity to unlearn and relearn. No doubt it is also partly due to some very real, tangible constraints of newswork. If you have two print columns at your disposal, or three minutes on the air, there is little chance of starting educating your audience from scratch. It is tempting to appeal to something already inscribed into its minds. Yet to the degree that the work of some foreign correspondents is less shaped by an appreciation of the diversity of things actually there on the beat, and more by the attitudes and ideas brought from home, any claim to cosmopolitanism would certainly seem to be weakened.

Making audiences feel at home in the world

That brings us from the question whether, or in what way, or to what extent, foreign correspondents themselves may be understood as cosmopolitans, to the question whether they exercise some kind of cosmopolitanizing influence on their audiences, cultivating some sense of belonging in the world.

We should not take it for granted that this is what they self-consciously would see as their mission. Some would say they are merely "doing their job." No doubt there are newspeople, too, who are drawn to whatever may shock their audiences. And then one comes across, at times, alarmist or rejectionist voices seemingly warning of too much involvement with the world, or at least with parts of it.

In a manner, Keith Richburg, the black *Washington Post* correspondent, has offered an example of this which for a while drew considerable attention and comment. In his memoir *Out of America* (1997), he detailed his reporting experiences in Africa during the violent early 1990s. Leaving his posting in Nairobi, after "three years walking around among the corpses," he wrote that he was

198 Foreign correspondents and cosmopolitanism

tired of the hypocrisy, double standards and ignorance concerning Africa he felt he was getting from some people who had often never been there. In particular, he was obviously out of sympathy with certain other Black Americans and their varieties of Black consciousness. "Talk to me about Africa and my Black roots and my kinship with my African brothers and I'll throw it back in your face," Richburg warned in his preface, "and then I'll rub your nose in the images of rotting flesh." He certainly would not defend slavery, as part of the history of America, and of his own family. But provocatively, he thanked God his ancestors had thus been taken out of Africa, and that in the end he was himself an American. On that note, he had moved on to Hong Kong.

When we met there, he acknowledged that his experience in Nairobi had not actually been all bad. He had had a good life in Nairobi, good friends, a large house, and he had enjoyed swimming in the Indian Ocean, and fishing. But in his book he had had a point to make, and he had felt strongly about it. He saw his book above all as a forceful affirmation of his American identity, a patriotic manifestation, polemically aimed especially at Afrocentrist fellow travelling.

One may still feel, however, that the line between patriotism and chauvinism is not always easily drawn. Indeed, as news of the world out there is so often bad news, of conflicts and catastrophies, it may seem to be above all a place to be wary of − one that on the basis of common sense the "man in the street" would want to have as little to do with as possible. You would prefer to keep your distance, and if people from out there knock on your door, you will want to have nothing to do with them. Pierre Bourdieu (1998: 8), in his critique of television and journalism, took this view: "Journalism shows us a world full of ethnic wars, racist hatred, violence and crime − a world full of incomprehensible and unsettling dangers from which we must withdraw for our own protection."

Isolationism, and even xenophobia, can thus be other reactions to bad news from abroad − "if the world is becoming a single place, for God's sake, let us take it apart again." I talked about this with Inger Jägerhorn, at the time the foreign news editor of *Dagens Nyheter* in Stockholm, the paper for which Göran Leijonhufvud also writes. She said she and her colleagues were aware of this danger. There should be more reporting which portrayed everyday life elsewhere. Moreover, she noted, television might naturally be committed to reporting the news through dramatic pictures. This did not have to be her priority as a newspaper editor.

There is, I believe, a kind of cosmopolitan turn here, an actual desire to make the vicarious experience of the world through the media a richer, more varied one. As it turned out when I talked to him, Keith Richburg, too, felt that, in the future of foreign reporting, there should be not merely a shift from safari jackets to pinstripes, but a more general broadening to deal with cultural issues, hi-tech, the environment. He hoped to do more of this in his remaining year in Hong Kong. When I came to meet him at the Foreign Correspondents Club, he had just been interviewing a film maker. And the *New York Times*, I learned, talking to several of its correspondents in different places, had been, if not a trend setter, clearly thinking along similar lines. The foreign editor who oversaw the paper's post–Cold War transition period, Bernard Gwertzman, had written an important internal memorandum which pointed to new directions for his correspondents.[6] In the coming period, he suggested, there would be a widening of reporting from political news to a wider variety of stories:

> We are interested in what makes societies different, what is on the minds of people in various regions. Imagine you are being asked to write a letter home every week to describe a different aspect of life in the area you are assigned.

Perhaps this oftentimes seems less like a first draft of history, and more like notes toward an ethnography.

The future of foreign correspondence

As I talked to Keith Richburg in Hong Kong, he pointed out that, at least in the United States, in the 1990s, there was less interest in foreign news. The TV networks had closed many of their foreign bureaus, and in the *Washington Post*, his own paper, there could easily be one or two days in a week without a foreign story on the front page. But then in November 2001, as a parachutist again, Richburg was also among the thousands of newspeople covering the war in Afghanistan. He could report vividly on a horse ride across the mountains, through ice and snow, with three cousins in the jewelry business, one relief agency worker, and two other foreign journalists. One horse slipped and fell into a river, taking sleeping bags, satphones, and laptops with him. "Of all the dumb things reporters have done to get a story, this definitely was one of the dumbest" (Richburg 2001). After September 11, it seemed, foreign news was back. The relative post–Cold War tranquility of the 1990s was over, and more sinister aspects of the understanding of the world as a single place insisted on attention. Certainly, foreign correspondence has always prospered in times of war – to the extent that the categories "war correspondent" and "foreign correspondent" seem sometimes to be understood as nearly synonymous. This is actually mistaken in two ways: both because many foreign correspondents, most of the time or even all the time, are actually peace correspondents, and because some war correspondence is really more like domestic news in that the coverage focuses on the boys and girls from home.

In a way that became clear once more in Iraq in March and April 2003, when many correspondents were "embedded" in the invading forces and thereby possibly tempted into some rather biased reporting. More patriotism, one might suspect, and less cosmopolitanism.

Yet if, as some now argue, the Cold War was World War III, and the War on Terrorism is World War IV, the implications for foreign news reporting may still not be so obvious. What is actually the future of this particular kind of migrancy in the contemporary world? When I began my study of foreign

200 Foreign correspondents and cosmopolitanism

correspondence as a way of life, I was perhaps inclined to assume rather innocently that, with globalization, the demand for foreign news must grow. Indeed, in times and places like Afghanistan in 2001 or Iraq in 2003, media organizations may well now and again be capable of massive instant efforts, turning the good, the bad, and the ugly into parachutists, and meanwhile largely ignoring what goes on elsewhere. Yet beyond and between such mobilizations, there is a fairly widespread concern that foreign correspondence as a skilled, continuous, comprehensive, localized, or regionalized craft is in some danger, in many news organizations although hardly in all.

"Remember that this is a dying occupation," said one of the first foreign correspondents I talked to, as we parted ways in a busy street in New York. Too dark a view, perhaps. But if in overall quantitative terms there really has been a decline in foreign coverage in recent years, notably in the United States although in many places elsewhere as well, it appears to have less to do with the coming of any more peaceful world, and more with the fact that the news business is indeed mostly a business. "The accountants are cracking their whips," said another news veteran to me in Jerusalem. It is certainly a widely shared view that, in times when economic considerations play a very large part in management minds, the down-to-earth question is raised whether the high cost of foreign news, especially in the form of a more extensive network of staff correspondents, mostly spiralists, is really balanced by more readers or advertisement revenue directly brought in by such coverage. For some organizations the answer may be simply "No," and thus they may seek alternative ways of reporting on the world – or just do very little of it. It is also true that we are in a period in which the media landscape is being reconfigured. One can now find one's way to more information, and more varied information, by consulting a range of more specialized publications of different kinds – and not least, on the Internet, an almost infinite number of websites from all over the world. Those in the news business who question the need to provide so much foreign news for general audiences are inclined to point this out.

Yet it may be precisely those general audiences that we hope will be able to stay in touch with the world, without aspirations to expertise but reasonably effortlessly through daily routines of consumption. In that case, despite all the weaknesses and limitations of contemporary mainstream foreign correspondence that we can identify, and sometimes like to dwell on, there is perhaps no simple substitute for the kind of global brokerage exercised by those spiralists and long-timers.

Notes

1 It is true, however, that Australian journalists have been rather numerous, and prominent, in reporting from Hong Kong and South-East Asia. One of them, and one of the legendary Asia correspondents of the twentieth century, Richard Hughes, also appears rather lightly disguised in le Carré's book, as one of the habitués of the Foreign Correspondents Club, under the name "Craw." The reason for taking a point of departure for this chapter in the encounter with a Hong Kong-based journalist from an Australian newspaper is that it was

first presented as a paper at the Conference on "Migrancy and its Futures" at the University of Western Australia, Perth, June 27–28, 2003. I am grateful to my fellow participants for comments made there, and especially to Nicholas Harney and Loretta Baldassar, for their part in organizing an extremely enjoyable conference, as well as for their hospitality. It was then published in *Journal of Ethnic and Migration Studies*, 33 (2): 299–311, 2007.

2 For representative recent work on cosmopolitanism, see for example the edited volumes by Cheah and Robbins (1998) and Vertovec and Cohen (2002).

3 I have reported on my entire study of foreign correspondents in Hannerz (2004a), on which this paper draws. The study was supported by the Bank of Sweden Tercentenary Foundation. For comments relating specifically to other field sites, see Hannerz (1998, 1999, 2001). I have discussed the related experience of multi-site fieldwork in Hannerz (2003). A more extended discussion of cosmopolitanism is in Hannerz (2004b).

4 Later yet, after this paper was first written, Leijonhufvud has in fact retired from foreign correspondence, but remains in China. He has returned to Beijing, where he engages in research, while his wife continues as a correspondent for a Swedish business newspaper.

5 Göran Leijonhufvud speaks Mandarin, and gets by in Cantonese. Keith Richburg noted, when I talked to him, that the *Washington Post* is fairly generous in allowing language study in preparation for postings where the dominant language is exotic: Russia, Japan, China … But as far as Hong Kong was concerned, it was defined as an Anglophone beat.

6 Gwertzman's memorandum is reprinted in a book by Japanese writers criticizing *New York Times* reporting from their country (Zipangu 1998).

References

Appiah, K.A. 1996. Cosmopolitan Patriots. In Joshua Cohen (ed.), *For Love of Country*. Boston, MA: Beacon Press.

Bourdieu, P. 1998. *On Television and Journalism*. London: Pluto Press.

Cheah, P., and R. Robbins (eds.) 1998. *Cosmopolitics*. Minneapolis, MN: University of Minnesota Press.

Friedman, T. 1998. Booting Up Africa. *New York Times*, May 5.

Hannerz, U. 1990. Cosmopolitans and Locals in World Culture. In M. Featherstone (ed.), *Global Culture*. London: Sage.

———. 1998. Reporting from Jerusalem. *Cultural Anthropology*, 13 (4): 548–574.

———. 1999. Studying Townspeople, Studying Foreign Correspondents: Experiences of Two Approaches to Africa. In H.P. Hahn, and G. Spittler (eds.), *Afrika Und Die Globalisierung*. Hamburg: LIT Verlag.

———. 2001. Dateline Tokyo: Telling the World about Japan. In B. Moeran (ed.), *Asian Media Productions*. London: Curzon.

———. 2003. Being There … and There … and There! Reflections on Multi-Site Ethnography. *Ethnography*, 4 (2): 229–244.

———. 2004a. *Foreign News*. Chicago, IL: University of Chicago Press.

———. 2004b. Cosmopolitanism. In D. Nugent, and J. Vincent (eds.), *Companion to the Anthropology of Politics*. Oxford: Blackwell.

le Carré, J. 1977. *The Honourable Schoolboy*. London: Hodder and Stoughton.

Richburg, K.B. 1997. *Out of America*. New York, NY: Basic Books.

———. 1998. I Sing the Body Politic – And Economic. *The Correspondent*, March 4–5.

———. 2001. A Trek through the Mountains to the Taliban Front Is A Chilling Experience. *Washington Post*, November 8.

Robertson, R. 1992. *Globalization*. London: Sage.

Vertovec, S., and R. Cohen (eds.) 2002. *Conceiving Cosmopolitanism*. Oxford: Oxford University Press.

Watson, W. 1964. Social Mobility and Social Class in Industrial Communities. In M. Gluckman (ed.), *Closed Systems and Open Minds*. Edinburgh and London: Oliver and Boyd.

Zipangu (ed.) 1998. *Japan Made in USA*. New York, NY: Zipangu.

11

TOURING SOWETO

Culture and memory in urban South Africa

In the spring of 1998 I made my first visit to South Africa: a country which for me, and for many in my generation, has taken up a large space in our awareness, but which for many years, until recent changes, we mostly did not go to.[1] On a Sunday morning, during a stay in Johannesburg, I joined a half-day tour of Soweto, the enormous combine of Black townships which during the apartheid era acquired a world-wide reputation as the preeminent urban form of that social and ideological system: a concentration in space of separation, oppression, and impoverishment.

Since the end of apartheid, Soweto has in fact become one of Johannesburg's major tourist attractions. That may seem strange, and in very bad taste: a view of human suffering from a tour bus. Indeed, the tours have been somewhat controversial, and I was a little ambivalent about the arrangement. Yet I felt that as an at least off-and-on professional city watcher, I could hardly come away from South Africa without having had at least a glimpse of Soweto. Besides, I was curious about the tour itself – at this point in South African history, how would Soweto be represented, what image of its past, present, and future would be promoted?

So we set off from the hotel, in a discreet unmarked minibus, with Desmond, Black and in fact himself a Sowetan, as tour guide and driver. And as it turns out, what we are shown in the next few hours is not just an exhibition of human misery, but something more complex. Entering Soweto, we pass the huge Baragwanath Hospital; then there is the campus of Vista University, and a teacher training college, and a technical college. We stop on a hill where one can look down on a squatter settlement, full of bustling life, but with extremely small shacks, in large part of corrugated zinc, although partly of rough planks and cardboard. Desmond points out that the inhabitants are mostly South Africans, but also that many are immigrants from neighboring countries: Mocambicans, Zimbabweans

204 Touring Soweto

and others. As a handful of small children assemble next to the minibus, Desmond takes a few ballpoint pens out of a briefcase to distribute among them.

We drive past street-side garbage dumps where neighborhood people are engaged in a cleanup campaign, putting the refuse into plastic bags, and then we stop in a rather unkempt open area which once won its place in South African history. This was where, during two days toward the end of June, 1955, more than 3,000 delegates of a multiracial, although mostly Black, Congress of the People adopted the Freedom Charter, a founding document of the struggle against apartheid. The meeting was broken up by the police; Nelson Mandela (1995: 201–203), who describes the event in his autobiography, reminisces that he had observed it from the outskirts of the crowd, as he was already banned from public appearances, and notes that like other similar documents – the American Declaration of Independence, the French Declaration of the Rights of Man, and the Communist Manifesto – the Freedom Charter was "a mixture of practical goals and poetic language."

The site may be rather unimpressive yet, but Desmond, our guide, tells us that the present government plans to build a monument there, with inscriptions of the names of the Freedom Charter signatories.

Our next stop is at Wandie's Place, in Dube Street. Wandie's Place used to be a shebeen, one of the illicit drinking spots with which South Africa's Black townships were long generously sprinkled. Now it has been upgraded to a restaurant with menus, wine bottles on the tables, a hot buffet, and an aquarium with goldfish. One wall at Wandie's is almost covered by the business cards of visitors from all over the world – some recent additions to the collection are from White House staff, who have presumably made their calls at Wandie's while reconnoitering for President Clinton's Africa tour, just about to take place. I add my card, too.

We stop briefly outside one of ex-wife Winnie Mandela's more recent homes, an elegant house surrounded by high walls. Apparently relatives of Winnie's live there now. And then we proceed to the museum based on President Mandela's modest original home in Soweto: a small, box-like brick house where he lived for a period from the 1940s. The address used to be No. 8115 Orlando West, and Mandela indeed returned there briefly with Winnie after he regained his freedom in 1990. By now, I had just read in the South African newspapers, the museum is involved in a controversy – it is run by Winnie, and Nelson wants her evicted. There is a smooth-talking museum guide, educated in part in the United States, who says nothing about that conflict but demonstrates various memorabilia assembled in the few rooms, invites visitors to the gift shop, and points out that the museum welcomes donations.

A little further down the street is the home of Archbishop Desmond Tutu, also surrounded by high walls. This narrow hillside street in Soweto, we are informed, is "the only street in the world with the homes of two Nobel Prize winners."

Our bus proceeds past the large Roman Catholic Cathedral of Regina Mundi, which opened its doors to large gatherings in the apartheid period when political rallies in more secular spaces were not possible. Now, according to our guide Desmond, the government wants to take it over and turn it into a historical monument. We pass enterprises said to be owned by Soweto millionaires, and in the area known as Diepkloof, we can admire, if we are not put off by, the ostentatious villas owned by the newly rich. In East Orlando, in contrast, we come across some of the remaining examples of the most primitive accommodation, from Soweto's early period; also some of the worst crowding in Soweto, as the architectonic bricolage work of squatters fills in the small spaces surrounding original legal housing. But here and elsewhere, we also see how, now that the occupants can acquire ownership rights to their houses, original small houses can be expanded and gentrified. Some have flowers in front, although the plots are usually small. Out of many houses enterprises are run: food stores, barber shops.

And then, toward the end of the morning's tour, we come to Hector Petersen (or is it Peterson? In different places, different forms are used) Square, named after the 13-year-old school boy who was the first person to die in the Soweto riots of June, 1976, when students rose in protest against a proclaimed expansion of teaching in the Afrikaans language in their schools. At present, large containers around the square offer a home for an exhibition of photographs from the events of 1976, by South Africa's master photographer, Peter Magubane, complemented by pages from contemporary newspapers. Presumably there will be a more permanent exhibit someday. Meanwhile, a few weeks after our tour, President Clinton also visits Hector Petersen Square.

Our Soweto sightseeing is over – so what was it all about? After this first visit, to Soweto and to South Africa, I should certainly not claim any instant expertise. What perhaps even these early impressions can be used for, on the other hand, are some reflections on kinds of urbanism and urban cultural process, and on the ways we attach meanings and memories to urban environments.

To begin with, clearly, the Soweto cityscape is a product of that large-scale attempt at racist social engineering which took systematic and explicit shape in South Africa a half-century ago. Apartheid was in very considerable part a policy of spatial separations: from the overall confinement of as many Blacks as possible to limited rural "Bantustans," by way of the Group Areas Act which delimited separate areas of residence for Whites, Colored, Blacks and Asians, to the micromanagement of access to things like buses, benches, and toilets in those areas which must inevitably be shared by groups. Preferably, according to this line of thought, even members of different Black ethnic groups should keep their distances from one another. In Soweto, the idea had once been to assign them to different quarters. Here, too, as in other planned townships, the assumption that Blacks were essentially rural beings, only sojourners in urban environments, was made obvious under apartheid by the public ownership of those simple box-like houses, and the limited development of facilities. Electricity took a long time coming to much of Soweto. Not even the name really lent itself to a sense of historical rootedness, of being at home. As a matter of administrative rationality, it was simply an abbreviation of South Western Townships.

206 Touring Soweto

The tour showed this, but at least as much it was about how apartheid rules had been subverted and resisted under the apartheid era itself, and then more or less ostentatiously discarded in the few years afterwards. It offered more than just vicarious wallowing in human misfortune. In the late 1990s, the Sowetan urban landscape is still in considerable part one of widespread poverty, but there are also public institutions of learning and welfare, and the more individualizing exhibitions of cumulative local rooting, enterprise, and upward social mobility. Not least are there the symbols of past heroic protest, systematically foregrounded by the post-apartheid city and nation. In the construction work of collective memory, Soweto, like some variety of other more or less urban spaces in South Africa, has at least a part of its future as a rather sprawling monument to the freedom-seeking human spirit.

Nevertheless, it would then seem to be still a monument largely of Black South Africans (disregarding, for the moment, for example, the fact that some of those signatories of the Freedom Charter were Colored, and Asian, and White). And even as apartheid is gone as a legal structure and as a planning ideology, it is glaringly obvious that as a matter of everyday practice, urban South Africans of different pigmentations tend to remain in separate spaces. The central business district of Johannesburg, "downtown," is a dramatic example. It is not so long ago that this area was, not all White, but firmly under White control, before apartheid began to crumble. Now, at least one's first impression is of a curiously vertically divided cityscape. Look up, and you see the steel and glass facades of high-rises which could be in North America, or here and there the monumental architecture of the British Empire. Look at sidewalk life, and you see the pedestrians and petty traders of urban Black Africa. Prosperous White Johannesburg, it appears, has in large part withdrawn to the shopping malls and office buildings in the northern suburbs, where homes are surrounded by high walls, and large signs warn that trespassers will be met with "ARMED RESPONSE."

Sophiatown/Triomf

I was actually in South Africa this time for the purpose of talking to news media foreign correspondents, as part of a research project, and when I mentioned to the Johannesburg correspondent of the London *Daily Telegraph* that I had taken one of the Soweto tours, it reminded him of a South African White acquaintance of his who had been sharply critical of these – but then it had turned out that she had never ever been to Soweto herself, or to any other Black township for that matter. He had thought that perhaps some time, in some way or other, as a citizen, she ought to go.

Yet there was another part of Johannesburg to which I was also drawn, with rather more personal preparation than I had for Soweto. Toward the end of the apartheid era, one of South Africa's best-known journalists, Alister Sparks (1997: 187), described the area this way:

> Take Bree Street out of central Johannesburg heading west, and you will come in time to one of the city's more colourless suburbs, little stucco-plastered

houses on eight-acre plots surrounded by prefab walls, many in wagon-wheel designs, and with concrete gnomes in the garden. A glimpse through the windows will reveal living rooms furnished with cheap modern furniture, plastic doilies, kitschy copper ornaments, and sentimental Tretchikoff prints, while the driveways, likely as not, will contain more than the usual number of powerful motorcycles and supercharged Volkswagens. This is lower-middle-class white suburbia, clean, conformist, macho, and dull.

At the time, as a product of apartheid urban planning, this area could seem like Soweto's better-off White counterpart. But Sparks (1997: 187) went on to draw attention to the name of the area – Triomf:

> As you may deduce from that, this otherwise unremarkable suburb is in fact a triumphant symbol of Afrikaner racial domination. Because here briefly in the 1930s, 1940s and early 1950s flourished South Africa's closest approximation to a free black society, a vital, vibrant community, a living example of what a free South Africa might have been and may yet be. But for precisely that reason it cut across what the apartheid visionaries had in mind and so they eliminated it and built Triomf in its place.

That "vital, vibrant community" which was destroyed in the late 1950s and replaced by Triomf was Sophiatown (named after the wife of the White speculator who had first acquired the land). And in a way it was not Triomf, but rather the mythical Sophiatown I wanted to visit, perhaps a bit oddly more in the nature of a pilgrimage.

I first learned of Sophiatown a few years after its destruction, in the early 1960s, when, at a theater in London's West End, I saw the export version of the musical *King Kong*, which, it has been said, "represented at once an ultimate achievement and final flowering of Sophiatown culture" (Coplan 1985: 175). *King Kong* was the story, with a basis in actual events, of a tragical hero, the heavyweight champion Ezekiel Dhlamini, taking his name as a star of the boxing ring from movie posters. King Kong the boxer became involved with gangsters, found his woman friend involved with another man, killed her, was sent to jail, and committed suicide there. And *King Kong* the musical had the street life, the shebeens, the violence, and something at least approximating the music of the township: jazz, penny whistles, the work songs of Black miners.

Then as time passed, I came upon Sophiatown again and again, at first stumbling on it in the works of a generation of Black South African writers, many of whom were at one time or other journalists at *Drum*, the popular magazine. And I also began looking for it a little more systematically, in places from Nadine Gordimer's novels to Nelson Mandela's and Miriam Makeba's autobiographies. Mandela, while not a resident of Sophiatown, had been involved in the attempts to save it from destruction; when *King Kong*, the musical, had premiered in Johannesburg, Makeba had played the female lead role. Until then, she

208 Touring Soweto

had been the vocalist of a leading township group. By the time I saw *King Kong* in London, she had left the cast, in pursuit of her own international career.

Indeed, Sophiatown saw a remarkable number of people pass through who would go on to make a name for themselves. During much of that period, which later became legendary, the preeminent local celebrity was no doubt Alfred Bitini Xuma, medical doctor, trained in America, Scotland, and England, sometime president of the African National Congress. His large house, almost palatial by local standards, with two garages, was a Sophiatown landmark. But among the pupils at the highly reputed local Anglican mission school were Oliver Tambo, later Nelson Mandela's law partner and ANC president in exile while Mandela was spending those decades in prison, and also Hugh Masekela, who achieved world fame as a trumpeter before returning to South Africa only as apartheid was coming to an end. (Masekela, too, started out with *King Kong*, where he was in the orchestra.) And then again there was Desmond Tutu, the later archbishop, anti-apartheid activist and Nobel Prize winner, but before that the son of a Sophiatown washerwoman.

And yet as Archbishop Tutu's mother's occupation suggests, by the standards of Black South Africa at the time this was not even some kind of elite district. For the African middle class Sophiatown was attractive not least because after land ownership had been severely restricted through the 1923 Urban Areas Act, it was one of few places where they could own their plots and houses. Moreover, as newer Black townships were built much further out, there was hardly anywhere else that Africans could live so conveniently close to the center of Johannesburg, in such relative freedom of control. Even so, the larger part of the Sophiatown population would be working class or lumpenproletariat, so it was a place where classes and lifestyles mingled. People had to sort each other out and find ways of co-existing. "Double-storey mansions and quaint cottages, with attractive, well-tended gardens, stood side by side with rusty wood-and-iron shacks, locked in a fraternal embrace of filth and felony" writes Don Mattera (1989: 74), gang leader turned writer, and the grandson of an Italian immigrant who became a prosperous transporter. "The communal water taps, toilets and showerhouses of Sophiatown, though insanitary and inadequate, are remembered today as casual meeting places where the better-off and educated mixed with their humbler neighbours," the anthropologist David Coplan (1985: 152) notes.

In the outside, powerful world, there were those who looked upon Sophiatown as a slum, and used this as a reason for doing away with it, removing its inhabitants to rapidly growing Soweto. Certainly Sophiatown with time became increasingly overcrowded. Houses had more and more occupants – owners, tenants, and subtenants; sometimes forty to a dwelling, and fifteen to a room – and new shacks were squeezed into the existing plots. By midcentury some 40,000 people lived there. The Johannesburg city government also provided fewer amenities than it would in areas more directly under its domination. And there was forever a danger of violence; while some would argue that the township

Touring Soweto **209**

gangsters, the tsotsis, would seldom bother ordinary people, in large part preoccupied with their own internecine battles (and otherwise engaging in a sort of
Robin Hood-like social banditry, stealing from White businesses and selling at
favorable prices in the townships), it can hardly be denied that their presence
was often felt to be quite menacing.

Cosmopolitanism and creativity

But the reason I became increasingly fascinated by the historical record of the
Sophiatown that was already gone was the kind of culture that had apparently
flourished there. By the time that I got around to collecting and organizing the
accounts and commentaries more systematically, I was engaged in a sort of comparative study of the peculiarities of urban cultural process, and of what makes
some cities, in some periods, more than usually culturally creative. I had been
looking, for example, at Vienna around the last turn of the century, Calcutta
during its nineteenth-century Bengal Renaissance, and at San Francisco in the
post-World War II years, in what was also described as a San Francisco
Renaissance.[2] What one could find in such places was for one thing a coming
together of people and cultural currents from many origins, and for another an
internal openness, so that the different kinds of people and their understandings
and modes of expression actually met, sometimes clashed, and certainly mingled
in a synergetic process, with rich opportunities for serendipity. In Calcutta there
was the encounter between Indian and western culture; in Vienna the meeting
ground of the many peoples of the crumbling Habsburg Empire, and frequently
the best and brightest of them, as well as some of their nastiest; in San Francisco,
a sanctuary of American nonconformism, White and Black, also found sources
of inspiration in Native American as well as Asian culture. Furthermore, in each
of them a conspicuous feature of the urban landscape was the more or less informal public spaces which allowed interaction and communication as an easy,
ongoing thing – the rich associational life and the *adda*, salons, of Calcutta, the
cafés of Vienna, the bars and coffee houses of San Francisco.

I felt I could discern some of the same conditions of cultural swirl in what
had been Sophiatown. True, this was not a separate urban community. Rather,
I understand it to have been the kind of part of a larger urban conglomerate
"where the action is," where cultural process is somehow intensified – the
Soho, the Greenwich Village, the Quartier Latin, the Kreuzberg, the North
Beach of Johannesburg; or perhaps what Harlem was to New York in the days
(and nights) of the 1920s Harlem Renaissance. There is a great deal going on in
such a place in terms of the local shaping and handling of ideas and symbolic
forms. But it also brings in culture from the outside, as working materials, and
then sometimes also exports something of its own to the surrounding world:
regionally, nationally, globally.

Sophiatown also brought people together in diversity. Alister Sparks, the
South African journalist comparing Sophiatown with the Triomf that followed

210 Touring Soweto

it, may have described it as "a free Black society," but although this is a large part of the story, it was not only that. Apart from the fact that there were both Black and Colored inhabitants, according to the historical South African distinction, there were some number of Indian and Chinese residents, as well as Indian, Chinese, and Jewish shopkeepers. Indeed, there seems to have been the occasional White resident Sophiatowner as well; the playwright Athol Fugard apparently lived there for a while.

And in any case, Sophiatown certainly did see more White visitors than most Black townships. It was not so far away, and its entrance was not controlled as some others (cf. Nicol 1991: 96). To the more adventurous, it was an attractive place.

The cosmopolitanism of Sophiatown is eloquently captured, I think, in a brief passage by Can Themba (1972: 107), one of the Black writers of the *Drum* generation:

> You don't just find your place here, you make it and you find yourself. There is a tang about it. You might now and then have to give way to others making their ways of life by methods which are not in the book, but you can't be bored. You have the right to listen to the latest jazz records at Ah Sing's over the road. You can walk a Coloured girl of an evening down to the Odin cinema, and no questions asked. You can try out Rhugubar's curry with your bare fingers without embarrassment. All this with no sense of heresy. Indeed, I've shown quite a few white people "the little Paris of the Transvaal" – but only a few were Afrikaners.

I am reminded here of the essayist Jonathan Raban's (1974) notion of the "soft city" – translated into the vocabulary of social theory, the role of agency in creating one's personal urban environment.

And then Sophiatown, too, had those free public spaces where people could mix and exchange news and views – places of different kinds, although the shebeens were surely not unimportant. Places like the *Back of the Moon*, the *Thirty-nine Steps* or the *Cabin in the Sky* seem to have been the kind of places where, in endless and probably noisy debates, reality as well as alternatives to it are continuously constructed, destroyed, and reconstructed again. According to the account of someone who was born and brought up in Sophiatown:

> In such places one could sit until the following day just as long as one bought liquor. The shebeens were one of the main forms of social entertainment. In old Sophiatown the shebeens were not simply made up of a gathering of drunkards. People came to the shebeens to discuss matters, to talk about things, their daily worries, their political ideas, their fears, and their hopes. There were various kinds of people who frequented the shebeens. But probably the most interesting and the most dangerous types were the politicians. Such people have always tried to influence others and

get them to conform to their way of thinking, and if one disagreed he immediately became suspect and classed as an informer ... Such were the Sophiatown shebeens, dirty dark little rooms, hidden away in some back alley, or smart posh joints furnished with contemporary Swedish furniture.

(deRidder 1961: 41)

Perhaps the classic shebeens were to 1950s Sophiatowners what the *Vesuvio Bar* and the *Caffe Trieste* were to the Beats and bohemians in San Francisco at much the same time, or what the *Greinstiedl* and the *Café Central* were to turn-of-the-century Vienna?

Conclusion: cityscapes of a rainbow nation

It is time, perhaps, to make some brief but more explicit comparative points about Soweto and Triomf as products of apartheid, and Sophiatown as a pre-apartheid phenomenon. To phrase the message in more general terms, let me quote one of the greatest scholars of city life in the twentieth century, the sociologist Robert Park, founder of the Chicago school of urban sociology which flourished between the two world wars. Park (1952: 47), in a statement drawing attention to the divisions within cities, suggested that "the processes of segregation establish moral distances which make the city a mosaic of little worlds which touch but do not interpenetrate." And this formulation indeed guided much of the work of the Chicago urban sociologists: the city was a "mosaic of little worlds," which its ethnographers could see as more or less well-bounded isolates. Yet some critics have later suggested that these "little worlds" did in fact not only touch, but interpenetrated rather more than the researchers of the pioneer generation cared to acknowledge.

The "mosaic" has indeed over the years been a favorite metaphor for describing not only the diversity within cities, but also the diversity of the world. Nevertheless, we should perhaps be a bit suspicious of its general applicability. In recent years, I have been more actively preoccupied with globalization and its cultural processes, while criticizing the widespread assumption that increasing global interconnectedness necessarily leads to cultural homogenization. I have often returned to a contrast between a view of the world as a "mosaic" and a view of it as an "ecumene" – where a relevant definition of an ecumene is "a region of persistent cultural interaction and exchange" (Kopytoff 1987: 10). Taking this contrast into an urban setting, one may well discern that some cities, and some parts of cities, may match more closely the metaphor of the mosaic with its enduring, well-demarcated pieces, while others are more ecumenical in their handling of cultural diversity.

There is another metaphor of social life I want to remind you of here, not so much out of academic social science but rather out of contemporary South Africa. In the years of post-apartheid enthusiasm, some South Africans, at least, have been happy to describe themselves as "the rainbow nation," and we could reflect a little

212 Touring Soweto

about how to understand this. A rainbow is of course a harmonious, esthetically pleasing, multicolor phenomenon, and this is what many South Africans may now want to identify with. One might add that a rainbow is something which emerges after some bad weather. Yet moreover, the stripes of the rainbow typically do not have sharp edges. Rather, they are gently blurred vis-à-vis one another. In that way, it seems to me that this is an imagery which shows greater affinity to the ecumene than to the mosaic.

Social life, and not least urban life, in apartheid South Africa may have approximated the mosaic model more closely than one would normally expect to find in the contemporary world. There was, in fact, a concern among those in power that those different social worlds in the city should not only not interpenetrate, as in Robert Park's formulation just quoted – they should preferably not even touch (an ideal which was of course impossible). Soweto and Triomf, as they existed for perhaps a third of a century or so, were parts of an attempt to take the mosaic metaphor quite literally. Sophiatown, on the other hand, seems to have been a neighborhood in the rainbow nation, where cultural interaction and exchange did take place.

It is interesting to see what kinds of memories are now consciously maintained and reconstructed in the South African city. In Soweto, we have seen, it is in large part a matter of protest and resistance. Again, this is largely a Black affair, and it could hardly be otherwise. Just next to Johannesburg's lively, somewhat nervous downtown, however, on Bree Street, which the journalist Sparks noted led toward Triomf, there is the new Museum Africa, devoted to a post-apartheid understanding of South Africa's political, social, and cultural history. And there, in the exhibits, one finds Sophiatown given a great deal of attention, including the reconstruction of one of its old-time shebeens. At the other end of the country, in Cape Town, there is another museum, a kind of participatory institution devoted to another urban area: the old District Six, close to the harbor, somewhat resembling Sophiatown in its diversity and cosmopolitanism, and likewise destroyed during the apartheid era, although still not quite replaced by anything else.[3] It seems, then, that the rainbow nation is seeking out those early cityscapes which were at one time in character with its present self-image, and reassembling them in memory even when the reality has been destroyed.

And what did I find, then, on my instant pilgrimage to what had been Sophiatown, but was still Triomf? Indeed a physical setting not so different from what Alister Sparks described from a decade ago. There is really nothing left materially of old Sophiatown; even its street pattern has been obliterated. Yet in the new South Africa, its population is changing. This is no longer an all-White piece in a mosaic. Indians and Blacks are moving in, even as some Whites remain. And when I pass the police station which my Johannesburg map still identifies as the General Johan Coetzee Police Station, linking law and order to a well-known Afrikaner name, I now read a new name on the wall: Sophiatown Police Station. Through the politics of naming and renaming, it seems, one pioneering moment of rainbow past is returning to the present.

Notes

1 This essay first appeared in *City and Culture: Cultural Processes and Urban Sustainability*, edited by Louise Nyström and published by the Swedish Urban Environmental Council (Boverket), Karlskrona 1991. In the part discussing Sophiatown, I draw on my earlier inquiry into its life (Hannerz 1994, 1996: 160 ff.).
2 See on this Hannerz (1992: 173 ff.).
3 On District Six in Cape Town see e.g. Western (1996: 137 ff.).

References

Coplan, David. 1985. *In Township Tonight!* London: Longman.

deRidder, J.C. 1961. *The Personality of the Urban African in South Africa*. London: Routledge & Kegan Paul.

Hannerz, Ulf. 1992. *Cultural Complexity*. New York, NY: Columbia University Press.

———. 1994. Sophiatown: The View from Afar. *Journal of Southern African Studies*, 20: 181–193.

———. 1996. *Transnational Connections*. London: Routledge.

Kopytoff, Igor. 1987. The Internal African Frontier: The Making of an African Political Culture. In Igor Kopytoff (ed.), *The African Frontier*. Bloomington, IN: Indiana University Press.

Mandela, Nelson. 1995. *Long Walk to Freedom*. London: Abacus.

Mattera, Don. 1989. *Sophiatown*. Boston, MA: Beacon Press.

Nicol, Michael. 1991. *A Good-Looking Corpse*. London: Secker and Warburg.

Park, Robert E. 1952. *Human Communities*. Glencoe, IL: Free Press.

Raban, Jonathan. 1974. *Soft City*. London: Hamish Hamilton.

Sparks, Alister. 1997. *The Mind of South Africa*. London: Arrow Books. (First published in 1990 by William Heinemann.)

Themba, Can. 1972. *The Will to Die*. London: Heinemann.

Western, John. 1996. *Outcaste Cape Town*. Berkeley, CA: University of California Press.

12

REFLECTIONS ON VARIETIES OF CULTURESPEAK

A sunny morning a few years ago, at my summer house in southern Sweden, with a national election season approaching, I found a leaflet in my mail box.[1] In blue letters against a yellow background (the colors of the Swedish flag), an extremist group in a nearby town argued that the country had turned from a *folkhem*, a "home of the people," into a "multicultural inferno."

One could reflect that this suggests two things about the place of the culture concept in contemporary discourse. One is that "culture" is no longer a notion occurring mostly among the well-educated, within the confines of their scholarly, intellectual and esthetic preoccupations. Increasingly it, and other concepts deriving from it, seem to be just about everywhere, from public commentary and political agitation through organizational consultancy to commerce and advertising. And there are no real barriers separating different uses, and different users. Researchers and policy makers now share the term "multiculturalism" with ethnic minority politicians, as well as with the xenophobic activists claiming to represent a silent majority. One has to be sensitive, consequently, to those refractions of meaning which may occur as a vocabulary of culture moves between contexts.

The other thing to note, with regard to that suggestion of a "multicultural inferno," is that while "culture" in the past was probably a term with mostly consensual and positive overtones, it now very often shows up in contexts of discord – "culture clash," "culture conflict," "culture wars"; and perhaps also, at a different level, "culture shock." A major reason for this, no doubt, is that culturespeak now very often draws our attention to what are taken to be the interfaces between cultures; a tendency which in its turn has much to do with that polymorphous global interconnectedness through which such interfaces become increasingly prominent in human experience. In what follows, I will comment on some of the ways we now talk of the meeting of cultures, and their implications for scholarship and public life.[2]

Clashing civilizations

The leaflet in my summer mailbox is obviously only some minor, parochial evidence here. Let me turn to, and to some extent dwell on, a weightier instance of writing about cultures in conflict. Since the end of the Cold War, there has been a certain rush to produce scenarios for what the world will now be like. One of the most conspicuous has been that of the political scientist Samuel Huntington, appearing first in an article in the influential American journal *Foreign Affairs* (1993), and later (1996) in book form. With major conflict over political ideology gone, Huntington argues, the next battle is between the large-scale cultural blocs of the world, a "clash of civilizations."

Attempting to enumerate such entities, Huntington refers to Spengler, Toynbee and other ancestral figures in civilizational scholarship, but appears uncertain as to how many civilizations there are now. Africa may or may not qualify, and he is not very clear or consistent about Buddhism, Judaism and Eastern Orthodox Christianity either, but at least there are Western, Latin American, Islamic, Hindu, Confucian (or Sinic) and Japanese civilizations. In any case, while states may be the major actors in the international order, the important thing about civilizations in Huntington's view is that they tend to determine who goes with whom in wider configurations of conflict. Peoples and nations now try to answer that most basic question – who are we? – and use politics not just to advance their interests but also to define their identity. "We know who we are only when we know who we are not and often only when we know whom we are against" (Huntington 1996: 21). Thus identity politics goes global; and, putting it bluntly in Huntington's worst scenario, it is the West against the Muslims and the Confucians.

In the preface to his book, Huntington suggests that it is "not intended to be a work of social science." It offers him an opportunity, however, to elaborate on some themes which he had only been able to touch on in his preceding article:

> the concept of civilizations; the question of a universal civilization; the relation between power and culture; the shifting balance of power among civilizations; cultural indigenization in non-Western societies; the political structure of civilizations; conflicts generated by Western universalism, Muslim militancy, and Chinese assertion; balancing and bandwagoning responses to the rise of Chinese power; the causes and dynamics of fault-line wars; and the futures of the West and of a world of civilizations.

In the wake of the 1993 article, he notes he not only became involved in innumerable meetings with academic, government and business groups across the United States, but also had the opportunity to participate in discussions of its thesis in "many other countries, including Argentina, Belgium, China, France, Germany, Great Britain, Korea, Japan, Luxembourg, Russia, Saudi Arabia, Singapore, South Africa, Spain, Sweden, Switzerland, and Taiwan" (Huntington 1996: 13–14). With enthusiastic blurbs on the back cover of the book by such major international policy

216 Reflections on varieties of culturespeak

makers of the past as Henry Kissinger and Zbigniew Brzezinski, there is probably a good chance that it, too, will draw some public attention – even as the more strictly academic reception has been rather unenthusiastic.[3]

"The Huntington thesis" appears, on the whole, to be a high-status variant of what the Barcelona anthropologist Verena Stolcke (1995) has described as "cultural fundamentalism" – human beings are, by nature, culture bearers; cultures are distinct and incommensurable; relations between bearers of different cultures are intrinsically conflictive; it is in human nature to be xenophobic. Such cultural fundamentalism, Stolcke notes, differs from traditional racism in that it does not necessarily carry with it assumptions of hierarchy. It may well proclaim a sort of cultural relativism, but then each culture should stay in its place. As they are incommensurable, they must be spatially segregated. Cultural fundamentalism thus now serves, not least in Europe, as an alternative doctrine of exclusion. In other words, we are back to the idea of the "multicultural inferno."

Quite possibly Huntington might be horrified by such associations, as this is not usually the language of the seminar room or the conference center. Yet with the kind of multifaceted impact his recent writings have had, it seems reasonable to be somewhat concerned about what series of echoes they may produce. There are commentators who even suggest that there could be an element of self-fulfilling prophecy in the thesis and its further propagation.

Scrutinizing culturespeak

Perhaps one would imagine that those of us who have long been occupied with questions of culture, in research and in policy, should now be very pleased with the current spread of culturespeak. It could appear that other people are finally realizing that we are concerned with something that is, after all, worthwhile and important. Instead it turns out that we have reason to be worried. In anthropology, there have recently been a number of scholars who for various, but partly political, reasons have felt that we would be better off without the culture concept, precisely because it may give too much emphasis to difference, and thereby could indeed lend support to cultural fundamentalist tendencies. I am afraid this is an ostrich response. The problem will not go away just because some rather small group of academics decide to banish a word from their own vocabulary (and besides, there are aspects of the culture concept which we probably still find quite valuable, and which are, at present, not communicated equally effectively by any alternative term). Insofar as academic scholarship on culture carries any intellectual authority outside our own institutions, we would do better to keep a critical eye on the varieties of culturespeak both among ourselves and in society at large – and try to blow our whistles when usage seems questionable or even pernicious.

I am suggesting, this is to say, that one kind of cultural research with a definite policy relevance involves scrutinizing the uses of "culture" and related concepts, and the assumptions underlying these uses, in public life. Cultural study is not only a summarizing label for all those inquiries we conduct into the wide range of

Reflections on varieties of culturespeak **217**

things we consider cultural, but also (not least in the present period) a study of popular theories, prototheories and quasitheories of culture.

Cultural fundamentalism is only one of these. They may develop in different contexts, shaping themselves to meet different requirements, and they need not be all malignant. I mentioned above the concept of "culture shock," diffusing widely in the late twentieth century as a way of referring to the kind of emotional and intellectual unease that sometimes occurs in encounters with unfamiliar meanings and practices. Rather facetiously, I have also occasionally referred to the growth of a "culture shock prevention industry." The proper term for its practitioners, I should quickly note, is "interculturalists" – a new profession of people working commercially as trainers and consultants, trying to teach sensitivity toward cultural diversity to various audiences through lectures, simulation games, videos, practical handbooks and some variety of other means. From an academic vantage point one may be critical of certain of the efforts – they may seem a bit trite, somewhat inclined toward stereotyping, occasionally given to exaggerating cultural differences perhaps as a way of positioning the interculturalists themselves as an indispensable profession. As Tommy Dahlén (1997) has recently shown, some of the peculiarities of interculturalist theory and practice are indeed shaped by the characteristics of the market place. Yet one may find much to think about in the experimentation with the modalities of communicating about experiences of cultural difference. And obviously interculturalists are not xenophobes. They are cultural technicians in an era of globalization, trying to assist clients practically in dealing with others "of a different cultural background."

We may see "multiculturalism" as another conspicuous late twentieth-century form of culturespeak. I refer here not merely to cultural diversity as such, but to that self-conscious preoccupation with cultural difference and collective identity which, although it undoubtedly has many sources, may have had a sort of recent historical take-off point in Black American cultural nationalism and separatism in the late 1960s, and the attention it received throughout much of the world. Clearly contemporary multiculturalism is very heterogeneous, much more so than its adversaries are likely to recognize. A common denominator, however, tends to be that culture is understood to be linked with power. A collectivity of some sort – mostly but not always ethnically or racially defined – makes its culture the source of internal solidarity and mobilization, and externally stakes claims to autonomy or special rights on the same basis. Multiculturalist persuasions vary in their concerns with boundary maintenance, but certain forms come to resemble cultural fundamentalism in their emphasis on separateness. The obvious difference is that cultural fundamentalism of the type initially identified above seeks spatial exclusiveness at some macro-level, such as that of a nation-state, to avoid the "multicultural inferno," whereas multiculturalists mostly seek their rights within a shared space and social order.

Yet another well-established form of culturespeak must be brought into the picture here. For at least a quarter-century or so now, Swedish discussions of

218 Reflections on varieties of culturespeak

culture, not least in policy contexts, have been prefaced by references to a contrast between, on one hand, "the anthropological concept of culture," and on the other hand, something which for a long time was the rather more prevalent understanding of the term, referring to particular intellectual and esthetic achievement.

That anthropological concept may never have been quite as homogeneous as this contrast made it out to be, but in the context of the distinction, it has obviously been taken to refer to something like collective ways of life. At this point, however, let us consider briefly the other concept, that relating to a more or less specialized domain of intellectual and esthetic activity, a "cultural sector" as understood in a rather traditional way. Here the emphasis is on innovation and originality, and while there are ever-debatable quality criteria by which some achievements are evaluated as greater than others, the overall attitude can perhaps be described as celebrationist: culture is a good thing, and cultural variety and change are also good things.

No need to repeat here the familiar recent arguments about the ways in which the involvement with (consumption and awareness of) such cultural materials have tended to become unevenly socially distributed, and turn into a "cultural capital" of mostly prosperous and well-educated classes, especially in western society. We also see that to the extent that there have been anything like state cultural welfare policies, they have been in large part concerned with making intellectual and esthetic products and activities, of what has somehow been defined as high quality, more broadly available, along class and regional dimensions – and especially taking them to some degree out of the framework of the market.

What I particularly want to draw attention to here, however, is the tendency of "cultural celebrationism" also to establish itself as a major variety of contemporary culturespeak; and not least its tendency to expand out of that domain of intellectual and esthetic achievement which seems to be its original home base. It would seem very likely that the polysemy of the term "culture" facilitates the spread of this stance into other areas of life and thought as well, including those where that "anthropological concept of culture," centering on differences between collectively based ways of life, is most strongly rooted. When it reaches into such contexts, we should note, cultural celebrationism may tend to merge with certain of the varied meanings of "cosmopolitanism" – defined for example in *Webster's International Dictionary* as "marked by interest in, familiarity with, or knowledge and appreciation of many parts of the world" or "a climate of opinion distinguished by the absence of narrow national loyalties or parochial prejudices and by a readiness to borrow from other lands or regions in the formation of cultural or artistic patterns." The attitude of intellectual and esthetic appreciation is extended here, then, to seeing entire collective ways of life and thought as something like works of art, and to enjoy the diversity of culture for its own sake.

Most people involved in cultural policy issues, in agencies at national and local levels as well as in international organizations such as UNESCO, are probably habitual users of a celebrationist variety of culturespeak, and it is well established in Academia as well, especially in the humanities and social sciences. Such habitual users may conceivably be somewhat ill at ease in seeing it relativized as a variety of culturespeak, insofar as they may be entirely convinced that it is the natural, or at least more enlightened, way of approaching cultural matters. Yet in the context of the wider field where different ways of looking at culture and cultural difference meet, it may be useful not to leave it as an unmarked variety.

Celebrationism in its cosmopolitan tendency is certainly strong among anthropologists; it is also widespread among interculturalists, who may have to start out from defining cultural difference as a practical problem, but are inclined to move on to helping clients become aware of "the wealth of human diversity" or some such formula. Multiculturalism and celebrationism may at times form a kind of symbiotic relationship, since celebrationists can appreciate the diversity fostered by multiculturalist policies and are frequently in positions from which they can give effective political and material support to the claims multiculturalists make. The real clash, on the other hand, is obviously with cultural fundamentalism, which may perhaps be celebrationist *within* a culture, but not across "cultural borders." The conversation between fundamentalists and celebrationists readily turns into a dialogue of the deaf, and consequently into a shouting match.

Confronting cultural fundamentalism

Can we identify a more persuasive way of talking about contemporary culture, which stands a better chance of engaging with at least some of the concerns now underlying cultural fundamentalism? It may be naive to expect that one could thus reach out for some all-inclusive consensus, embracing even the activists behind a "multicultural inferno" leaflet, but it would seem that there are now, in Sweden and elsewhere in Europe and the world, those who simply find celebrationism unpersuasive in their own everyday situations, and partly for lack of a better alternative fall back on at least mild versions of cultural fundamentalism, as a readily available, easily comprehensible default solution; something that appears more like "common sense" than celebrationism may do.

It is always difficult to compete with simple formulae for public attention. The subtleties of cultural research are frequently not readily packageable as attractive goods in a more general marketplace of ideas. Nevertheless, it would seem that the effort has to be made to seek out the kind of working understandings of culture which we as researchers now find productive in our scholarly activity, and which may also resonate with the personal experiences of laymen, so that they can stand as a credible alternative to fundamentalist views of the world. Perhaps it could be instructive here to look again at Samuel Huntington's "clash of civilizations" thesis; after all, one of the more elaborated and intellectually sophisticated statements of a fundamentalist position. Certainly Huntington's main concern is with large-scale political, and ultimately military, conflict,

220 Reflections on varieties of culturespeak

rather than with a cultural mapping of the world *per se*. Yet the listing of topics at least touched on in his book, as quoted above, suggests that there is at least an outline of a more all-embracing view of the global situation. And to repeat, it is a view which draws attention in board rooms, government offices and newsrooms, and which is likely to spread from there as well.[4] Where, then, would one want to take issue with his arguments and assumptions about the present cultural order?

The late twentieth century turn of a senior theorist of the Cold War to civilizations, and to the preoccupations of Spengler and Toynbee, may appear surprising, even quaint. Indeed he has some rather more recent sources of inspiration as well (such as Carroll Quigley, Rushton Coulborn, Fernand Braudel and William McNeill). But many of these later points of reference in the area of comparative civilizational thought are still midcentury or so.

Yet we must note not only where, and in what periods, he finds his intellectual companions, but also who his adversaries are. And these are not only the potential enemies of his country (or his civilization) but are also closer at hand, in more recent western academic theory and intellectual debate. On the one hand, they include the variety of proponents of arguments to the effect that the world is becoming more culturally uniform. Here are those who assume that modernization equals westernization. Here are also all those who either celebrate or regret, but mostly do not doubt, the pervasive global influence of western popular culture and the media. And here, too, are the people who believe in a "universal civilization" – a set of assumptions, doctrines and values held by many people in Western civilization, Huntington notes, and by some people in other civilizations. But we might as well, he suggests, call it "Davos Culture," after the 1000 government officials, bankers, businessmen, intellectuals and journalists who meet annually at the World Economic Forum – outside the West, its adherents hardly make up as much as 1% of the people in any civilization.

Among Huntington's adversaries are also, on the other hand, the multiculturalists at home. In the domestic culture wars of his own country, that is, Huntington is obviously a partisan. The "divisive siren calls of multiculturalism," he argues, not only threaten to turn the United States into a United Nations. In so doing, they furthermore undermine that western civilization in which the American component is now of vital importance.

One may be inclined to sympathize somewhat with Huntington's rejection of some of the more far-reaching claims and forecasts of global cultural homogenization, and yet feel that he has little to offer in the way of an understanding of the interplay between longstanding regional characteristics and especially more recent global and transnational influences. The point of much recent writing (mine included) on the cultural aspects of globalization, after all, is not to depict or predict a uniform world culture, but to portray the new complexity brought about by the coexistence and the intertwining of what tends to be labeled "the global" and "the local," and the new experiences and cultural forms generated through interconnectedness.[5] And here the skirmishes over multiculturalism in the United States may not, after all, stand out as such an aberrant case. There is certainly a fair amount of cultural debate now going on in others of Huntington's civilizational entities as well; debates brought about not least by expanding transnational markets, changing media configurations, new migration streams, clusters of rights-oriented social movements, or other of those phenomena which now tend to blur the borders of the past.

Perhaps a key word in pulling together another approach is "process." In a way, the problem of Huntington's civilizational emphasis is its strong bias in the handling of the time dimension of culture: "civilizations are mortal but also very long-lived; they evolve, adapt, and are the most enduring of human associations, 'realities of the extreme *longue durée*'" (Huntington 1996: 43). Despite those "evolve" and "adapt," it shares with other versions of cultural fundamentalism the tendency to naturalize cultural immutability and persistence. The point of emphasizing process is not to shift to the opposite bias, and discern only change, change, change. It is rather a matter of destabilizing the privileged assumptions of continuity and timelessness, to make reproduction and change in principle equally problematic. This could seem like a good idea at any time, but it appears especially desirable now, insofar as globalization in major or minor ways increasingly affects more locally encapsulated processes of reproduction and makes their continued functioning less self-evident.

A more processual view tends to "bring people back in." In recent times, there has been a considerable amount of attention in social and cultural theory to issues of "agency" and "structure." It seems characteristic of civilizational thinking of the type that Huntington draws on, as well as of cultural fundamentalism generally, that the greater weight is usually placed on structure.[6] (Or somehow, culture itself becomes some sort of superhuman agent.) It would seem helpful to make more continuously visible how both persistence and change in culture depend on human activity; and how in contemporary, complex social life, the combined cultural process, and the overall habitat of meanings and practices in which we dwell, is the outcome of the variously deliberate pursuit by a variety of actors of their own agendas, with different power and different social and spatial reach, and with foreseen or unanticipated consequences. Such an approach to cultural process would be a challenge to each of us, layperson or scholar, to try and work out what ingredients go into situations that may puzzle us or annoy us. For one thing, it may reveal to what extent conflicts over cultural identities, xenophobia, and ethnic cleansing are initiated and reinforced by political entrepreneurs with megaphones and printing presses (and, by now, websites).

The attention to processes and people may also help unpack the assumption of the unitary, integrated culture which may not be unique to cultural fundamentalism but which goes well with it. We have an old habit of speaking about "cultures," in the plural form, as if it were self-evident that such entities exist side by side as neat packages, each of us identified with only one of them – this is indeed a timeworn implication of at least one "anthropological culture concept." And the notion of "cultural identity" often goes with it. It may well be that some considerable number of people

222 Reflections on varieties of culturespeak

really live encapsulated among others who share most of the same experiences, ideas, beliefs, values, habits, and tastes. Nonetheless, it appears increasingly likely that many people have biographies entailing various cross-cutting allegiances – they share different parts of their personal cultural repertoires with different collections of people. And if there is an "integrated whole," it may be a quite individual thing. Under such circumstances, people may well value some parts of these personal repertoires more highly than others, identify themselves particularly in terms of them, and identify in collective terms more strongly with those other people with whom they share them. It could also be, on the other hand, that they may resist attempts to categorize them unidimensionally in terms of any single cultural characteristic.

This has some bearing on Huntington's manner of classifying civilizations, where the emphasis is largely on major religions as central institutional and ideational complexes. The temporal bias is implicated here as well, to the extent that major religious doctrines and rituals are mostly characterized by relatively slow change. Yet precisely how each of them, in the civilizations which they presumably define, at present fit into current social life and serve as major construction materials for personal and collective identities is hardly made very clear in his line of argument, and the point here must be that whatever is most enduring is not necessarily also at any one time most central to people's cultural preoccupations, and to their sense of who they are. There are now surely many different ways of being more or less Christian, more or less Muslim, more or less Confucian; and of being at the same time some number of other things.

Most significantly, finally, an emphasis on process may entail a subversion of a kind of mystique of cultural difference which seems to be an important part of cultural fundamentalism. When it is understood that human beings are forever cultural, information-handling animals, dealing with their surroundings by way of interpreting and making signs, then culture can be seen to a degree as fluid and permeable, not entirely independent of a variety of practical and material conditions. We may sense that all kinds of interests and pressures in human life tend to take the shape of culture, cultural identity, and cultural difference, and we may better realize that cultural turbulence may be a response to changes in power equations, redistributions of physical assets, and demographic shifts. When on the other hand persistence is natural and taken for granted, cultures tend to be decontextualized and seen more as species. And once they are more like species, quasibiological notions and racism are nearer at hand.[7]

Conclusion: scholars, citizens and cultural understanding

These days the notion of "citizenship" is coming into prominence again; not only in a legal sense, but as a key word in debates over desirable combinations of rights, responsibilities, and competences in the late twentieth century, soon twenty-first century, world. These are debates over the limits of uniformity as well as diversity, over the difference between nationalism and patriotism, over what it means to identify with one country, or with two countries, or with humanity, or with oneself and one's credit cards. Clearly a large part of what is being said about citizenship also has to do with culture.

As scholars we are also citizens, but there are other citizens who are not scholars (or at least not in our fields). Again, it would seem that one particular civic responsibility we could take on, especially now that varieties of culture-speak proliferate and spread, would be to try to draw on our research interests and experiences to offer other citizens as well the tools to think about culture in the world around them.

Apparently this task of offering useful cultural understanding has at least two identifiable levels. The Huntington example, even if it is not entirely one of which we approve, suggests that there is a demand for the larger-scale syntheses, the "future scenarios" or whatever we may want to call them. They offer the Big Picture of the world, satisfying some yearning for a "sense of the whole" into which particular events and experiences can be fitted. (And even when they claim to be about the future, it is one of their interesting characteristics that they may sometimes be self-fulfilling prophecies, and sometimes self-destructive.) We may debate how intellectually satisfactory any such synthesis may be. It is not likely, however, that we can really compete with them only with a myriad of miniatures, or long lists of exceptions. Is it worth pondering here the fact that Huntington goes back to what is largely a midcentury way of thinking about culture in the world to summarize the present, and sound alarms about the near future? Indeed it may fit with his political agenda, but he may not have had to confront so many particularly well-articulated, updated alternatives.

So the work of putting things together is there for us. It will no doubt require an amount of interdisciplinary effort for which our academic structures are not especially well equipped. It would appear to me that in cultural research, there is not least a need for closer contact between the humanities and the social sciences; partly because the relationships between culture, power and the economy are more intricate than can be handled by those ideas about the latter with which humanists tend to become enamored, and partly because humanists are also too often weak in dealing with what is socially complex, aggregate, and large-scale. Their attempts to move quickly from the miniature and personal to the national or civilizational have not seldom turned out a bit embarrassing.

People need "the Big Picture," arguably, as a framework for concrete experiences; it can help take citizenship beyond the local and national contexts. At the other, surely not altogether separate level, the task is rather one of making everyday, piecemeal reasoning about culture a resource readily at hand for responsible civic conduct. Such a civic understanding of culture can hardly be compressed into any very simple recipe, but perhaps some ingredients could be identified.

I have suggested that it ought to be processual – not only for researchers, but for other people as well. It is a way of arguing that we are not necessarily stuck forever with either our own culture or those of other people, including those of our neighbors. Culture is in no small part a matter of cumulative experience,

224 Reflections on varieties of culturespeak

and exchanges about that experience. Meanings and practices can be changed; culture is a matter of doing as well as being. (Which is not to say that we will always want it changed.)

That civic understanding of culture, and cultural difference, should also be interactionist, and as a part of this, it may offer some more explicit recognition to the fact that cultural differences may indeed entail some minor or major nuisances. These days, people of different cultures are prone to come in each other's way. For those not "sharing a culture," in the form of everyday expectations and guidelines for interaction, contacts may well appear more opaque, less predictable, even threatening; certainly at times inconvenient. It sometimes seems to me that cultural celebrationism mostly disregards such interactional experiences. Drawing perhaps on the more esthetic understanding of culture, it may be inclined to see cultural diversity rather in terms of differing performances – to be enjoyed at a certain distance, from a good seat in the audience – rather than as a matter of ongoing, active, not always smooth mutual adaptation. Unless we offer some recognition to the difficulties sometimes involved, possibly some people could even assume that "multicultural infernos" are created on purpose by mad celebrationist cultural engineers, as supposedly enriching experiences.

Here the interculturalists I referred to above at least realize that they have some practical problems to solve, some bridges to build. It would seem far from certain, however, that their techniques could ever remove all frictions from intercultural encounters. Perhaps as at least a complementary attitude, one might cultivate a readiness to cope with them such as they are, in the same way as one expects mature people to cope with differences and tensions between generations, or between the sexes, or between the parties in a number of other relationships which they also handle on a regular basis. Life may be tough sometimes, but we do not expect to solve problems in such relationships by telling the others to go back to where they came from. Rather, we muddle through.

Such an interactionist stance might also lead to some nuanced consideration of the room for cultural diversity in a society. We may sympathize with the idea that each human being has a right to his/her "own culture," and on this idea policies of multiculturalism may be based. Yet such rights tend to face certain limits in those social contexts where for reasons not least of effectiveness and justice there must be shared rules of the game (and where the rules can hardly be negotiated anew in each relationship). What situations are necessarily of this sort, and which are not? Where do the rules come from, and how can they be made readily accessible to everyone affected, instead of being rooted in layers of implicit assumptions? Multiculturalism can hardly be an either/or thing, but to define its reasonable place, one has to work on such questions.

And then, as a matter of that right to one's own culture, we must also confront the problems of clashes between collective and individual rights. A group may well find strength in its own culture. Along the lines of multiculturalist thought, that culture may offer resources for solidarity and mobilization, and it may be a haven of security and trust in contexts where by internal consensus its

Reflections on varieties of culturespeak **225**

own "rules of the game" apply. Yet from the perspective of the individual, it would follow from the processual argument sketched before, the right to one's own culture is also a right to change it or even give it up, making it no longer "one's own," if one finds an attractive and viable alternative; and that may also entail downgrading one's commitment to the group with which the culture is associated, or even abandoning it.[8] We need to think carefully about any acceptance of an institutionalized, corporate multiculturalism which could somehow be seen to limit anybody's rights to cultural choice and mobility.

To sum up an already very briefly stated point of view: as researchers on culture, we can hardly distance ourselves from the way conceptions of culture circulate in public life. We may want to influence the latter to accept our ways of culturespeak, try to make these accessible, and hope that they can be found credible. This cannot be an obligation to conceal difficulties and offer an entirely rosy imagery in their place, but it should be an attempt to help dealing constructively with existing circumstances. And thus, at the very least, we must not support fear-mongering, giving it a veneer of academic authority. Some years ago, a young immigrant in Stockholm, who is now a graduate student in my department, was one of those shot by a xenophobic desperado, the "Laser man." I would not want to contribute, and much prefer not to see other scholars contributing, to a social climate where such acts can occur.

Notes

1 This paper is a slightly revised version of a lecture given at the conference "Culture, Cultural Research, and Cultural Policy", organized by the Swedish Academy of Letters, History and Antiquities, the Swedish Research Council for the Humanities and Social Sciences (HSFR), and the Tercentenary Foundation of the Bank of Sweden in Stockholm and Friibergh, August 25–27, 1997.
2 Several of the arguments sketched here are more fully elaborated elsewhere (Hannerz 1996, 1997); with regard to immigration and cultural diversity in Sweden. I also still find my earlier comments reasonably to the point (Hannerz 1981a, 1981b).
3 For some of the comments occasioned by Huntington's recent publications, see e.g. Ajami (1993), Bartley (1993), Binyan (1993), Kirkpatrick and others (1993), Hartmann (1995), Ignatieff (1996), McNeill (1997) and Pfaff (1997).
4 In a conversation I had in March, 1997, with the foreign editor of the *New York Times*, Bill Keller, he took note of the "Huntington thesis" (even if somewhat skeptically) as he pointed out that the most recently opened news bureau of his paper was in Istanbul – chosen partly because this was a meeting point, or in Huntington's phrasing, at the fault line, between Islam and the West.
5 See e.g. Appadurai (1996) and Hannerz (1996).
6 It is worth noting here that one reviewer, the prominent political commentator William Pfaff (1997: 96), finds a streak of fatalism in Huntington's thesis: "His argument that wars in the future will be conflicts of civilization shifts the responsibility for those wars from the realm of human volition and political decision to that of cultural predestination."
7 Yet we may sometimes have to watch out for such implications even in more processualist language – when culture is said to be passed down "from generation to generation", are we not again a little susceptible to assimilating this notion to one of biological ancestry, in determining who is and who is not counted as belonging to the previous age grouping?

226 Reflections on varieties of culturespeak

8 One may consider in this context those highly publicized cases where young immigrant women in Sweden have chosen a life style out of line with the traditions of their ethnic groups, and have suffered violent treatment by their male kin as a consequence. When such cases end up in court, with the aggressor as defendant, there is sometimes an attempt to resort to what has become known as the "cultural defense plea" – it is argued that it is a mitigating circumstance that the defendant has behaved "according to his culture" (for a relevant discussion in an American context, see Koptiuch 1996). Perhaps some observers will at such times be inclined to shake their heads and think, "that must be a bad culture"; and others, to ward off such conclusions, will object that "this had nothing to do with culture". The latter claim does in fact seem to be somewhat lacking in credibility, but one major problem of a "cultural defense plea" is that its acceptance would mean that some people are held less responsible than others for a particular kind of action, and that some other people, the typical victims of such action within the networks of the aggressors, would be less well protected, and thus more vulnerable. They would be placed, in other words, within the domain of a culture which they probably do not accept.

References

Ajami, Fouad. 1993. The Summoning. *Foreign Affairs*, 72 (4): 2–9.

Appadurai, Arjun. 1996. *Modernity at Large*. Minneapolis, MN: University of Minnesota Press.

Bartley, Robert L. 1993. The Case for Optimism. *Foreign Affairs*, 72 (4): 15–18.

Binyan, Liu 1993. Civilization Grafting. *Foreign Affairs*, 72 (4): 19–21.

Dahlén, Tommy. 1997. *Among the Interculturalists*. Stockholm Studies in Social Anthropology, 38. Stockholm: Almqvist & Wiksell International.

Hannerz, Ulf. 1981a. Leva med mångfalden. In *Att leva med mångfalden*. Stockholm: Liber.

———. 1981b. Sverige som invandrarsamhälle: Några antropologiska frågeställningar. In Eva M. Hamberg and Tomas Hammar (eds.), *Invandringen och framtiden*. Stockholm: Liber.

———. 1996. *Transnational Connections*. London: Routledge.

———. 1997. Borders. *International Social Science Journal*, 49: 537–548.

Hartmann, Heinz. 1995. Clash of Cultures, When and Where? Critical Comments on a New Theory of Conflict – And Its Translation into German. *International Sociology*, 10: 115–125.

Huntington, Samuel P. 1993. The Clash of Civilizations? *Foreign Affairs*, 72 (3): 22–49.

———. 1996. *The Clash of Civilizations and the Remaking of World Order*. New York, NY: Simon & Schuster.

Ignatieff, Michael. 1996. Fault Lines. *New York Times Book Review*, December 1, p. 13.

Kirkpatrick, Jeane J., et al. 1993. The Modernizing Imperative. *Foreign Affairs*, 72 (4): 22–26.

Koptiuch, Kristin. 1996. "Cultural Defense" and Criminological Displacements: Gender, Race, and (Trans)nation in the Legal Surveillance of U.S. Diaspora Asians. In Smadar Lavie and Ted Swedenburg (eds.), *Displacement, Diaspora, and Geographies of Identity*. Durham, NC: Duke University Press.

McNeill, William H. 1997. Decline of the West? *New York Review of Books*, January 9, pp. 18–22.

Pfaff, William. 1997. The Reality of Human Affairs. *World Policy Journal*, 14 (2): 89–96.

Stolcke, Verena. 1995. Talking Culture: New Boundaries, New Rhetorics of Exclusion in Europe. *Current Anthropology*, 36: 1–13.

13

A DETECTIVE STORY WRITER

Exploring Stockholm as it once was

Recently I noticed that my friends and colleagues in Vienna, Cape Town, and Chapel Hill had all been reading the same few books; moreover, that they had shared this reading with my neighbor the plumber, across the road in the south Swedish village where I spend the summer. And then, on a flight somewhere, far from home, when I glanced sideways at what the man in the seat next to mine was reading, it was again one of these same books. They have been reviewed respectfully in the *New York Review of Books*, and parodied in the *New Yorker*.[1] I am referring to the "Millennium Trilogy" by the Swedish writer Stieg Larsson: *The Girl with the Dragon Tattoo, The Girl Who Played with Fire*, and *The Girl Who Kicked the Hornets' Nest*.

So my dispersed anthropologist friends, aware of my own interest in detective stories, ask me what I think about these books, and their remarkable success, and indeed the international reception of a number of Scandinavian authors in the same genre in recent years.

Mostly, in fact, I have not read them. I went into anthropology in no small part because I like to travel; that also goes for my taste in detective stories. So I hang out in Chicago through the writings of Sara Paretsky, in Cajun country and New Orleans with James Lee Burke, on and off the Indian reservations of the U.S. Southwest with Tony Hillerman, and revisit Washington, D.C, where I did my first field work, with George Pelecanos.[2] I can make return visits to Sicily with Andrea Camilleri, to Shanghai with Qiu Xiaolong, and to Vientiane, Laos, with Colin Cotterill, and I can even travel in time to Tokugawa-era Japan with Laura Joh Rowland, and to late Ottoman Istanbul with Jenny White.

I have felt no strong need, on the other hand, to read so much of the recent detective writing set in Sweden, the country that surrounds me anyway. Yet I did get around to reading the Millennium trilogy, as my brother-in-law gave it to me for Christmas, and as shortly thereafter, my wife and I fled the Swedish winter to spend two weeks on the beach in Goa, India. I rather liked the first book, and got increasingly irritated at the latter two. But I could sense that the heroine, Lisbeth Salander, has the transcultural appeal of a trickster figure – cunning, seemingly weak but actually strong (good with her fists, training occasionally with the young men in a local boxing club; and when you place her at a computer, you find that she is also an expert hacker), sexually ambiguous, distrustful of authorities, and with her own sense of morality. Probably the more or less global success of the stories built around her has much to do with this.

Yet then, as again and again I find other detective story readers among my colleagues and exchange reading tips with them, I come to wonder if there is some kind of affinity between detective stories and anthropology. In a way, perhaps, a detective story is like a field situation. There may be some rather limited number of people – a dozen? twenty? – that you get to know quite well, although which these are may not be obvious at the start. You have to work out the relationships between them. But meanwhile, there is also a wider setting which is part of the ethnography, with its tangible characteristics providing a sense of place. Reading detective stories, for anthropologists, may be a variety of "studying sideways," observing the workings of a parallel craft.[3] Here, however, we are not competing, as with some of the people in neighboring disciplines, or some journalists. We read these stories in a relaxed mood, winding down, during vacation (perhaps on the beach), or late in the evening before going to sleep.

For this affinity there is some occasional tangible evidence. Sara Paretsky was at one time one of George Stocking's students at the University of Chicago; Tony Hillerman received an award from the American Anthropological Association for spreading knowledge of American Indian culture through his novels; Jenny White is herself a professional anthropologist.[4]

It is an affinity which is probably closer with some detective stories than with others. P.D. James (2009: 84), one of the most successful British mystery authors of recent times, who has also written reflectively on her line of work, notes of her predecessor Agatha Christie that her natural world is

> a romanticized cosy English village rooted in nostalgia, with its ordered hierarchy: the wealthy squire (often with a new young wife of mysterious antecedence), the retired irascible colonel, the village doctor and the district nurse, the chemist (useful for the purchase of poison), the gossiping spinsters behind their lace curtains, the parson in his vicarage, all moving predictably in their social hierarchy like pieces on a chessboard.

The stories which now appeal most to anthropologist readers, I believe, are set in another kind of world – complex, mostly urban, not so seemingly transparent but more unpredictable, with more anonymity.

Moreover, the plot is frequently interwoven with a strong element of social critique. Paretsky, Burke, and Pelecanos do not find contemporary American society faultless. Corruption, organized crime, racism, and sleazy business deals are built-in

A detective story writer **229**

parts of the environments they depict. And part of the international popularity of several Swedish authors in the genre, not least in the United States, I also believe, is based on the kind of critical portrayal of Swedish society they offer – the darker sides of an imperfect welfare society, where the heroes are anti-heroes, tired cogs in a bureaucratic machine. This was true of the writing couple, Maj Sjövall and Per Wahlöö, first to break into an international market in the 1970s or so, and is also true of Henning Mankell, whose success story extends into the present. And most recently, it was true in Stieg Larsson's case.[5]

Anyhow, the central figure of detective stories – a police officer, a private eye, or some amateur who just has a habit of stumbling onto strange happenings – is now a recurrent urban social type in fiction; and the detective story writer may be recognized as a social type of real, non-fiction urban life. The fiction character may appear in the stories as a "he" or "she," or sometimes as "I," the narrator. The person who really tells the story, who actually makes the plot and selectively re-creates its milieu, however, is the author – an influential interpreter, consequently, of some slice of life in our cities.

To repeat, I have mostly not been drawn to the recent Swedish detective story writers myself. Further back, on the other hand, there was one I read consistently, for particular reasons. Stieg Trenter was for several decades, from the early 1940s to the late 1960s, undoubtedly Sweden's most successful author in the genre, with some twenty-five books. He was also a good friend of my parents when I grew up, so I knew him well. And even before his novels were published, they usually circulated in the family in page proofs.

Trenter had a habit of using real people in his circle of friends and acquaintances as more or less close models for persons in his novels. It was widely understood that the hero in most of his stories, Harry Friberg, was the fiction version of his close friend, the well-known photographer K.W. Gullers (with whose children I and my siblings were schoolmates) (Figure 13.1). His senior police officers were similarly identifiable, and in addition other people, more discreetly and fleetingly portrayed, could at least recognize themselves. At different times, this included, as I remember it, my father, my sister, and myself; and my parents were just a little concerned once when their good friend had used our family telephone number in one of his stories. (It only led to one or two calls from curious readers.) My father, a doctor whose private practice in the Old Town of Stockholm drew a notably diverse clientele, would normally not take much time out for lunch, but Stieg liked to time his visits around mid-day, and then come directly from the renowned delicatessen nearby, bringing some freshly baked bread, fresh shrimps, smoked salmon, interesting cheeses or whatever, for them to sit down and share in a back room. My father, for his part, occasionally offered medical advice that could be useful in Trenter's murder plots.

Trenter was very much a Stockholm boy. His widowed mother ran a grocery in a periurban area then south of Stockholm, now a suburb – a square has been named after him there. His schooling was not particularly extensive but he wanted to write and started out as a journalist (it seems many detective story writers do). Briefly he was a war correspondent for a minor Stockholm

FIGURE 13.1 Stieg Trenter, on the right, with the photographer K.W. Gullers, model for his amateur detective hero Harry Friberg

newspaper, at the time of Italy's conquest of Ethiopia. He then had his beginnings in fiction writing with short stories for rather downmarket popular magazines. One of the first novels was a bit of a World War II spy story, starting in the borderlands between Sweden and German-occupied Norway, and involving both Gestapo and the Norwegian resistance. But from then on, Stockholm was the main scene of his stories.

Trenter's skill in exploring the urban landscape, portraying it both vividly and with precision, has drawn much praise. He took great care in inspecting locales to get the details just right (often asking his friend Gullers to take photographs for him to have at hand when writing), and his authority as an observer was underpinned by the way he mixed depictions of sites which every Stockholmer would know well with close-up views of places which they would know *of*, but might have less direct familiarity with – islands just offshore, neighborhoods a little out of the way. The quite intricate puzzles of his stories mostly involved little real violence, but there were critical situations and rapid movements, in and between concrete settings. If you as a reader knew the city, you might also recognize this peculiar building at the corner, or that crossing where irritating traffic jams were likely to occur.

Mostly this was a man's world. His central figure, the photographer Friberg, was a tall but gentle bachelor (the actual model, Gullers, was six-foot-six, but actually married and the father of six), mostly surrounded by male company,

A detective story writer **231**

talking the colorful talk of their times (more or less midcentury jargon). There might still be some close attention to women's appearance and clothing, and there is a young, pretty, smart woman somewhere in the midst of stories, often exposed to some risk, but she is not portrayed with much complexity, is usually chaste, and most likely will not reappear in another story. (Not much like Lisbeth Salander.)

As his improvised catering at the back room of my father's office suggests, Trenter was a foodie. Friberg actually makes his first appearance as one early novel opens at the Restaurant Cattelin, in the Old Town. Friberg asks for snails, a specialty of the house, but the waitress tells him they are not yet in season. So instead she suggests calf's brain – "you do like that, Mr. Friberg." Which is a way of making clear immediately that he is a steady patron of the establishment.

Some number of Stockholm restaurants show up in his novels, as sites of enjoyable meals. Cattelin, one of few French-inspired restaurants in the city at the time, is probably revisited most often, and it is noted that many of its guests can be overheard speaking foreign languages – this restaurant actually had the reputation of having been a place where spies mingled, in neutral Sweden, during World War II. Yet the meals which Trenter takes pleasure in describing mostly do not involve particularly intricate or exotic menus. There is a lot of herring. This was still a time when there was very little in the way of foreign cuisines in Stockholm – not even the pizzerias had arrived yet, and certainly no sushi, or fusion experiments.

That, of course, is not unrelated to the fact that there were as yet, during most of Trenter's writing career, few people living in Stockholm other than native Swedes. The larger number of newcomers, first labor migrants, then refugees from troubled corners of the world, only started becoming a more conspicuous part of the urban scene in the late 1960s. Their arrival, and the increasing mobility and worldliness of the natives themselves, made for a very different culinary scene toward the end of the century.

If in that earlier period there were not yet so many people from elsewhere moving in, Trenter himself more and more often moved out, personally and in his writings. He became very attached to Italy, particularly to Florence, and spending just over half the year there was also a good idea for tax reasons. So his own life style became that of a seasonal migrant; and while Stockholm remained a dominant scene, the stories often became multi-sited. In Italy, in his own life, he at least at one time had plans to get involved in wine-growing, but I am not sure what actually came out of that. What is certain is that he cultivated friendships with a number of the Swedish soccer players, national heroes who had become professionals in Italian major-league teams. Whether in Italy or Sweden, Trenter was an intense soccer fan. Very occasionally I went with him to games of his favorite Stockholm team, AIK, which was supposedly also mine. For some reason, this enthusiasm of his does not show up in the books.

Italy does, however – easily enough, as Friberg also expanded to work internationally. Much of his photography business involved the pictorial celebration

232 A detective story writer

of large industrial enterprises, and he had major customers abroad. At times the trips to Italy and elsewhere were perhaps mostly diversions, but at other times they had their part in a plot. In an era when trains were often more important than planes, moreover, one gets a sense, in Friberg's company, of some of the features of traveling overland in Europe: finding a home country newspaper (most likely in a kiosk close to the station), changing currencies every so often (no Euros yet, and no ATMs).

The calendar of Swedish publishing in those times depended greatly on the Christmas season – popular fiction was typically a Christmas gift. (My brother-in-law, giving me the Millennium trilogy, still followed this tradition.) So detective stories by the major authors in the field were typically in the book-shops by mid-fall, at which time advertising campaigns were also launched; and soon after that the reviews would appear in the newspapers. In Sweden, for a number of years, this season involved a battle for sales and reviews between Trenter and Maria Lang, a mystery writer of a type more like Agatha Christie's, with her stories placed mostly in quaint small-town settings. By the end of the season, Trenter's book, and perhaps Lang's as well, may have been printed in some 40,000 copies – a considerable success by local standards at the time, although the Larsson trilogy, with its international sales combined, has apparently now sold about a thousand times as many.

In a way both Lang and Trenter had constructed their identities – "Maria Lang" was widely known to be the *nom de plume* of Dagmar Lange, who thus distanced her detective story writing from her highly respectable work as principal of one of Stockholm's best-known private girls' schools. "Trenter" was the new surname invented for himself by Stig Johansson, who thereby created a brand name much more distinctive than what he had had before. "Johansson" probably was then, and is still, the most common last name in Sweden – at present the name of over a quarter-million Swedes, which means that approximately every thirty-fifth person in the country is a Johansson. The eighteen most frequent surnames in Sweden all end with "-son", a vestige of the country's peasant society past where every son of a Johan became a Johansson, the son of every Bengt a Bengtsson, and so forth. But having so many people named Johansson, Larsson, Nilsson, Hansson, Bengtsson, Eriksson, Svensson or whatever became a nuisance in the urbanizing society of the twentieth century, and the patronymic custom by which the last name would change with every generation was no longer practicable (as it had been when people tended to be identified primarily with their farms anyway). So a great many people, not least those with ambitions of upward social mobility, invented new family names – some so inventive that they became subjects of ridicule. And thus Stig Johansson became Trenter. It was a name inspired by a detective story he had read, E.C. Bentley's classic *Trent's Last Case*. Moreover, Stig became Stieg, a mere change of spelling which was also fairly original.

Trenter enjoyed the good life and was very generous, toward himself and his friends (and the children of his friends); his publisher occasionally grumbled that this highly valued author was inclined to live a little beyond his means. Probably he would show up, somewhat reluctantly, in the fall rush period to do his book signing sessions in the bookshops, although he preferred to be in Italy during Stockholm's cold, dark season. He was a warm presence in small gatherings, but appallingly awkward the couple of times when my father, with a certain activist streak, mistakenly involved him in rather modest public appearances – very different from many contemporary writers who have to get used to, and develop some skill for, events and appearances of various kinds.[6] His own circle, at least as I understood it, apart from those people in the world of soccer, was probably not so different from those appearing in various combinations in his books. There were people from the arts, some business people, professionals; bourgeois, bohemian, or some combination thereof. The police officers of a senior level who interacted with Friberg in the novels and took part in the handling of mysterious murders performed very competently or even brilliantly. They were certainly honest, while one of them recurrently showed a certain vanity, wearing rather high heels to compensate for an unimpressive stature.

Friberg and friends often traveled by taxi, slightly extravagantly by local standards, more seldom by streetcar; but both means of transportation allowed further comment on Stockholm landmarks, literally in passing. So mostly they were above ground – they did not use the Stockholm subway system much, but then it did not exist yet when he began writing, and only developed gradually during his later life, reaching its current state of completion only after he had departed from the scene. The streetcars, for their part, mostly disappeared from Stockholm streets in September 1967, in connection with Sweden's shift from left hand to right hand driving. That was two months after Trenter's death, at the age of 53.

Like the somewhat limited choice in Stockholm restaurants, the greater presence of streetcars and absence of the subway in Stieg Trenter's novels are signs of the times. His Stockholm was still a rather compact city. Then from the 1960s and 1970s, the new subway lines would take you to the massive, hastily constructed suburbs made up of large, undistinguished apartment buildings; and these were also where immigrant populations came to live in considerable numbers, so that Stockholm became an increasingly diverse but segregated city. (The term "suburbs", consequently, has by now mostly come to be understood in Swedish as rather like the recent French *banlieues*; or, paradoxically, "the inner city" in America – even the term "ghetto" is occasionally heard.)

At much the same time, the central business district of Stockholm went through massive, ruthless urban renewal. It has left some foreign visitors wondering how it was that they had not known how heavily this city had been bombed during World War II – which, of course, it had not been, as Sweden did not actually take part in that war. Those parts of the city, rather, were flattened by the city fathers: its politicians and its business elite together. The result has been that a fairly sizeable part of the city that Stieg Trenter so carefully depicted is no longer there.

234 A detective story writer

That makes him a figure not so much *of* an urban transformation, but of the period just before, waiting for change, beginning to show the signs of it. But where can we place him in the changing history of his genre, as a writer of detective stories? Where does he fit into that lineage which has lately also come to include authors like Stieg Larsson?

As far as I know none of Trenter's books were translated into English (a few of them did appear in German, and one in Spanish). At one time, it seems, Alfred Hitchcock was interested in making a movie out of one of them, and visited him in Stockholm to look into the project, although nothing came out of it. Some of them were turned into films for Swedish television. Many of his books have appeared repeatedly in new editions, although there are also connoisseurs who collect the first editions.

With regard to that contrast between the classics of British detective literature and current American masters which I hinted at before, it seems to me that Stieg Trenter is in a way in the middle, transitional, but also a figure of his place and time. Let us return to the authoritative British insider P.D. James again. Born in 1920 herself, James could recognize the world in which her compatriot predecessors had lived and written:

> a cohesive world, overwhelmingly white and united by a common belief in a religious and moral code based on the Judeo-Christian inheritance – even if this belief was not invariably reflected in practice – and buttressed by social and political institutions which, although they might be criticized, attracted general allegiance, and were accepted as necessary to the well-being of the state: the monarchy, the Empire, the Church, the criminal justice system, the City, the ancient universities.
>
> *(James 2010: 70)*

By and large, this was an existing social order which they had accepted, or perhaps rather taken for granted. And so, in this period,

> the British detective story is concerned with bringing order out of disorder, a genre of reconciliation and social healing, restoring the mythical village of Mayhem Parva to prelapsarian tranquillity.
>
> *(James 2010: 72)*

To me at least, this looks like one of the darker varieties of Victor Turner's (e.g. 1969) conception of liminality, as a phase of structural uncertainty in between the more extended periods of order. Incidentally, Turner was also born in 1920, like James – some generational British pattern of thinking here?

Stieg Trenter's outlook hardly shared the particular elements of this British world, but I believe there is a parallel in that he, too, was surrounded in Sweden, during most of his productive years, by a society which had its streak of largely satisfying taken-for-grantedness. It had mostly come out of poverty, and a great

A detective story writer **235**

many people felt that they were doing better than before, and better than their parents had done. It was a class society, but without much overt class conflict. Again, Sweden had stayed out of World War II, but as neighboring lands were drawn into it, the country was on guard, and that also brought its people together. It was an ethnically largely homogeneous country, with a state church, a unitary state school system, one radio channel, and TV arriving with its single channel in the late 1950s – in other words, an apparatus for cultural cohesion. Politics was in large part consensual, or at least negotiable. There was a national coalition during the war years, leaving only the small Communist party outside; as the Cold War got going, Sweden remained officially neutral, but the Russians were the traditional enemy since centuries back. The country had the same prime minister for 23 years, during most of Stieg Trenter's writing life.

It seems to me that like his classic British colleagues, Trenter was largely uncritical of the existing social order – not the same one as theirs, but still a tightly woven reality. His world had treated him well (even as he knew how much effort had gone into taking him where he was), and while he might grumble about a thing or two, he did not reject it. He did not scrutinize institutions much, but focused on relationships, networks and milieux. Yet in this, as an essentially urban animal, he was more like the later American detective story writers than those British predecessors and contemporaries who lingered in Mayhem Parva.

In Trenter's own country, those internationally more celebrated detective story writers which appeared in later years had, I believe, a rather different life experience, and view of the world. Both members of the Sjövall-Wahlöö duo, and Stieg Larsson, indeed had a past as journalists, like Trenter; but they had made early political commitments on the left, as had Henning Mankell, whose parallel interest was in theater. This, in large part, was in the period of much more dramatic political cleavages which, particularly in the later 1960s and early 1970s in Sweden, were linked to a greater engagement with the outside world, and to the aroused awareness of younger cohorts of what was going on there – anticolonial wars in Asia and Africa; the struggle against right-wing and military dictatorial regimes in southern Europe; the growth (or revival) of racism and xenophobia on a number of dispersed national and local arenas; and the generational Western student protest which also found its Swedish expressions. Young Mankell was apparently a Maoist, young Larsson a Trotskyite. For Mankell, the engagement became primarily anticolonial, for Larsson anti-racist and anti-fascist. But in a more general way, this also provided an intellectual setting for a darker, more opaque view of Sweden – even, toward the end of Larsson's work, as a locus for a kind of secrecy and conspiracy in high places which I must confess to finding bizarre. Perhaps one should note here that several of these Swedish detective story writers died rather prematurely: Trenter, to repeat, at age 53, Wahlöö at 48, Larsson at 50. For the latter two, this meant that their active careers as major writers were fairly brief, and somewhat compressed, while Trenter's extended, as we have seen, over a quarter-century. Indeed, Larsson's

236 A detective story writer

three books were only published after his death. So perhaps if he had had a chance to continue writing, he would eventually have made it back to a more credible Sweden.

For all the differences between Larsson and Trenter, perhaps one can catch a glimpse of some connections. A collection of Trenter's short stories, from 1962, had the title *Flickan som snavade på guldet*, "The Girl who Stumbled on the Gold" – the similarity to Larsson's later English-language titles is noteworthy (although it is true that only one of the titles of the Swedish originals had this form). And then Stieg Larsson also shifted his first name from the original, but much more common, spelling "Stig". Again, "Larsson" was another of these very common surnames, and there was already another Stig Larsson writing. But adopting the spelling which could bring strong reminiscences of his predecessor might have been a bow of recognition, and to some extent a branding strategy.

Those visitors to Stockholm who now take guided walking tours through the neighborhoods of Stieg Larsson's trilogy will sometimes cross paths, too, with Stieg Trenter's stories as well. (Not least in the district known as "Södermalm," or briefly "Söder" – an old working-class district later bohemianized and, to a degree, gentrified.) Yet a tour of Trenter's Stockholm is no longer an entirely viable project. Reading Trenter now, for many in his enduring as well as new audiences, carries a strong element of nostalgia. It is not only that the sense of place is there. It is also the sense of time, of Stockholm only as it once was.

Notes

1 See Ephron (2010) and Parks (2011).
2 I would like to acknowledge here that I first made my way to several of these authors after reading the travel reportage of the British journalist John Williams (1991).
3 On "studying sideways," see Hannerz (1998) and Ortner (2010). The notion is, of course, inspired by Nader's (1972) "studying up."
4 George Stocking (2010: 214), the historian of anthropology, notes in his recent autobiography that Paretsky was in one of his classes. I had the pleasure of meeting Jenny White at a conference of the Turkey Anthropological Association, in Istanbul.
5 In April, 2011, it drew some attention in Sweden when King Carl XVI Gustaf, on a state visit abroad, a trip certainly intended to promote a favorable view of his nation, had to respond to a foreign journalist's question that Sweden was really not the way Stieg Larsson described it. A few months later, when I ran into a former Swedish (Social Democratic) prime minister at a conference, I asked him whether he had read the Larsson trilogy. He had, but did not like it very much.
6 But note what one more recent, successful writer, David Foster Wallace (1997: 21) said:

> a majority of fiction writers, born watchers, tend to dislike being objects of people's attention. Dislike being watched. The exceptions to this rule – Mailer, McInerney – sometimes create the impression that most belletristic types covet people's attention. Most don't. The few who like attention just naturally get more attention. The rest of us watch.

References

Ephron, Nora. 2010. The Girl Who Fixed the Umlaut. *New Yorker*, 86 (19), July 5: 30.

Hannerz, Ulf. 1998. Other Transnationals: Perspectives Gained from Studying Sideways. *Paideuma*, 44: 109–123.

James, P.D. 2010. *Talking about Detective Fiction*. London: Faber and Faber.

Nader, Laura. 1972. Up the Anthropologist – Perspectives Gained from Studying Up. In Dell Hymes (ed.), *Reinventing Anthropology*. New York, NY: Pantheon.

Ortner, Sherry B. 2010. Access: Reflections on Studying Up in Hollywood. *Ethnography*, 11: 211–233.

Parks, Tim. 2011. The Moralist. *New York Review of Books*, 58 (10), June 9–22: 8–12.

Stocking, Jr., George W. 2010. *Glimpses into My Own Black Box*. Madison, WI: University of Wisconsin Press.

Turner, Victor W. 1969. *The Ritual Process*. Chicago, IL: Aldine.

Wallace, David Foster. 1997. *A Supposedly Fun Thing I'll Never Do Again*. New York, NY: Little, Brown.

Williams, John. 1991. *Into the Badlands*. London: Paladin.

14

NEIGHBORS IN A SOUTH SWEDISH VILLAGE

Globalization: small-scale and unexpected

Really, I never expected I might be invited to give a Douglass Lecture for this society.[1] For I may be a sometime Africanist, and a sometime Americanist (depending on what that means), even briefly a Caribbeanist, but I was never actually a Europeanist. I do read a fair amount of the Europeanist literature, for pleasure and illumination, and indeed some of my best friends are Europeanists. But I believe I was drawn to anthropology in large part because I like to travel, and so while I have nothing against "anthropology at home," I have not really practiced it myself.

On the other hand, I am of course a European. So this will in a way, to an extent, be autoethnography; a postcard from one corner of Europe. Last year my wife and I, and our neighbors in the south Swedish village where we spend summers, came together to celebrate that our house had then belonged to my family for a hundred years. Our neighbors live in the village the year around. There are very few people in this village apart from us who come there for the summer. But since I retired from my university post, I have been extending these summers; I tell my neighbors that I will nowadays arrive in the spring to see the apple trees in our garden in flower, and then stay around to harvest the apples. (Before that, there will also have been some rather tiny plums, black-berries, two kinds of cherries, and two kinds of gooseberries.)

This is a village in the countryside, close to the seashore, in the province of Scania, Skåne; historically in the contested borderlands between Sweden and Denmark. When I fly south from Stockholm, on my way out into the world somewhere, I try to get a window seat on the left side of the plane, because on a clear day, after an hour's flight or so, I can see the village down there, easily recognizable next to the estuary of a small river. There is a town nearby, and a small city not so far away. The nearest ferry to Denmark leaves from that city, about half an hour away. (Across the straits is the castle where Shakespeare placed

Hamlet.) The village is in a reasonably prosperous farming area, but historically most farms were rather small. There have been people in this neighborhood since prehistoric times. Carl Linnaeus, the renowned naturalist, mentions in a diary that he passed by on July 15, 1749, on his comprehensive tour of Skåne, and offers some notes on plants and bird life, but nothing about the people (Linnaeus 1975: 360). A century and a half or so later, in the latter part of the nineteenth century, my maternal great-grandfather had one of these small farmsteads, but he and his wife had eleven children, so these could not possibly all stick around. This was an emigration area at the time, and three of the sons left for America. Only belatedly did we in fact discover that they were three. Why my elderly relatives had only talked about two of them, and left out any mention of the third, who was the eldest of them but the last one to leave, remains a bit of a mystery. Perhaps there was some conflict involved, as he would have seemed to be in a good spot to take over the farm. My own grandfather left at an early age to make a living as a sailor, and eventually became a sea-captain with a major shipping line. And by the time my great-grandfather, the farmer, realized he had nobody left in the family to take over the farm, the household consisted of him, his wife, and two spinster daughters. So he sold the farm, and acquired that house surrounded by a garden in the nearest village, the house that is now ours.

I did not go there so frequently during my youngest years, but we always enjoyed our occasional visits with those two aunts of my mother who spent most of their lives there. My brother, sister, and I thought they made wonderful pancakes and told wonderful ghost stories – only in retrospect I am not so sure that what were ghost stories to us were always ghost stories to them. I still have a number of letters which the youngest of these grand-aunts wrote to my mother, about changing seasons, the arrival and departure of birds of passage, and the pleasures of work in the garden.

Now the village has a little over 200 inhabitants. Its main enterprise, employing a fair number of villagers, was for a long time a small brick factory, which could make use of the excellent local clay. Its tall chimney was the most visible landmark, but the factory closed in the early 1970s, and the chimney was torn down. There is no school. When the youngest children stand around in the village road in the morning, next to a row of neighborhood mailboxes, waiting for the school bus to pick them up, they remind me of a *Peanuts* comic strip. The only grocery store closed down some time in the 1990s. From the perspective of the city, some twenty miles away, this would seem to be a very ordinary, nondescript village, probably in decline.

A witch and a spaceship

The most famous person from this vicinity, for a long time, may in fact have been someone whose actual presence there seems difficult to date – probably it was many hundreds of years ago (Thysell 1914). This was the local witch Potta Långhaka; that translates as Pottie Longchin. Pottie was a specialist in the black arts, and

240 Neighbors in a south Swedish village

had many kinds of odd creatures working for her. One was a milk hare, which was capable of emptying the udders of the best cows of nearby farms and leaping home to the witch with the fresh product. People tried to shoot the milk hare, but it could only be hit with a silver bullet. When it was finally killed, however, it turned out to consist only of a fur sleeve and the handles of four silver spoons.

Finally, Pottie Longchin herself died, and she was buried at the local cemetery – but as those who had attended the funeral returned from it and passed by her ramshackle cottage, the witch was standing outside it, laughing at them. So they buried her again, and once more she was there in front of her house, laughing. Only the third time did she fail to escape out of her coffin, and presumably remained dead. That time they had not rung the church bell. And by then she was buried not in the church yard but in an open field, and an oak pole was stuck through her heart so she would not have a chance to move. In later years, however, when young people played in that field and sometimes would hit that pole, a voice could be heard from deep in the ground: "Shake the pole, so Pottie can come up!"

Some years ago a local theater group put on a play about Pottie Longchin, so you might say that in the imagined world she is even now alive and well. And by the standards she has set, our village in its present-day version may seem rather prosaic. But wait – there is more to say about it. Scratch, scratch the surface. What follows is mostly about our village neighbors now. Over the last few decades, many of them have become close friends.

Although they are people who would seem quite different from me and my wife, who is also a professional anthropologist, by now we feel very much at home with them. When we invited them to that party to mark my family's hundred years in the village, it seemed like a nice way to remind them that my roots in the village go as deep as just about anybody else's, but I think our neighbors have really long accepted our curious double life, as world-roaming teacher-scholars from the university in the capital city and as neighbors whose garden will probably never be a match for their own.

In fact the village grew noticeably in the early 1970s, with a number of new small family homes being built on what had until then been a grazing field in its middle. The builder was an entrepreneur who had risen from modest beginnings to become, by local standards, quite wealthy. I never met him personally, although I saw him once or twice before he died some years ago; he was not a villager himself but lived at the outskirts of the town a few miles away. The core of his business was an herbal medicinal product based on extracts from locally collected pollen and used not least for the treatment of benign prostate conditions. Over time, this became a successful small export industry, with considerable sales, especially in Japan.

This gentleman, referred to widely as "the Pollen King", had a couple of unusual obsessions. One was that he liked ice hockey, and was prepared to spend a part of his fortune putting together a top-quality team, with some local talent, but otherwise with players recruited from all over Sweden. Ice hockey had not really been much of a local sport until then, since this is a part of Sweden with mild winters, and in the past you would only play ice hockey for a very short and unpredictable season on naturally frozen surfaces. So this project seemed a little odd. Now, however, he built an indoor stadium, and the open space below the seating could be used to store the harvests of pollen. And some of these ice hockey stars were placed in the new houses in our village; mostly they would soon move on to other clubs. One of them left to play professionally in Canada, in the National Hockey League, but he is still remembered for his mean temper, and the booming voice sometimes to be heard across the village green.

Our entrepreneur's other obsession was an experience he claimed to have had an early summer evening in 1946, when he was a young man. He had been out alone for a walk in a forest outside the town when he saw that a large flying object had descended from the sky and had landed on a glade next to him. Some live creatures had come out of this flying machine; when they saw him, they made an unmistakable sign that he should stay away. He looked at them for a moment, then walked away only to return a little later to watch the machine disappear into a distant sky. When he came back the next morning he took careful measurements of the traces it had left on the ground, and even of the marks of the travelers' boots.

What was it he had seen, he wondered? It was just a year after the end of World War II, and Denmark, which was nearby, had been occupied by Nazi Germany for a large part of the war, so people in the area had had the war close at hand. Consequently he had first thought it had something to do with that. Perhaps these were German soldiers escaping from some camp? But then he thought these visitors must be from much further away. Anyhow, they were never seen again, by anybody.

I thought that was an interesting story because this encounter with a ship from outer space would have taken place just over a year before the much more famous sighting of an unidentified flying object in Roswell, New Mexico, and might thus have been more of an original. But as I understand it, our entrepreneur did not start circulating his account until much later, by which time UFO lore was a rather more established genre. Nonetheless, he set aside some money to build a sizeable model of the visiting spacecraft on the glade where it supposedly landed – I sometimes take visitors on a walk to see it. And the Pollen King also found a ghostwriter to help him with his autobiography, with his encounter with the extraterrestrial visitors as the high point (Carlsson and Svahn 1995). By now this volume has become an item eagerly sought after in used bookstores. Moreover, in 1996, in time for the fiftieth anniversary of the landing, the merchants' association in the nearby town printed shopping bags for the affiliated retail businesses with the spacecraft on it, further safeguarding its place in local history.

Yet in a way, I should admit, I find the story a little disappointing. The young man who had observed the visit and who later became the Pollen King described the strange technical features of the spaceship in some detail, but those

242 Neighbors in a south Swedish village

travelers appeared rather remarkably ordinary. They had white uniforms, the men had some sort of caps. But the women were young, pretty, in modern hairdos, and had shining white teeth. So, attractive maybe, but ordinary. No unexpected shapes or traits – judging from those marks he measured on the ground, even their boots had been of rather average human sizes. Pottie Long-chin actually comes across as a more striking figure than those extraterrestrials. But then of course perhaps he just saw what he saw.

A plumber, two motorcycle gangs, and an early Hollywood star

Anyway, back on the ground again, to the Pollen King's later invention, the ice hockey team. The one member of that first generation of players on the team who really had local roots – who was indeed born in the village – is now one of our nearest neighbors. Fifty years have passed since those times, when season after season he was triumphant in scoring more goals for the team than anybody else. Since then he has mostly spent his time running his own plumbing business. He comes from an old blacksmith family, and one of his sons has recently taken up this family heritage, with a small smithy in one part of the old brick factory. His own physical presence is still impressive – big, tall, with muscular arms, and a nose signaling some past experience of contact sports, observing his surroundings, with a slightly mischievous smile seldom far away. I suspect this played a part in one of his more remarkable work encounters, in another nearby village, as he commented on it.

What had happened was that in two other neighboring villages, Hasslarp and Kattarp – both of them in some real decline – a sugar mill had closed in one of them, after the production of beet sugar was no longer so profitable, and a dairy had closed in the other. So there were some industrial buildings no longer in use. In one of the villages, a part of the sugar mill was taken over by the local branch of Hell's Angels, the internationally infamous motorcycle outlaws. And in the other village, the new occupants of the old dairy were the Bandidos, likewise an ill-reputed motorcycle gang. These two gangs were rivals, with some preoccupation with turfs, and no strangers to violence. Indeed, skirmishes between them took place on that one-kilometer stretch of road across the fields between the two villages. Our neighbors would comment and shake their heads in disbelief at the fact that Hasslarp and Kattarp had made it on world news, as reported by CNN International. But our neighbor the plumber, and former ice hockey player, was not so impressed. It had been his business to take some of the equipment apart and remove it from the old dairy, and while working on that he had met some of the Bandidos who were just moving in. They had seemed like rather meek young men to him, he reported. But then they might also have had a sense that this big, old, rugged, ice hockey player was not to be messed with.

I should insert here that Hasslarp, the village where the local branch of Hell's Angels made their home, has another claim to fame. One of the Hollywood stars in the era of silent movies, Anna Q. Nilsson, grew up there, as her father worked precisely at that sugar mill where later the motorcycle gang had its headquarters. But then already in her teens, she left for the United States – about the same time as my grandfather's brothers. If her south Swedish dialect came through in her English, it presumably did not matter since her movies were silent anyway, and one prominent artist in her new homeland described her as "the most beautiful woman in America." No doubt she was prettier than Pottie Longchin. You can check Anna Q. Nilsson out online if you want to.

But back to our neighbor, the ice hockey player/plumber. Occasionally, nowadays, he takes time out to write down his recollections from times since which local life has changed a great deal, for the future benefit of his children and grandchildren. He writes in longhand, in a large notebook, in hand writing that may be much the same as in his school days – no typing, no laptop for him. His wife (who has turned out to be a relative of mine, from six generations back) on the other hand, now has a website of her own – although I suspect it would not have come about were it not for her children. She came from a larger village a few miles away, and then after she left school she was in London briefly as an au pair. For much of her working life she taught domestic science – "school kitchen" in the Swedish vocabulary of the times – in an area school. But she became dissatisfied with that, and left to turn more full-time to her real vocation as a sculptress, with her studio next to the family home. Every Easter weekend artists in the region, mostly painters and sculptors, have a kind of decentered exhibit where small galleries and studios show their work to the public; this draws quite a few extra cars into our village for a few days, while neighbors of course also come around to offer some moral support. The area has always been strong on earthenware goods and pottery – again, that local clay is excellent for such purposes. Our sculptress neighbor's recent specialty shows her own variety of feminism, also on display on her website. In a way her women are heroic figures in the everyday conquest of modernity, as it was in Sweden around the mid-twentieth century. There is the young woman on a bicycle, the housewife with a vacuum cleaner, a speaker in a small, tight-fitting hat addressing an early women's rights meeting – "Dear sisters!" But they are at the same time endearingly funny – large feet, slightly clumsy bodies, small heads.

A former bank robber next-door

On the other side of our house we have had a series of different neighbors over the years. One year, as we arrived in the village at the beginning of summer, we went over to say hello to the elderly widow in the house across the village road. She mentioned that a new neighbor had moved into the house to the left of ours. "Well, you will probably hear more about that," she said, adding only that he was apparently from a good family. She was characteristically discreet, a habit she may have acquired during the many years when she and her mother had run the manually operated telephone switchboard for the village, and probably inevitably learned a fair amount about the private lives of the villagers.

244 Neighbors in a south Swedish village

We did quickly hear more about this new neighbor. He was in fact someone who had made it on world news for his fifteen minutes of fame, a decade earlier or so, when his attempted bank robbery in central Stockholm drew a great deal of attention. Some of you may have heard of "the Stockholm Syndrome," a term which denotes a situation where victims of a crime come to sympathize with its perpetrator. In this case, some of the young female bank employees formed a positive bond with the robber who had taken them hostage inside the bank, and made this plain to the police who were in the public square outside. The Swedish prime minister, too, got a piece of their minds when he was on the telephone. The affair dragged on for some time, with the police sharing the large square with the television crews. The robber issued an ultimatum that he wanted another of Sweden's best-known criminals to be released from prison and allowed to join him at the bank, but when this colleague was indeed permitted to come to the crime scene he apparently played some part in persuading the robber that the game was over. So this young bank robber went off to serve a long prison sentence, and the news-media concentrated their attention on what else was at hand. (It was in September, 1973, the old King of Sweden had also just died, and far away in Chile, General Pinochet had just seized power in a coup. So just what should go into the major headlines may have posed a bit of a dilemma.)

The bank robber had served his time in prison and was now our new village neighbor in the house next door. Before we got to the village for the summer, he had made his rounds in the village, explained who he was, and said he had served his sentence – and so "he did not want to hear more about that." I had still thought this would be an interesting neighbor, for small talk across the hedge between our gardens, and thought this might just provide the opportunity to turn to topics other than the weather, or the used car business he was now in, or how our berry bushes were doing. Unfortunately, I was disappointed. He was not much of a gardener, and tended to get quickly out of his car and into the house. A girlfriend, who had moved in with him for a while, complained about his conduct to one of our other neighbors, so he was apparently not always as charming as he had been to those young bank employees at one time. But this other neighbor chose not to get involved. The only time I even had a chance to say hello to the ex-bank robber was once when a baker's truck came on its rounds to sell fresh bread in the village, but that was an encounter very much in passing. Then, rather soon, he moved away, and now he lives in Thailand, with a new Thai wife, and a new business. That much I know because he, too, like the Pollen King with the ice hockey team and the space ship, has had his ghostwritten autobiography published. I gave it to my wife as a Christmas gift when it had just been published, although I might add that I was the first to read it (Olsson 2009).

When the bank robber was ready to sell his house, he had a special reason to call his neighbors on the opposite side from ours, who lived in a large house where the village grocery store had also once been, on the bottom floor. Before the store had closed down, the local authority had insisted that the store must have an appropriately sized parking space for mobile customers. So the store owner had acquired some space in front of what slightly later became the bank robber's house. Now the elderly couple who were interested in buying the bank robber's house from him had said they would only want to do so if they could also get that parking lot in front of their house. It was in any case no longer in use, so he wanted to know if the neighbors now owning the former shop building would possibly agree to return that space to the property next door. But then, the former bank robber in his telephone call to those neighbors said they did not really have to. He also had another prospective buyer for his house, who might alternatively become their new neighbors ... a Gypsy family.

The couple who now had the house with the former shop, and its additional parking lot, were in fact perfectly pleased to get rid of that unused space. But as they told the story of that phone call later on, they were rather amused. The suggestion that a Roma family might move in next to them was most likely a veiled threat, they thought: an imaginative trick to get them to agree to the parking lot deal more readily; making them an offer they could not refuse. And as the wife in that couple, a veteran school teacher who also taught adult classes on "intercultural communication" in the nearest city, considered the incident, it gave her one more interesting case study as she would be discussing varieties of ethnic prejudice. (It had already turned out she was using something I had written on cultural diversity in one of her classes.)

Swimming across the Nile

That other neighbor in the village – to whom the former bank robber's more recent girlfriend took her complaints – did not want to get involved. Although much older, he had himself grown up in the nearest city in that same rather tough neighborhood that the bank robber came from, and he had a sense of what kind of company he did not want to keep. But we have come to know him quite well. Now in his late seventies, he lost his mother, who died when he was twelve, and then his father had moved to Stockholm soon after that, leaving him alone in an apartment – functionally orphaned, one might think, although his neighbors had promised to keep an eye on him. But he had really managed quite well on his own. He finished the seven years of schooling which was the basic educational offering at the time, took various kinds of jobs, and then found an apprenticeship in a printing and publishing company which happened to be one of the more important businesses in the city. He worked his way up there, and was the head of a graphic design department when he retired.

Meanwhile, he also cultivated a wide range of other interests. He has been to visit a cousin whose father migrated from southern Sweden long ago, and who now has a *finca* in the Guatemalan highlands. A local newspaper has done the occasional story about him as he continues to compete quite successfully in international swimming contests for seniors. For one thing, this has taken him to swim across the Nile. Moreover, he has theatrical inclinations, knows a lot of

246 Neighbors in a south Swedish village

old Swedish hit tunes by heart, and makes the occasional appearance as an impromptu stand-up comedian in our neighborhood gatherings. At the party I mentioned, where we celebrated the centennial of my family's move to our house, he contributed a series of brief speeches in English, German, French, and Russian, most of which are languages he does not know, although they came out sounding just right. The Russian version ended with his banging his shoe on the table – as you may realize, a reminder of a famous speech by Nikita Khrushchev in the United Nations some fifty years earlier.

The refugee from East Prussia

Now the couple who bought the ex-bank robber's house next to ours have also become good friends. The first time they walked by with their dog, as my wife and I were doing some garden work, they introduced themselves, and we noticed that underneath the wife's cultivated local dialect, there were the slight traces of a German accent. It turned out that they had just retired from the fairly large farm some distance away, closer to the city, which Carl, the husband, had inherited from his father and had just turned over to his only son. During the years that we have now known them, Carl has in large part continued with what would be a prosperous farmer's pursuits – keeping the garden in excellent shape, going back to help his son on occasion, going hunting and fishing with old friends, offering helpful practical hints to that urban academic in the next house who is not always so good at such things. I particularly remember the time when he helped me remove a large, lively wasp nest, which I had discovered in our hedge as I was cutting it. At late dusk, when all the wasps had returned home, we set the nest afire. The hedge remained wonderfully intact, but all the wasps perished in an instant. Except one, which survived to sting me the next day.

Carl's wife, with that ever-so-gentle German accent – I will call her Angela here – has a wider, and often quite surprising, range of interests. Now in her early eighties, she watches international soccer games on television, and has very actively supported her grandson's involvement with one of the stronger area soccer teams. She takes a trip to the lake district in northern Italy every summer with her daughter, usually by bus, and it seems that most of the year, she takes an extended morning walk with her neighbor the sculptress – apparently they always have much to talk about, even in the winter when they may hardly see anybody else on the move in the village.

But what about that German accent, then? The story of that has only come out in installments, over time, even as it then turns out that Angela is an accomplished story teller. To begin with, yes, she had come to Sweden after World War II, as Germany lay in ruins, and many young German women came to Sweden to look at least for a temporary escape from the harsh life in their home country. But Angela had met this young farmer's son, and as he took over the family farm, she became a south Swedish farm wife.

Neighbors in a south Swedish village **247**

It turned out it was a life, and a round of activities, she was very well prepared for. The region of Germany where she had had her childhood and early youth is in fact no longer part of that country. It was in East Prussia, now a part of Poland, where her father had been a significant land owner, basically a *Junker* of the kind that Max Weber and others have told us about, and where her family had deep roots. An early installment of Angela's story we got one of the times when she and Carl have been over for dinner, was about the winter of 1945, when Angela was in her early teens. Her mother and a little sister left their home, escaping in a carriage over the ices of the frozen Baltic Sea just slightly ahead of the approaching Soviet troops, and then huddling under the deck as the guns of enemy aircraft strafed the ship on which they were being taken further westward along the German coast. Angela's father, already too old to be a soldier, but still drafted into war-related efforts somewhere in Germany, could only be located long after the war had come to an end, traced through the upheavals of foreign occupation and refugee migration streams, so that the family could be reunited. Yet before all that, in her early years, Angela had had the experience of farm life, harvests, and cows and horses, which came in usefully in her new life as an immigrant in Sweden.

In some passing conversation, I got another piece of her early family history. Before one set of her ancestors came to East Prussia, they had actually lived in Austria, as members of a Protestant community in the strongly Catholic Habsburg Empire. It was a time, Angela said, apparently in the eighteenth century, when those Protestants were under strong pressure to either convert to Catholicism or get out. And so her headstrong ancestors had pulled out, moving northward and eventually taking up that land in East Prussia – offered, I take it, by the King of Prussia as part of his expansionist effort to colonize areas otherwise inhabited mostly by Slavs. Another segment of that same Protestant kin group in Austria, however, submitted to the demand that they must become Catholics, and could thus remain where they were. A couple of centuries or so later, a young descendant of that group did leave Austria, however; he took his powerful body to America, became a movie star, a politician, and eventually governor of California – Arnold Schwarzenegger. Angela told me the story with an amused smile, and possibly with a little pride.

And then it was over another dinner at our house that she offered more details of life as it was in East Prussia in the early twentieth century, and perhaps before. It was actually a border area between Germany, Poland, and Russia, but the borders were really not so important. The better-off families socialized across them, in festivities, hunting parties, and intermarriage. For Angela's family and people of their kind, it had been a good life.

"So Angela, what was actually your family name before you married?" I asked. In marriage she had acquired one of those last names that thousands and thousands of Swedish people have, Persson, or Svensson, or Larsson, or Nilsson, the kind of names that in the old peasant society would change with every generation, as the son of Per becomes a Persson. If only names mattered, you could hardly be more

248 Neighbors in a south Swedish village

anonymous in a modern, more urban society. But now, Angela exchanged a long glance with her husband before she responded to my question. "Romanov," she said.

So here, in Mrs. Persson, in the house next-door in my village, I had a neighbor who was actually a remote relative of the last Russian imperial dynasty. She hurried to point out that there were actually a lot of Romanovs in Russia. It was a clan, or whatever we should appropriately call it, with its homes dispersed in the country, and one or other of its members had apparently married across that rather unimportant border and become Prussian rather than Russian, if you could not just as well be both. And later on, as Angela offered more details of her family's immediate post-war experiences, it turned out that the family name had been useful. A Soviet officer in the invading troops, needing a local interpreter, found a dislocated German who indeed spoke Russian. The officer had been startled to find that this German gentleman, Angela's father, was a Romanov. But he was apparently not so much of a committed Communist, so he struck up a rather friendly and protective relationship with this new helper; until, of course, the latter left for a life outside what was becoming the Soviet zone, and successfully tracked down his wife and daughters.

Conclusion: a village and the world

So there are some stories from my seemingly ordinary, non-descript south Swedish village, and its immediate surroundings. On a sunny summer day, with several of the neighbors in sight or within earshot, in their gardens, it all seems utterly idyllic. But then on an August night, as the moon shines over the silent village and I look out over it and think about the backgrounds and life stories of my neighbors, those who are there now or those who have left or passed away, I have a sense that this is village ethnography with a dash of magical realism, so unlikely do they and their stories sometimes seem: an ancient witch refusing to stay in her grave, an early UFO, the world-famous bank robber, the man who swam across the Nile, the elderly soccer-loving lady who is a relative of the Russian czar. Up the road, an internationally famous (or infamous) biker gang.

Then, too, there are other neighbors who, like my great-aunts in their day, have never in their lives moved very far away. When I go into that nearest town to do some errands, however, I find that the faces I encounter in the shops and in street life have changed over the years. Now my barber is from Beirut, for one thing, and for some decades, there have been a noticeable number of Vietnamese refugees and their descendants – they run several enterprises. Recently one of these families took over the old assembly hall of the Salvation Army and turned it into a very successful coffee shop named Piece of Cake.

So let me turn now to some straight academic anthropology, and a couple of classics or near-classics, for some final reflections about my village neighbors and the world. I am reminded that quite long ago now, Clifford Geertz (1973: 21–22) pointed out that anthropologists characteristically approach large issues by way of "exceedingly extended acquaintances with extremely small matters" – they study *in* villages (or similar settings), but they do not study villages. By now, of course, they do not quite so typically study in villages either. It seems that now more than half of humanity live urban lives, and we anthropologists have in large part followed after. If you go to the villages and do not now find quite so many of us there, go and look for us in squatter settlements, refugee camps, shopping malls, hospitals, laboratories, studios, on trading floors, or for that matter in the archives, or in front of computer screens.

But then in another of his reflections on the anthropological experience, Geertz (1995: 94–95) also noted that as much as anthropologists may have been inclined to try and circumscribe field sites so as to make them conveniently local, it may happen again and again that these contexts explode. Geertz himself could remember being sought out, in the late 1950s, by a group of earnest Balinese who wanted to have it confirmed by an American that the Soviet Union had indeed put a moon up in the sky. For if even an American would admit it, it must be true.

Now I have certainly not been much involved in studying villages, or even *in* villages; from the very beginning I have been mostly a city kind of person, in my anthropology as well. And I cannot really say that what I have done in my village, with my neighbors, has been "studying". Here immersion in the local has been rather more a matter of getting away from the habitus of academic life. What I have learned about them has come my way in casual conversations over garden hedges, or in the village road, or over coffee or dinner tables, not through anything I would call "interviews." My neighbors pretty much take for granted that my real research is something that goes on in other places, and if they express any interest in it, it is mostly very fleetingly. Possibly I could describe this as some forty summers of low-intensity field work, half-deep hanging out. Occasionally, I can now add something to what I learn from these conversations, and from browsing among the old photographs that have accumulated over generations on the attic of our house, by reading those couple of ghostwritten autobiographies by recent but now departed local celebrities, or by looking up the Hollywood silent movie star from Hasslarp, or that bank robber neighbor in the archives of the *New York Times*. You can even look up Pottie Longchin.

But that means that Clifford Geertz' other point, about local contexts exploding, is more to the point. Yet is "exploding" really the right word here? Perhaps I should say rather that I find the outside world there in my village again and again, mostly undramatically subverting its boundaries, penetrating into its life. I hope my rather diverse collage of illustrations to this talk has helped convey a sense of this. My neighbors are not any self-conscious cosmopolitans, harping on again and again about those outside linkages, in their present, recent past, or further back in their family histories. Some of these connections come up anecdotally and become more generally familiar, some may even have been described in greater detail only to me. But they are there, I think, somewhat discreetly as a dimension of village microculture. When I first came to the United States as an exchange student close to fifty years ago, I came across a small book by Anthony Wallace (1961), the psychological anthropologist, where he argued that culture might be better understood as an organization of

250 Neighbors in a south Swedish village

diversity than as a replication of uniformity. That is a formulation that has been on my mind ever since, and now I again wonder if it does not help me understand some of the interactions of my village neighbors. There may actually be a mix of that organization of diversity with a fair amount of replicated uniformity, but one reason why these people keep finding each other good, interesting company seems to be that they keep having a wide range of things to talk about.

Moving out from the village scene, however, I think it tells us something about the way the world hangs together now. No doubt we have to pay attention to these large-scale structures and processes, for which over the years we have tended to borrow key words and analytical frames from elsewhere, outside the discipline: modernization, world-system theory, cultural imperialism, neoliberalism ... I sometimes get impatient with my fellow anthropologists for not doing more on their own to contribute to the Big Picture – perhaps more as a matter of identifying themes and processes rather than systems. But then, to come back to the Geertzian vocabulary, as I also reflect on my village and my neighbors there, as a matter of "extended acquaintance with small matters," I see that the density of the global ecumene is built up in considerable part through the sedimentation of contingencies over time – a density of actions, movements, relationships, and memories. It may draw on the larger patterns and events of religious persecution, continent-wide conflicts, transnational migration, and the globalization of some subcultures. For one thing, one can sense the present-day power of the media in creating micro–macro connections, when words and pictures move between local sites and global screens, in both directions. But the way all these things come together, as ancestries, biographies, and imaginaries, and interweave in particular contexts, is often opaque rather than transparent, and can continue to surprise us as we encounter them in the small worlds of our everyday lives.

So these are some of the things I have learned and thought about over those forty-some summers of getting together with my village neighbors. Perhaps it is indeed an unusual village, despite its outward ordinariness – I cannot really tell. But then again you just might find another set of comparable stories in the next village over. In fact, a well-known American anthropologist, and now a good friend, flies over from his home in Florida every year to spend the summer in his cottage here; this I discovered only through a serendipitous encounter at another American Anthropological Association meeting here in California a few years ago. Recently we have been spending a series of Midsummer Eves there together, so he and I can exchange academic gossip and reminiscences while the village children perform the "Small Frogs" dance around the Maypole. Now that, clearly, is also part of globalization, small-scale and unexpected.

Note

1 This chapter was originally presented as a William A. Douglass Distinguished Lecture for the Society for the Anthropology of Europe, at the annual meeting of the American Anthropological Association, San Francisco, CA, November 14–18, 2012. I remain grateful for the invitation, and the memorably pleasant reception.

References

Carlsson, Gösta, and Clas Svahn 1995. *Mötet i gläntan*. Nyköping: Parthenon.

Geertz, Clifford. 1973. *The Interpretation of Cultures*. New York: Basic Books.

———. 1995. *After the Fact*. Cambridge, MA: Harvard University Press.

Linnaeus, Carl. 1975. *Skånska Resa År 1749*. Carl-Otto von Sydow (ed.). Stockholm: Wahlström & Widstrand.

Olsson, Janne. 2009. *Stockholmssyndromet*. Stockholm: Telegram Bokförlag.

Thysell, Ernst. 1914. *Från flydda tider i Välinge och Kattarp*. Rögle: Författarens förlag.

Wallace, Anthony F.C. 1961. *Culture and Personality*. New York: Random House.

INDEX

Abacha, Sani 28, 33
Abrahams, Roger 11, 42
Abu-Lughod, Lila 27, 46, 154, 174
acculturation 43, 125, 137, 140, 142, 149, 150, 153
Achebe, Chinua 22
Adams, Richard 132, 153
Ade, Sunny 130
Afghanistan 199–200
Africa, in Black American identity 57–58
Afropolitans 27, 46
Agier, Michel 46–39
Ahmadu Bello 127–128, 131
Ajami, Fouad 225
Alex, Nicholas 77, 80, 81
Alvarez, Robert 147
Amado, Jorge 27. 135, 140, 143, 149
Amit, Vered 45
American Anthropological Association (AAA) 5, 13, 14, 28, 33, 173, 228
Anderson, Malcolm 154
Andersson, Ruben 45, 46
Angrosino, Michael 155
Anikulapo-Kuti, Fela 120, 130
Apollonian–Dionysian contrast 76, 86, 91, 93
Appadurai, Arjun 45, 138, 140, 166, 183, 225
Appiah, Kwame Anthony 195
Archer, Dane 93
Archilochus 194
Ash, Chris Myers 44
audiences, for anthropological writing 7–8

audit culture 37, 47
Augé, Marc 37

Bahia 135, 137, 140, 143, 144, 149
Bakhtin, Mikhail 150
Baldassar, Loretta 201
Bandele, Biyi 45
Bandidos 242
Banton, Michael 78
Barber, Karin 155
Barnes, John 44
Barth, Fredrik 139, 142, 153, 154
Bateson, Gregory 138, 143, 153
beaches 148
Becker, Howard 178
been-to, Nigerian type 27, 123
Beijing 193
Beirut 248
Bell, Daniel 72
Ben, field assistant in Nigeria 25
Benedict, Burton 102
Benedict, Ruth 4, 76, 150, 162
Ben's Chili Bowl 14
Berkeley, University of California 31, 186
Berlin, Isaiah 194
Berry, Sara 128
Bethlehem 166
Bhabha, Homi 150
Biafra 6, 63
Bittner, Egon 81
Björklund, Ulf 185
Black American culture 9, 52–59
Black Panther Party 90

Index **253**

Bloch, Maurice 37, 154, 174
Boas, Franz 5, 8, 28, 160, 173
Bohannan, Laura 45
Bohannan, Paul 45
borders *see* boundaries
Borneman, John 46
Boskovic, Aleksandar 45
Boston 16, 44
boundaries 27, 28, 46, 141–148
Bourdieu, Pierre 198
Bowen, Elenore Smith 45
Bradburd, Daniel 42
Brathwaite, Edward 132
Braudel, Fernand 220
Brazilian Anthropological Association 27
Broom, Leonard 140, 142, 143, 149
Brown, James 15, 56
Brown, Richard 93
Bruner, Jerome 114
Brussels 123, 181
Brzezinski, Zbigniew 216
Buchler, I.R. 104
Burckhardt, Jacob 110, 113
Burke, James Lee 227
Burke, Peter 129

Calcutta 33, 46, 209
Callick, Rowan 189–190, 192–196
Camilleri, Andrea 227
Canton 193
Cape Town 73–75, 212, 213
Carmichael, Stokely 29
Castells, Manuel 153
Cayman Islands 19–21, 29, 34, 45, 96–104
Center for Advanced Study of the
    Behavioral Sciences 26, 45
Center-periphery structures 26, 123–132,
    151, 179
Chapel Hill 227
Cheah, Peng 201
Chevalier, Louis 72
Chicago 12, 13, 69, 85, 227
Chicago School of Sociology 16, 44, 148,
    178, 211
Chirot, Daniel 132
Christie, Agatha 228
Citizenship 222–225
Claiborne, William 93
Clark, Kenneth 12
Clarke, Johan 91, 93
clash of civilizations thesis 38, 215–216
Clifford, James 160
Clinton, Bill 44, 205
CNN 14, 33–34, 179, 195, 242

Cohen, Anthony 154
Cohen, Robin 201
Cohen, Stanley 84
Coimbra 37
Collins, Randall 132
columnist experience 36–37
Comaroff, Jean 174
Comaroff, John 174
Comitas, Lambros 97
Coplan, David 207, 208
cosmopolitanism 31–32, 46, 191–199,
    209–212
Cotterill, Colin 227
Coulborn, Rushton 220
creolization 26, 33, 45, 126–132, 151
cultural apparatus 127, 161, 172
cultural celebrationism 218–219
cultural defense plea 226
cultural fundamentalism 154, 216, 219–222
cultural intimacy 44
culture concept 26, 38, 62, 124–126, 142,
    214–225
culture of poverty 10, 12, 53, 61
culture shock 214
Czikszentmihalyi, Mihaly 153

Dahlén, Tommy 174, 183, 217
DaMatta, Roberto 153
danger 17–18, 71–95, 167
Daniel, Susie 82, 93
Darley, John 93
Davos Culture 220
Dening, Greg 148
DeRidder, J.C. 210
detective stories 39, 227–236
Dhlamini, Ezekiel 207
Dore, Ronald 127
Douglas, Mary 83
Droogers, André 155
Drummond, Lee 126, 155
DuBois, W.E.B. 11, 27, 43, 54, 55,
    148–149
Duneier, Mitchell 44

EASA (European Association of Social
    Anthropologists) 37
East London, South Africa 73–74
East Prussia 247
East Timor 192
ecumene, global 42, 136, 159, 178, 211
Eickelman, Dale 132
Eisenstadt, Shmuel 37
Ekwensi, Cyprian 123
Eliot, T.S. 120, 122

254 Index

Ellis, Stephen 46
Ellison, Ralph 99
Eriksen, Thomas Hylland 155
ethnicity 38, 58, 63, 82, 122
Evans-Pritchard, Edward 176, 180–183, 186

Fabian, Johannes 126, 132, 139
Fanon, Frantz 122
Farjean, Herbert 40
Featherstone, Mike 155
Ferguson, James 177, 184
Ferguson, Niall 44
Ferlinghetti, Lawrence 13
field assistants 25, 65–66
field work 6–7, 60–67, 176–186
Firth, Raymond 139
Fish, Stanley 11
Florence 231
Flow 27, 45, 139–141
foreign correspondents 29–34, 164–172, 178–186, 189–200
Frankfurt am Main 12
Franklin, Aretha 14, 15
Freyre, Gilberto 149
Friberg, Harry 229–232
Friedman, Thomas 197
frontiers 145–147
Fugard, Athol 210
Fulani 23, 24, 105–106
future scenarios 38–39, 47

Gans, Herbert 15, 44, 69, 93
Garsten, Christina 180
Gbulie, Ben 128
Geertz, Clifford 6, 37, 42, 44, 107, 187, 248
Gellner, Ernest 45
Genovese, Kitty 88–89, 93
Gershenhorn, Jerry 43
ghetto concept 7, 11–13, 43, 44, 52–59, 233
Gingrich, Andre 47
globalization, concept 27, 135–137, 220
Goffman, Erving 75
Golding, Peter 124
Golovensky, David 155
González, Roberto 46
Goodenough, Ward 132
Goodhart, David 47
Goody, Jack 107
Gordimer, Nadine 207
Graburn, Nelson 126
Granovetter, Mark 40

Great Divide 109
Green, Arnold 155
Greenbaum, Susan 43
Guatemala 245
Gupta, Akhil 177
Gullers, K.W. 229–230
Gusterson, Hugh 185
Gutwirth, Jacques 70
Gwertzman, Bernard 199, 201

halfies, concept 27–28, 46
Hall, Thomas 132
Hamelink, Cees 132
Hammond, Peter 43
Hammoudi, Abdellah 42
Hansen, Edward 99
Harlem Renaissance 9, 209
Harney, Nicholas 201
Harre, Rom 118
Harris, Marvin 37
Hart, Keith 132
Hasslarp 242
Haugerud, Angelique 46
Hausa 23, 63, 65, 122
Hayakawa, S.I. 55
Heller, Agnes 110
Hellman, Peter 93
Hell's Angels 82, 86, 242
Hennessy, Alistair 154
Henslin, James 78
Herskovits, Melville 8–10, 27, 43, 59, 137
Herzfeld, Michael 44
hidden curriculum 128
Hillerman, Tony 227, 228
hippies 77, 84
Hitchcock, Alfred 234
Hofstadter, Richard 154
Hollingworth, Clare 31
Hong Kong 31, 112, 178, 189–200
Hoosiers (natives of Indiana) 5
Howard Theatre 14–15, 25, 61
Howell, Signe 140–141, 154
Hughes, Everett 178
Hughes, Richard 200
Human Terrain Systems 29
Huntington, Samuel 38, 215–216, 219–225
Hunton, Alphaeus 43
hybridity 27, 148–152
Hyra, Derek 44

Ibo 63
Identity concepts 105–118, 142
Igbo *see* Ibo
Ignatieff, Michael 225

Index **255**

Imperiale, Anthony 89
Indiana University, Bloomington 4–5
informants and interviews 66, 67, 178–180, 249
Ingold, Tim 154
interculturalists 159, 163–164, 183, 217, 224, 245
intifada 166
Ionescu, Ghita 45
Iron Curtain 37
Istanbul 227

Jägerhorn, Inger 198
Jackson, Jean 155
Jacobs, Jane 80, 88, 90
Jakarta 192
James, P.D. 228, 234
Janowitz, Morris 91
Japan 167–172, 181
Jefferson, Margo 44
Jerusalem 179, 181, 182, 192
Johannesburg 32–33, 46, 74, 179, 181, 182, 192, 203–211
Johansson, Göran 173
Johnson, Lyndon 10, 43
Jones, LeRoi 44
Jorgensen, Joseph 160

Kafanchan 16, 22–25, 30, 33–34, 62–67, 105–106, 111–113, 116–118, 121, 124
Kaje 25, 63
Karachi 178
Kattarp 242
Kearney, Michael 143, 147
Keesing, Roger 174
Keil, Charles 10, 45, 59
Keiser, Lincoln 90
Keller, Bill 225
Kennedy, John F. 4, 145–146
Khanna, Parag 44
Khosravi, Shahram 47
Khrushchev, Nikita 246
King, Martin Luther 34
King of Sweden 40, 236, 244
King Kong, the musical 207
Kingston, Jamaica 71, 78, 82, 87
Kinshasa 79
Kissinger, Henry 216
Kleinman, Arthur 174
Kleinman, Joan 174
Klor de Alva, Jorge 155
Kobe 167–172
Koptiuch, Kristin 226
Kopytoff, Igor 146–147, 211

Kreml, William 93
Kristof, Nicholas 46, 167–172, 174
Kroeber, Alfred 1, 5, 42, 139, 153
Kulick, Don 163

La Fontaine, Jean 79
Lagos 123
Lang, Maria 232
Lamont, Barbara 88
Lantis, Margaret 79
Larsson, Stieg 227, 229, 235, 236
Lash, Scott 138, 140, 143
Latané, Bibb 93
Lauterbach, Preston 44
Lave, Jean 154
Leach, Edmund 146–147
Leacock, Eleanor 43
LeCarré, John 189
Lederman, Jim 165–166
Leenhardt, Maurice 160
Leijonhufvud, Göran 193–194, 198, 201
Lejeune, Robert 77, 80, 81
Lévi-Strauss, Claude 160
Lewis, Oscar 10, 53, 59, 86
Leyburn, James 154
Lifton, Robert Jay 115
Linnaeus, Carl 239
Lips, Julius 140
Lipset, Seymour 154
Linton, Ralph 140, 143, 145
Löfgren, Orvar 174
London 1, 141, 177, 181, 243
Longchin, Pottie 239–242
Los Angeles 179
Lowie, Robert 4, 144

Mabley, Moms 15, 18
Mafeje, Archie 33, 73–74
Magubane, Peter 205
Mailer, Norman 13, 14
mainstream culture 53–55
Mair, Lucy 153
Makeba, Miriam 40, 207–208
Malinowski, Bronislaw 150, 153, 177
Manchester School, in anthropology 16, 44, 192
Mandela, Nelson 32, 204, 207
Mandela, Winnie 204
Manila 192
Mankell, Henning 22–29, 235
Marcus, George 177, 184, 187
marginal man 148–149
Markham, Pigmeat 15
Marriott, McKim 139

256 Index

Marx, Gary 93
Masekela, Hugh 208
Masemann, Vandra 129
Matory, Lorand 44
Mattera, Don 208
Matza, David 76
Mauss, Marcel 160
Mayer, Philip 74–75, 83
Mazrui, Ali 42
McGuire, Pete 82, 83
McLuhan, Marshall 29, 36, 55, 84, 136
McNeill, William 220, 225
Mead, Margaret 162
media, in anthropology 29–30, 48,
   130, 185
Merriam, Alan 43
Merry, Sally 81, 87, 93
Métraux, Rhoda 162
Meyer, John 127
Miami 123
migration studies, in Sweden 37–38, 47
Milgram, Stanley 40, 47
military service 18–19, 128
Mills, C. Wright 127, 161
Miner, Horace 44
Mintz, Sidney 42, 153, 155
mirrors 105, 116, 118
missionaries 28, 160, 163
modernization concept 125, 137, 220
Moeran, Brian 46
Moore, Carlos 130
Morgan, Jane 118
Morin, Edgar 85
Morris, Aldon 43
Morris, Colin 110
motorcycle gangs 82, 83, 87, 242
Moynihan, Daniel Patrick 10, 43
Mphahlele, Ezekiel 42
multiculturalism 142, 154, 214–225
multi-site field studies 30, 176–186
Murphy, Robert 46, 153
Musgrove, George Derek 44
Myrdal, Alva 11, 39, 44
Myrdal, Gunnar 8–13, 36, 39, 43–44

Nader, Laura 159, 173, 178, 184
Naipaul, V.S. 122
Nairobi 33, 192, 197–198
Nakane, Chie 37
Narayan, Kirin 46
Nash, June 132
national anthropologies 18, 45
Nederveen Pieterse, Jan 155
neighbors, in Swedish village 41, 238–250

neonationalism 47
networks 16, 40–41, 44, 66, 183
New Orleans 227
New York 72, 77, 88, 89, 91, 93, 165,
   177, 178
Newman, Oscar 80, 88
nicknames 112
Nigeria 6, 22–26, 28, 45, 105,
   120–132
Nile River 245
Nilsson, Anna Q. 242–243
n-word 12, 44, 55
Nzekwu, Onuora 22, 28

Obiechina, Emmanuel 111
occupational multiplicity 97
O'Neill, Christopher 118
Onitsha publishing 111–112
Oreh, O.O. 130
Ortiz, Fernando 150
Ortner, Sherry 236
Oslo 141

Paden, John 118
Padilla, Elena 91
Palmié, Stephan 152
Papastergiadis, Nikos 155
Papua New Guinea 189, 190
Paretsky, Sara 227, 228
Paris 72–73, 123, 177, 192
Park, Robert 148–149, 211
Parkin, David 186
Parks, Tim 226
participant observation 6, 52,
   60, 64
Pauw, B.A. 73, 93
Peel, J.D.Y. 128
Pelecanos, George 227
Pfaff, William 225
photography 113, 116–117, 205
Pierce, Steven 46
plural societies 45, 125–126
Poland 247
political correctness 12
populism 21, 46
Port Moresby 189, 190
poverty, culture of 10, 12
poverty, war on 10
Prague 37
Pratt, Mary Louise 150, 173
Presley, Elvis 13, 21
Price, David 46
Price, Richard 153
Project Camelot 5, 28

protean man 115
Purdom, Judy 155

Queen of Sweden 135
Quigley, Carroll 220
Qiu Xiaolong 227

Raban, Jonathan 210
Rabinow, Paul 46
Rainwater, Lee 43, 93, 118
Ramirez, Francisco 127
Ramo, Joshua Cooper 44
Rather, Dan 187
Reader, D.H. 73
Redfield, Robert 43, 139, 143, 153
Reich, Robert 46
Renaissance men 110–114
Richburg, Keith 190–192, 197–199, 201
Richelson, Jeffrey 162
Riesman, David 155
Riesman, Paul 106–107
Riviere, Peter 86
Robbins, Bruce 201
Robertson, Ronald 153, 154, 163, 191
Rockefeller, Stuart 45
Romanov clan 248
Rosaldo, Renato 147
Rose, Arnold 43
Rose, Peter 42
Rowland, Laura Joh 227
Rubenstein, Joseph 132
Ruble, Blair 44
Rushdie, Salman 149
Russia 247–248

Saberwal, Satish 37
Sahlins, Marshall 5, 42
Said, Edouard 122
Saint Augustine 110
Salander, Lisbeth 228
San Francisco 26, 33, 41, 77, 209–211
Sauvant, Karl 124
Schiller, Herbert 132
Schneider, Jane 99
Schneider, Peter 99
school essays, as field materials 67
Schudson, Michael 154
Schwartz, Theodore 132
Schwarzenegger, Arnold 247
Seedman, Albert 93
Selasi, Taiye 46
Seoul 31
serendipity 2, 33, 177, 209
Sharo, ritual battle 23, 105–106, 116, 118

Shaw, Rosalind 152
Shultz, George 26
Sicily 227
Sinatra, Frank 109
Sjövall, Maj 229, 235
skinheads 82, 84, 87, 93
Slaughter, Anne-Marie 44
Smith, Daniel Jordan 46
Smith, M.G. 45
sociology of knowledge 26
Sontag, Susan 116–117
Sophiatown 33, 40, 46, 207–212
soul concept, in Black American culture
    55–59
soul food 55–56
soul music 25, 55–56, 59
South Africa 203–212
southern heritage, of Black Americans 56
Soweto 32–33, 203–212
Sparks, Alister 206–207, 209, 212
Spengler, Oswald 139, 220
Sperber, Dan 132, 144
spies 28–29, 160–162
spiralists 192–194
St. Louis 78
Sterngold, James 170
Stewart, Charles 45, 152
Stipe, Claude 173
Stockholm 39, 80, 177, 229–236
Stockholm Syndrome 244
Stockholm University 4, 18, 35–39, 193
Stocking, George 173, 218, 236
Stolcke, Verena 154, 216
Stoller, Paul 174
Stonequist, Everett 155
story lines 166
Stowe, Harriet Beecher 42
Strathern, Marilyn 47, 136
Strauss, Anselm 118
studying sideways 28, 159–175, 228, 236;
    Suttles, Gerald 85, 90
Swartz, Richard 47
Sweden 227–250
Swedish Institute for North American
    Studies 42
Sykes, Gresham 76
symbolic interactionism 26
syncretism 152
synergy 150
Szwed, John 42, 59

Tambo, Oliver 208
Taylor, Ian 93
terrorism, in Stockholm 39

258 Index

Tett, Gillian 47
Thailand 244
theater state, in Bali and America 42
Themba, Can 93, 210
Thompson, Hunter 86
Thrasher, Frederic 90
Timbouctou 197
time 2, 183–184
Tiv 23–24, 45, 122
Tokyo 179, 181
Tourism 97–104, 164
Toynbee, Arnold 220
transculturation 150
transnational, concept 27
traffic relationships 18, 75–76
travel industry 164
Travers, Jeffrey 47
Trenter, Stieg 39, 227–236
Triomf 206–212
Tsing, Anna 44
Tsotsis 17, 32, 73–75, 82, 83, 84,
    93, 209
Tuchman, Gaye 165
Turner, Frederick Jackson 145–149
Turner, Stephen 154
Turner, Ted 195
Turner, Terence 154
Turner, Victor 147, 153, 234
Tutu, Desmond 204, 208

UFOs 241–242
underclass, concept 12
Urban, Greg 154
urban anthropology 15–17, 44,
    60–70
Urry, John 138, 140, 143
Useem, John 155
Uwaifo, Victor 130

Valentine, Charles 43, 59
Van der Geest, Sjaak 173
Velho, Otávio 154
Verdery, Katherine 154
vernacular culture 79
Vertovec, Steven 201
Vienna 33, 46, 209–211, 227
Vientiane 199
vigilantism 89–92

Vincent, Joan 70, 153
violence, in cities 71–92

Wahlöö, Per 229, 235
Wall, David 93
Wallace, Anthony 26, 132, 21, 114, 249
Wallace, David Foster 236
Wallerstein, Immanuel 132, 154
Walter, Greg 86
Ware, Caroline 91
Washington, DC 2, 14, 35, 52–62, 77, 78,
    176, 192, 227
Waterman, Christopher 154–155
Watson, C.W. 187
Watson, James 153, 177
Watson, William 192
Weber, Max 247
Weiner, Eric 46
Welles, Orson 39
Wenger, Etienne 154
White, Jenny 227, 236
White, Josh 40
Whyte, William 44
Wikan, Unni 174
Williams, John 236
Williams, Raymond 137, 152, 154
Willwerth, James 78, 81
Wilson, James 92
Wilson, Monica 73–74
Winston Street (pseudonym) 6, 8, 14, 29,
    34–35, 60–62
Wirth, Louis 12, 16, 68–69
Wolf, Eric 37, 102, 132, 147, 160
Wolfgang, Marvin 92
World Economic Forum 220
WuDunn, Sheryl 169, 174
Wulff, Helena 180, 185 159, 162, 163

Xhosa 73–74
Xuma, Alfred 208

Yancey, William 43
Yoruba 63, 122, 128
Young, Jock 84
Young, Robert 155
youth culture 111–113

Zaire 126
Zambia 184